MW01593746

Introduction by the Editor

ffore\word

THE Renaissance in Italy, the heart of Christendom, sent something of a pulse even as far as that member of the body of Europe called England. For there such men as More, Fisher, Colet, Lilly, Linacre, and Grocyn lived, studied, and taught. Erasmus speaks most flatteringly of King Henry VIII., surrounded by a chosen, able coterie of savants and litterateurs, the modern Mæcenas, who himself contended for and won his laurels—and that from the hands of the cultured Pope Leo X.—in reward for the royal literary feat, the "Assertio Septem Sacramentorum," i. e., the "Defence of the Seven Sacraments."

"The evil that men do lives after them; the good is oft interred with their bones. So let it" *not* be with Henry. Generally he is remembered as one who "spared neither man in his hate, nor woman in his lust."* But this is the roué, the non-Catholic, the Protestant, the schismatic Henry. Let us not forget that at least once he had been the beau-ideal Henry; in body, tall, straight, broad-shouldered, a master of every gentlemanly accomplishment; in mind naturally clever, an accomplished linguist, a learned theologian, a faithful son of the Church. As such he wrote his famous book, the "Defence of the Seven Sacraments." In reprinting this work several topics of interest seemed to need notice and explanation, and these have grown and shaped themselves into an Introduction grouped under the following heads:

* Carwithen's Hist. of the Church of England, I., p. 38.

1. A Synopsis of the "Assertio."
2. Its Occasion, Origin and Motive.
3. Its Authorship.
4. The Various Editions and Versions.
5. The Presentation of it to the Pope.
6. Was the Title "Defender of the Faith" Hereditary?
7. Criticism and Influence of the "Assertio."
8. Bibliography.

Following this Introduction comes the "Assertio" proper, preceded by a few documents reprinted in English, some of them in the Latin too, in the following order:

1. The Introduction to the English version here reprinted, in English only.
2. Henry's Letter to Leo, in English and Latin.
3. The Oration of John Clark, in English only.
4. Leo X.'s Reply, in English only.
5. Leo X.'s Bull, in English and Latin.
6. Leo X.'s Letter to Henry, in English and Latin.
7. Henry's Dedicatory Epistle, in English and Latin.
8. Henry's "To the Reader," in English and Latin.
9. Henry's Two Preliminary Chapters, on Indulgences and the Papacy, respectively, in English and Latin.
10. Henry's "Assertio Septem Sacramentorum," or "Defence of the Seven Sacraments," in English and Latin.
11. The Index to the "Assertio," in English and Latin.

The first reason for reprinting this work is a moral one—namely, that the readers may see, from so illustrious an example, that loss of faith comes from loss of morals. The second reason is that non-Catholics, those

"other sheep which are not of this fold," may return to
the rich, green pastures which they left four hundred
years ago, and which are still as rich, as green, because
still watered by the perennial streams of the seven sacraments, just as in the days of Henry; they are "ever
ancient, yet ever new."

The editor regrets that this piece of work has been
made much after the manner of the good housewife's
rag carpet—composed of pieces and patches, at different times and places, when and where a busy ministry
would permit. There is no pretence at style. Indeed,
while trying to be brief, and yet give all the testimonies
collected, the matter has, it is feared, often grown
heavy; while trying to teach one is apt to forget to
amuse. All that the editor asks is a careful reading
and indulgence for his defects.

The writer takes pleasure in acknowledging his in-
debtedness to the rich treasures of the Library of the
Peabody Institute of Baltimore; the kind loan of one
edition of the "Assertio" from the Catholic University
of America; also Dr. Healy's old English version of
the "Assertio," here reprinted; above all, the encour-
aging interest and learned advice of that richly gifted
historian — that gentle, hard-working teacher — Very
Reverend Thomas J. Shahan, S.T.D., Professor of
Ecclesiastical History in the Catholic University of
America. To the Rev. Lucian Johnston, S.T.L., of
Baltimore, the writer is grateful for helpful criticism
and advice; also to the Rev. Charles Hogue, S.S., of
St. Charles' College, Maryland; to Rev. Henry J.
Shandelle, S.J., of Georgetown, and Rev. Fr. Ehrle,
S.J., of Rome. And though last, not least, most pro-
foundly does the writer appreciate the graciousness of
that providential modern defender of the FAITH OF

OUR FATHERS, who has been good enough in his busy, latter days to introduce this book—His Eminence James Cardinal Gibbons, Archbishop of Baltimore.

THE CATHEDRAL, BALTIMORE,
    FEAST OF PENTECOST, 1907.

Synopsis of the "Assertio"

THIS Synopsis of the "Assertio" sums up the gist of the English version reprinted further on *in extenso*.

And first comes the rather quaint "Advertisement," bespeaking the merits of this English version. It is as follows:

I

Advertisement

ALL readers of English history know that Luther started and Henry established "those fatal confusions, animosities and devastations . . . in these three kingdoms."

Wealth, sloth, looseness of morals, ignorance made a reformation of the manners of some of the clergy desirable. Luther's first intention to reform abuses of churchmen was good, but later he set himself above the whole Church to reform religion itself. The German princes helped Luther with arms, and Catholics repelled force by force. Henry "had well studied philosophy and theology," but his style is abusive, imitating that of his adversaries. "Luther was inflamed by the censures of the University of Paris;" still more by those of Henry. Henry was a "devout Roman Catholic" till the Pope refused him a divorce. However, "his 'Defence of the Seven Sacraments' is a work of considerable merit. Its orthodoxy we cannot doubt of. . . .

The work . . . may not only be very profitably perused, but is also extremely curious, when we consider
its author's very remarkable and inconsistent character.
The London edition, from whence the present is taken,
has been carefully corrected throughout, in the orthography and punctuation, and the text, obscure in some
parts, has been elucidated. . . . This edition is
vastly preferable to all former ones in the English
tongue. . . . The publication of a work, hitherto so
extremely scarce, will be satisfactory to the curious."

II

"Letter of Henry VIII. to Leo X.

On the Subject of the 'Assertio,' 1521.

"Most Holy Father:"

As We Catholic sovereigns should uphold religion,
when We saw Luther's heresy running wild, for the
sake of Germany, and still more for love of the Holy
Apostolic See, We tried to weed out this heresy.

"Seeing its widespread havoc, We called on all to
help Us to eradicate it, particularly the Emperor and
the Electoral Princes. Lest, however, this be not
enough to show Our mind on Luther's wicked books,
We shall defend and guard the Holy Roman Church
not only by force of arms, but also by Our wits. And
therefore We dedicate to Your Holiness Our first fruits,
confident that an abundant harvest will be gathered,
should Your Holiness approve Our work.

"From Our Royal Palace at Greenwich, May 21st,
1521.

"Your Holiness' most devoted and humble son,
Henry, by the grace of God King of England and
France, and Lord of Ireland."

III

"Oration of Mr. John Clark,

Orator for henry VIII., king of England, France and
Ireland, Defender of the Faith; on his exhibiting
this Royal Book, in the Consistory at Rome, to Pope
Leo X.

"Most Holy Father:"

What great troubles from the Hussites! What from
Luther's works! especially from " 'The Babylonian
Captivity of the Church,' in refuting which many grave
and learned men have diligently laboured."

"Henry VIII., most affectionate son of Your Holiness and of the sacred Roman Church, hath written a
book against this work of Luther's, which he has dedicated to Your Holiness, . . . which I here present, but
before You receive it, most holy Father, may it please
You, that I speak somewhat of the devotion and veneration of my King towards Your Holiness, and this most
Holy See; as also of the other reasons which moved
him to publish this work." . . .

"Luther rends the seamless Coat of Christ, makes the
Pope a mere priest, condemns all ministers, and calls
Rome Babylon, makes the Pope a heretic and himself
[Luther] equal to St. Peter. He burnt the decrees and
statutes of the Fathers and published his Book of the
Babylonian Captivity. It condemns Pope, hierarchy
and 'the Rock' and the Church; abolishes most sacred
practices; institutes sacraments after his fancy, reducing them to three, if not to none at all. What ills are
yet to be added to those started by the Hussites? My
King moved the Emperor to exile Luther.

"My . . . England . . . hath never been behind in
. . . due obedience to the Roman Church, either to

Spain, France, Germany or Italy; nay, to Rome itself;
so no nation more impugns this monster. . . . King
Henry, Your Holiness' most devoted son, undertook
this pious work himself," . . . the most learned clergy
of this realm have endeavoured to remove all doubts, "so
that amongst us the Church of God is in great tranquillity; no differences, no disputes, no ambiguous
words, murmurings or complaints are heard amongst
the people." . . .

"The reason that moved my most serene King," who
has defended with the sword the Catholic Faith and
Christian Religion, to undertake this work, is his
piety:—"his accustomed veneration to Your Holiness;
Christian piety in the cause of God; and a royal grief
and indignation of seeing religion trodden under foot;"
also "the desire of glory" might have induced him "to
discover by reason the Lutheran heresies. . . . This
raging and mad dog is not to be dealt with by words,
there being no hopes of his conversion, but with drawn
swords, cannons, and other habiliments of war." And
this "work of his, though it had the approbation of
the most learned of his Kingdom; yet he resolved
not to publish until Your Holiness (from whom we
ought to receive the sense of the Gospel, by your quick
and most sublime judgment) deem it worthy to pass
through the hands of men. May therefore Your Holiness take in good part and graciously accept this little
Book."

IV

Leo X.'s Reply

"NOTHING could have been sent more acceptable to
Us." We praise and admire that most Christian King,
having the knowledge, will, and ability of composing

this excellent book, who "has rendered himself no less
admirable to the whole world by the eloquence of his
style, than by his great wisdom." May the Creator
bless him, and we shall do "anything that may tend to
the honour and dignity of his Majesty and to his and
his kingdom's glory."

V

The Pope's Bull

" **Leo, X. Bishop and Servant of the Servants of God: To
our most dear Son in Christ, henry, the illustrious
King of England, and Defender of the Faith, sends
Greeting, and gives his Benediction.**"

"As the other Roman Bishops have bestowed particular favours upon Catholic Princes" for constancy in
Faith, and unspotted devotion to the Church in tempestuous times: so also We, for your Majesty's most
excellent works. "Our beloved son John Clark did,
in Our Consistory, in presence of Our venerable
Brethren, Cardinals of the Church, present Us a book
which your Majesty . . . did compose as an antidote
against the errors of divers heretics, often condemned
by this Holy See, and now again revived by Martin
Luther."

"Having found in this book most admirable doctrine
We thank God and beg you to enlist like workers.
We, the true successor of St. Peter, presiding in this
Holy See, from whence all dignity and titles have
their source, have with our brethren maturely deliberated on these things; and with one consent unanimously decreed to bestow on your Majesty this title,
namely, 'Defender of the Faith.' . . . We likewise command all Christians, that they name your

Majesty by this title. . . . Having thus weighed . . . your singular merits, we could not have invented a more congruous name.

"And you shall rejoice in Our Lord, showing the way to others, that if they also covet to be invested with such a title, they may study to do such actions, and to follow the steps of your most excellent Majesty, whom, with your wife, children, and all who shall spring from you, we bless.

"Given at St. Peter's in Rome, the fifth of the Ides of October; in the year of Our Lord's Incarnation 1521, and in the ninth year of Our Papacy."

VI

"Letter from Leo X.

To Henry VIII. respecting the 'Assertio Septem Sacramentorum,' in reply to the book written by the King against Luther.

"To Our dearest Son in Christ health and Apostolic benediction."

We are deeply grateful for your defence of this Holy See, and all but welcome Luther's crime as the occasion of Your noble championship. Such virtue must not lose its reward. For if praise is due to those who protect our liberty, as well as to those who defend our sacraments, both of these noble virtues are united in You.

What return can We make for Your good will towards Us?

Your learning, cleverness and charity should convince and gain back the heretics.

For Your service "for the great God, and this Holy See, We give infinite thanks to Your Majesty, Defender of the Faith."

"In a bull of Our Own, with the assent of Our Venerable Brethren, We have forwarded to You this title of 'Defender of the Faith.' "

Forget not, dearest Son, to act in accordance with Your new and honourable title, remembering that far greater rewards, from Our Lord and Saviour, await You in heaven. Let Your defence of the Spouse of Christ here on earth remind You of, and prepare You for, an eternal reward hereafter.

VII

The Epistle Dedicatory

To Our Most Holy Lord Leo X., chief Bishop, Henry, King of England, France and Ireland, wisheth perpetual happiness.

"Most Holy Father:"

You will wonder at a man of war and affairs writing against heresy, but love for the faith and respect for You urge me, and God's grace will aid me. "Religion bears the greatest sway in the administration of public affairs and is likewise of no small importance in the commonwealth," . . . and so we have spent much time in the contemplation thereof, and now we "dedicate to Your Holiness what we have meditated therein. . . . If we have erred in anything, we offer it to be corrected as may please Your Holiness."

VIII

To the Reader

Though of limited ability I feel it my duty to defend the Church and Catholic Faith to the best of my power. I arm myself with a twofold armour, celestial and ter-

restrial, to overcome him who perverts Scripture, the
Sacraments, ecclesiastical rites and ceremonies—the infernal wolf, who tries to disperse the flock of Christ
with his Babylonian Captivity.   If Luther do not repent and "if Christian princes do their duty these
errors and himself, if he perseveres therein, may
be burned in the fire."

CHAPTER I

Of Indulgences and the Pope's Authority

*"Indulgentiæ sunt adulatorum Romanorum ne-
quitiæ."**

Luther attacks not only the abuses but the doctrine
of indulgences: "they are nothing but mere impostures,
fit only to destroy people's money and God's faith."
. . . As he denies "indulgences to be profitable in this
life, it would be in vain for me to dispute what great
benefits the souls in Purgatory receive by them, . . .
whereby we are relieved from Purgatory itself." . . .
"The words of Christ remain firm: . . . 'Whatsoever
thou shalt loose on earth, shall be loosed in heaven.'   By
which words, if it is manifest that any priest has power
to absolve men from sins, and take away eternal punishment due thereunto, who will not judge it ridiculous,
that the Prince of all priests should be denied the taking away of temporal punishment?"

"What concerns it me what that man admits, or
denies, who alone rejects all things which the Holy
Church has held during so many ages?"

* Luther's words, quoted by Henry.

CHAPTER II

Of the Pope's Authority

"Papatus est robusta Venatio Romani Pontificis.

"First, he [Luther] denied the Pope's supremacy to be of divine right, or law, but allowed it to be of human right. But now, (contrary to himself) he affirms it to be of neither of them. . . . He now embraces what he then detested. . . . He preached that excommunication is a medicine and to be suffered with patience and obedience: he himself being (for every good cause) awhile after excommunicated, was so impatient of that sentence that (mad with rage) he breaks forth into insupportable contumelies, reproaches and blasphemies." . . . "He cannot deny that all the faithful honour and acknowledge the sacred Roman See for their mother and supreme." . . . "The Indies themselves . . . do submit to the See of Rome. If the Bishop of Rome has got this large power, neither by command of God, nor the will of man, but by main force, I would fain know of Luther when the Pope rushed into the possession of so great riches. . . . By the unanimous consent of all nations, it is forbidden to change, or move the things which have been for a long time immovable. . . . Since the conversion of the world, all churches in the Christian world have been obedient to the See of Rome. . . . Though the Empire was translated to the Grecians, yet did they still own, and obey the supremacy of the Church, and See of Rome, except when they were in any turbulent schism.

"St. Jerome . . . openly declared . . . 'that it was sufficient for him that the Pope of Rome did but approve his faith, whoever else should disapprove it.' "

* Luther, quoted by Henry.

He is "endeavouring to draw all others with him into destruction, whilst he strives to dissuade them from their obedience to the Chief Bishop, whom, in a three-fold manner, he himself is bound to obey, viz., as a Christian, as a priest, and as a religious brother. . . . Luther . . . refuses to submit to the law of God, but desires to establish a law of his own."

CHAPTER III

The Defence of the Seven Sacraments

THE preceding two chapters of Luther are but a flourish to his real work. "Of seven Sacraments he leaves us but three ; . . . of the three he takes away one immediately after in the same book, . . . he says 'that if he would speak according to Scripture, he would have but one Sacrament and three sacramental signs.' "

CHAPTER IV

The Sacrament of the Altar

"LET us begin where he began himself, with the adorable Sacrament of Christ's Body. The changing of the Name thereof, calling It the sacrament of bread, shows" Luther's intentions. As "St. Ambrose . . . says . . . 'Though the form of bread and wine is seen upon the altar, yet we must believe that there is nothing else but the Body and Blood of Christ.' " Next comes the *consubstantiation theory* of Luther, who was determined with himself to draw the people to worship the bread and leave out Christ's Body.

Luther reopened the old sore of the Bohemian trouble,

i. e., that the people should receive Communion under both forms. Luther's charge that the clergy forcibly took away the chalice from the laity against their will is disbelieved by Henry. If Luther objects to the change from the primitive way of giving Communion, he should object also to children not receiving at all, and to our receiving in the morning instead of after supper. And what authority in Scripture has he to put water in the wine, if not tradition? The change is made by the Holy Ghost. "He that pretended to stand for the communicating under both kinds recommends the quite contrary, to wit, that it may be lawful for them never to receive under any kind."

Luther also inculcates that "the substance of true bread and true wine remain still after Consecration."

"He esteems this to be his greatest and chiefest argument, to wit, 'That Scripture is not to be forced, . . . but to be kept in the most simple signification that can be.' . . . But," says he, "the Divine Words are forced if that which Christ calls bread be taken for the accidents of bread, and what He calls wine for the form of wine. . . . The evangelists so plainly write that Christ took bread and blessed it. . . . We confess He took bread and blessed it, but that He gave bread to His disciples, after He had made It His Body, we flatly deny, and the evangelists do not say He did." Luther says: "Take, eat, this, that is, this *bread,* (says He, which He had taken and broken) is My Body. . . . This is Luther's interpretation, but not Christ's words, nor the sense of His words. . . . If the rod" [of Aaron] "could not remain with the serpent, how much less can the bread remain with the Flesh of Christ?"

"Christ does not say '*Hoc est Sanguis Meus,*' but '*Hic est Sanguis Meus.*' . . . Though wine is of the neuter gender, yet Christ did not say '*hoc,*' but '*hic est*

Sanguis Meus.' And though bread is of the masculine gender, yet, notwithstanding, he says, *'Hoc est Corpus Meum,'* not *'hic,'* that it may appear by both articles that He did not mean to give bread or wine, but His own Body and Blood." So "bread is not in the Eucharist," concludes Henry. If the Acts speak of the Eucharist as bread, it is because It *was* formerly, or still appeared as bread; just as Aaron's rod, though changed to a serpent, is still called a rod. Christ said "This is My Body," not "My Body is in this," or "With this which you see, is My Body." Luther says the word "transubstantiation" has risen up inside the last 300 years. Henry replies that 400 years ago "Hugo de Sancto Victore writ a Book of the Sacraments," and said: " 'By the word of Sanctification the true substance of bread and wine is turned or changed into the true Body and Blood of Christ, only the form of bread and wine remaining, and the substance passing into another substance.' "

"Eusebius Emissenus, dyed about 600 years since, . . . said, 'Now the invisible Priest converteth, by His secret power, the visible creatures into His own Body and Blood, saying, "Take and eat, this is My Body." ' "

St. Augustine: "We honour (says he) invisible things, viz., the Flesh and Blood in the form of the bread and wine."

"St. Gregory Nissenus says, 'That before the consecration it is but bread; but when it is consecrated by mystery, it is made, and called the Body of Christ.' " ·

"Theophilus . . . says, 'The Bread is not a figure only of the Body of Christ, but is changed into the proper Body of the Flesh and Blood of Christ. . . . Our Lord, condescending to our weakness, preserves the forms of the bread and wine, but changes the bread and wine into His own true Flesh and Blood.' "

"St. Cyril . . . says, 'God, condescending to our frailties, lest we should abhor flesh and blood on the holy altars, infuseth the force of life into what is offered, by changing them into the truth of His own proper Flesh.' "

"St. Ambrose . . . said, 'Although the form of bread and wine is seen, nevertheless we are to believe that there is nothing else after the consecration but the Body and Blood of Christ.' "

So the Fathers teach, not consubstantiation, but transubstantiation.

Luther "denies it [the Mass] to be a good work," though "he sees and confesses himself that the opinions of the Holy Fathers are against him, as also the Canon of the Mass, with the custom of the universal Church, confirmed by the usage of so many ages, and the consent of so many people. . . . He strives . . . to excite the commonalty against the nobility. . . . He says that we ought to receive the 'Communion with faith alone. . . . The more clear, pure, and free from the stain of sin our consciences are, in the worse capacity are we to receive. . . . Mass is no sacrifice: it is only profitable to the priest, not to the people; that it is nothing available either to the dead or the living.' "

Henry expounds the Mass and shows "Christ to be the eternal Priest: . . . on the cross He consummated the sacrifice which He began in the supper. . . . The consecration in the supper and the oblation on the cross is celebrated and represented together in the sacrament of the Mass."

Henry then shows that the Mass said by priests is a good work. "The Mass of every priest helps those to salvation who, by their faith, have deserved." . . . The Mass is a sacrifice, for "the priests do not only perform

what Christ did in His last supper, but also what He
has afterwards done on the cross." We must accept not
only the words of Scripture, but also the tradition of
the Church.

The Mass is a true sacrifice to God, despite Luther's
objection that it is received by the priest; for so were
all of Moses' sacrifices received by priests. St. Ambrose and St. Gregory are quoted to prove the Mass a
sacrifice, and Augustine, who says: "The Oblation is
every day renewed, though Christ has but once suffered." . . . "Other sacraments are only profitable
to particular persons receiving them; this, in the Mass,
is beneficial to all, in general." Moreover, even "the
wickedness of the minister, be it never so great, is not
able to lessen or avert the benefit of It from the people."
It is to be adored, and also received at least once a year.
Henry sums up this chapter and shows that Luther
tries to draw people and even clergy from receiving
Communion.

CHAPTER V

Of Baptism

"HE has treated of Baptism itself after such a manner, that it had been better he had not touched it at all."
Have faith and baptism, and then no matter what sins
you commit. "He [Luther] says, 'The baptized man
. . . cannot lose his salvation, though willing to do it,
by any sin whatsoever, except infidelity.'" Penance is
not necessary, though St. Jerome said, "Penance is the
board after shipwreck." Next Luther says that faith
without the sacrament suffices. The two theories of the
causality of sacramental grace are contradicted by
Luther; he makes faith a cloak for a wicked life; he

would undo all authority and order. "Why does he thus reproachfully raise himself against the Bishop of Rome? . . . To demolish Christ's Church, so long founded upon a firm rock; erecting to themselves a new church, compacted of flagitious and impious people."

CHAPTER VI

Of the Sacrament of Penance

FORGIVENESS is no new doctrine, as Luther would imply, but a very old and common practice indeed.

CHAPTER VII

Of Contrition

LUTHER says that "after they are loosed by the word of man here on earth, they are absolved by God in heaven."

If God "has promised forgiveness only to those who are as contrite as the greatness of their crimes requires, then Luther himself cannot (as he commands all others to be) be assured and out of doubt that his sins are forgiven him. If God has promised pardon to such as are less contrite—attrites—by that Luther agrees with those he but now reprehended. But if God has promised it to such as have no manner of sorrow for their sins, He has surely much more promised it to such as are attrite. . . . If he admits but only contrition, that is, a sufficient grief, then can nobody be assured that he is absolved."

Besides, Luther's motives for contrition are not even as good as those always inculcated.

CHAPTER VIII

Of Confession

LUTHER says public sins are to be confessed; he is not clear on private sins. Ecclesiasticus, St. John Chrysostom, Numbers, St. James, Isaias, St. Ambrose, St. Augustine, and custom, all prove confession of secret sins by "the divine order of God. . . . Confession was instituted and is preserved by God Himself, not by any custom of the people, or institution of the Fathers."

"Now Luther is condemning the reservation of some sins . . . so as not to discern jurisdiction from Order. Luther says Christ's words, conferring the power of forgiving sins, apply to the laity; Augustine, Bede, Ambrose, the whole Church deny it; which do you believe?"

CHAPTER IX

Of Satisfaction

LUTHER says satisfaction is a renewal of life, and asserts that the Church does not teach this. He asserts that faith without good works suffices: "God does nothing regard our works." Henry exhorts Luther to repent and make satisfaction for his undervaluing Penance, and, indeed, denying it to be a sacrament at all.

CHAPTER X

Of Confirmation

LUTHER denies this to be a sacrament. Tradition, Henry shows, is authority for our faith. Then Henry expounds the sacrament of Confirmation.

CHAPTER XI

Of the Sacrament of Marriage

"MARRIAGE . . . is . . . denied by Luther to be any sacrament at all. Luther says, 'Marriage was amongst the ancient Patriarchs and amongst the Gentiles, and that as truly as amongst us, yet was it not a sacrament with either of them.' Divorcement was not lawful in former times amongst the people of God."

Henry, quoting from Ephesians, declares: "He tells you 'that the man and wife make one body, of which the man is the head; and that Christ and the Church make one body, of which Christ is the head.'" Adam's words, "A man shall leave father and mother and cleave to his wife," show the dignity of marriage —a "great sacrament in Christ and His Church." Moreover, says Henry, "Observe that the Apostle's business, in that place, to the Ephesians, is not about teaching them how great a sacrament Christ joined with the Church is; but about exhorting married people how to behave themselves one towards another, so as they might render their marriage a sacrament, like, and agreeable to, that so sacred a thing of which it is a sacrament." Luther's saying the Greek *word* is mystery does not change the sense of the *thing* named, "seeing it is taught so to be by the circumstance of the whole matter. . . . There is no sacrament but what is a mystery." Augustine and Jerome disagree with Luther. . . . "Augustine, above a thousand times, calls it the sacrament of marriage."

"The Apostle says, 'This sacrament is great, but I speak in Christ and the Church.' What sacrament is that that is great in Christ and the Church? Christ and the Church cannot be a sacrament in Christ and

the Church; for none speaks after this manner. It is therefore a necessary consequence that this sacrament, which he says is great in Christ and the Church, is that conjunction of man and wife which he has spoken of."

Luther denies that matrimony gives any grace. The Apostle calls it "a bed unspotted," and Henry argues that "marriage should not have an immaculate bed, if the grace, which is infused by it, did not turn that unto grace, which should be otherwise a sin."

"The Apostle saith, 'If any brother hath a wife, an infidel, and she consent to live with him, let him not put her away. And if any woman hath a husband, an infidel, and he consent to dwell with her, let her not put away her husband. For the man, an infidel, is sanctified by the faithful woman; and the woman, an infidel, is sanctified by the faithful husband; otherwise your children should be unclean, but now they are holy.' Do not these words of the Apostle show that in marriage . . . the sanctity of the sacrament sanctifies the whole marriage, which before was altogether unclean ?"

When it is said of the first marriage, "God blessed them [Adam and Eve], did He give no grace to their souls ?" . . .

" 'What God hath joined together, let no man put asunder.' . . . There must be understood sure something more holy than the care of propagating the flesh, which God performs in marriage; and that, without all doubt, is grace; which is, by the Prelate of all sacraments, infused into married people in consecrating marriage."

So reasoning and tradition both prove marriage to be a sacrament.

CHAPTER XII

Of the Sacrament of Orders

LUTHER denies Orders to be a sacrament. "There is no difference of priesthood between the laity and priest: all men are priests alike. . . . The sacrament of Orders is nothing else but the custom of electing a preacher in the Church . . . whose wicked doctrine all men may see tends directly to the destruction of the faith of Christ by infidelity."

"The Church," says Luther, "can discern the word of God from the word of men." Luther's fundamental reduced *ad absurdum*. Did not the Apostle warn Timothy, "Impose not hands lightly upon any man"? Were not Aaron and his sons made priests of the Old Law? Luther reviles St. Dionysius, who calls Orders a sacrament. Testimonies of St. Jerome, St. Gregory and St. Augustine as to Orders being a sacrament, and of a permanent character. Luther shown to be wrong in saying laymen are equal to priests, for priests only can consecrate. Luther had even said: "That the people without the bishop, but not the bishop without the people, can ordain priests." Why, then, says Henry, does the Apostle warn Timothy, " 'Neglect not the grace which is in thee, and which has been given thee by prophecy, by the imposition of the hands of the presbytery'? And in another place, to the same, 'I admonish thee that thou stir up the grace of God that is in thee, by the imposition of my hands.' " Résumé.

CHAPTER XIII

Of the Sacrament of Extreme Unction

"If ever Luther was mad at any time, . . . he is certainly distracted here, in the Sacrament of Extreme Unction," says Henry. "You see how he here endeavours in two ways to weaken the words of the Apostle. First he will not have the epistle to have been writ by the Apostle. Secondly, though it was by him written, yet will he not have the Apostle to have authority of instituting sacraments. . . . They are the chief weapons by which he intends to destroy this sacrament." But Luther is confuted by St. Jerome and by Luther himself. When Extreme Unction should be administered. It is a sign of grace for the soul; not necessarily to give health to the body. " 'This Unction,' he says, 'is no sacrament, because it does not always heal the body.' " Luther has reason to deny St. James' Epistle, for it denies Luther's teaching. But Luther goes farther and denies and defies the whole Church. "I advise all Christians that, as the most exterminating of plagues, they shun him who endeavours to bring into the Church of Christ such foul prodigies, being the very doctrine of anti-Christ. For, if he who endeavours to move a schism in any one thing is to be extirpated with all care, with what great endeavour is he to be rooted out who not only goes about to sow dissension, but to stir up the people against the chief Bishop, children against their parents, Christians against the Vicar of Christ." Though he shows signs of death, yet he will not let the pious Vicar of Christ act as the Good Shepherd and save him from the wolf of hell. If Luther had spoken privately to the Pope of the errors he condemned, the Pope had doubtless blessed him. But no! He publicly

exposed and pointed to the shame of his father. "After which he was summoned to Rome, that he might either render reasons for his writings, or recant what he had inconsiderately written, having any security imaginable offered him, that he should not undergo the punishment which he deserved, with sufficient expenses offered him for his journey. But . . . he refused to go. And . . . made his appeal to a general council, yet not to every council, but to such as should next meet in the Holy Ghost; that in whatsoever council he was condemned, he might deny the Holy Ghost to be present therein. The most conscientious shepherd has at length been forced to cast out from the fold the sheep suffering with an incurable disease, lest the sound sheep be corrupted by contact."

Henry wishes Luther might repent, and exhorts all Christians to unity: "Do not listen to the insults and detractions against the Vicar of Christ, which the fury of this little monk spews up against the Pope . . . this one little monk, . . . in temper more harmful than all Turks, all Saracens, all infidels everywhere."

Occasion, Origin and Motive of the "Assertio"

In this chapter the Occasion, Origin and Motive of the royal *tractate* will be set forth in the words of reputable chroniclers and historians. It is hoped that the reader will not be repelled by the series of quotations—their excuse is the not unreasonable one that it has cost time and labour to bring them together, some from rare and at times inaccessible books; in a very few cases the writer has been obliged to take them at second-hand.

To begin, then, with—

I. *The Occasion of the "Assertio"*:

Audin* tells us that across the sea "Germany now, for the first time, beheld her ancient faith attacked, not by arguments, but by ridicule, for that was the weapon used by Luther." . . . That, moreover, "This apostate monk . . . would recognize the existence of no law for his own personal acts, either moral or physical; . . . that Luther . . . asserted that a single individual might be right, though opposed to popes, councils, doctors, the past and the present; . . . that he compared the syllogism to the ass."

Luther's "Babylonish Captivity" was sent by Luther to the Pope, "with expressions of personal respect, and invoking him to set about a work of reformation in his corrupt court."†

*Henry VIII., Ch. IX., pp. 88, 89.
†Beckett's English Reformation, XVII.

James Gairdner* says that "Luther in his 'Babylonish Captivity' repudiated the Pope's authority entirely, attacked the whole scholastic system, . . . and declared four of the reputed seven sacraments to be of only human origin."

As to *England* the situation is briefly but clearly stated by Paton :† "The long reign of Henry VIII., 1509-1547, falls practically into two periods of nineteen years each: in the former of which he was the champion of Popery against all comers, against Luther among the rest, under the title still worn by our sovereigns, 'Defender of the Faith.' "

It was in the former half of his reign that the composition of the King's treatise took place; a few quotations from the best sources will give a reliable outline of the situation which occasioned the "Assertio." Polydore Vergil,‡ a contemporary Italian historian of England, says of Henry's book and its title:

"Quocirca Henricus rex, qui habebat regnum suum maxime omnium religiosum, veritus ne uspiam labes aliqua religionis fieret, primum libros Lutheranos, quorum magnus jam numerus pervenerat in manus suorum Anglorum, comburendos curavit, deinde libellum contra eam doctrinam luculenter composuit misitque ad Leonem pontificem, . . . tum Henricum defensorem fidei appellavit, quo ille deinceps titulo usus est."

Confirming this statement of the large quantity of Luther's books already in England, is the injunction

---

*English Church in the Sixteenth Century, p. 78.

†James Porter, British History and Papal Claims, Vol. I., p. 40.

‡Polydori Vergilii Urbinatis. Angliæ Historiæ Libri Vigintiseptem, lib. XXVII., fol. 664. As to Polydore Vergil's reliability, Mr. H. Ellis, in the Preface to Polydore Vergil's English History, published by the Camden Society, says: "That Polydore Vergil's History is entirely without mistakes cannot be asserted, but they are very few."

against their being read, sent by Leo to Wolsey; it is as follows:*

"Et quia dicti errores et plures alii in diversis libellis per Martinum Lutherum hæresiarcham compositis, continebantur, libellos ipsos in quocumque idiomate reperiebantur, damnavimus, ne libellos, hujusmodi errores ipsos continentes legere, imprimere, publicare, seu defendere, aut in domibus suis, sive aliis publicis vel privatis locis tenere quomodo præsumerent; quinimmo illos, statim post literarum nostrarum, super his editarum publicationem ubicumque forent per ordinarios et alios in dictis literis expressos diligenter quæsitos, publice et solemniter in præsentia cleri et populi, sub pœnis in iisdem literis expressis, comburentur, ipsique Martino, ut ab omni prædicatione desisteret, jussimus."

The following extract describes the condemnation and burning of Luther's books at St. Paul's Church, London, and complements the foregoing quotation; it shows also that the Pope's mandate was promptly and solemnly executed. It is from the Cottonian MSS. in the British Museum (Vitell. b. 4, p. 111) and is entitled: "Pope's Sentence against Martin Luther, published at London."

"The xij daye of Maye in the yeare of our Lord 1521, and in the thirteenth yeare of the Reigne of our Soveraigne Lord Kinge Henry the eighte of that Name, the Lord Thomas Wolsey, by the grace of God Legate de Latere, Cardinal of Sainct Cecely and Archbishop of Yorke, came unto Saint Paules Churche of London, with the most parte of the Byshops of the Realme, where he was received with procession, and sensid by

* Rymer, Fœdera, Vol. XIII., p. 742. "Bulla Leonis X. Cardinali Eborum, de potestatibus super lectione librorum Martini Lutheri."

Mr. Richard Pace, then beinge Deane of the said Church. After which ceremonies done, there were four Doctors that bare a canope of cloth of gold over him goinge to the Highe Alter, where he made his oblacion; which done, hee proceeded forth as abovesaid to the Crosse in Paules Church Yeard, where was ordeined a scaffold for the same cause, and he, sittinge under his cloth of estate which was ordeined for him, his two crosses on everie side of him; on his right hand sittinge on the place where hee set his feete, the Pope's embassador, and nexte him the Archbishop of Canterbury: on his left hand the Emperor's embassador, and nexte him the Byshop of Duresme, and all the other Byshops with other noble prelates sate on twoe formes outeright forthe, and ther the Byshop of Rochester made a sermon, by the consentinge of the whole clergie of England, by the commandment of the Pope, against one Martinus Eleuthereus, and all his workes, because hee erred sore, and spake against the hollie faithe; and denounced them accursed which kept anie of his bookes, and there were manie burned in the said church yeard of his said bookes duringe the sermon, which ended, my Lord Cardinall went home to dinner with all the other prelates."

Not only was London infected with Luther's errors, but they had reached Hereford at least, for in Wilkins' "Concilia"* we read of Wolsey's order to the Bishop of Hereford about Luther's books and a catalogue of forty-two errors contained in them: it is entitled as follows: "Mandatum cardinalis Wolseii episcopo Herefordensi, de exquirendis libris M. Lutheri prohibitis; cum catalogo XLII errorum in iis contentorum ex. reg. Episc. Heref., fol. 66."

* Vol. III., p. 690.

Lord Herbert of Cherbury, a seventeenth-century historian of Henry VIII., says :*

"Our king, being at leisure now from wars, and for the rest delighting much in learning, thought he could not give better proof either of his zeal or education, than to write against Luther. In this also he was exasperated, for that Luther had often times spoken contemptuously of the learned Thomas of Acquine, who yet was so much in request with the King, . . . that, as Polydore hath it, he was called Thomisticus."

And Roscoe, in his Life of Leo X.,† adds to this and says :

"Such was the reception they [the new opinions of the Reformation] met with in this country [England], that Henry VIII., who had, in his youth, devoted some portion of his time to ecclesiastical and scholastic studies, not only attempted to counteract their effects by severe restrictions, but condescended to enter the lists of controversy with Luther, in his well-known work, written in Latin, and entitled 'A Vindication of the Seven Sacraments.' "

Henry, then, loved theological learning in general, and St. Thomas in particular, as its most gifted exponent; for this reason alone Luther must have been odious to the royal English theologian.

Audin‡ says :

"Luther again republished his insulting tirade against the 'Angel of the Schools' in his 'Captivity of the Church at Babylon.' . . . All Henry's knowledge of theology, and he was no bad theologian, he was indebted for to St. Thomas Aquinas, his inseparable companion, who, beautifully bound, occupied the most

---

*Life and Reign of Henry VIII., p. 85.
†Bohn ed., II., p. 231.
‡Henry VIII., p. 89.

prominent place in his library, and which he read over
and over again, and each time with fresh ardour; and
his chief advisers, Fisher, Wolsey, and More, were as
enamoured with St. Thomas as himself. . . . Happily for Henry, the monk, in his 'Captivity of the
Church at Babylon,' had created a new dogma, whence
he had excluded the sacraments of order, extreme unction and penance; indulgences, purgatory and the papacy. . . . His [Henry's] address, 'Ad Lectores,'
which he placed at the commencement, might have been
taken as the production of a theologian of the twelfth
century. His aged mother had been insulted, and therefore, as an affectionate son, he had hastened to her defence."

II. *The Origin of the "Assertio."*—On this subject
Bishop Creighton's* remarks are rich and graphic:

"But besides ecclesiastical ceremonies (in London)
and bonfires of Luther's books, Wolsey discussed with
his master (Henry VIII.) the theological aspect of Luther's teaching. Henry showed such knowledge of the
subject that Wolsey suggested he should express his
views in writing. The result was that the English King
entered the lists of theological controversy. . . . In
August the book was printed, though it was not published till it had been formally presented to the Pope.
Alexander received an early copy. He found the work
to be a collection of precious gems. 'If kings,' he writes,
'are of this strength, farewell to us philosophers.' . . .
Henry felt aggrieved that the English King had no
title to set by the side of 'Catholic' and 'Most Christian,'
which were enjoyed by the Kings of Spain and France.
Wolsey represented to the Pope that the English King
deserved some recognition of his piety and the claim

*History of the Papacy during the Period of the Reformation,
Vol. V., pp. 163, 164.

engaged the serious attention of a consistory on June
10. There was no lack of suggestions: 'Faithful,'
'Orthodox,' 'Apostolic,' 'Ecclesiastical,' 'Proctor,' are
some out of the number. . . . The King's book ar-
rived at Rome, and on September 14 was presented to
the Pope, who read it with avidity and extolled it to
the skies. But this was not enough to mark the importance of the occasion, and it was formally presented in a
consistory. After this the Pope proposed 'Defender of
the Faith' as a suitable title; some demurred on the
ground that a title ought not to exceed a single word,
and still hankered after 'The Orthodox' or 'Most Faithful'; but the Pope decided in favor of 'Defender of the
Faith,' and all agreed. . . . In a letter written by
Pace to Wolsey, November 19 (Brewer, Calendar,
1772), the King's thanks are conveyed to Wolsey for
having suggested this work. Doubtless the King consulted with others, chiefly with Fisher, but there is no
reason to doubt that the work was substantially his own."

Pallavicini* also declares that Cardinal Wolsey
asked the Pope for some extraordinary title for Henry.

An interesting and rare account of the origin of the
"Assertio" is given in the quaint old book entitled
"The Annals of England."† It says:

"The King having written a booke against Martin
Luther, sent it as a present to Pope Leo the
Tenth. . . .

"Henry being offended with Luther's new (as the
world then deemed them) tenets, thought it would
prove to his honour, by writing against Luther, to manifest his learning and piety to the world. Herupon
under his name a book was set forth, better beseeming

*Hist. du Con. de Trente, I., col. 676.

†In Latin, by Francis Lord Bishop of Hereford. **Englished by**
Morgan Godwyn, p. 47.

some antient and deep divine, than a youthful prince, (whom although he earnestly endeavoured it, yet his affairs would not permit to bury himselfe among his books) which many thought to have been compiled by Sir Tho. More, some by the Bishop of Rochester, and others (not without cause) suspected to be the worke of some other great scholler. . . . This booke was so acceptable to the Pope, that according to the example of Alexander the Sixt, who entituled the King of Spain Catholic; and of that Pope whosoever he were, that gave the French King the title of Most Christian; he decreed to grace King Henry and his successors with that honourable one of 'Defender of the Faith,' which severall titles are by these princes to this day."

The historian Speed* seems to belittle the worth of the title and the King's personal merit. He says:

"Carolus, Henricus, vivant, defensor uterque,
Henricus fidei, Carolus Ecclesiæ.

"Why the titles Defender of the Church and Faith were attributed unto these two Princes, is no marvell; for Charles chosen Emperour, was scarcely confirmed, but to purchase the Pope's favour, he directed forth a solemne Writ of outlawry against Martin Luther, who then had given a great blow to the Papal Crowne. And King Henry likewise was renowned in Rome, for writing a Booke against the said Luther, unpropping the tottering or downe-cast countenance of the Pope's pardons; which Luther shrewdly had shaken; the Pope therefore, to show himselfe a kinde father unto those his sonnes, gave them these titles; which in truth were none other, then the same which they sware unto, when the Crownes of their empires were first set upon their heads."

Luther had said in his "Babylonian Captivity": "I

*Hist. of Great Brit., p. 991.

must now deny that there are seven Sacraments, and bind them to three—baptism, the Lord's Supper, and penance." Apropos of this denial, Canon Flanagan gives the following account* of the occasion of the King's treatise:

"Henry VIII. himself, assisted, it is thought, by Wolsey, and Fisher the bishop of Rochester, and Sir Thomas More, wrote a treatise upon the seven Sacraments against Luther. The latter speedily answered, never being at a loss, if not for arguments at least for fitting words. His answer was replied to by Sir Thomas More. Again he [Luther] took up the pen. . . . It was in acknowledgment of this defence of the Church's doctrine that Henry received from the Pope what his successors have tenaciously retained, the title of 'Defender of the Faith.' It appears that sometime before writing the treatise, he had sued for the title of 'Most Christian' which Julius II. had threatened to withdraw from the schismatical Louis XII. Disappointed in this, he presented his treatise to Leo X. for his examination and approval, and petitioned for the other title, promising to be equally zealous against Luther's followers in England as against Luther himself. It was granted after 'mature deliberation' by Leo in 1521, and again by Clement in 1524."

III. *The Motive of the "Assertio."*—As to the motive for which the "Assertio" was composed, Mr. John Clark, Orator for Henry VIII., in his address to Leo X. at the presentation of the "Assertio" at the papal court, says:

"Only first be pleased that I declare the Reason that moved my most serene King to undertake this Work. For I believe it will cause Admiration in several, that a Prince . . . should now, for the Glory of God, and

*Vol. II., pp. 24, 25, of his " History of the Church in England."

Tranquillity of the Roman Church, by his Ingenuity and Pen, put a Stop to Heresies, which so endanger the Catholic Faith.

"These, most holy Father, are the chief Reasons, of his entering upon this Work: his accustomed Veneration to Your Holiness; Christian Piety in the Cause of God; and a royal Grief and Indignation of seeing Religion trodden under Foot. I confess the Desire of Glory might have been able to have induced him to these Things . . . in the field of learning against Martin Luther."

Henry himself, in his "Epistle Dedicatory" to Leo, states "the Reasons that obliged Us to take upon Us this Charge of Writing. We have seen Tares cast into our Lord's Harvest; Sects do spring up, and Heresies increase, . . . also to declare Our great Respect towards Your Holiness, Our Endeavours for the Propagation of the Faith of Christ, and Our Obedience to the Service of Almighty God." And in his "To the Reader," Henry declares: "I cannot but think myself obliged . . . to defend my Mother, the Spouse of Christ."

In the "Archæologia," Vol. XXIII., page 69, Ellis, quoting John Bruce, says: "Henry's book was not *written* to get the title but was *seized upon as a clinching argument* for obtaining the title which *had been asked*—the book being all the while in preparation, but not formally for that purpose."

Father Bridgett thinks that Henry acted from a high and pure intention, i. e., the defence of the Church. He says:* "In 1520 Luther published his treatise called 'The Babylonian Captivity,' in which he finally broke with the Church, railed at the Pope, and called on the world to embrace an entirely new religion, under the name of genuine Christianity.

*Sir Thomas More, pp. 210–212.

"In 1521, Henry printed his book called 'Defence of the Seven Sacraments.' Luther replied in a treatise so scurrilous that it has probably no parallel in literature. Certainly such language had never before been addressed to a King or Prince. It cannot be said that Henry had drawn this upon his own head. He had not attacked Luther, but stepped in as the Church's champion, to ward off the blows Luther was aiming at her. On the whole his defence is dignified, and he uses language no stronger than had been used in all ages, by saints and doctors, against inventors of novelties and disturbers of unity. In this book of Henry's More had no other share than that, after it was written, he had arranged the index. But against his will he was drawn into the controversy. . . . The King, however, in all probability, himself suggested to More that his wit would be well employed in chastising the insolent friar. This I gather from More's own words: . . . 'Nothing could have been more painful to me than to be forced to speak foul words to pure ears. But there was no help for it.' . . . His book is not a treatise on Lutheranism, for Lutheranism as a system had not yet been enunciated, and was still incomplete in the brain of its author. He refutes indeed both the denials and assertions of Luther as they occur, but it is with Luther himself and Luther's language to Henry that he is dealing. . . . He did not consider that his own book was to have any permanent value."

Finally as to Henry's motive in writing the "Assertio" a most clever and interesting piece of literary detective work, whether convincing or not, has been done by Seebohm. It is this: Gairdner, in his "History of the English Church,"* says that Henry "declared to More a secret reason for maintaining it [the Pope's

* P. 79.

supremacy] so strongly; of which reason Sir Thomas
had never heard before, and which must remain to us
a matter of speculation."

Seebohm has tried to fathom this secret. He says:
"I propose in this paper* to inquire what was the motive which induced Henry VIII. to write his celebrated
book against Luther. The motive hitherto assigned—
that of earning the title of 'Defender of the Faith'—
does not, upon consideration, seem to me a sufficiently
strong one. . . . Henry, knowing that the validity
of his own marriage [with Catharine of Aragon] and
Mary's legitimacy depended upon the validity of the
Papal power of dispensation, would be likely to regard
the attack of Luther upon the Papal power, when in
1521 it assumed so dangerous an attitude, as a question of personal importance to himself. He had, indeed, abundant reason to insert in his book against
Luther passages which appeared unwisely strong to the
mind of Sir Thomas More, as yet uninitiated into royal
secrecy, and at the same time skeptical of the divine
authority of the Papal jurisdiction. What, then, was
this 'secret cause' of which More 'had never heard before,' and which, when divulged, proved the turning-
point in his views on this subject? The conjecture
may at least be hazarded that it also related to the
King's marriage. It is not only possible, but also most
probable, that More, relying upon Catharine's assertion previous to her marriage, shared in the popular
view that the impediment to the marriage was one
merely of ecclesiastical law, and not an impediment
'jure divino.' And it is obvious that in this popular
view of the nature of the impediment it was one which

*In the *Fortnightly Review*, edited by John Morley, vol. for Jan.
—June, pp. 509 and fol., 1868, " Sir Thomas More and Henry VIII.'s
Book against Luther," by Frederic Seebohm.

the Pope could well be considered as able to dispense
with by virtue of the power vested in him by the common consent of Christendom, whether the Papal supremacy were of divine institution or not.   The secret
which Henry divulged to More may therefore have
been, what afterwards became the ground for the divorce, viz., that the previous marriage with Prince
Arthur having been consummated was an impediment
'jure divino,' and consequently, could not be dispensed
with by the Pope unless the Papal power of dispensation were held to be 'jure divino.' "*

Mr. Brown† seems inspired by the same idea when
he writes that Henry was not sincere in his book, especially about the authority of the Pope, but that he had
an "ulterior aim."

What truth is in this alleged motive it is surely difficult, not to say impossible, to decide, for while Henry's
after life would incline one to believe him capable of a
deep ulterior purpose, his earlier life would lead one to
believe him sincere and earnest.   Was his motive in
writing the "Assertio" to save his own English people
and Europe from the new religious movement?   Was
it to check Luther, or at least to be avenged on him?
Was it to obtain a Papal title?   Was it to strengthen
the foundation of the Papal authority?   The latter may
have been the predominant motive in the King's mind,
without exclusion of the others; the relative force of
each it would be difficult now to estimate with any degree of accuracy.

*Conf. "The Era of the Protestant Revolution," by Seebohm,
pp. 172 and fol., *Scribner's*, 1874. The execution of the Duke of
Buckingham at this time by Henry is attributed by Seebohm to
Buckingham's having spoken of the invalidity of Henry's marriage
with Catharine.

†Roy. Hist. So. Transactions, VIII., 257.

Authorship of the "Assertio"

WHO wrote the "Assertio"? That is, who composed or compiled it? For the authorship is far from a settled question.

The chief testimonies adverse to Henry's authorship are first given and then those maintaining it, that the reader may be convinced by both the greater authority and number of the latter that, to say the least, it is *more* probable that Henry *wrote* the book: *very* probable that he *compiled* it, at any rate.

First, then, the testimonies *against* Henry's authorship. In the "Calendar of State Papers between England and Spain,"* edited by Bergenrath, we read the following:

"The King of England has sent a book against Martin Luther to the Pope. It is said that all the learned men in England have taken part in its composition. Hears that it is a good book. The Pope has given to the King of England the title of 'Defender of the Christian Faith.' This title prejudices no one, as all Christian princes are, or ought to be, defenders of the faith.

"[Written on the margin by Gattinara:] It is true that all princes ought to be defenders of the Christian faith. As, however, this title has been given to the King of England, it makes it seem as if he deserved it more than others, and as if others do not defend the faith so well as he does."†

*Henry VIII., Vol. II., p. 381.
†See also Lives of the English Cardinals, by Folkstone Williams, Vol. II., p. 870, note, who quotes: "Juan Manuel writes, 17th October, 1521: 'The King of England has sent a book against Mar-

While personally Pocock believes Henry to be the author, yet he is fair and honest enough to quote the following :*

"A letter of Cardinal Wolsey's to King Henry with a copy of his book for the Pope.   An original.

". . . 'I do send Mr. Tate unto your Highness with the book bound and dressed which ye purpose to send to the Pope's holiness. . . . I do send also unto your highness the choice of certain verses to be written in the book to be sent to the Pope of your own hand: with the subscription of your name. . . . By your

'Most humble chaplain,

'T. Car^{lis} Ebor.' "

This is certainly rather strong testimony, and adverse to Henry's authorship.   And yet its corrective swung Pocock's decision to the other side of the question.

But judgment must be suspended till all the evidence, both against and for Henry, is fully and fairly heard. So, then, to proceed.

Audin† says: "The literati of the day were supposed to have had a hand in the composition of the work," and he continues, in a note, saying that Calvin said: "This book was written by some monk well versed in cavilling, and the King, having been influenced by his advisers, consented that it should be printed in his name, and though he has since repented of his rash and inconsiderate act, he allowed it to pass under his name for thirty years."

tin Luther to the Pope.   It is said that all the learned men of England have taken part in its composition.   He hears that it is a good book. The Pope has given to the King of England the title of " Defender of the Christian Faith." '   Written on the margin by Gattinara."— London, Allen, 1868.

*Burnet's Reformation, by Pocock, Vol. VI., No. 3.

†Henry VIII., p. 92.

A humorous confession, in frankness characteristic of its authors, is said by Worsley* to have been made by Luther's countrymen. It is as follows:

"To the Germans especially it appeared marvellous that a crowned head should contain so much learning."

In the "Catalogue of the Noble and Royal Authors of England," in two volumes (London, MDCCLIX.), Vol. I., p. 9, we read an insidious innuendo:

"HENRY THE EIGHTH. As all the successors of this Prince owe their unchangeable title of Defender of the Faith to his piety and learning, we do not presume to question his pretensions to a place in this catalogue. Otherwise a little skepticism on his Majesty's talents for such a performance, mean as it is, might make us question whether he did not write the defence of the Sacraments against Luther, as one of his Successors [Charles I.] is supposed to have written the Εἰκὼν Βασιλική; that is, with the pen of some court-prelate."

Mr. Richard Watson Dixon, in his "History of the Church of England," Vol. I., page 4, says rather disparagingly of Henry, that he was "a man of force without grandeur, . . . of great ability but not of lofty intellect, . . . cunning rather than sagacious." In other words, that on the principle "nemo dat quod non habet," Henry did not write the "Assertio."

How did it come about then? How did Henry's name get to be popularly appended to it as the author? Here is one answer:† "Cardinal Wolsey, having a mind to engage the King to act against Luther, whose opinions daily spread and got ground here in England, contrived that an answer should be written to this book, which the King should own for his, and be presented to the Pope in his name." This is also stated by

*Worsley, Dawn of the Reformation, p. 160.
†Lewis's Fisher, Vol. I., p. 107.

Turner in his "History of England,"* where he says that Henry's book "is not unlikely to have originated, less from Henry's literary conscience, than from Wolsey's crafty contrivances."

The famous John Foxe, in his "Acts and Monuments,"† says:

"This book, albeit it carried the King's name in the title, yet it was another that administered the motion, another that framed the style."

And here ends the direct testimony against Henry's authorship. For though what follows—i. e., the grounds on which rest the claims of others to be the author of the "Assertio"—might at first sight be expected to tell against Henry, yet eventually it will prove in favour of the King of England. Because as none of these other claims can be substantiated, they only add, by elimination, a new indirect argument in favour of Henry's being the author.

But if not Henry who else could have composed the "Assertio"? Passing by the allusion to Wolsey's having a hand in the authorship, as not sustained by authorities, Blessed John Fisher, the Bishop of Rochester, is the most likely, and for the following reasons: The "Assertio" is bound up with his works in the Wirceburg edition.‡

Pallavicini says:§ "Some have attributed to him [Fisher] the book which King Henry had had printed against Luther."

The Bishop of La Rochelle, Clement Villecourt, says

*Henry VIII., Vol. I., p. 280.

†Vol. IV., p. 293.

‡R.D.D. Joannis Fischerii Roffensis in Anglia episcopi opera (Wirceburgi, 1597) : "Assertio Septem Sacramentorum adversus Martinum Lutherum, ab Henrico VIII., Angliæ Rege, Roffensis tamen nostri hortatu et studio edita."

§Tome I., col. 848.

most decidedly that Henry was not the author, but that Fisher very probably was. His words are: "Je crois volontiers qu'il [Henri] est mort sans en avoir bien connu une seule page [de la Captivité de Babylone].

"Si la Défense des sept Sacrements a été écrite par ce prince [Henri], ma conviction bien prononcée est qu'il n'en a été que le copiste, ou qu'il s'est borné à l'écrire sous la dictée de quelqu'un.

"Ce n'est pas à quinze ans, et avant cet âge, qu'on peut être capable de quelque succès dans celle étude.

"Je suis persuadé que Henri n'a jamais ouvert un volume du docteur angélique."

Further, the bishop says that Fisher could write the "Assertio" in a few months, whereas it would take Henry as many years; that Henry's life was so different from the principles of the "Assertio" that he could not have written it.

With this unhesitating statement of Villecourt, Thomson, in his "Memoirs of the Court of Henry VIII.,"* agrees partly, adding another name to the list of probable authors. He says: "The world . . . has attributed all that is valuable in this work to the assistance of Bishop Fisher and of Sir Thomas More."

So much for Fisher's claims; those of More may be given next. And there are indeed strong testimonies in favour of More's authorship, as may be seen from the following citations.

The "Annals of England"† says of More: "Thomas More . . . cultivated literature, and being introduced at court about 1521, he soon became a favourite with the King, whom he assisted in the composition of his work against Luther."

But this is not the only testimony in favour of More's

*Vol. I., p. 380.
†3 vols., Oxford, 1856, Vol. II., p. 137, note.

authorship. In the "Archæologia," published by the
Society of Antiquaries of London, in Volume XXIII.
there is a transcript of an original MS. containing a
memorial from Geo. Constentyne to Thos. Lord Cromwell, etc. (p. 55 and note). It speaks of "the doubt
which he entertains as to the authorship of the book
against Luther, which bears Henry's name—a doubt
which appears to have arisen partly from common report, but more directly from his knowledge of the extent
of the King's scholarship. It may be seen that he attributes the work to Sir Thomas More."

Again W. H. Hutton, in his "Sir Thomas More,"*
says: "He [More] had assisted him [Henry] in his
book against Luther."

A fourth author, or co-worker at least, has been suggested. Schaff† says: "Henry VIII. wrote in 1521
(probably with the assistance of his chaplain, Edward
Lee) a scholastic defence of the seven Sacraments,
against Luther's 'Babylonish Captivity.' " Schaff probably bases this statement on the words of Luther, who
"believed it to be the book of Dr. Edward Lee, afterwards Archbishop of York, . . . and he struck at Lee
through the King."‡ Luther says:§ "There are some
who believe that Henry is not the author of the work.
. . . My opinion is that King Henry, perhaps, gave
one or two yards of cloth to Lee, . . . and that Lee had
made thereof a cape, to which he has sewed on a lining.
What is there so wonderful in a King of England having written against me ? . . . If a King of England spits
forth his lying insults in my face, I have the right, in
self-defence, to thrust them down his throat."

*P. 189.
†History of the Christian Church, VI., § 70.
‡Gairdner, English Church in Sixteenth Century, p. 80.
§Audin, Henry VIII., pp. 96, 97.

To the names of Wolsey, Fisher, More and Lee a fifth one, Gardiner, is added by Fuller in a pretty, even if not very serious way. "King Henry had lately set forth a book against Luther, endeavouring the confutation of his opinions as novel and unsound. None suspect this King's lack of learning (though many his lack of leisure from his pleasures,) for such a design; however, it is probable that some other *Gardiner* gathered the flowers, (made the collections,) though King Henry had the honour to wear the posey, carrying the credit of the title thereof."*

A sixth probable associate-author is presented because of his style, the claimant being Pace, and his supporter being Hutton, who "thinks that the aid of More and *Pace* 'at most extended to the composition and correction of the Latin style.' "†

Indeed, a seventh candidate might be added, were it not that the principal himself withdraws his claim; for Erasmus says (Epist. Jo. Glapioni, Edit. Leid. p. 743) that "in Germany he [Erasmus] was thought to be the author of it." But in the preface of Jortin's edition his apologies and refutation of this statement may be seen.

Such are the statements supporting these different claimants: now for their sifting, criticism and refutation.

And first of all, to be the author of a book need not mean that one has no quotations from others, no ideas from others, no suggestions, criticisms and helps of this kind. It must be admitted that Henry was very probably helped, that he has many quotations from the Bible and the Fathers, that it seems likely that More assorted, and not improbably made the index to the "Assertio."

*Church History of Britain, by Thomas Fuller, Vol. II., p. 13.
†Overton, The Church in England, Vol. I., p. 357, note 3.

"Quoique Henri se réputât un des plus solides théologiens de son temps, il avait, avant de le publier, soumis son écrit à l'examen et à la correction du cardinal Wolsey, de Fisher, évêque de Rochester, et surtout du savant Chancelier Thomas Morus."* This is admitted, but it would be a groundless deduction to conclude that Henry did not write the "Assertio."

We are told by the most recent and decided of Henry's adversaries, the Bishop of La Rochelle, that before Henry was fifteen he was too young to have acquired the knowledge; that after that age he had not leisure from his duties of state. As to the first, remembering that Henry had wise, capable parents, and would have the best tutors and aids that the kingdom could give, that he had been prepared, at least remotely, to be Archbishop of Canterbury, that if he simply knew the sources where to go for his materials and arguments, e. g., St. Thomas's "Summa," that with this granted—and it is certainly probable enough—one can see, if he will read the "Assertio," no very great difficulty in Henry's authorship. As to the objection of the Bishop of La Rochelle, that it would take Henry three years to write the "Assertio," this is exactly what Mr. Hutton and Mr. Brewer say was the case, i. e., that as early as 1518 Henry had begun the work, and finished it in 1521. After all, it is a simple treatise, probably almost all culled from some standard work, e. g., St. Thomas, St. Bonaventure, Peter Lombard, etc., as D'Aubigné says, some breviary of collected texts on the subjects treated.

But to answer the suggested authorships other than that of Henry: Wolsey can hardly claim a refutation. As to Fisher being the author, it is to be supposed that

*Dictionnaire de la Théologie Catholique, Wetzer et Welte, art. Henri VIII.

he ought himself to know whether he wrote it; and as he was a man who laid down his life for the truth, it is to be further supposed that we may believe him when he denies emphatically that he is the author.

"It had been rumoured abroad that the prelate had dictated while Henry wrote; 'this,' exclaimed Fisher indignantly, 'is a calumnious falsehood. Let Henry enjoy his meed of praise without any participation in it.'"

As to the "Assertio" being bound up with Fisher's works, at least in the Wirceburg edition, and while it is said to be edited by "the care and zeal of ours of Rochester," yet it is said first to be by the King of England: "Assertio . . . Angliæ Rege, Roffensis tamen nostri hortatu et studio edita."

Moreover, if Fisher, not Henry, were the author, Fisher, not More, would have been "the sorter-out and indexer," for the humble bishop would hardly ask the Chancellor of England to make an index for him. And yet More says that he [More] was the "sorter-out,"* etc.

Furthermore Collier criticized the style of the "Assertio," saying that the King "leans too much on his character as monarch, argues in his garter robes, and writes, as it were, with his sceptre." Now surely the gentle Fisher would write in any style but this, would not rely on character, but give a cold, calm reason for the faith that was in him, as his other works show he did.

But if not Fisher, More, the glory of the age,† was perhaps the author, for "French and English, keen logic, wide knowledge, merciless wit make More an unsurpassed controversialist of his kind."‡ In rebuttal

*Audin, Henry VIII., p. 92, quotes Saconay's introduction to the " Assertio."
†Pocock's Burnet's Reformation, Vol. III., p. 172.
‡More, by Mason, p. 85.

of this, More, who, if anything, was an honest, "plain,
blunt man," replied: "I was only a sorter-out and placer
of the principal matters therein contained." So he is
quoted by his son-in-law, Wm. Roper, Esq.*

Pocock, in his edition of Burnet's "Reformation,"
says:† "It is plain More wrote it not."

A long, full passage in Collier‡ is interesting and
strong, and is quoted here at length:

"Fisher and More are reported by several of the
Church of Rome to have made the book which goes under King Henry's name against Luther; but the Lord
Herbert is not of this opinion. He only thinks they
might look it over at the King's instance, and interpose
their judgment in some passages. But that the King
after all was governed by his own sentiment, and that
More had no hand in the composition appears pretty
plainly from this gentleman's letter to Cromwell dated
March, 1533. He acquaints this minister 'twas formerly his opinion that the Pope's supremacy stood only
on Councils and præscription, and was not jure divino.
That when the King showed him his book against Martin Luther he desired his Highness either to omit the
point of the Papal supremacy or touch it more tenderly
at least. For the asserting the privilege of the Pope's
see to that height might afterwards prove unserviceable,
in case any disputes should happen between the court
of Rome and his Highness: that the stretch of the Pope's
pretensions had been unfortunate to some princes, and
that it was not impossible the same occasions might be
revived.

*Life of Sir Thomas More, Singer, p. 65. See also Lewis's Fisher,
Vol. I., pp. 109, 110.

†III., p. 171.

‡Pt. II., Bk. II., p. 99. See also Turner, Henry VIII., Vol. I.,
p. 281, note.

"To this the King answered he had resolved not to alter anything upon that head, and gave Sir Thomas a reason which was altogether new. This book of the King's, it seems, and his farther reading upon the controversy, made him change his opinion in some measure, and rather conclude, the Pope held his Primacy by divine right. However, as he continues, he still thought the Pope under the jurisdiction of a general council, and that he might be deposed, and another set up, at the pleasure of such an assembly. By this letter it appears More had no share in the book against Luther: and that he believed the King the author of that tract."

Finally, as summing up, we quote from Mr. Brown, who says:*

"Mr. Brewer seems to believe the book to have been written by Henry because it is so bad. The Bishop of La Rochelle, who wrote an introduction to the French edition of 1850, considers it impossible that he could have produced the work, because it is so good. Horace Walpole pronounces the book a bad one, and yet too good for Henry to have written." May not these three opinions be explained on the ground of subjective religious bias? Mr. Brewer deeming it *"bad"* for *Protestants* because so Catholic; the Bishop of La Rochelle *"good"* for *Catholics* because so Catholic; and Mr. Walpole *"bad"* because against Protestants, and yet too *"good"* for Henry, lest Henry be shown to have been so thoroughly Catholic.

As for the claims of Lee, Gardiner, Pace and Erasmus—if Luther believed *Lee* to have written it, why did Luther excoriate not Lee, but the King? For Luther needed the King's aid in the new religious fight, and if he did not believe Henry an enemy of his, in all shrewdness he should have tried not only not to attack him un-

*In Royal Historical Society's Transactions, Vol. VIII.

necessarily, but to placate him. Besides Luther later apologized to Henry, showing that he believed him and not Lee to be the author.

As to Gardiner's claim—it is a mere pretty pun. And Pace was only *hinted* at by Hutton as *possibly,* with More, having corrected the Latin mistakes.

Erasmus, as said above, disclaimed the authorship, and, besides, we may add, by way of explanation, that Erasmus had visited Henry when Henry was nine years old and Henry studied Erasmus as a master and model, hence the similarity of Henry's style to that of Erasmus might be explained, if indeed there be any need of an explanation.

These are the main reasons why neither Fisher, nor More, nor Lee, nor Gardiner, nor Pace, nor Erasmus wrote the "Assertio." Probably not all objections have been answered: difficulties may still exist in some minds; doubtless not all are convinced; but Henry's claims have not yet been presented. This will now be done. For the sake of clearness the various testimonies have been grouped under the following heads of proof:

I. Henry's own statements, found in his writings most closely connected with the "Assertio."

II. Statements of others in documents closely connected with the "Assertio."

III. Other works of Henry, showing in a general way his ability to have written the "Assertio."

IV. The great number of witnesses declaring that Henry wrote the "Assertio."

V. A summary of the arguments.

I. As to Henry's own words in the documents most closely connected with the "Assertio," the following quotation is taken from Henry's letter to Leo X., printed elsewhere in this volume. He says:

"We have thought that this first attempt of *our*

modest *ability* and *learning* could not be more worthily
dedicated than to your Holiness."

In the "Epistle Dedicatory" sent with the "Assertio"
to Leo is found the following passage, unquestionably
claiming the authorship for Henry:

"We . . . now undertake the task of a man that
ought to have employed all his time in the studies of
learning. . . . We . . . have proposed to ourself to
employ our force and power in a work so necessary and
so profitable. . . .

"Though We know very well, that there are every-
where several more expert, especially in Holy Writ, who
could have more commodiously undertaken this great
work, and performed it much better than We, yet are
We not altogether so ignorant as not to esteem it our
duty to employ with all our might, our wit and pen in
the common cause. For having, by long experience,
found that religion bears the greatest sway in the administration of public affairs, and is likewise of no small
importance in the commonwealth, We have employed
no little time, especially since We came to years of discretion, in the contemplation thereof; wherein We have
always taken great delight: and though not ignorant of
our small progress therein made; yet, at least, it is so
much, as, We hope, . . . will suffice for reasons to discover the subtleties of Luther's heresy. We have therefore . . . entered upon this work, dedicating to your
Holiness what we have meditated therein. . . .

"If We have erred in any thing, We offer it to be
corrected as may please your Holiness."

The next quotation, likewise clearly and strongly implying that Henry wrote the "Assertio," is from Henry's
"To the Reader." It says: "I cannot but think myself obliged . . . to defend my mother, the Spouse of
Christ. Which, though it be a subject more copiously

handled by others, nevertheless I account it as much my own duty, as his who is the most learned, by my utmost endeavours, to defend the Church, and to oppose myself to the poisonous shafts of the enemy."

That there were disputes as to the author of the work even in Henry's own day is clear from what we have already quoted and that, when Henry's own ears had heard them, he promptly took occasion flatly to deny these reports is clear from the following quotation from the King's letter to Luther. He says:* "And although ye sayne your self to thynke my boke nat myne owne, but to my rebuke (as it lyketh you to affyrme) put out by subtell sophisters, yet it is well knowen for myn, and I for myne avowe it." And again from the same document, quoted by Audin:† "As to my letter, which in your opinion was the work of a captious sophist, it is my own production, as many witnesses worthier of credit than yourself can testify, and the more it displeases you, the greater pleasure do I feel in acknowledging myself its author."

So that Henry's own words show that he claimed, and proved, or certainly tried to prove, that he was the author of the "Assertio."

II. And to confirm this may be adduced in the second place the words of others who were very close to Henry and knew the inner history of the writing of the "Assertio." These words are found in the documents connected with the "Assertio," and published in full elsewhere in this volume. Here are a few passages from Mr. John Clark's Oration at the presentation of the "Assertio" to Leo X.: Henry, "under the charge of the best tutors, and a father none of the most indulgent,

*Dibdin, II., pp. 488 and fol., No. 619, "A copy of the letter, etc.," of Henry to Luther.
†Henry VIII., p. 101.

having passed his younger days in good learning, and
afterwards so well versed in Holy Scriptures that, confiding in his own abilities, he often (not without great
glory) disputed with the most learned in Britain." . . .

"My most serene and invincible Prince, Henry VIII.,
King of England, France and Ireland, and most affec-
tionate son of Your Holiness and of the sacred Roman
Church, hath *written a book* against this work of
Luther's which he has dedicated to Your Holiness." . . .

Henry "undertook this pious work himself," . . .
and, Clark continues: "The pious, and Your most devoted Prince, has, with all his power, endeavoured . . .
and hopes to have acquitted himself." . . .

Lastly, says Clark: "I believe it will cause admiration
in several that a prince . . . should undertake such
things [as this book] as, according to the common saying, might require to employ wholly all the thoughts of
a man. . . . By his *ingenuity* and pen [he] put[s] a
stop to heresies."

So much from Henry's ambassador, Clark; now for
the Pope himself. In his reply to Clark's Oration, Leo
implies that the form as well as the substance, the style
as well as the matter were Henry's. He said:

"His Majesty, having the *knowledge, will and ability
of composing* this excellent book, against this terrible
monster, has rendered himself no less admirable to the
whole world, by the eloquence of *his style,* than by *his
great wisdom.*"

In Leo's letter to Henry, acknowledging the book
written by the King against Luther, several passages
may be used to prove Henry's authorship.

The very title itself contains the first: "De gratiis pro
libro *per regem* contrà Lutherum *scripto.*" And in the
body of the letter the Pope says of Henry: "Tu fidem
Christianam thesauris *tuæ* et pietatis et scientiæ adver-

sum impias hæreses munitam esse voluisti." And the
Pope further speaks of the book as a "Nobilem *partum
ingenii tui.*" And again he goes on to say that men
"tuis scriptis ad sanitatem debeant reduci." Finally,
exhorting Henry to continue ever faithful, the Holy
Father says: "Fides quoque Christiana quæ nunc doctrinæ *tuæ clypeo* adversus sceleratas hæreticorum insanias communita est."

This personal, spontaneous and therefore very strong
testimony is confirmed by Leo's Bull to Henry,
"Bulla de gratiis pro libro per regem contra Lutherum
scripto."* In this Bull Leo wrote apropos of Henry's
authorship:

"John Clark . . . in our consistory . . . did present
unto Us a book which *your Majesty . . . did compose."* . . .

"Your Majesty has with *learning and eloquence writ*
against Luther." . . .

"Render your Majesty so illustrious and famous to
the whole world, as that our judgment in adorning you
with so remarkable title may not be thought vain or
light by any person whatsoever."

Really, these documents should be first-class proofs,
and they could scarcely be stronger and clearer in trying to show that Clark and Leo believed the author of
the "Assertio" to be Henry.

III. In the third place, besides the "Assertio," there
are other works attributed to Henry, and showing that
consequently he might well have written the "Assertio"
also. In Dibdin† and the "Dictionnaire de Bibliographie Catholique"‡ we read of "Henrici VIII., Angliæ regis, ad Saxoniæ principes de coercenda abigen-

*Rymer, Fœdera, printed elsewhere in this volume.
†II., p. 485.
‡Tome I., col. 868 ; Tome III., col. 431, and Tome III., col. 675.

daque Lutherana factione, et Luthero ipso *epistola;*
cum Georgii, Saxoniæ ducis, ad eundem rescriptione;
Argentorati, 1523 in 4to." Also Leipsiæ (sine anno)
in 4to. That is, "The *epistle of Henry VIII.,* King of
England, to the princes of Saxony about checking and
doing away with the Lutheran faction, and Luther himself: with the reply of George, Duke of Saxony, to the
same."

Again Dibdin* records: "Henrici Octavi Regis Angliæ et Franciæ. . . . Ad Carolum Cæsarem Augustum," etc. "An Epistle of . . . Henry VIII. . . .
to the Emperour's Maiestie, to all Christian princes,"
etc.

Then there are other works by Henry recorded:†
"Exemplum litterarum Henrici VIII. ad Lutherum, et
Lutheri ad ipsum; 1525 in 4." Also edited by Pynson
in 1526, small 8vo, and by Pynson 1527, in small 8vo,
and at Cologne by Quentell in 1527, in 4to.‡

Besides these, in the "Dictionnaire de Bibliographie
Catholique," we read:§ "Opus eximium de vera differentia regiæ potestatis et ecclesiasticæ, et quæ sit ipsa
veritas ac virtus utriusque; Londini, in ædibus Thom.
Bertheleti, 1534, pet. in 4 de 63 ff. Ouvrage attribué
par Bale à Henri VIII., roi d'Angleterre, et par Leland
à Fox, évêque de Winchester. Brunet."

Gasquet, "Eve of the Reformation," p. 101, note 1,
refers to a book called "A Glass of Truth," written in
favour of the divorce, and says: "The work was published by Berthelet anonymously, but Richard Croke,
in a letter written at this period (Ellis, Historical Let-

---

*III., p. 308, Nos. 1207, 1208.
†Dic. de Bib. Cath., I., 868.
‡Lowndes, Biog. Manual, Part IV., p. 1089. See also Dibdin, II.,
616.
§Tome III., col. 1099.

ters, 3d Series, II., 195), says that the book was written by King Henry himself. It was generally said that Henry had written a defence of his divorce."

Watts speaks of it in the following entry as Henry's work: "Opus eximium de vera differentia regiæ potestatis et ecclesiasticæ, et quæ sit ipsa veritas, ac virtus utriusque, Henrico VIII., Angliæ reg. auctore. Lond. 1534, 4to."

"A necessary doctrine and erudition for any Christian man. Lond. 1543, 4to. Lond. 1545, 8vo. In Latin, Lond. 1544, 4to."

So that from these several writings, stated on good authorities to be Henry's, we may conclude that Henry might well have written the "Assertio," thus solidifying and confirming the direct statements of Henry himself, as well as those direct or implied statements made by Clark and Leo.

IV. In the fourth place come the great number of first-class testimonies of historians of recognized ability and trustworthiness, who either imply or say directly that Henry is the author of the "Assertio." And first of all should be placed the following statement in the "Advertisement" to the old English translation of the "Assertio" that is here reprinted. It says: "Henry the Eighth was a Prince of great learning, considering the age in which he lived. He had well studied both Philosophy and Divinity in his youth, his father, Henry the Seventh, having intended him for the ecclesiastical state. His writings against Luther (I mean the following work, so much approved of by Leo the Tenth), shew a fund of ecclesiastical erudition, and a strength of understanding uncommon in persons in his high station."

Next should come the remarks of Gabriel de Saconay in his Preface to his Latin reprint of the "Assertio,"

done at Lyons, 1561. In his title Saconay wrote: "Henricus, octavus Angliæ Rex, inter paucos reges literarum et multarum rerum cognitione commendabilis, hunc librum conscripsit. Lugduni, apud Guliel. Rovillium sub scuto Veneto. MDLXI."

On page LXXI he says: "Christiana tunc pietate illustrissimus Anglorum rex Henricus, hujus nominis octavus raro nimis, et cunctis seculis admirando exemplo, ex regali fastigio in literariam descendit arenam, contra maledicum decertaturus mendicantium fratrum apostatam. Scripsit itaque assertionem septem sacramentorum adversus captivitatem Babylonicam Lutheri ad Leonem, hujus nominis decimum Papam, adeo sane diserte, erudite ac copiose, ut eo labore promeruerit ipsius Papæ omniumque cardinalium judicio, perpetuæ laudis titulum, ut publica deinceps appellatione, fidei catholicæ defensor nuncuparetur." On p. LXXII Saconay quotes Luther as saying: "Hîc insulto papistis, Thomistis, *Henricistis*, . . . divina majestas mecum facit ut nihil curem si mille Augustini, mille Cypriani, mille ecclesiæ *Henricianæ*, contra me starent." . . . And p. LXXIII: "Itaque extorsimus, et triumphamus adversus assertorem sacramentorum. . . . Quis est ipse Henricus novus Thomista? . . . sit ipse defensor ecclesiæ, sed ejus ecclesiæ, quam tanto libro jactat et tuetur."

On p. LXXIV Saconay continues to quote Luther: "Recte conjungitur simul Papa, et Henricus de Anglia: ille papatum suum tam bona habet conscientia, quam hic suum possidet regnum. Interea dum sic fureret Lutherus, quidam Germani, piam et eruditam *regis Angliæ assertionem* cœperunt a Lutheranis calumniis asserere."

On p. LXXVIII Saconay says: "Hæc sunt quæ huic libello præponenda duxi, ut noscas, lector, quo impulsu

Rex iste manum huic operi apposuerit." On pp.
LXXXIII and LXXXIV Saconay says: "Perlege
igitur, lector, hoc opusculum antequam aliquod judicium temere feras, videbis *principis animum,* qui multum ornavit nostra studia, et religionis causam et pie
suscepit, et diserte defendit. Olim summa pietas judi-
cabatur, si Reges armis tutati fuissent Christianam
tranquillitatem, hic autem *ingenio et calamo* propug-
navit. Quomodo ergo non pudeat ecclesiasticos plerosque tam ociose vitam degere? cum videant tantum
principem in his studiis eo progressum esse, ut libris
etiam editis catholicæ religioni patrocinaretur. Ac-
cipe itaque piam sacramentorum assertionem." . . .

This encomium of Henry's ability is confirmed by
Speed in his "History of Great Britain,"* where he
says of Henry: "His youth so trained up in literature
that he was accounted the most learned Prince of all
Christendom, indued with parts most befitting a
king. . . .

"His Councellors hee chose of the gravest Divines,
and the wisest nobility, with whom hee not onely often
sate, to the great encrease of his politicke experience,"
etc., etc.

And Hutton, in his "Sir Thomas More," says that
among such chosen ones the lovable, religious More was
the favourite. His words are:† "So from time to time
was he [More] by the Prince [Henry VIII.] advanced,
continuing in his singular favour and trusty service
twenty years and above. A *good part whereof* used the
King upon holidays, when he had done his own devo-
tions, to send for him into his travers, and there sometime in matters of Astronomy, Geometry, Divinity,
and such other Faculties, and sometime in his worldly
affairs, to sit and confer with him."

*Pp. 982, 983.   †P. 93.

Paradoxical as it may seem, we might say that even after death More affords testimony to Henry's authorship, for to the tomb of More was affixed an inscription composed by Erasmus, and in it Henry VIII. is spoken of: "To whom alone of all kings the hitherto unheard of glory has happened that he should be *deservedly* called the *'Defender of the Faith,'* and he has proven himself to be such both by the sword and the pen."*

Moreover, in More's reply to Luther in defence of Henry's "Assertio" Henry is spoken of as "Invictissimum Angliæ Galliæque regem, Henricum ejus nominis octavum, Fidei Defensorem, haud *litteris* minus quam regno clarum." As Henry was indeed a great king, probably in one sense the most influential England had ever seen, this statement of More surely implies that Henry had written something more than ordinary letters—that he was the author of the "Assertio."

"When one sees the various MSS. in the British Museum," says Audin,† speaking of Henry, "it is impossible to doubt the theological attainments of the monarch . . . who knew the Bible by rote." Henry's alleged inability as a Latinist has been made an argument against the possibility of his having written the "Assertio," but the following will show that Henry was quite proficient in this language, surely enough to have written the simple Latin of the "Assertio." First, as to his tutor and Latin master, Tytler‡ says:

---

*See Erasmi Opera, III., pars 2, col. 1441, Epistola MCCXXIII., Thomas Morus Erasmo Roterodamo : " Tabula affixa ad sepulchrum Thomæ Mori. . . . Ab invictissimo Rege, Henrico octavo, cui uni Regum omnium gloria prius inaudita contigit, ut fidei defensor, qualem et gladio se et *calamo vere præstitit, merito* vocaretur."

†Henry VIII., pp. 91, 92, note e.   ‡Henry VIII., p. 29.

"Linacre, a man infinitely superior to André [Arthur's tutor], who had studied the purest models in Italy, was afterwards selected by Henry the Eighth as his own master; but the monarch, although an *able Latinist,* does not appear to have made much progress in the other language" [Greek].

Although perhaps a bit flattering, yet the following testimonial to Henry's ability and even fluency in Latin is very interesting, coming as it does from no less a personage than Giustinian, the Venetian ambassador at the court of Henry VIII. He says:* "His majesty [Henry VIII.] is twenty-nine years old and extremely handsome; nature could not have done more for him; . . . he is very accomplished; . . . speaks good French, *Latin,* and Spanish; is *very religious;* hears three Masses daily when he hunts, and sometimes five on other days; he hears the *office* every day in the Queen's chamber, that is to say, vespers and compline."

Id. p. 77, fol. Letter of Secretary of Sebastian Giustinian, Knight Ambassador in England, to Alvise Foscari, May, 1515: "His Majesty [Henry VIII.] sent for the ambassadors, and addressed their magnificences, partly in French and partly in *Latin,* as also in Italian."

Id. p. 86, Giustinian's letter saying of Henry VIII.: "He speaks French, English and *Latin,* and a little Italian."

"To the Council of Ten, London, July 3, 1515: "The King [Henry VIII.] answered us *very suitably in Latin."* . . .

In general, several quotations of the King *speaking Latin,* or quoting Scripture in Latin, are given in this same work.†

*Vol. I., pp. 26, 27.
†Id., p. 101.

Probably basing his remarks on the authority of Giustinian, Brewer, in his "Reign of Henry VIII.,"* says: "He [Henry VIII.] spoke French, Italian, and Spanish. Of his proficiency in *Latin* a specimen has been preserved among the letters of Erasmus. All suspicion of its genuineness is removed by the positive assertion of Erasmus, that he had seen the original and corrections in the Prince's own hand."

Jeremy Collier† agrees with and even adds to these statements, saying: "He was a very promising prince, both as to person, capacity, and improvement. . . . His genius was lively, and his education push'd, and well manag'd; for besides the customary exercises and accomplishments of a prince, he had made considerable advances in learning. He was a good *Latinist,* a philosopher and divine; and as for music, his progress in that science was so unusual, that two entire Masses of his own composing were sung in his chapel. His inclination to letters was early perceived, and if his elder brother had lived, 'tis said his father design'd him for the see of Canterbury."

To add to this and recount briefly what many other weighty writers have said on the subject, Lilly, in his "Renaissance Types," says‡ of Henry: "He was highly educated, according to the standard of the times; a *good Latin scholar,* well versed in theology, the scholastic philosophy and the canon law."

John Richard Green, in his "History of the English People,"§ says: "He was a trained theologian and

---

*Vol. I., p. 4.
†Eccles. Hist. of Gt. Britain, Part II., Bk. I., beginning.
‡Ch. VI., p. 328.
§Vol. II., p. 124. See also A. L. Moore, Lectures and Papers on the Reformation, p. 25.

proud of his theological knowledge." He "liked the society of men of letters."*

"He received the benefit of as learned an education as the age could bestow, the King [Henry VII.] contemplating his accession to the primacy of England."†

Thomson, in his "Memoirs of the Court of Henry VIII.," says:‡ "The instructions bestowed upon Prince Henry by his preceptor, Skelton, were calculated to render him a scholar and a churchman, rather than an enlightened legislator. He was tutored in the philosophy of the schools, especially the Aristotelian, then the most in credit with the learned; he was *skilled in the Latin.* . . . To theological studies Henry devoted his attention in early life with ardour, and with success; at least this part of his attainments is not to be despised, since it enabled him in after times to procure for himself and his successors the title of Defender of the Faith."

Beckett, in his "English Reformation," says:§ "He [Henry] had been carefully educated by good scholars, and he believed himself to be a special master of theology."

Henry William Herbert, in his "Memoirs of Henry VIII.,"‖ says: "He had been studiously educated a theologian; . . . he really was more than a tolerable divine." Again:¶ "Henry VIII. . . . received a learned education. Having been destined for the Church, he had studied the writings of Aquinas and cultivated a taste for controversial divinity, which sharpened his intellect."

<hr>

*Lilly, Renaissance, Ch. III., p. 135.
†Sir Thomas More, W. J. Walter, Baltimore, p. 29.
‡Vol. I., p. 213.
§Ch. XV.
‖P. 121.
¶Tytler, Henry VIII., p. 111.

Not only had Henry had able schoolmasters and wisely selected studies to make him a theologian, but he had profited by the opportunities and delighted to use his powers: "He was fond of learned discussions and scholastic sophistry."*

James Gairdner, in his "English Church in the Sixteenth Century,"† says:

"From early days Henry had shown a taste for theological discussion, and the story that his father had intended once to make him Archbishop of Canterbury is not at all incredible. In 1518, as we learn from Erasmus and some allusions in State papers, he composed a treatise on the question whether vocal prayer was necessary to a Christian. . . . Indeed, putting tradition aside, we know quite well that Henry VIII. had all his days a taste for theological subtleties, and probably could not have done the things he did but that he was fully competent to argue points—of course with most royal persuasiveness—against Tunstall, Latimer, Cranmer, and any divine in his kingdom."

Overton, in his "Church in England,"‡ says:

"His abilities and attainments were so much above the average that long before he had reached the prime of life, he could contend on equal terms with the ablest and most learned writers of the day."§

Samuel Gardiner, in his "English History for Students,"‖ says Henry "took a real interest in learning."

*Häusser, Period of the Reformation, Vol. I., p. 212.
†Pp. 78 and 5.
‡Vol. I., p. 335.
§"More writes to Erasmus in the early part of Henry's reign, when he had become connected with the court: 'Such is the virtue and learning of the King, and his daily increasing progress in both, that the more I see him increase in these kingly ornaments, the less troublesome the courtier's life becomes to me.'"
‖By Mullinger, p. 105.

This seems true of even his youngest days, for Erasmus
was "presented to Henry VIII., then a boy of nine
years old, who asks for a tribute of verses, afterwards
duly paid. . . . He came back to England again, in the
hope, which proved delusive, of patronage and employ-
ment from the young Henry VIII., in whose love of
learning all humanists put their trust."* And yet he
was sometimes more generous in reward of literary effort, for the "Censura Literaria"† says: "And King
Henry the Eighth . . . for a few psalmes of David
turned into English meetre by Sternbold, made him
groome of his privy chamber and gave him many other
good gifts."

"Henry had been educated to some extent in the new
learning."‡ No wonder, then, that "there was a moment in the reign of Henry VIII. when it appeared not
impossible that English scholars might, north of the
Alps, lead the van in the restoration of the new learning. . . . King Henry, too, was within an ace of gathering into our libraries those treasures of Greek manuscript which Francis I. secured and placed at Fontaine-
bleau."§

Naturally enough, "the Classicists might expect
everything from one who at nine years old had written
good Latin, uncorrected by tutors, the church reformers
from a prince with so strong a turn for theology."‖

And he was practical, preparing the way, laying a
foundation in the young by establishing lower schools at
the same time that he encouraged the universities. Indeed he had the most recent American ideas of educa-

*Martin Luther and the Reformation in Germany, Charles
Beard, p. 87.
†Vol. I., p. 342.
‡Oxford Reformers of 1498, Seebohm, p. 124.
§Old English Bible, Gasquet, p. 314.
‖The Early Tudors, Moberly, p. 100.

tion—that of subsidizing students to go abroad to study, as we learn from Collier:*

"Henry founded a great many grammar schools; . . . he likewise founded lectures in both universities, where those who read in the faculties of divinity, law and physic were encouraged with a considerable settlement. The same countenance was likewise given to professors of Greek and Hebrew. . . . He built and endowed the famous Trinity College in Cambridge. . . . Lastly, he maintained a great many young scholars in foreign countries."

The brightest star of the new learning was Erasmus, and this star is drawn to be a satellite of Henry and to sound his praises and declare that he believed Henry truly to be the author of the "Assertio." Worsley† says of him in connection with the "Assertio":

"Erasmus believed, or affected to believe, that Henry himself was 'parent and author.' 'His father,' he [Erasmus] wrote, 'was a man of the nicest judgment; his mother possessed the soundest intellect, etc. When the King was no more than a child he was sent to study.' " But whoever will take up Erasmus's own works will see that he praises Henry's ability, as well as his actual work, implying that Henry wrote the "Assertio," and answering objections against the King's authorship, by denying any help from his—Erasmus's—hands, either as to matter or style. Here are his words:

"Tom. iii^{us}., Pars 1^a, col. 7. Epistola X. Gulielmus Montjoius Erasmo Roterodamo S. D.

"Verum si scias‡ . . . quam sapienter se gerat . . . quod studium in literatos præ se ferat. . . . Noster Rex

*Pt. II., Bk. III., p. 214.
†Dawn of the Reformation, p. 160, note.
‡Desiderii Erasmi Roterodami Opera Omnia. Lugduni Batavorum, cura et impensis Petri Van der Aa. MDCCIII.

non aurum, non gemmas, non metella, sed virtutem, sed
gloriam, sed æternitatem concupiscit."

Id. col. 145, Erasmus calls Henry "aurei sæculi
parentem."

Id. col. 187, he says of Henry, "Nec ipse literarum
imperitus."

Id. col. 253, Erasmus writes to Henry: "Nullus tibi
pene dies abeat, in quo ncn aliquam temporis portionem
libris evolvendis impertias, cumque priscis illis sapien-
tibus colloqui gaudeas." . . .

Id. col. 402, Erasmus to Paul Bombasius says of
Henry, "bonis libris delectatur."

Id. col. 440, Erasmus to Henry, Antwerp, May 15,
1519: "Et tamen in literis quas olim, felicissime degus-
tavit tua majestas, . . . ut eruditissimis etiam theologis
miraculo sit sanitas et acumen ingenii tui. Siquidem in
disputatione, quam nuper animi causa *tua majestas instituit cum* acutissimo simul et doctissimo *theologo, de-
fendans.* . . . Quis *invenire poterat argutius?* quis colligere *nervosius? quis explicare venustius."*

Id. col. 463, Erasmus writes to Jacob Banisius:
"Triumpharent bonæ literæ, si Principem haberemus
domi, qualem habet Anglia. Rex ipse non indoctus,
tum ingenio acerrimo, palam tuetur bonas literas, rabu-
lis omnibus silentium indixit. . . . Aula Regis plus
habet hominum eruditione præstantium, quam ulla
Academia." Bruxellis, 21 Junii, anno 1519.

Id. col. 533, Erasmus to John Faber, Vicar of the
Bishop of Constance, writes: "Ipse Rex felicissime phil-
osophatur. Regina literas amat, quas ab infantia feliciter didicit."

Id. col. 660, Erasmus writes to Richard Pace: *"Librum, quem Regia majestas conscripsit adversus Lutherum,* vidi tantum in manibus Marini nuncii Apostolici.
Vehementer aveo legere. Nec enim dubito quin dig-

nus sit illo longe felicissimo ingenio, quod mire valet,
ubicunque sese intenderit. . . . Henricus octavus *in-*
genio, calamoque propugnat pro Christi sponsa. . . .
Porro, confido fore ut hoc pulcherrimum planeque ra-
rissimum exemplar multos principes provocet ad æmula-
tionem. An non pudebit post hoc sacerdotes, monachos,
episcopos nihil scire rei theologicæ, quum viderint Regem tantum juvenem, tot negociis districtum, eo progressum in cognitione sacrarum Literarum, ut libris editis periclitanti Christianæ religioni patrocinetur?"
Brugis, 23 Augusti, 1521.

Id. col. 732, Erasmus Roterodami Georgio duci
Saxoniæ. "In scholasticorum theologorum libris versari
gaudet, et in conviviis aliquid de re theologica disserere
solitus est. Nonnunquam in multam noctem profertur
contentio literata. Habet Reginam eleganter doctam.
Quod si qua in parte fuisset adjutus in eo libro, *nihil*
erat opus meis auxiliis, quum aulam habeat eruditissimis pariter ac eloquentissimis viris differtam. Quod *si*
stylus habet aliquid non abhorrens a meo, nihil mirum
aut novum, quum ille puer studiose volverit meas lucu-
brationes." . . .

Lastly, among the proofs showing in a general way
Henry's ability to have written the "Assertio," are the
records of his interest in, and use of, books. Although
these instances occurred some years later and in another connection, yet they may fairly be adduced as in-
dicating his trend of mind and ability. There are
many entries for books brought to King Henry VIII.,
or inventories of books, or books bound for him, or
for vellum, etc., told of in detail in N. H. Nicolas's
"Privy Purse Expenses of King Henry VIII."*

And now for the more definite and formal statements
of Henry's authorship, though it is difficult to draw a line

*London, 1827.

accurately separating these many witnesses into distinct classes.

D'Aubigné, in his "Reformation," says:* "Henry the Eighth had just composed a book against the monk of Wittemburg.

"The King himself was no stranger to the Romish doctrines. Indeed, it would appear that if Arthur had lived, Henry would have been destined to the archiepiscopal see of Canterbury. Thomas Aquinas, St. Bonaventure, tournaments, fêtes, Elizabeth Blount, and other court ladies, were all mingled together in the thoughts of this monarch, while masses of his own composition were being sung in his chapel. . . . He searched through Thomas Aquinas, Peter Lombard, Alexander de Hale, and Bonaventure."

"Doubtless the King consulted with others, chiefly with Fisher, but there is no reason to doubt that the work was substantially his own."†

Hutton, in his "Sir Thomas More,"‡ has an original and interesting statement: "As early as 1518 Henry VIII. had been preparing a book against the heretics, which, if the conjecture of Mr. Brewer be correct, was the original draft of the attack upon Luther, published in 1521. It was natural that Pace and More should be frequently consulted during the progress of this work, but it does not appear that they took any actual part in the authorship, their aid extending at most to the composition and correction of the Latin style."

The following from Lord Herbert of Cherbury is about as strong and clear a declaration of Henry's authorship as could be asked:§

*Translated by Gill, Part III., Ch. IV.
†Creighton, History of the Papacy, pp. 163, 164, note 3.
‡P. 196, ed. London, 1895.
§England under Henry VIII., published by Murray, London, 1870.

"Besides his being an able Latinist, philosopher and divine he was . . . a curious musician." (P. 110.)

"Our King thereupon *compiles* a book, wherein he strenuously opposes Luther in the point of indulgences, number of sacraments, the papal authority, and other particulars, to be seen in that *his* work, entitled 'De Sept. Sacramentis'; a principal copy whereof, richly bound, being sent to Leo, I remember myself to have seen in the Vatican Library." (P. 199.)

Dodd,* in his "Church History of England," says: "They [the clergy consulted about Henry's divorce] appealed to *his own book* against Luther," etc.

In the "Annals or General Chronicle of England, begun by John Stow, by Edmund Howes, Gent.,"† it is said:

"King *Henry wrote a book against Luther* in Germany and therefore Pope Leo the Tenth named him Defender of the faith. To the which book Luther answered very sharply, nothing sparing his authority or majesty."

In Burnet's "Reformation"‡ it is said: "When King *Henry wrote this book* of the seven sacraments it seems it was at first desired to send it over in manuscript," etc.

Arthur Mason, in his "Lectures on Colet, Fisher and More,"§ says: "Henry VIII., who was well read in theology for a layman of those days, had been negotiating at Rome for some complimentary title. . . . He composed, the next year [1521], a work on the seven sacraments against Luther."

*Vol. I., p. 95, col. 1, Brussels, 1737.
†Londini, impensis Ricardi Meighen, 1631, p. 514.
‡Part III., Bk. I., 18, Oxford, 1865.
§P. 81.

Bossuet speaks of "Henry VIII., King of England, who refuted his [Luther's] book."*

Rohrbacher declares flatly:† "Le roi d'Angleterre, Henri VIII., fit plus encore; l'anne suivante (1521) *il composa lui-même* une defense des sept sacrements contre l'ouvrage de Luther, de la Captivité de Babylon."

Moberly says:‡ "Before the end of 1521 Henry VIII. wrote his book on the Seven Sacraments. . . . The King . . . was stimulated to authorship."

Audin graphically expresses the situation:§ "Closeted with his chancellor, the archbishop of York; with Fisher, bishop of Rochester, and other prelates, he wrote the Defence of the Seven Sacraments."

"Henry was at the acme of animation while defending the Papacy."‖

In Seckendorf's "History of Lutheranism" we read:¶ "Rescivit etiam, Henricum VIII. Angliæ regem pulchrum librum a se pro septem sacramentorum defensione, adversus tractatum Lutheri de captivitate Babylonica conscriptum pontifici misisse, quo meritus est, ut condita ob id bulla gloriosum defensoris fidei titulum acciperet." . . .

Another source says:** "Ayant dans sa jeunesse étudié les sciences pour embrasser l'état ecclesiastique, à une époque où vivait encore son frère aîné, il voulut donner au monde une preuve de *son* mérite scientifique

*History of the Variations of the Protestant Church, Kenedy, 1896, Vol. I., p. 47.

†Hist. Univ. de l'Église Cath., XII., 105.

‡Epochs of Mod. Hist., Early Tudors, p. 151.

§Audin's Luther, Vol. II., p. 50, in Alzog's Universal Ch. Hist., III., p. 62.

‖Audin, Henry VIII., p. 91.

¶Comment. de Lutheranismo, lib. I., § CXII.

**Price, Vol. I., p. 13, quotes Lingard, VI., 142.

dans une cause si célèbre. Il *composa* donc un livre savant contre beaucoup des propositions erronées de Martin Luther, le fit presenter au pontife en consistoire le second jour d'octobre, par son ambassadeur, et le termina par ce distique, dont nous n'avons pas à juger le merite :

> Anglorum rex Henricus, Leo decime,
> Hoc opus, et fidei testem, et amicitiæ.
>
> > (Bzovius.)"

This statement is found in Price's "Nonconformity," taken from Lingard :* "After all, the probability is that the basis of the work was supplied by Henry ; . . . his explicit assertion of the fact, in his reply to Luther's answer, requires an admission to this extent. Had it been wholly the work of others the King would scarcely have ventured so open an assertion of his authorship."

Gairdner in the "Dictionary of National Biography," article "Henry VIII.," says : "As an author, Henry was by no means contemptible. His book against Luther ('Assertio Septem Sacramentorum,' published in 1521) was a scholastic performance of a rather conventional type, but it was the coinage of his own brain."

A rich and rare old book is Polydore Vergil's "History of England." In it we read :†

"Quocirca Henricus rex, qui habebat regnum suum maxime omnium religiosum, veritus ne uspiam labes aliqua religionis fieret, primum libros Lutheranos, quorum magnus jam numerus pervenerat in manus suorum Anglorum, comburendos curavit, deinde *libellum* contra eam doctrinam luculenter *composuit,* misitque ad Leonem Pontificem. Delectavit multum opus

---

*Price, Vol. I., p. 13, quotes Lingard, VI., 142.
†Polydori Vergilii Urbinatis. Angliæ Historiæ Libri Viginti-septem, Henrici VIII., lib. XXVII.

Leonis animum, partim quia plenum erat ipsius defensionis causæ, partim vero ob tale patronum consecutus foret, qui librum sua auctoritate probavit, legendumque decrevit, ac ut memoria tam grati beneficii aliquo nomine perpetuaretur, tum Henricum regem *defensorem fidei* appellavit, quo ille deinceps titulo usus est."

Audin gives a graphic picture of the inside history of the making of the "Assertio": "Henry, divested of the insignia of royalty, shut up in his study, was spending the night in consulting the great doctors of the Catholic schools."* As to the style, the same author says :† "The formal language of the schools might have crippled him, and consequently Skelton's pupil cast it off, and fell back on ancient history, for it was highly necessary that Luther should be aware that Henry knew something more than the 'Summa' of St. Thomas," for " . . . he knew the Bible by rote."‡

"Henry repeatedly amused his friends by reading to them portions of his MSS. More was one of his favourites, but he did not always flatter his royal master. 'Your Grace should be guarded in your expressions,' remarked More one day, 'for the Pope, as a temporal sovereign, may one day be opposed to England, and here is a passage wherein you exalt the authority of the Holy See to too high a pitch, and which Rome would surely adduce in case of a rupture.' 'No, no,' rejoined Henry, 'that expression is by no means too strong, nothing can equal my devotion to the Holy See, and no language can be sufficiently expressive, in my opinion, to speak my sentiments.' 'But, Sire, do you not remember certain articles in the Præmunire?' 'What matter,'

*Henry VIII., p. 88.
†P. 90, id. op.
‡P. 91, id. op.

retorted Henry, 'do I not hold my crown from the Holy See ?' "*

So that Henry's views, private whims even, are expressed in the "Assertio," and that without brooking the censure of even his nearest counsellor.

Seebohm, in his "Era of the Protestant Revolution," says: "Whilst the Diet of Worms was sitting, he [Henry] wrote his celebrated book against Luther and in defence of the divine authority of the Pope, for doing which the Pope rewarded him with the title of 'Defender of the Faith.' "

Natalis Alexander speaks of the Pope's rewarding Henry for having written the book in the following terms: "Henricum VIII. Angliæ Regem, ob egregium Librum contra Martini Lutheri Hæresim editum, illustri titulo Defensoris Fidei donavit, Diplomate dato quinto idus Octobris ejusdem anni (1521). Has constitutiones et diplomata legere est Tom II Bullarii."†

Pallavicini most briefly says of Henry: "Il composa donc un livre savant."‡ Though Sample, in his "Beacon Lights of the Reformation,"§ is as short, declaring that Henry "sat down and wrote a book."

Milner, in his "History of the Church of Christ," says that Henry "wrote in Latin his book on the seven sacraments."||

Hergenroether, in his "Histoire de l'Église," Tome V., p. 246, says: "Il fit presenter *son* ouvrage à Leon X."

Charles Butler declares that "considering his theological and classical education it is not to be wondered

*Henry VIII., p. 92.
†Historia, Vol. IX., p. 28.
‡Trente, Tome I., col. 675. Migne, 1844.
§P. 199.
||Vol. V., p. 161.

at that the spirit of authorship should fall upon the monarch; or that he should choose for his subject a theological theme."* More indirectly Janssen, in his "History of the German People," says: "So, too, the King of England vaunts himself that he is a protector of the Christian Church and people."†

So that really one could hardly ask for more or weightier testimonies than these presented, declaring that Henry wrote — composed — was the author of the "Assertio." Let it not be forgotten, however, that there are those who qualify somewhat the sense of the word "author"; for while Hallam says:‡ "Henry had acquired a fair portion of theological learning, and on reading one of Luther's treatises, was not only shocked at its tenets, but undertook to refute them in a formal answer," yet a foot-note§ qualifies this, particularly in regard to the diction: "From Henry's general character and proneness to theological discussion it may be inferred that he had at least a considerable share in the work, though probably with the assistance of some who had more command of the Latin language."

Then, too, in Allies's "History of England,"‖ it is said:

"The pen at least was Henry's own, and did the work well. Sir Thomas More furnished it with an index, which was his sole part in the book. . . . As far as genuine authorship went Henry had fairly won his honours. He possessed sufficient theological knowledge and acumen to explain the seven sacraments dogmatically.

---

*Historical Memoirs respecting the English, Irish and Scottish Catholics, Vol. I., p. 23.
†Vol. IV., pp. 41, 42.
‡Constitutional History, p. 44.
§Id. op., p. 80.
‖P. 13.

. . . His example belied his pen." And yet this is but a slight qualification of the term.

Du Pin does not say Henry actually wrote it, but that he might have :*

"Henry VIII., King of England, made most rigorous Acts to hinder the heresy [of Luther] from coming into his realm. This prince did something more to show his zeal for religion and the Holy See, for he *caused to be made* in his own name a treatise about the Seven Sacraments. . . . But Henry VIII. might very well write it, having studied divinity in his younger years."

Pocock's Burnet's "Reformation" gives a good argument in favour of Henry's authorship; at first stating an objection, but then also an answer to it :†

"It was also a masterpiece in Wolsey to engage the King to own that the book against Luther was written by him, in which the secret of those who, no doubt, had the greatest share in composing it was so closely laid, that it never broke out. Seckendorf tells us, that Luther believed it was written by Lee, who was a zealous Thomist, and had been engaged in disputes with Erasmus, and was afterwards made Archbishop of York. If any of those who still adhered to the old doctrines had been concerned in writing it, probably, when they saw King Henry depart from so many points treated of in it, they would have gone beyond sea, and have robbed him of that false honour and those excessive praises which that book had procured him."

If Luther assailed Henry so, he must have been the author of the "Assertio," or at least been believed such by Luther, for Luther would hardly attack the King of England unless he believed it to have been Henry who

*Ecclesiastical History of the Sixteenth Century, Bk. II., Ch. XII.

†Vol. III., p. 171.

struck at him in the "Assertio." If Henry were not
the author, Luther would probably have heard, at least
by a secret hint from England, but yet, "a *few years
afterwards*," when Luther began to suspect that the
King was not indisposed to favour his opinions, he
wrote to him to excuse the violence and abuse contained in his book, which he attributed to the advice of
others.*

Indeed, Du Pin says† that "the King of England
was chiefly angry because he [Luther] had said that his
book upon the Sacraments was made by another, and
put out in his name." . . .

The case is summed up thus by Lingard, in his "History of England":‡ "That the treatise in defence of the
Seven Sacraments, which the King published, was his
own composition, is forcibly asserted by himself; that
it was planned, revised and improved by the superior
judgment of the cardinal and the bishop of Rochester,
was the opinion of the publick."§

As for the author, then, of the "Assertio," it must be
admitted that there are some difficult objections and
weighty names against Henry's having written it; that
not all of these objections have been satisfactorily answered, and by the very nature and circumstances
of the case they could not be answered. However, the
great weight of the evidence is decidedly on the side of
Henry's claim. Certainly, he approved and claimed the
work and in this sense no one will deny his authorship. Very probably he selected and composed the ma-

*Roscoe's Leo X., Vol. II., p. 231, note 168.
†Bk. II., Ch. XVIII.
‡Vol. IV., p. 466.
§" Sir Thomas More confirms this opinion by saying that 'by his
grace's appointment, and consent of the makers of the same, *he* was
only a sorter-out and placer of the principal matters therein contained.' See a note on this subject by Mr. Bruce, Arch., XXIV., 67."

terials. Indeed, it is quite likely that the very style is Henry's.

V. And now, in the fifth place, here are several summings up of the arguments for Henry's authorship.

J. M. Brown, in the "Transactions of the Royal Historical Society," VIII., says that "we have the opinion of Erasmus (Jortin's Erasmus, Vol. I., p. 254 and fol.) that the King was capable of writing as good Latin as was contained in the disputed book." He quotes Lord Herbert of Cherbury (Hist. of H. VIII., fol. 85) as saying: "Henry was so associated with St. Thomas Aquinas as to be nicknamed Thomisticus."

"All those who could know anything about what was doing at court say that the book was the King's, with qualifications. If any one knew who wrote the 'Assertio' Fisher must have, and he says in the 'Defense' of the 'Assertio,' 'We may here remark the wonderful ingenuity of the King's mind.'"

"The only man besides the King whom we know positively to have had any hand in the book is More, the 'sorter-out and placer.'" (P. 257.) Thus far Brown.

In the "Archæologia," Ellis quotes from John Bruce and sums up a number of the weightiest reasons for Henry's authorship. He says:* "There is very little evidence upon which the authorship of this volume can be assigned to any particular person. . . . On the part of those who maintain the King's proper authorship there are: The book itself, and the King's reply to Luther's letter to him, in both of which the whole merit is assumed by the King. On this side of the question may also be produced the authority of Polydore Vergil (Angl. Hist., p. 664, edit. 1570); Speed (Hist., p. 759, edit. 1611); Fisher, who published a defence

*P. 67 and fol.

of the work, and attributes it to the **King** of **England** 'not less famous in arms than in letters' (Defensio Reg. Ass. dedicat.); Herbert (Life of Henry VIII., p. 94, ed. 1672); Holinshed, who . . . does not seem to impeach Henry's authorship (Vol. II., p. 872, edit. 1587); Strype (Eccles. Mem., Vol. I., p. 33) and many other authors, who treat the 'Assertio' as the work of him whose name it bears, without even mentioning any rumour of a doubt upon the subject.

"The circumstances under which the book was written . . . will be found to support Henry's claim to the authorship.

"Pace, in a letter addressed to Wolsey (Cotton MSS. Vitellus, B. IV., No. 59), dated 15th April without any year, but evidently written in 1521, gives an account of an interview he had that day had with the King. Pace found his Majesty 'lokyng upon a book of Luther's, and upon such dispraise as his Grace did give unto the said book,' Pace took occasion to deliver a Bull which he had lately brought from Rome. . . .

"The King remarked 'that it was joyous to have this tidings from the Pope's Holiness at such time, as he had taken upon him the defence of Christ's Church, with his penne.' . . . The King promised 'to take more pain to make an end' of his book within a specified time.

"In a letter from Wolsey to Clerk the Cardinal tells of 'what pain, labour, and studie his Highness hath taken in devising and making a book for the confutacion of his [Luther's] said erroneous opinions;' . . . 'the said booke is by his Highness perfected;' . . . 'the King's Highness has this [way] declared himself as the veray defender of Catholique faith [of] Crist's Churche as well w^t his preysence as w^t his lernyng.' "

So far Ellis's summary.

Lewis, in his "Fisher,"* by way of summing up the argument for Henry's authorship of the "Assertio" says that:

I. Henry in his letter to Luther owns it to be his.

II. More to Cromwell says he knows it to be by Henry's own pen and that "in the composition of it he was governed by his own sentiment."

III. Erasmus says: (a) "he could never find out by whose labour the King was assisted;" (b) "that the phrase was his own" [Henry's]; (c) "that he had a happy and ready genius for everything;" (d) "that but a few years before he wrote a theological disputation on the question 'whether a lay-man was obliged to vocal prayer';" (e) "and took delight in the books of the school divines, and would often at meals discourse on subjects in divinity."

So that while it is not a settled question, yet, considering Henry's own statements, those of others connected with the "Assertio," Henry's other works, and the statements of very many historians, it is more probable that Henry wrote, composed, was the author of the "Assertio." Not that he had no help, took no counsel, consulted no one (though it is known how he rejected More's advice about the strong praise and divine origin Henry attributed to the Primacy of the Papacy), but, as Mr. Overton† says of the "Assertio": "It at any rate expressed Henry's sentiments and he was quite competent to write it."

*P. 109.
†Church in England, Vol. I., p. 357.

Editions and Versions

It is of primary interest to know where the "Assertio" has appeared in print; and, first of all, where the original that Henry sent Leo now is.

Roscoe[*] answers the query. He says: "The original in an elegant MS. is still preserved in the Library of the Vatican, and is usually shown to Englishmen on their visits to Rome. Vide Dr. Smith's 'Tour of the Continent,' Vol. II., p. 200."

Strype[†] tells us of the book: "This book the King, by the Cardinal's advice, thought fit to have presented to Pope Leo. . . . This was brought about by the means of Cardinal Wolsey; who procured some copies of the book to be written in a very fair and beautiful character; and one of them to be bound up splendidly, namely, that that was to be sent to the Pope; and the said Cardinal sent that especially to the King, for his liking of it, before it went."

Perhaps no less interesting is what Rohrbacher writes:[‡] "C'est un beau volume in quarto sur velin, écrit par une calligraphe d'une rare habileté. Le roi se fait peindre sur la première page du manuscrit; il est dans l'attitude de la dévotion, à genoux; Léon X, sur son trône, semble écouter l'enfant qui vient offrir à son père le livre qu'il a composé pour la gloire du Christ. L'acte d'hommage est signé de la main du prince. À la fin du volume sont deux vers latins dont le sens est: 'Léon X!

[*]Leo X., p. 167.
[†]John Strype, Eccles. Memorials, Vol. I., p. 51.
[‡]Histoire Eccles., Vol. XII., p. 112.

Ce roi des Anglais, Henri, vous envoie cet ouvrage, témoin de sa foi et de son amitié.' . . . Un autograph du Pape Leo X, daté de Saint Pierre, le 11 Octobre 1521, et que l'on conserve dans les archives de la couronne d'Angleterre, donne à Henri VIII et à ses successeurs le titre de Défenseur de la Foi."

From this original an early copy was printed, as the following notices of Dibdin* show:

"613. Assertio Septem Sacramentorum adversus Martin. Lutherū, etc. Apud inclytam urbem Londinum in ædibus Pynsonianis. An. MDXXI. Quarto Idus Julij. Cum privilegio a rege indulto. Quarto."

To this Brunet adds:† "Édition trés rare; la première de cet ouvrage célèbre; . . . de 78 ff. . . .

"Jos Van Praet en cite trois exemplaires imprimés sur vélin."

And to this again Watts‡ adds a notice of apparently two other editions of the same year 1521, and in London; he says: "Et cum epistolâ ad Saxoniæ duces pie admonitoria. Lond. 1521, 4to;" and also: "Et cum summa indulgentiarum libellum ipsum legentibus concessarum. Lond. 1521, 4to."

Dibdin gives us details of the contents of one of the London editions of 1521. He says:§

"615. Libello huic Regio insunt, etc. Apud inclytam urbem Londinum in ædibus Pynsonianis MDXXI. Quarto.

"Herbert seems to have been indebted to Ames for the following account of this volume:

*Typograph. Antiq., Vol. II., p. 484. See also Audin's Henry VIII., note to p. 92. Alzog, Univers. Church Hist., Vol. III., p. 62, note 3. Worsley's Dawn of the Reformation, p. 159, note.

†Jacques Charles Brunet, Manuel du Libraire, Tome III., col. 100.

‡Biblioth. Britannica, Vol. I., Authors—article Henry VIII., King.

§Typograph. Antiq., Vol. II., p. 484.

" 'Libello huic regio hæc insunt.

" '1. Oratio Joannis Clerk apud Ro. pon. in exhibitione operis regii.

" '2. Responsio roman. pont. ad eundem ex tempore facto.

" '3. Bulla ro. pon. ad regiam majestatem, pro ejus operis confirmatione.

" '4. Summa indulgētiarum libellum ipsum regium legentibus, concessarum.

" '5. Libellus regius adversus Martinum Lutherum hæresiarchon.

" '6. Epistola regia ad illustrissimas saxoniæ duces pie admonitoria.' The colophon as above. In the public library, Cambridge."

Lastly, Thomson says* of this 1521 London edition: "It was printed in 1521 by Richard Pynson, in FRENCH, in *Latin* and in *English,* by order of the King."

So much for the publications of the "Assertio" that year in *London;* down in *Rome* Brunet† says it was printed, and an indulgence of ten years and ten quarantines was granted the readers of it. Here are his words: "Parmi les nombreuses reimpressions qui ont été faites de cette réfutation de Luther, une de plus rares, et sans doute la plus remarquable, est celle de Rome, opera Steph. Guilliereti, 1521, in 4, dont le titre porte: 'Librum hunc Angliæ regis fidei defensoris . . . legentibus, decem annorum et totidem XL indulgentia apostolica authoritate concessa est.' "

Panzer, "Annales Typographici," also mentions this edition of Rome 1521 as in quarto.

I may add that a recent catalogue of second-hand

*Court of Henry VIII., Vol. I., p. 381, note.
†Manuel du Libraire, Tome III., col. 100.

books rates a copy of this edition at 130 lire, though
Lowndes* mentions one sold for £3. 13. 6.

In 1522 there were several editions. Lowndes†
and Brunet‡ mention one in 4to of this date in
London.

Lowndes§ and Roscoe‖ speak of one at Antwerp, the
former (Lowndes) saying it was in 4to. The catalogue
of the British Museum says this edition was printed by
Hillen (see "Henry VIII.").

Lowndes,¶ Dibdin** and the "Bibliotheca Erasmiana"†† tell of one of the same year at Strasburg with
a commendatory epistle by Erasmus; Lowndes adds
that Archbishop Warham also commended it. Dibdin
and the "Bibliotheca Erasmiana" say it was in 4to; and
the "Bibliotheca" also says of it: "cum registro nuper
addito."

Dibdin further says that Ames speaks of an edition
"at Bruges by Erasmus," and that "Earl Spencer pos-
sesses a magnificent copy of this book, printed upon vellum, with the title-page elegantly illuminated. I have
seen an edition," he says, "of the date 1522, XVII Ka-
lendas Februarij cum privilegio a rege indulto."‡‡

Audin speaks of "two editions at Antwerp, with re-
prints at Frankfort, Cologne and many other places."§§

A 1523 edition is spoken of by Lowndes,‖‖ no place
given, in 4to, £1. 10. 0 in price. Twenty years
later it was published at Rome, according to Lingard¶¶

---

*Bibliographical Manual of English Literature, by Wm. T.
Lowndes, London, 1859, Part IV., p. 1039.

†Opus citat.	**Loco cit.
‡Opus citat.	††3ᵉ Serie, p. 28.
§Loco citato.	‡‡Op. cit., p. 485.
‖Leo X., loco citato.	§§Henry VIII., p. 92, note e.
¶Loco cit.	‖‖Loco citato.

¶¶Hist. of England, IV., 468.

and Walter,* Roscoe† adding that "From this" [i. e.,
the original copy sent to Leo X.] "copy it was printed
at Rome, in ædibus Francisci Priscianensis Florentini,
1543, as appears by the colophon."

Eighteen years later at Lyons another edition was
brought out by Gabriel de Saconay, "præcenteur" of the
cathedral at Lyons. The "Dictionnaire de Bibliographie Catholique" of Migne‡ says: "Præfixa est Gab.
de Saconay præfatio: accedunt exempla litterum Henrici VIII. ad Lutherum, et Lutheri ad Henricum; Lugduni, Guill. Rovillius 1561, in 4to." And Lowndes§
calls it a "valuable historical preface."

The editor has been able to locate only two copies of
this edition, one in the British Museum and the other
in the Vatican Pontifical Library respectively. From
the latter he has had a manuscript copy made, and finds
that, for the present purpose, out of the 84 pages of
Saconay's Preface p. lxxi is the first after the title-page
that speaks very distinctly of Henry's "Assertio." And
on p. lxxviiii he says that Henry's book had become so scarce "quod jam pene de manibus omnium
elapsum, et ab amico non obscura erga me benevolentia
comparatum, rursus in lucem emisi."

The next year, 1562, it was printed at Paris by William Desboys, in 12mo, "cui subnexa est ejusdem regis
epistola, assertionis ipsius contra eumdem defensoria;
accedit quoque P. Joan. Roffensis contra Lutheri
captivitatem Babylonicam assertionis regiæ defensio."‖

It may also be seen at the beginning of the "Opera"

---

*SirThomas More, by W. J. Walter, published by Lucas, Baltimore.
†Leo X., note 167.
‡Tome I., col. 751.
§Op. cit.
‖ Migne, Dic. de Bibliog. Cath., Tome I., col. 751.

of Bishop Fisher's works, published by Fleischman at Würzburg 1697.

Another edition appeared at Naples 1728, in 12mo.

Lowndes* speaks of a 16mo edition without place or date, and then says there are several other editions.

In 1850, at Angers, in France, it was published by Pottier in both Latin and French, 8vo, with an introduction on the authenticity of the "Assertio" by Clement Villecourt, the Bishop of La Rochelle.

The editions of Paris 1562,† Naples 1728, Angers 1850, and the English edition‡ to be described later have been used in this re-edition.

The "Assertio" was translated from the Latin into several of the modern languages. Luther reproduced it freely in German; Walch gives a translation by Frick, in 1522; Hergenroether§ mentions a translation in German this same year by H. Emser. Saconay in his Preface, p. lxxii, also speaks of "hoc libro regio, per Hieronymum Empserum in linguam Germanicam translato."

The catalogue of the British Museum, under "Henry VIII.," records this: "Schutz und handthabung der siben Sacrament. Wider M. Luther, etc. [Translated from the Latin by H. Emser.] Erfurt? 1522. 4°."

Audin's mention (Calvin, II., 425) of a French version is questioned, for the first and only French translation, except that mentioned by Thomson,‖ that Henry himself had it put into French, seems to have been that of Pottier, for although, as the Bishop of La Rochelle¶

*Loco citato.

†Kindly loaned by the Catholic University at Washington.

‡Dr. Healy, of the Catholic University, kindly loaned this, and allowed it to be reprinted.

§Hist. de l'Église, V., p. 247.

‖Court of Henry VIII., Vol. I., p. 381, note.

¶XIX., 158 seq.

says in his Introduction to it, "vit-on bientôt non-seule-ment l'Angleterre, mais l'Italie, l'Allemagne et la France *reproduire* ce chef-d'œuvre," yet he also says: "Je ne connais aucune *traduction* française de l'ouvrage, qui fut publié en 1521, a Londres, sous le nom de Henri VIII., roi d'Angleterre."

Gabriel de Saconay had *reprinted, but not translated* the "Assertio" at Lyons. Moreri* in his "Grand Dictionnaire Historique" says: "Dès l'an 1561, il avoit fait réimprimer l'ouvrage de Henri VIII., contre Luther, avec une belle et longue préface de sa façon."

After considerable patience and expense the editor has been able to confirm this statement, having at length secured a manuscript copy of Saconay's "Introduction" to the "Assertio."

The French version mentioned by Audin,† Main-waring Brown,‡ Brunet,§ and the "Dictionnaire de Bibliographie Catholique,"‖ is thus entitled on its fly-leaf:

"Défense des Sept Sacrements publiée contre Martin Luther par Henri VIII., Roi d'Angleterre et Seigneur d'Irland, traduite par R. J. Pottier, Licencié es-lettres. Précédée d'une préface par L'Abbé Maupoint, Vicaire-Général du diocèse de Rennes. D'une Introduction sur l'Authenticité de ce livre, par Mgr. l'Evêque de la Rochelle. Et suivie de la Constitution de Pie VI., 'Auctorem fidei,' traduite par le même prélat. Angers: Imprimerie et Librairie de Laine Frères 1850."

*Tome IX., Saconay.
†Henry VIII., p. 92, note b.
‡Henry VIII.'s Book, etc., in the Royal Hist. So.'s Transactions, VIII., p. 242 and fol.
§Op. cit., III., col. 100.
‖Migne, Tome I., col. 507.

And now, last, but not least, the English versions! Collier* has this entry: "Henry the Eighth.—A copy of the letters, wherein the most redouted and mighty price, our souerayne lorde, Kyng Henry the eight, Kyng of Englande and of Fraūce, defēsor of the faith, and lord of Irlāde; made answere unto a certayne letter of Martyn Luther, sent unto hym by the same, and also the copy of ye foresayd Luther's letter, in suche order as here after foloweth. B. L. 8vo. 49 leaves.

"The colophon to this volume runs thus: 'Imprinted at London in Fletestrete by Richarde Pynson.' . . . At the back of the title-page is the list of contents.

" 'Fyrst a preface of our souerayne lorde the Kynge . . .

" 'Copye of the letter, whiche Martin Luther had sent.

" 'The copye of the answere of our sayd souerayne lorde.' . . . The preface fills the first fifteen, and Luther's letter the next seven, pages. The answer of Henry VIII. occupies the rest of the volume."

An edition in 1687 in 4to is mentioned by Gasquet† and Watts;‡ and Lowndes§ in this connection has the following entry: "Assertion of the Seven Sacraments with his epistle to the Pope, Mr. John Clark's oration, the Pope's answer and Bull, etc., translated by T. W. Lond. 1687, 4to. Bindley, pt. II., 518, date 1688, morocco, 18s. 6d."

Substantiating the correctness of this is the entry in the catalogue of the British Museum, wherein, under article "Henry VIII.," one may read: "Assertio Septem

---

*A Biographical and Critical Account of the Rarest Books in the English Language, J. Payne Collier, F.S.A., Vol. I., p. 368.
† Eve of Reformation, p. 95, note.
‡Ubi supra.
§Bibliog. Man.. loco citato.

Sacramentorum: or, an assertion of the seven sacraments, against Martin Luther by Henry the VIII. . . .
To which is adjoyn'd his epistle to the Pope; Mr. J.
Clark's oration; and the Pope's answer thereunto. As
also, the Pope's Bull, by which his Holiness was pleas'd
to bestow upon K. H. VIII. . . . that most illustrious
. . . title of Defender of the Faith. Faithfully translated into English by T[homas] W[ebster]. Gent.
pp. 133. Eug. N. Thompson: London, 1687. 4°." And
also a "Second edition, revised and corrected. London,
1688. 12°."

As for other English versions, the writer knows of
none printed in England, for this English version, now
and here reprinted, was, he believes, done in Ireland;
·and this belief is based on the following reasons:
1. One might readily suspect that after Henry had
changed his morals—even if not his faith—and had not
only left, but shamefully pillaged and assaulted, the
Church, naturally he would not *allow* the "Assertio" to
be printed.* Neither would any subsequent sovereign, save Mary, in her brief and busy reign, and that
for the same obvious reasons. 2. In the "Advertisement" of the present edition, here reprinted, the writer
speaks of "The London edition from whence the present
is taken." Now, that sounds as if this edition were
not done in London, but somewhere else; and where?
3. In this same "Advertisement," page 247, note (a),
the writer refers to the "Historical Account of the
Reformation (from Fleury's Ecclesiastical History)
printed in *Corke* 1764." Now, at this date in *England* one would hardly expect to see a Catholic so dar-
ing as to break the laws and not only *have*, but print, a
book so decidedly pro-Catholic as the "Assertio." And

*The version just told of, by "T. W.," would seem to be the excep-
tion that proves the rule. It had doubtless been done surreptitiously.

if it were some non-Catholic, he would hardly quote
Fleury, a Catholic and a Frenchman. Furthermore,
whether Catholic or not, if an *Englishman,* he would
not likely use an edition of Fleury "printed in *Corke.*"
4. This English edition here reprinted, kindly loaned
by Dr. Healy, of the Catholic University of America,
was presented to him by an *Irishman* in *Ireland.*

Now, while this is not an apodictical argument, yet it
gives a great probability that the edition here reprinted
was printed not in England, but in Ireland. This edition seems to be simply a reprint from the first English
version, for the writer has compared several passages
quoted by Foxe, in his "Book of Martyrs"* (who, in all
probability, quoted from the first English version),
with the corresponding passages in the edition here reprinted, and the wording agrees perfectly.

As the first few pages and the last page are missing
in this copy of Dr. Healy's no further or surer details of
place or date or printer of the edition here reprinted
can be given save that it is the second half of a second
volume in 12mo, with, of course, the spelling "our,"
long s's, a guide-word at the foot of each page, and capi-
tals to nouns within sentences, even though not proper
names. It is bound in leather, and preceding it in the
same volume is a "Discourse on the Seven Sacraments,"
but without any clue as to author, place or date. The
writer knows nothing of the first volume, but this second
volume is entitled "Sacraments Explained."

Note. Since the above was written the editor has
found in the British Museum catalogue, article "Hornihold," the following entry:

"Hornihold (John), Bishop of Philomel. The Commandments and Sacraments Explained in fifty two
discourses, to which is added, King Henry the Eighth's

*Edited by Cummings, Vol. II., p. 79, note.

Defence of the Seven Sacraments, against Martin Luther. 2 vols. Dublin, 1821. 12°."

The same catalogue makes entries of "[another edition] Dublin 1836, 12°," and "[another edition] Baltimore [1858 ?], 8°" and "The Decalogue explained, etc., 1750, 12°." From the library of St. Mary's Seminary, Baltimore, the editor has secured a copy of the 1821 edition, entitled "The Commandments and Sacraments Explained in Fifty two Discourses by the Rt. Rev. Doctor Hornihold, to which is added, King Henry the Eighth's Defence of the Seven Sacraments against Martin Luther. In two volumes. Dublin: Richard Coyne, 16 Parliament St., Catholic Bookseller. 1821. Price 11s. 4½d." The work is in 16mo and bound in calf. On page 215 of Volume II. is the following: "Assertio Septem Sacramentorum, or a Defence of the Seven Sacraments against Martin Luther, by Henry the Eighth, King of England, France and Ireland, to which are adjoined His Epistle to the Pope, The Oration of Mr. John Clark, (Orator to His Majesty) on the Delivery of this Book to His Holiness, and the Pope's Answer to the Oration, as also the Pope's Bull, by which His Holiness was pleased to bestow upon that King (for composing this book) that most illustrious, splendid, and most Christian-like title of Defender of the Faith. Faithfully translated into English from the original Latin edition. By T. W. Gent."

This edition of Dr. Hornihold's work is different from the one which is here reprinted, though the latter is evidently by Dr. Hornihold.

The catalogue of the British Museum says there was "another edition of Hornihold, Dublin, 1836, 12°." Probably this latter is the edition here reprinted. The same catalogue records "another edition, Baltimore, 1858 (?), 8°."

From this narration of the various editions we may readily see how widely spread and read the "Assertio" was.

"Copies were sent to all the principal courts of Europe and to the universities. Two copies . . . are still in the Vatican Library."*

This statement must yield to a personal letter from Rev. Fr. Ehrle, S.J., from the Vatican Library, wherein he says there are now in the Vatican four copies of the edition of London 1521, all printed on parchment, and also the editions of Antwerp 1523, Florence 1543, Lyons 1561, and Paris (?) 1562 (?).

In the British Museum there are sixteen editions and ten copies of dates as follows: 1521, two editions and two copies; 1522, five editions and three copies; 1543, one edition; 1561, one edition and one copy; 1562, one edition and two copies; 1687, one edition and two copies; and one edition for 1688, 1821, 1836, 1850, and 1858.

Here at the end of the list of the editions of the "Assertio," for the sake of clearness and by way of supplement, is inserted a chronological summary taken from Walter's "More."

1521. May, "Assertio" begun. (?)
   October, "Assertio" published.
1522. July, Luther replied to Henry.
   Henry complained to the Elector.†
1525. September, at the entreaty of Christian, King of Denmark, Luther apologized to Henry.

---

*English Catholic Truth So.'s publication, "Popery on Every Coin of the Realm."

†Audin, Henry VIII., p. 101, gives the title of the letter of Henry to the Princes complaining about Luther, as follows: "Contra Lutherum ejusque hæresim epist. scr. regis Ang. ad illustrissimas Saxoniæ duces pie admonitoria."

1526. More's "Vindicatio Henrici VIII. a calumniis Lutheri" by "Gulielmus Rosseus."

So that besides the "Assertio" Henry sent out as *his* other documents, for Henry wrote a reply to Luther.* . . . "These letters have been published without note of place or date, and are prefixed, in the copy, now before the writer, of *the treatise of Henry* on the seven sacraments."†

As for Luther's writings in reply to the "Assertio," Roscoe, in his "Leo X.," says:‡

"Luther replied to this book in his treatise 'Contra Henricum VIII. Angliæ Regem'; which he addressed to Seb. Schlick, a Bohemian nobleman, in a dedication which bears date 15th July, 1522. In this work he treats the King, without any ceremony, as a liar and a blasphemer. 'Nunc quum prudens et sciens mendatia componat adversus mei Regis majestatem in cœlis, damnabilis Putredo ista et Vermis, jus mihi erit pro meo Rege, majestatem Anglicam luto suo et stercore conspergere, et coronam istam blasphemam in Christum pedibus conculcare.' But whilst he stigmatizes the book of Henry VIII. as *stolidissimum* and *turpissimum*, he acknowledges it to be 'inter omnes qui contra se scripti sunt *latinissimum.*' He insinuates, however, that it was written by some other person in the name of the King."

This criticism is not peculiar to Roscoe: Hutton, in his "More,"§ speaks of "an answer from Luther which no one denies to be violent and indecent to the last de-

* "Invictissimi principis Henrici VIII., regis Angliæ et Franciæ, ad Martini Lutheri epistolam responsio."
†Roscoe, Leo X., Vol. II., note 168.
‡Note 168.
§P. 198.

gree." Stapleton* says of Luther's reply, "spurcissimum librum spurcus Lutherus evomuerat."

As to this letter, it is worth while noting that: "His [Erasmus'] best friends . . . and some in England, suspected that Erasmus' hand and spirit were to be detected in the reply that Luther made to King Henry's book against him [L.]."†

As said above, Luther's apology to Henry was sent September, 1525; it was printed in German and afterwards also in Latin. Hallam attributes this recantation of Luther's to some derangement of the intellectual faculties.‡ Audin assigns some other reason.

But now turn back from this unhappy German to the quiet peaceful Englishman—Sir Thomas More.

Roscoe§ says that "An answer to the work of Luther was published or re-published, London, 1523, under the following title: 'Eruditissimi viri Gulielmi Rossei opus elegans, doctum, festivum, pium, quo pulcherrime relegit ac refellit insanas Lutheri calumnias; quibus invectissimum Angliæ, Galliæque Regem Henricum ejus nominis octavum, Fidei defensorem haud litteris minus quam regno clarum scurra turpissimus insectatur,' etc. In this work, which is attributed to Sir Thomas More, the author has not only endeavoured to refute the arguments, but to equal the abuse of the German reformer. . . . A few years afterwards . . . Luther wrote to him to excuse the violence in his book, which he attributed to the advice of others. . . . To this Henry condescended to write a long and argumentative reply, in which he advises Luther to retract his errors. . . . These letters have been published without note of place or date, and

---

*Tres Thomæ, p. 186.
†Gasquet, Eve of Reformation, p. 185.
‡Note to Audin's Henry VIII., p. 101.
§Op. citato, note 168.

are prefixed, in the copy now before me, to the treatise of Henry on the Seven Sacraments."

This work of More was in Latin,* and, says Burnet,† "He wrote according to the way of the age, with much bitterness." However, Maitland‡ may be quoted, who says: "I do not want to defend the Romish writers and I hope I have no partiality for them, . . . but it really appears to me only simple truth to say that, whether from good or bad motives, they did in fact abstain from that fierce, truculent, and abusive language, and that loathsome ribaldry, which characterized the style of too many of the Puritan writers."§

Besides Sir Thomas another wise and holy man defended the King: that was John Fisher, Bishop of Rochester, who wrote also in 1523.‖ Lingard¶ says: "Fisher, Bishop of Rochester, in a more argumentative style, undertook the defence of the King in his work, entitled 'Defensio Assertionum regis Angliæ de fide Catholica adversus Lutheri Captivitatem Babylonicam.'" Audin says of it:** "It is a controversial work, where no passionate expression can be perceived, and were the bishop alive nowadays, and about to publish it, he would not require to erase a single word. Luther must have suffered most acutely on reading a work of such candour and merit." Fisher's argument is that "men may err in interpreting Scripture, and therefore they must obey the Holy Ghost, Who ex-

*Eve of Reformation, p. 90.
†Hist. of Reformation, Vol. I., p. 31.
‡The Reformation, p. 48.
§Conf. Lingard, Hist. of Eng., IV., p. 468, note 2. Stewart, Life and Letters of Sir Thomas More, p. 119. Henri Bremond, Thomas More, Ch. V., note 2.
‖Mason, p. 81, op. cit. in Bibliog.
¶Hist. of England, Vol. IV., p. 468.
**Henry VIII., pp. 99, 100.

pounds Scripture infallibly in the Church by the mouths of the Fathers and Councils and Tradition."

Besides More and Fisher we are told that in 1523 "appeared [Wolsey's] elaborate defence of Henry VIII. entitled 'Adsertionis Lutheranæ confutatio,' and also Powell's 'Propugnaculum.' "* Of this latter, Collier tells us :†

"One Dr. Powell of Oxford was a second to the King in this controversy. . . . The tract was divided into two books; the first was entitled 'De summo Pontifice et Eucharistiæ sacramento;' the other 'De Sex Sacramentis.' The King was extremely pleased with Powell's management. . . . But he lost the King's favour by appearing strongly against the divorce and the new supremacy."

Over the Channel, even in the land of the enemy, Henry had apologists. Du Pin, in his "Ecclesiastical History," says :‡

"Several divines thought it an honour to defend the King of England, by confuting Luther's book, which he wrote against him. In Germany, John Eckius answered it in Latin, and Thomas Muncer in High-Dutch."

*Hardwick's Christian Church, p. 165, note 1.
†Op. cit., Pt. II., Bk. I., 17.
‡Sixteenth Century, Bk. II., Ch. XIV.

The Presentation to the Pope

THOUGH I have found nothing in the records, yet one may fancy the feelings of Henry as he waited in England for news of how his book had been received at Rome.

Lingard, in his "History of England," tells something of the outward presentation and of the inward private history, too. He says* that "Clark, dean of Windsor, carried the royal production to the pontiff, with an assurance, as his master had refuted the errors of Luther with his pen, so was he ready to oppose the disciples of the heresiarch with his sword, and to array against them the whole strength of his kingdom. Leo accepted the present, . . . but Henry looked for something more pleasing to his vanity than mere acknowledgments. The Kings of France had long been distinguished by the appellation of 'Most Christian,' those of Spain by 'Catholic.' When Louis XII. set up the schismatical synod of Pisa it was contended that he had forfeited his right to the former of these titles, and Julius II. transferred it to Henry, but with the understanding that the transfer should be kept secret till the services of the King might justify in the eyes of men the partiality of the pontiff. After the victory of Guinegate Henry demanded the publication of the grant; but Julius was dead; Leo declared himself ignorant of the transaction, and means were found to pacify the King with the promise of some other, but equivalent, distinction. Wol-

*IV., 446.

sey had lately recalled the subject to the attention of the papal court; and Clark, when he presented the King's work, demanded for him the title of 'Defender of the Faith.' This new denomination experienced some opposition; but it could not be refused with decency; and Leo conferred it by a formal bull on Henry, who procured a confirmation of the grant from the successor of Leo, Clement VII."

Another very interesting and somewhat different account is that given by Roscoe.* He says:

"This work Henry dedicated to Leo X., and transmitted a copy to Rome with the following distich:

'Anglorum Rex Henricus, Leo Decime, mittit
  Hoc opus, et fidei testem et amicitiæ.'

It was presented to the pontiff in full consistory, by the ambassador of the King, who made a long and pompous oration; to which the Pope replied in a concise and suitable manner. The satisfaction which Leo derived from this circumstance, at a time when the supremacy of the Holy See was in such imminent danger, may be judged of by the desire which he showed to express to the King his approbation of the part he had taken. After returning him ample thanks, and granting an indulgence to every person who should peruse the book, he resolved to confer upon him some distinguishing mark of the pontifical favour, and accordingly proposed in the consistory to honour him with the title of Defender of the Faith. This proposition gave rise, however, to more deliberation, and occasioned greater difficulty in the Sacred College than perhaps the Pope had foreseen. Several of the Cardinals suggested other titles, and it was for a long time debated whether, instead of the appellation of Defender of the Faith, the

*Leo X., II., 231.

sovereigns of England should not, in all future times, be denominated the Apostolic, the Orthodox, the Faithful, or the Angelic.* The proposition of the Pope, who had been previously informed of the sentiments of Wolsey on this subject, at length, however, prevailed, and a bull was accordingly issued, conferring this title on Henry and his posterity;† a title retained by his successors to the present day, notwithstanding their separation from the Roman Church; which has given occasion to some orthodox writers to remark that the Kings of this country should either maintain that course of conduct in reward for which the distinction was conferred, or relinquish the title."‡

Audin adds that Pace also went with Clark "to the Vatican to present the 'Assertio' to His Holiness."§

Pallavicini, in his "History of the Council of Trent,"‖ says: "Il composa donc un livre savant contre beaucoup des propositions de Martin Luther, le fit presenter au pontife en consistoire, le second jour d'octobre, par son ambassadeur. . . . Ce fut pour Leon le sujet d'une grande joie."

He further tells us that among the titles suggested as a reward for Henry were "Apostolic," "Orthodox," "Faithful," "Angelic" (Anglican), "Most Faithful," "Glorious"; . . . that on the 26th of October, 1521, the Consistory agreed on the title "Defender of the Faith."

"Thereupon a bull was drawn up on this subject, and a brief which was to be joined to the bull, . . . and these two pieces were approved in a consistory 26 Oct.

*Pallavic., Concil. di Trento, lib. II., cap. 1, Sec. VIII., p. 177.
†Vide App., No. X.
‡Seckend., lib. I., p. 183. (Luther Op.)
§Henry VIII., p. 93.
‖Bk. II., Ch. I., par. 7.

1521."* Pope Clement confirmed the title in a bull of March 5, 1523.†

Humanly speaking, what a boon this book of Henry's, and all that it stood for in the eyes of the world, must have been to the Pope! Protestantism was about to break out in Germany, and this embassy from England must have indeed cheered the drooping spirits of the Sovereign Pontiff. This is well put by Speed:‡ "But with what acceptance his Holinesse received King Henrie's booke, his own oration solemnly made at the delivery thereof unto M. John Clarke, the presenter and King's ambassador, in his Consistory, and in the presence of his Cardinals, sufficiently doth show, the translation whereof we have inserted as we find it in the Originall it selfe." [Translation follows.]

"To manifest which his readinesse, himself among his Cardinals decreed an augmentation unto King Henries royall style, to bee annexed unto his others; confirming the same by his Bull, which that it perish not by the devouring teeth of time wee have here published from the originall Parchment, and Leaden Seale it selfe, as follows: . . . "

Last, but not least, is Brewer's edition of the "Letters and Papers, Foreign and Domestic,"§ concerning Henry VIII.'s book being presented to the Pope. The account says:

"1592. Campeggio to Wolsey:

"1521   "Is overcome with joy at reading the
19 Sept.   King's 'aureus libellus.' All who have seen
R. O.   it say that, though so many have written
           on the same subject, nothing could be bet-
ter expressed or argued, and he seems to have been in-

*Part I., Bk. II., Ch. I.
†Schaff, Christian Church, Ch. VI., § 70.
‡Hist. of Great Britain, p. 992.
§Vol. III., Part II.

spired more by an angelic and celestial than by a human spirit. We can hereafter truly call him 'Lutheromastica.' I send also congratulatory letters to the King. You will hear the account of the war in Italy from the King's ambassador and the Pope's nuncio with you. Rome 19 Sept. 1521. Signed. Lat. p. 1, Add."

So much for the preliminary presentation. As to the presentation in Consistory the records say :*

"1607. Clerk to Wolsey:

"The Pope has appointed next week for receiving the King's book in open Consistory. Would have sent a copy of his proposed oration, but was prevented by the hasty departure of the carrier. Rome. 25 Sept. 1521.

"Hol. My Lord Cardinal's grace."

However, we have soon after the omitted speech, at least in substance; it runs thus :†

"1656. JOHN CLARK.

"His speech in the consistory on presenting the King's book.

"The King has written this book to counteract the pernicious and widespread heresies of Martin Luther, and commissioned the speaker to offer it to his Holiness. Enlarges on the virulence of Luther and his disrespect for the Pope, his making himself equal to St. Peter, and his contempt for the authority of the Fathers. Luther has broken the rule of continence and reduced the sacraments to 3, 2, 1, would probably reduce them to nothing some day. Points to the misery of Bohemia caused by the Hussite heresy, as a warning. The new enemy equals all heresiarchs in learning, exceeds all in wickedness of spirit.

"The Pope, however, has done his best to stifle the flames, aided by learned men in all countries, of which

*Brewer, State Papers.
†Brewer, op. cit. 13th Henry VIII.

England, though most remote, is not the least devout. There, among other fast friends of the Holy See, the most conspicuous is Wolsey, a member of that college, who has caused the Pope's rescript against Luther to be published everywhere, and Luther's book to be burned, called an assembly of learned men to write against him, and supported them at his own cost for some months. In more simple times error was plucked up by the roots, and the quiet of the Church was undisturbed. Many wonder how a prince so much occupied was led to attempt a work that demanded all the energies of a veteran man of letters; but having already defended the Church with his sword, Henry felt it needful to do so with his pen, now that she is in much greater danger. Not that he thought it glorious to contend with one so despicable as Luther, but he wished to show the world what he thought of that horrible portent, and to induce the learned to follow his example, by which Luther might be compelled himself to retract his heresies. The King, however, has no hope of convincing him; he should be assailed with those weapons which, if the time permitted, the King would use against the Turks.

"Finally, the King desires the work not to be published otherwise than with the approval of the Pope, from whom we ought to receive the sense of the gospel.

"The Pope's answer, saying that he thanked God the Holy See had found such a prince to defend it."

Further items are also entered:

"11 Oct. 1659. Fidei Defensor.

"Bull of Leo X. conferring upon the King, in full Consistory, the title of 'Fidei Defensor.'

"Rome 5 id Oct. 9 pont 1521. Signed by the Pope and Cardinals. Vellum, mutilated.

"Wolsey's speech on presenting the bull for the title of Defender of the Faith.

"When John Cl[erk], the King's ambassador at Rome, presented the King's book against Luther to the late Pope Leo X., in presence of the College of Cardinals, it was beautiful to hear with what exultation the Pope and Cardinals broke out into the praises of Henry, declaring that no one could have devised a better antidote to the poison of heresy, and that Henry had with great eloquence completely refuted Luther by reason, Scripture and the authority of the Fathers. He had thus devoted his learning to the support of religion, and shown an example to Christian princes. As an imperfect acknowledgment of this service, the Pope, with the unanimous assent of the Cardinals, a little before his death, ordained, by letters under the hands of himself and them, that Henry should henceforth be called 'Defender of the Faith,' and ordered a bull to be sent, which Wolsey now presents. Congratulates Henry on the honour, and himself on having induced him to undertake the work.

"Lat. pp. 2 mutilated."

It is pertinent to ask about the Bull *now*, which was conveyed to Henry with such "fulsome parade and pomp."[*] It "is still in the British Museum, as also an autograph letter[†] from the Pope praising Henry and his work in the highest terms."[‡]

Fuller, in his "Church History of Britain," Vol. II., p. 13, says:

"There is a tradition that King Henry's fool, . . . coming into the court, and finding the King transported with an unusual joy, boldly asked him the cause thereof; to whom the King answered it was because that

*Worsley, Dawn of the Reformation, p. 160.
†See Pope's Letter to Henry, p. 175.
‡English Catholic Truth Society, pamphlet "Popery on Every Coin of the Realm."

the Pope had honoured him with a style more eminent than any of his ancestors. 'O good Harry,' quoth the fool, 'let thou and I defend one another, and let the faith alone to defend itself.' "

Finally, there is an amusing as well as interesting statement made by Lowndes,* who says that the Roman edition of 1521 had four leaves prefixed, declaring: "Librum hunc Invictiss Angliæ Regis, Fidei Defensoris contra Mart. Lutherum Legentibus, decem annorum et totidem XL Indulgentia apostolica Auctoritate concessa est."

*Biograph. Manual, Part IV., p. 1039.

The Title "Defender of the Faith"— Was It to be Hereditary?

EDWARD VII. is the seventeenth "English sovereign who has borne that title. . . . It is the only title besides that of 'King' of England he thinks it worth while to put on his coinage. In other words, his proudest title, after 'King of England,' is that given by the Pope—'Defender of the Faith.' "*

Now, the question is, has the present King, had any king or queen other than Henry VIII., the right to the title "Defender of the Faith" which the Pope gave Henry?

The question must be divided in two, thus:

1. Did the King of England ever have this title before Henry VIII.?

2. Was *Henry VIII.'s* title given to him by the Pope to be hereditary?

1. As to the first, there are several reliable witnesses for the affirmative.

In the "Archæologia," published in London, Vol. XIX., p. 1, Luders presents very interesting testimony. He says: "According to Henault, Pepin had received the title of 'Most Christian' in A.D. 755 from the Pope, and Charles the Bald in 859 from a Council. Charles the Sixth, in a charter of 1413, refers to ancient usage for the same." Continuing, he says that Richard II. and Henry IV. both speak of themselves as "Defenders of the Faith."

*English Catholic Truth Society, pamphlet "Popery on Every Coin of the Realm."

Further proof of this assertion is found in the work "A History of the Christian Church during the Reformation, by Charles Hardwick, M.A., [edited] by W. Stubbs, M.A."* Apropos of Henry's title, it is said that "the title itself, however, was not new, having been applied to previous kings, e. g., to Henry IV. (1411)."

Confirming this statement, that Henry IV. used the title, is the following extract from Wilkins' "Concilia," Vol. III., p. 334, wherein under the title "Convocatio Prælectorum et Cleri Prov. Cant. Anno Christi 1411. Reg. Angliæ Henric. IV. 13. Primo die Decembris in ecclesia S. Pauli, London. Ex reg. Arundel II., fol. 22," we read that the Archbishop of Canterbury, Thomas Arundel, says: "Quod ipse [Thomas Arundel] pro parte sua, singulique confratres sui, et tota ecclesia Anglicana tenebantur, et semper tenerentur cum omni devotione specialius et devotissime habere recommissum prosperum statum domini regis, tamquam pugilis, athletæ, et præcipui *defensoris fidei* orthodoxæ; qui maxime ad extirpandum errores et hæreses, ac herbas venenosas, et plantulas infectivas, jam nimis diu per regni latitudinem seccrescentes, novitatis Lollardicæ pravitatis animadversionem suæ regiæ majestatis, tamquam rex catholicus, cum omni assistentia prebuit gratiosam."

Again, in Lewis' "Fisher"† it is said: "And yet it's certain this was no new title, but had been claimed and used long before by King Richard II. in the commissions granted by him for the apprehending and imprisoning those who taught or maintained the conclusions of Dr. Wiclif. Nos zelo *fidei* Catholicæ cujus sumus et esse volumus *Defensores* in omnibus commoti."

Further, Croly, in his "Luther and the Reformation,"‡ speaks of "The title of 'Defender of the Seven

*P. 165, note 3.   †Vol. I., p. 108.   ‡P. 222.

Sacraments,' a title which had been borne by former kings, but which he [Henry VIII.] exulted in as a personal distinction."

So that one may reasonably conclude that the title "Defender of the Faith," or at least a title similar in wording, if not in idea, was used before Henry VIII. received it from Leo. And, moreover, while it is not so stated in the authorities consulted, yet this title, used before the time of Henry, would seem to have been hereditary.

2. And now as to the second part of the question: Was the title given by the Pope to Henry VIII. intended by the Pope to be perpetual and hereditary?

The evidence is not all on one side, and hence the testimonies declaring the title hereditary are here given first.

Butler, in his "Church History of Britain,"[*] says of Henry VIII.: "To requite his pains the Pope honoured him and *his successors* with a specious title, 'A Defender of the Faith.'"

Thomson agrees with this in his "Court of Henry VIII.,"[†] and says: "His theological attainments enabled him in after times to procure for himself and *his successors* the title of 'Defender of the Faith.'"

So, too, Lewis, in his "Life of Dr. John Fisher,"[‡] speaks of "An Acte in bull under lead declaring His Grace to be the 'Defender of the Christian Faith' and *his successors forever.*"

The "Annals of England," page 47, says of Leo: "He decreed to grace King Henry *and his successors* with that honourable one of Defender of the Faith."

Concurring with this is Cobbett in his "History of the Protestant Reformation in England and Ireland,"[§]

[*]Vol. II., p. 13.   [‡]Vol. I., p. 108.
[†]Vol. I., p. 3.   [§]Phila., 1825, p. 69.

who makes the translation of the Pope's Bull declare that he, the Pope, does "grant unto Your Majesty, your *heirs and successors,"* the title.

In Edward Hall's "Lives of the Kings"* is the following very interesting and detailed entry: "The second day of February, the Kynge beyng at Grenewiche, came thether the Cardinall with a legacion from Leo, bishop of Rome. . . . And finally the Cardinall declared how the sayd bishop of Rome had sent his highnes an Acte in Bull under leade, declaryng therein his grace to be defendor of the Christian fayth, *and his successors for evermore.* And when his grace had received the sayd Bull and caused it to be redde and published, he went to his chapell to heare Masse."

"Holinshed's Chronicle of England, Scotland, and Ireland"† has the following to say on the title being hereditary: "On the second daie of Februarie, the King, as then being at Greenewich, received a bull from the Pope, whereby he was declared Defendor of the Christian faith, *and likewise his successors forever.* . . .

"The title was ascribed unto the King because he had written a booke against Luther in Germanie; whereunto the said Luther answered verie sharpelie, nothing sparing his authoritie nor majestie. Of which booke published by the King, I will not (for reverence of his roialtie), though I durst, report what I have read: bicause we are to judge honourablie of our rulers, and to speake nothing but good of the princes of the people. Onelie this briefe clause or fragment I will adde (least I might seeme to tell a tale of the man in the moone) that King Henrie in his said booke is reported to rage against the divell and antichrist to cast out his some against Luther, to raise out the name of the Pope, and

*Henry VIII., Vol. I., p. 235.
†Vol. III., England, p. 675.

yet to allow his law, etc. I suppresse the rest for shame, and returne to our historie."

John Foxe, in his "Acts and Monuments,"* says the same: "But whosoever had the labour of this book, the King had the thanks and also the reward; for consequently upon the same the bishop of Rome gave to the said King Henry, for the style against Luther, the style and title of 'Defender of the Christian Faith,' and to *his successors forever.*"

Baronius, in his "Annales Ecclesiasticæ,"† sides with the foregoing: "Tam gratum accidit Leoni id munus Henrici Regis, ut non modum illum laudibus celebrarit, verum etiam defensoris Ecclesiæ titulo decoraverit, quem veluti perpetuum et immortale regiæ gloriæ monumentum in *ejus posteras transfundendum* constituit."‡

This is certainly a rather formidable array of historians in favour of the title being hereditary, and yet there are others, best of all the Bull itself, in comparison with which all other witnesses are of little weight, which seem to disprove the hereditary character of the title, at least in the Pope's intention as implied in the Bull.

Mainwaring Brown, in the Royal Historical Society's Publications, Vol. VIII., has an article on "Henry VIII.'s Book, 'Assertio Septem Sacramentorum,' and the Royal Title of 'Defender of the Faith.' " He says: "Old writers, such as Holinshed, Lever, etc., say that it [the title] was granted to the King *and his successors,* but the words of the bull" are [see elsewhere in this volume]. "This bull, then, so far from making the title hereditary, especially set forth that it was not so, and

*Vol. IV., pp. 293, 294.
†Cum Pagi, Tom. XXXI., p. 343, ad an. 1521, parag. LXXIV.
‡IV., 468, note 1.

that if Henry's successors desired to bear it they must earn it as he had done. . . .

"Henry did not at first see that the personal title which he held from Rome was inferior in dignity to the hereditary titles which they [Kings of France and Spain] held."

And he furthermore says: "In 1523 the King obtained a confirmation of [the title] from Clement VII. The original grantor, Leo X., had died before the bull containing the title reached England. . . . It is likely that Henry desired to have the title made hereditary. . . . Several old writers (e. g., Burnet) speak of the second bull actually making it so. . . .

"The Pope so ambiguously worded [the bull] that Henry might be privately told that he could make the title hereditary on its authority.

"It must not, however, be forgotten that there is no evidence more than presumptive in favour of this view. . . .

". . . Henry will keep a title which he ought to have dropped, and will grant to his descendants a distinction which neither he nor his Parliament had any right to bestow. . . .

"There is a vast difference between the authority which granted the title and that which made it hereditary. The Pope commanded all Christian people to call Henry Defender of the Faith; the English Parliament could only require his own subjects to address him by that title."

Lastly, from this same author we read the following: "Titulum illum et cognomen Fidei Defensoris . . . approbamus confirmamus tibique perpetuum et proprium deputamus."

Circumstances confirm this interpretation, for the Pope would hereby please Henry by his title, yet not

arouse the jealousy of the others by a hereditary one. Strangely enough, Parliament declared the title hereditary (see State Papers, 35 Hen. VIII., c. 3). It was repealed by Parliament in 1554, yet the crown still used it. Elizabeth revived it by act of Parliament.

But the weightiest witness in this question is surely the Pope's Bull itself; so that we should carefully read the following passage of it, which decides that the title is not hereditary:

"As we have by this title honoured *you,* we likewise command all Christians that they name *your Majesty* by this title, and that in their writings to *your Majesty,* immediately after the word King they add Defender of the Faith. Having thus weighed and diligently considered *your singular* merits, . . . which [title] as often as you hear, or read, you shall remember your *own* merits and virtues; nor will you, by this title, exalt *yourself,* . . . but become more strong and constant in your devotion to this Holy See, by which you were exalted. And you shall rejoice in our Lord, who is the Giver of all good things, for leaving such a perpetual and everlasting monument of *your* glory *to posterity,* and showing the way *to others* that if *they also covet to be invested with such a title,* they may *study to do* such actions, and to follow the steps of *your* most excellent Majesty; whom, with your *wife, children, and all who shall spring from you,* we bless with a bounteful and liberal hand."

Leo's other communication to Henry, dated Rome, Nov. 4, 1521, and found elsewhere in this volume in both Latin and English, does not say that the title was to be hereditary. Certainly, if the Pope had meant it to be hereditary, one cannot but think that he would have said so, as he seems overflowing with kindness and marks of affection for Henry. Besides, the Bull alludes

to the title and hopes "that you may be able to sustain that singular and indescribable glory, which your Majesty has quite justly merited by your very great deeds, even to the very last day of this life, and leave it to be *told of* to all your posterity [et eam in omni posteritate prædicandam relinquere]."

Peter Heylin, in his "Ecclesia Restaurata" (2 vols., Cambridge, 1849), Vol. I., p. 44, says of the hereditariness of the title: "But then, considering with himself that it was first granted by that Pope as a *personal* favour, and *not intended to descend upon his posterity*," etc.

In the "Archæologia," Vol. XIX., p. 1 and fol., published in London 1819, Luders writes: "Our Kings do not bear this title under the authority of Leo X.'s bull to Henry VIII., or that of Clement VII., his successor, who confirmed it. . . . This grant, we should say, according to our law, has no proper words of limitation and inheritance, for the blessing alone is conferred upon the wife and children, and not the title. The inheritance seems not to be conveyed. So that none but the King himself could claim the honour, as peculiar to his person, unless in the opinion of His Holiness the descendant should be thought to inherit the virtues of his ancestor.

"The Bull of confirmation, granted two years afterwards by Clement VII., . . . in respect of the title earned by his extraordinary merits, simply confirms the grant of Leo to the King himself: 'Approbamus, confirmamus, *Tibique perpetuum* et proprium deputamus.' "

How, then, can the statements of so many historians who declare the title hereditary be explained? Possibly flattery was their motive; very probably assumption, not having carefully read the Bull; or perhaps the wish

was father to the thought. So for the older historians. For the later ones, the continued use of the error would lead these to fancy that their monarch had a perfect right not only "de facto" but "de jure," and consequently they would infer that the Pope had made it hereditary.

At any rate, there is one very reliable historian who stands against the title's being hereditary "de jure"; it is Lingard, who, in his "History of England," says most plainly and decidedly: "It should be observed that in neither of the bulls is there any grant of inheritance. The title belonged to the King personally, and not to his successors—Tibi perpetuum et proprium . . . Ibid. But Henry retained it after his separation from the communion of Rome, and in 1543 it was annexed to the crown by act of Parliament, 35 Henry VIII., 3."

It might be added by way of negative argument, that as Polydore Vergil says nothing of the hereditary character of the title, we might also conclude that it was for Henry alone and personally.

So that, though "the King's grace would not lose that stile (defender of the faith) for all London and twenty miles round about,"* yet even this he had no right to hand down to posterity; the assumption of the title by the subsequent sovereigns of England was without right and without good taste.

*Christopher Wordsworth, Ecclesiastical Biography, Vol. II., p. 476, note 2, of London edition, 1837.

Criticism and Effects of the "Assertio"

As to the merits of the "Assertio," critics differ widely, apparently somewhat influenced by religious bias. "Henry VIII.'s treatise 'Assertio Septem Sacramentorum' is an example of exactly the opposite disposition [to Dean Colet's treatise on the seven sacraments], that of adhering exactly to received tradition. It has no particular merit, literary or theological."* So wrote Blunt.

Collier† is a little more favourable: "As to performance, the King seems to have the better of the controversy; and, generally speaking, to be much the sounder divine. Generally speaking, I say, his principles are more catholic, and his proofs more cogent. He seems superior to his adversary in the vigour and propriety of his style, in the force of his reasoning, and the learning of his citations. But then, with due regard to his memory, it must be said that his manner is not altogether unexceptionable. He leans too much upon his character, argues in his garter robes, and writes as 'twere with his sceptre. He gives rough language sometimes, treats Luther with contempt, and drives his invective pretty strong upon him. . . ."

The greater part of the criticism is favourable:

Butler‡ says: "It is written with order and perspicuity."

*The Reformation of the Church of England, by J. H. Blunt, M.A., F.S.A., Vol. I., p. 429.

†Eccles. Hist. of Great Britain, Part II., Book I.

‡Historical Memoirs, Vol. I., p. 24.

Leo calls the doctrine set forth in the "Assertio" "remarkable," and "permeated with the dew of heavenly grace," and he "thanked Almighty God most deeply, Who moved your mind, so able and prone to every good work, and, as it were, designed to pour grace from above into your mind, that you should write these things."*

"It was throughout an appeal to authority,"† is the criticism of a professor in a great American university, which he intended to be unfavourable, but which appears quite the contrary to one who believes that every good comes down from the Father of light and the Giver of all good gifts, and knows that every one should be subject to authority.

Hergenroether's estimate is calm and just: "Cet ouvrage, qu'on a beaucoup surfait de son temps, etait conçu dans une forme populaire, et faisait habilement ressortir les contradictions de Luther sur la confession, les indulgences et la primauté."‡

Saconay, on p. lxxii of his Preface to the "Assertio," says: "Postea quam autem sensit Lutherus hoc libro regio, per Hieronymum Empserum in linguam Germanicam translato, multum existimationis apud Germanos detrahi evangelio suo."

One who reads the "Assertio" cannot fail to be impressed with the common sense and cool reason displayed, and will not unlikely be won over to Henry and the faith he defends. He quotes the Scriptures very frequently, and several of the Fathers and theologians aptly and tellingly. To be more accurate, he quotes the Old Testament forty-two times: Genesis 5, Exodus

---

*Bull of Leo, printed in this volume.

†George Fisher, Prof. Eccles. Hist. in Yale, in his " The Reformation," p. 126.

‡Hist. de l'Église, V., 247.

3, Leviticus 1, Numbers 1, Deuteronomy 3, I. Kings 2, Psalms 9, Proverbs 3, Wisdom 1, Ecclesiasticus 2, Ecclesiastes 1, Ezechiel 4, Isaias 3, and Zachary 1. The New Testament is quoted one hundred and one times: Matthew 11, Mark 3, Luke 10, John 18, Acts 4, Romans 7, I. Corinthians 12, Galatians 1, I. Thessalonians 1, Colossians 1, Ephesians 3, I. Timothy 10, II. Timothy 2, Titus 2, Hebrews 4, James 8, I. Peter 2, I. John 1, Apocalypse 1.

The style is simple and direct, and appropriate to the subject.

Disparaging criticism can easily come from the biassed prejudice and à priori decision of one who has not read it, or who hates the faith Henry so well defends, or who would expect too much of an amateur.

No wonder, then, that so able and practical and timely a work should have had the effect that it did. Audin* says: "Never did a controversialist, even to this hour, win such laurels of glory as Henry; . . . praise daily laid at his feet from Germany, Italy, France, the Netherlands, and Spain." And in his "Calvin" (II., 424) the same author asserted: "Or, l'Assertio septem sacramentorum du monarque anglais, accueillie à Rome avec enthousiasme, avait ému le monde théologique."

The Bishop of La Rochelle, in his Introduction to the "Assertio," says as much and even more: "Un livre qui fit tant de bruit dans l'Éurope entière, qui excita tant de joie dans l'Église, qui produisit, parmi les savants, une admiration si general, et qui jeta la terreur dans le camp de l'hérésie."

As to the reception it received at the Court of Rome, Pallavicini† says: "Ce fut pour Leon le sujet d'une grande joie."

---

* Henry VIII., p. 92.
† Trente, Bk. I., Ch. I., sec. 8, par. 177.

Better still, we have a really beautiful, fatherly criticism of the worth of the "Assertio" in the Pope's Bull of November 4, 1521, wherein he says so many kind things in such a beautiful way. The Bull is printed elsewhere in this volume in both Latin and English, so I quote from it only a few lines: "What seriousness in the theme itself! What order! How great force of eloquence, so that the Holy Spirit seems to be in it! Everything is full of judgment, of wisdom, of piety; there is kindness in teaching, meekness in admonishing, truth in arguing," etc.

As to the *effects* it had at Rome, Sample* says: "He accomplished his main purpose, for he received from the Pope the title of 'Defender of the Faith.'" However, this was not done hurriedly and without forethought, for Brewer† says that only "after months spent in deliberation, Henry, the new candidate for spiritual honours, was admitted into the narrow and exclusive orbit of the Church's patrons: 'Defender of the Faith.'"

A less selfish, more generous, and far wider purpose is attributed to Henry by Worsley in his "Dawn of the Reformation."‡ He says: "As a theological work, although not destitute of polemical ingenuity in argument, it missed the main point [stopping Luther and the Reformation]. It was hailed as a prodigy. To the Germans especially it appeared marvellous that a crowned head should contain so much learning."

Still, Henry is declared to have deeply influenced a great—and very great—man, his own Prime Minister, for "There is no reason to doubt the statement that at least one illustrious convert [More] was brought over to a belief in the Pope's supremacy by the very con-

*Beacon Lights of the Reformation, p. 199.
†Reign of Henry VIII., Vol. I., p. 302.
‡P. 160.

troversialist who was afterwards to behead him for retaining it."* And this despite the statement that "Sir Thomas [had] spent seven years considering the claims of the Papacy to be a divine institution," as says Mary Allies.†

As to Henry's *faith,* Gairdner, in the "Dictionary of National Biography," article "Henry VIII.," says: "Henry showed himself every day more zealous for ancient doctrine. In November, 1537, he issued a proclamation for Anabaptists to quit the kingdom. In the same month he signally illustrated his position as head of the Church by hearing personally an appeal from the Archbishop of Canterbury by a heretic named John Lambert, otherwise called Nicholson, who denied the corporeal presence in the sacrament. From the account of an eye-witness, preserved, and certainly not weakened in effect, by Foxe (Acts and Monuments, ed. Townsend, 1838, V., 230-6), he seems to have shamefully browbeat the accused. Cromwell, on the other hand, in a contemporary despatch, reports with admiration how benignly His Grace essayed to convert the miserable man. Collier's 'Ecclesiastical History,' ed. 1852, IV., 428."

But Henry did not live up to his ideals, and this failing to practise what he preached has been assigned as the reason of his inability to check the cataclysm of the Reformation, for Henry "answered Luther by his pen, not by his life, and this is the whole secret of his failure."‡ He still had faith; indeed, it seems to be admitted that to his death Henry was a Catholic in belief, for "To his doctrine on the sacraments Henry consistently held fast for the rest of his life."§

*Epochs of Mod. History, Moberly, p. 152.
†The Church in England, A.D. 1509-1603, p. 10.
‡M. Allies, Ch. in Eng., p. 13.
§Worsley's Dawn of the Reformation, p. 159.

As to Henry's faith outwardly manifested even at the end of his life, Luders, in the "Archæologia," XIX., p. 1 and fol., says: "Our Henry indeed proved an ungrateful child of the Holy See, but his character had nothing to disgrace the donor at the time of the gift; and though he renounced the Pope, he may be said to have defended the Catholick faith to the last."

And Sander* has the following interesting notice: "In the year of our Lord 1541 the imperial Diet was held in Ratisbon, and thereto the King [Henry VIII.], weary, after the manner of the world, not only of the wickedness of others, but also of his own, sent Sir Henry Knyvett, and Stephen Gardiner, bishop of Winchester, a man of great learning and marvellous sagacity. One of his reasons for sending them was his desire to justify his caution in matters of religion before certain princes of Germany, who were charging him with being lukewarm in his prosecution of the new gospel. But his chief reason was this: He knew that if neither Catholics nor Protestants were satisfied with him, seeing that he fully agreed with neither, he therefore determined that his ambassadors should, in concert with the emperor, devise some means by which he might be reconciled to the Roman Pontiff, and openly observe the perfect rule of the Catholic faith, which he knew to be more true and more certain than any other. He was driven to this by the pressure of his conscience,

---

*Rise and Growth of the Anglican Schism. Notes by David Lewis, pp. 152, 153. As to Sander's trustworthiness, Nicholas Pocock, in his Preface to "The Pretended Divorce between Henry VIII. and Catharine of Aragon," in the Camden Society's Transactions, 1878, has the following tribute to Sander: "Whom it has been the fashion ever since the days of Burnet to disparage as eminently untrustworthy. At one time I was of the same opinion, but the more intimately I became acquainted with Sander's work the more reason I found to change my judgment about him."

which, as the ancients have justly observed, is equal to a thousand witnesses."*

But these pretty speculations are well-nigh vain now. Poor Henry! What a change from the "Defender of the Faith" to him who drew England—the land of Augustine, Bede, Lanfranc, Anselm and Thomas—away from the pulsing heart of unity and the sacramental system of grace!

In "A Treatise on the Pretended Divorce between Henry VIII. and Catharine of Aragon, by Nicholas Harpsfield, LL.D., by Nicholas Pocock, M.A.," the Camden Society's publication for 1878, is an interesting domestic scene and a prophecy said to have been made by Henry VII. respecting the gigantic mischief his son was to consummate. It says: "I credibly understand himself [Henry VIII.] was beaten of his father, saying to Alcock, Bishop of Ely, then present and entreating for him: 'Never entreat for him, for this child shall be the undoing of England.' "

And yet, despite his bad life, Green says of him in his "History of the English People":† ". . . To the end his convictions remained firmly on the side of the doctrines which Luther denied."

In the "Chronicle of King Henry VIII. of England, written in Spanish by an unknown hand, translated with notes and instructions by Martin A. Sharp Hume,

---

*"Burnet (Hist. Reform., IV., 578, ed. Pocock) says that 'this is another ornament of the fable, to show the poet's wit; but it is as devoid of truth as any passage in Plautus or Terence is.' . . Sander had better opportunities of learning the truth on this point, both in Rome and in Spain, and Gardiner confesses it (Foxe, VI., 578): 'Master Knevett and I were sent ambassadors unto the emperor to desire him that he would be a mean between the Pope's Holiness and the King, to bring the King to the obedience of the See of Rome.' "

†Vol. II., p. 124.

Knight of the Royal Spanish Order of Isabel the
Catholic, London, 1889," p. 152, it is said of Henry on
his death-bed: "The next day he confessed and took the
Holy Sacrament, and commended his soul to God." A
foot-note amplifies and confirms this statement. And
this firm faith was probably, in part at least, the effect of
the "Assertio," the studying out and composing of which
so clearly and deeply convinced Henry of the truth of
the faith he then defended that even after his morals had
changed yet his faith was in much still staunch and
true. The English Catholic Truth Society's tract,
"Popery on Every Coin of the Realm," says: "Protestantism can claim the last and worst part of his [Henry
VIII.'s] life; but in his earlier and better years, both
as prince and king, he was a staunch Catholic."

Those earlier, better, Catholic days were looked back
to with pleasure by the people who later saw and suffered by his unhappy change. To quote the great Catholic historian of Henry VIII. and the Reformation,
Dom Gasquet, in his "Henry VIII. and the English
Monasteries":* "They remembered Henry in his
earlier days, when he was never so immersed in business

*Vol. II., pp. 331, 332.

By way of parenthesis it may be interesting to recall the various
wives of Henry and their respective children, who later succeeded to
the throne.

Henry's six wives (?) and children: Catharine of Aragon, repudiated 1533—Mary; Anne Boleyn, beheaded 1536—Elizabeth;
Jane Seymour, died 1537—Edward VI.; Anne of Cleves, repudiated
1540; Catharine Howard, beheaded 1541; Catharine Parr, died 1548.

Apropos of Catharine's "divorcement" by Henry, Mr. John Strype,
in his "Memorials of Thomas Cranmer," Vol. I., p. 4 and fol., has
the following interesting details: "Not long after this, King Henry
being persuaded that the marriage between him and Queen Catharine, daughter to King Ferdinand of Spain, was unlawful and
naught, by Dr. Langland, Bishop of Lincoln, his confessor, and
other of his Clergy; he sent to six of the best learned men of

or pleasure that he did not hear three or five Masses a day. . . . He had at bottom a zeal for the faith." So that the "Assertio" affected Henry himself. But, moreover, it doubtless had an influence on thousands, millions of others who, during those days that tried men's souls, were defended and strengthened and calmed in their old, Catholic faith by the "Assertio Septem Sacramentorum."

May it not be hoped that his work, now reprinted, may perhaps be in some way helpful in leading back again some of those whose forefathers Henry led or drove from the Church?

Cambridge, and as many of Oxford, to debate this question, Whether it were lawful for one brother to marry his brother's wife, being known of his brother ? . . . These learned men agreed fully, with one consent, that it was lawful, with the Pope's dispensation, so to do." And page 6: " This was about August, 1529. Henry learning of Cranmer's opinion, that the devines should leave it to the King, sent for him and lodged him with the ' Earl of Wiltshire and Ormond,' named Sir Thomas Bolen, . . . esteeming him a fit person for Cranmer to reside with, who had himself been employed in embassies to Rome and Germany about the same matter."

As to Cranmer's *opinion*, it was as follows : " There is but one truth in it ; which no men ought, or better can discuss than the devines ; whose sentence may be soon known, and brought so to pass with little industry and charges, that the King's conscience may thereby be quieted and pacified. Which we all ought to consider, and regard in this question of doubt ; and then his highness, in conscience quieted, may determine himself that which shall seem good before God. And let these tumultuary processes give place unto a certain truth." Id., p. 5.

Bibliography

I. Sources

Assertio VII. Sacramentorum adversus Mart. Lutherum. Henrico VIII. Angliæ Rege Auctore. [Herein reprinted.]

Assertionum Regis Angliæ de Fide Catholica adversus Lutheri Babylonicam Captivitatem defensio. Authore R. D. Johanne Roffensi Episcopo. [To be found in Fisher's Works, and also bound up with many editions of the Assertio, e. g., that of Paris 1562.]

Brewer. Letters and Papers, Foreign and Domestic. Henry VIII. Longmans, 1867.

Bullarium Magnum Romanum. Tom. I., col. 620. Luxemburgi 1727.

Clark, John. Oration to Leo X. [Herein reprinted.]

Erasmiana Bibliotheca, 3e Serie. Erasmus, Desiderius. Roterodami: Opera Omnia. Lugduni Batavorum. Cura et impensis Petri Van der Aa. MDCCIII.

Fischerii, Joannis Roffensis, in Anglia Episcopi. Opera. Wirceburgi 1597.

Giustinian. Court of Henry VIII. London 1854.

Henry's Letter to Leo X. [Herein reprinted.]

Henry's Letter to Luther. [Herein reprinted.]

Leo X.'s Reply to Clark's Oration. [Herein reprinted.]

Leo X.'s Letter to Henry. [Herein reprinted.]

Leo X.'s Bull to Henry. [Herein reprinted.]

Polydori Vergilii Urbinatis. Angliæ Historiæ Libri Vigintiseptem. Basiliæ, apud Mich. Isingrinium: Anno MDLV.

Roper, William. Life of Sir Thomas More, by his son-in-law, by Singer. Chiswick 1822.

Rymer, Thomas. Fœdera. Churchill, London MDCCXII.

State Papers between England and Spain, Calendar of. Vol. II., Henry VIII. Edited by Bergenroth. Longmans, London 1866.

Wilkins. Concilia Magnæ Britanniæ et Hiberniæ. Londini 1737.

II. *Secondary Literature*

Allies, Mary A. The Church in England, 1509-1603. London 1895.

Alzog, John. Manual of Universal Church History. 3 vols. Clarke, Cincinnati 1874.

Annals of England. 3 vols. Oxford 1856.

Annals of England. Henry VIII., Edward VI., Queen Mary. In Latin, by Francis, Lord Bishop of Hereford. Englyshed by Morgan Godwyn. Islyp Stansby, London 1630.

Annals or General Chronicle of England; begun by John Stow; by Edmund Howes, Gent. Impenses Ricardi Meighen, Londini 1631.

Archæologia. Society of Antiquaries of London.

Audin. Henry VIII. Dolman, London 1852.
  Life of Luther. London 1854.
  Calvin. 2 vols. Paris 1843.

Baronii. Annales Ecclesias. Cum Pagii. Tom. XXXI., pag. 343. Lucæ 1755.

Beard, Charles. Martin Luther and the Reformation in Germany. London 1889.

Beckett. English Reformation. London 1890.

Blunt, J. H. The Reformation of the Church of England. Rivington, London 1882.

Bossuet. History of the Variations of the Protestant Church. 2 vols. Kenedy, New York 1896.

Bremond, Henri. Thomas More. Licoffre, Paris 1904.

Brewer. Reign of Henry VIII. 2 vols. Murray, London 1884.

Bridgett. Sir Thomas More. Burns & Oates, London 1891.

Brown, J. Mainwaring. "Henry VIII.'s Book 'Assertio Septem Sacramentorum,'" in the Royal Historical Society's Transactions, Vol. VIII., p. 242 and fol.

Brunet, Jacques Charles. Manuel du Libraire. Tomes V. Didot Frères, Paris 1862.

Burnet. History of the Reformation. Oxford 1865.

Butler, Charles. Historical Memoirs Respecting the English, Irish, and Scottish Catholics. 2 vols. London 1819.

Carwithen. History of the Church of England. Parker, Oxford 1849.

Catalogue of the British Museum.

Catalogue of the Noble and Royal Authors of England. 2 vols. London MDCCLIX. Vol. I.

Censura Literaria. London 1805.

Cobbett, William. History of the Protestant Reformation in England and Ireland. Philadelphia 1825.

Collier, Jeremy. Ecclesiastical History of Great Britain. Keble, London 1714.

Collier, J. Payne. A Biographical and Critical Account of the Rarest Books in the English Language. 2 vols. Lilly, London 1865.

Craly. Luther and the Reformation. London 1858.

Creighton, M. History of the Papacy during the Period of the Reformation. Oxon. and Cambridge 1882.

D'Aubigné. The Reformation. Translated by Gill. London 1890.

Dibdin, Thomas Frognall. Typographical Antiquities, or The History of Printing in England, Scotland, and Ireland, by Joseph Ames, William Herbert, etc. London 1812.

Dixon, Richard Watson. History of the Church of England. London 1884.

Dodd. The Church History of England. 3 vols. Brussels 1737.

Du Pin. Ecclesiastical History of the Sixteenth Century. London 1703.

Ellis, H. Preface to Polydore Vergil's English History, in the Camden Society's Publications.

English Catholic Truth Society. Popery on Every Coin of the Realm.

Facciolati, Forcellini. Totius Latinitatis Lexicon. 4 vols. Patavii 1771.

Fisher, George P. The Reformation. Scribner, New York 1884.

Flanagan, Thomas. A History of the Church in England. Baker, London 1857.

Foxe, John. The Acts and Monuments of. 8 vols. Religious Tract Society, London.

Fuller. Church History of Britain. 3 vols. London 1842.

Gairdner, James. History of the English Church in the Sixteenth Century. Macmillan, London 1903.

Gardiner, Samuel R. English History for Students, by J. Bass Mullinger. Holt, New York 1881.

Gasquet, Francis Aiden. The Eve of the Reformation. Nimmo, London 1900.

Henry VIII. and the English Monasteries. 2 vols. Hodges, London 1893.

Old English Bible. Nimmo, London 1897.

Green, John Richard. History of the English People. Macmillan, London 1878.

*f*rüninger, Jean. Répertoire Bibliographique Stras-
bourgeois. Jusque vers 1530.

*f*all, Edw. Henry VIII. 2 vols. Grafton Press,
New York and London 1905.

*f*allam. Constitutional History of England. New
York 1857.

*f*ardwick, Charles, M.A. A History of the Christian
Church during the Reformation: by W. Stubbs, M.A.
Macmillan, 1877.

*f*arpsfield, Nicholas, by Pocock. A Treatise on the
Pretended Divorce between Henry VIII. and Catharine of Aragon. Camden So., 1878.

*f*äusser, L. The Period of the Reformation. 2 vols.
London 1873.

*f*enry VIII. of England, Chronicle of King. Translated by Martin A. Sharp Hume. London 1889.

*f*erbert of Cherbury, Lord. England under Henry
VIII. London 1870.

    Life and Reign of Henry VIII. London 1741.

*f*erbert, Henry William. Memoirs of Henry VIII.
Porter & Coates, Philadelphia 1880.

*f*ergenroether, Joseph. Histoire de l'Église. Tomes 8.
Delhomme et Briguet, Paris et Lyon 1894.

*f*eylin, Peter. Ecclesia Restaurata. 2 vols. Cambridge 1849.

*f*olinshed's Chronicles of England, Scotland, and Ireland. 6 vols. London 1808.

*f*utton, W. H. Sir Thomas More. London 1895.

*f*anssen. History of the German People. St. Louis
1903.

*f*ewis, John. Life of Dr. John Fisher. 2 vols. London 1855.

*f*illy. Renaissance Types. Longmans, New York
1901.

*f*ingard. History of England. Dolman, London 1849.

Lowndes, William T. Biographical Manual of English Literature. In 8 parts, 4 vols. London 1859.

Luders, in Archæologia, XIX., p. 1.

Maitland, S. R. The Reformation. Rivington, London 1849.

Mason, Arthur J. Letters on Colet, Fisher, and More. London 1895.

Mayor. Fisher's Works. London 1876.

Migne. Dictionnaire de Bibliographie Catholique. Tom. I. Paris 1858.

Milner. History of the Church of Christ. 5 vols. Mallory & Co., Boston 1811.

Moberly. Epochs of Modern History. The Early Tudors. Longmans, London 1887.

Moore, A. L. Letters and Papers on the History of the Reformation in England and on the Continent. Kegan Paul, Trench, Trübner & Co., London 1890.

Moreri, Louis. Le Grand Dictionnaire Historique. 10 vols. Paris 1759.

Natalis, Alexandri. Historia Ecclesiastica. Tom. X. Venetiis 1778.

Nicolas, N. H. Privy Purse Expenses of King Henry VIII. London 1827.

Overton. The Church in England. Gardner, London 1897.

Pallavicini. Histoire du Concile de Trente. Tomes III. Migne 1844.

Panzer, G. W. Annales Typographici. 11 vols. Norembergæ 1803.

Paton, James. British History and Papal Claims. 2 vols. London 1893.

Pocock, Nicholas. Burnet's History of the Reformation. Oxford 1865.

Preface to "The Pretended Divorce between Henry VIII. and Catharine of Aragon." Camden So., 1878.

'rice, Thomas. History of Protestant Nonconformity in England. 2 vols. London 1838.

ℓohrbacher, Renatus. Histoire Universel de l'Église Catholique. Cinquième édition. Gaume Frères et Duprey, Paris 1868.

ℓoscoe, William. The Life and Pontificate of Leo X. 2 vols. Bohn, London 1885.

ιaconay, Gabriel de. Preface to the Assertio. Lyons 1561.

ιample. Beacon Lights of the Reformation. Philadelphia 1889.

chaff, Philip. History of the Christian Church. New York 1895.

eckendorf. Lutheranismi Historia. Francofurti et Lypsiæ MDCXCII.

eebohm, Frederick. Oxford Reformers of 1498. Longmans, 1867.

    Sir Thomas More and Henry VIII.'s Book against Luther. Fortnightly Review, Vol. III., new series, January—June, 1868.

    The Era of Protestant Revolution. Scribner, New York 1874.

peed, John. The History of Great Britain. Dawson, London 1632.

tapleton, Thomas. Tres Thomæ Coloniæ Agrippinæ. MDCXII.

teuart, Agnes M. Life and Letters of Sir Thomas More. London 1876.

trype, John. Ecclesiastical Memorials. 6 vols. Oxford 1822.

    Memorials of Thomas Cranmer. 2 vols. Oxford 1840.

ʼhomson, A. T. Memoirs of the Court of Henry VIII. 2 vols. Longmans, 1826.

ʼurner. Henry VIII. London 1827.

Tytler. Henry VIII. London 1854.

Walter, W. J. Sir Thomas More. Lucas, Baltimore.

Watts, Robert. Bibliotheca Britannica. In 2 parts. Edinburgh 1824.

Wetzer et Welte. Dictionnaire de la Théologie Catholique. Vol. X. Paris 1864.

Williams, Folkstone. Lives of the English Cardinals. Allen, London 1868.

Wordsworth, Christopher. Ecclesiastical Biography. 4 vols. 3d edition. London 1839.

Worsley. Dawn of the Reformation. London 1890.

THE "ASSERTIO"
IN
ENGLISH AND LATIN

Advertisement

Every Person in the least conversant with ecclesiastical History, or indeed with the civil History of *England*, must know that *Martin Luther* himself, remarkable a Man as he was, was not more so than the royal Author of the following Work: Nor can a Reader of either Species of History be unacquainted with those fatal Confusions, Animosities and Devastations, that were consequent of, and owed their Rise to, that Mode of Religion introduced by the former, and in a great Measure established by the latter in these three Kingdoms.

We shall not enter into a Detail, at large of those Springs and Motives that were the efficient Cause of the *Reformation* (as it is called) in the old Religion: We shall only observe, very briefly, that, antecedently to that most remarkable Revolution, some of the Clergy, sunk in that Sloth which great Affluence is but too apt to generate in the human Mind, became so relaxed in Discipline, and in the Duties in general of their holy Profession, that there was a real Necessity for a Reformation of *Manners*. Pampered Sloth not only begets a Looseness of Morals, but is often the Father of Ignorance; and thus too many of the sacred Order, not only did not practise, but were really, even in Speculation and Knowledge, Strangers to their Duty. The few (comparatively the few) Learned and Virtuous saw and lamented the almost general Depravity of the Times; and it is probable that *Luther*, at first, meant no more than to expose and correct the Enormities which he every where saw practised: But, puffed up with a Con-

ceit of his own Abilities; (which indeed were far from being contemptible) he, from endeavouring to reform particular Abuses, which no way concerned the *Essence* of Religion, (though they threw a Stain on many of its Members) at length set about a Reformation of Religion *itself;* and came to think his own Knowledge in Divinity superior to that of the whole aggregate Church. The Ambition of, and Contests between some of the *Germanic* Princes, concerning Matters of a civil Nature, were favourable to his Views; and, in the Career of his newly-broached Opinions, inconsistent as they were, one with the other, he prevailed so far as to engage the Power of Magistracy in their Propagation and Defence. All *Europe* stood astonished, when it beheld Armies of military Apostles enforcing an Obedience to the wild and incoherent Notions of a vain, obstinate, self-willed and enthusiastic Clergyman. The People that were determined not to quit the old Road to Heaven, thought themselves obliged to defend the antient Religion, by the *like Means;* and thus a general Warfare sprang, from the Petulancy and fiery Zeal of an Individual. The learned and virtuous Part of the Clergy employed their Zeal, and exerted their Talents, on this alarming Occasion; and demonstrated to the World, that the Deviations from good Morals could be no just Foundation for a Separation from that Religion, which had the Promise of *Christ* for its Support and Existence, *whilst the World should last.*

Henry the Eighth was a Prince of great Learning, considering the Age in which he lived. He had well studied both Philosophy and Divinity, in his Youth; his Father, *Henry* the Seventh, having intended him for the ecclesiastical State. His Writings against *Luther,* (I mean the following Work, so much approved of by Pope *Leo* the Tenth) shew a Fund of ecclesiastical Erudition, and a Strength of Understanding, uncom-

mon in Persons of his high Station. It must, indeed,
be acknowledged, that they breathe too much of the
Spirit of Acrimony, and run into a Latitude of Abuse,
ever disgustful to Readers of Taste, Moderation and
Candour: But let it be remembered, at the same Time,
That extreme Virulency, Insolence and Self-sufficiency,
almost every where, mark the Writings of *Luther* and
his Fellow-reformers: That those Reformers having
thus led the Way, their Opponents thought themselves
justified in retaliating the Abuse, with which they had
been attacked: And that the Manners of those distant
Times, wherein polemical Disputes about Religion were
so strongly and warmly agitated, differ very widely
from those of the present more enlightened and more
moderate Age.

Luther was not less inflamed, by the Censure of the
University of *Paris* (*a*), to whose Judgment he had
submitted his Writings, with great Elogies, and who
had condemned his Doctrine in above an hundred Propositions; than he was to find that the King of *England*
had written against him. His Answer abounds with
(*b*) "heinous Affronts and injurious Lies, in almost
every Page.———This Writing did its Author no
Honour, even among those of his own Party; even his
Friends were scandalized at the injurious Contempt,
with which he treated all that was most august in the
Universe, and at the whimsical Manner, in which he
judged of Points of Doctrine."

Henry was a pious and zealous *Roman Catholic,* until
such Times as he suffered himself to be borne away by
an immoderate Passion for Women, and found his
Sollicitations at *Rome* for a Divorce from his Queen,
Katherine of *Arragon,* absolutely fruitless. Then it
was that he broke all Measures with the holy See; and

(*a*) *Historical Account of the Reformation* (from Fleury's *Ecclesiastical History*,) printed in *Corke*, 1764. (*b*) Id. p. 136.

he, who had been a powerful and firm Defender of the Church, became the Corner-stone, in *England,* of that Reformation which he had so warmly and strenuously opposed.

Notwithstanding this Falling-off, however, his Defence of the *seven Sacraments* is a Work of considerable Merit. Its Orthodoxy we cannot doubt of, when we read the Pope's Bull, granting him the most honourable and glorious Title of DEFENDER OF THE FAITH; a Title still retained by his Successors on the Throne, though of a contrary Religion. Although it is not to be doubted but that subsequent Writers have handled the Subject-matter of this Book with more Accuracy, Clearness and Precision; yet the Work before us may not only be very profitably perused, but is also extremely curious, when we consider its Author's very remarkable and inconsistent Character. The *London* Edition, from whence the present is taken, has been carefully corrected throughout, in the Orthography and Punctuation, and the Text, obscure in some Parts, hath been elucidated, without deviating, however, from the Sense of the Author. Upon the Whole, we may venture to affirm, that this Edition is vastly preferable to all former Ones, in the *English* Tongue; and we flatter ourselves with the Hope, that the Pains we have taken, in the Publication of a Work, hitherto so extremely scarce, will be satisfactory to the Curious.

Henry VIII.'s Letter to Leo X. on the Subject of the "Assertio"

Most Holy Father: I most humbly commend myself to you, and devoutly kiss your blessed feet. Whereas we believe that no duty is more incumbent on a Catholic sovereign than to preserve and increase the Christian faith and religion and the proofs thereof, and to transmit them preserved thus inviolate to posterity, by his example in preventing them from being destroyed by any assailant of the faith or in any wise impaired, so when we learned that the pest of Martin Luther's heresy had appeared in Germany and was raging everywhere, without let or hindrance, to such an extent that many, infected with its poison, were falling away, especially those whose furious hatred rather than their zeal for Christian truth had prepared them to believe all its subtleties and lies, we were so deeply grieved at this heinous crime of the German nation (for whom we have no light regard), and for the sake of the Holy Apostolic See, that we bent all our thoughts and energies on uprooting in every possible way, this cockle, this heresy from the Lord's flock. When we perceived that this deadly venom had advanced so far and had seized upon the weak and ill-disposed minds of so many that it could not easily be overcome by a single effort, we deemed that nothing could be more efficient in destroying the contagion than to declare these errors worthy of condemnation, after they had been examined by a convocation of learned and scholarly men from all parts of our realm. This course of action we likewise recom-

Letter to Leo X. on the Subject of the "Assertio," 1521

Beatissime pater. — Post humillimam commenda-
tionem et devotissima pedum oscula beatorum. Quoniam
nihil magis ex Catholici principis officio esse arbitra-
mur, quàm ut christianam fidem et religionem atque
documenta ita servet et augeat, suoque exemplo posteris
sic intemerate servanda tradat, ut à nullo fidei eversore
tolli, seu quovis pacto ea labefactari sinat; ubi primùm
Martini Lutheri pestem atque hæresim in Germania
exortam, ubique locorum cohibente nullo sensimus
debacchari, adeo ut suo veneno infecti plures contabes-
cerent, et hi præsertim qui odio potius intumentes quàm
christianæ veritatis zelo ad ipsius versutiis atque men-
daciis credendum omni se ex parte aptaverant; atrox
istud scelus tùm germanicæ nationis (cui non medio-
criter afficimur), tum verò sacrosanctæ apostolicæ sedis
gratia sic indoluimus ut cogitationes omnes nostras,
studium et animum eo diverteremus, hanc zizaniam,
hanc hæresim e dominico grege, quacumque ratione fieri
posset, funditus tollere nitentes. Sed cum exitiale hoc
virus eo progressum imbecillosque multorum ac male
affectos animos sic jàm occupasse videremus, ut uno im-
petu haud facilé tolli posset; nihil æque huic delendæ
pesti censuimus expedire, quàm si doctoribus eruditiori-
busque hujus regni viris undique excitis trutinandos hos
errores, ac dignos qui perderentur esse declararemus,
aliisque compluribus hoc idem faciendum suaderemus;
in primisque Cæsaream Majestatem, ob fraternam quam
illi gerimus affectionem, omnesque principes electores ut

mended to a number of others. In the first place, we
earnestly entreated His Imperial Majesty, through our
fraternal love for him, and all the electoral princes, to
bethink them of their Christian duty and their lofty
station and to destroy this pernicious man, together with
his scandalous and heretical publications, after his re-
fusal to return to God. But convinced that, in our
ardor for the welfare of Christendom, in our zeal for
the Catholic faith and our devotion to the Apostolic See,
we had not yet done enough, we determined to show
by our own writings our attitude towards Luther and
our opinion of his vile books; to manifest more openly
to all the world that we shall ever defend and uphold,
not only by force of arms but by the resources of our
intelligence and our services as a Christian, the Holy
Roman Church. For this reason we have thought that
this first attempt of our modest ability and learning
could not be more worthily dedicated than to your
Holiness, both as a token of our filial reverence and an
acknowledgment of your careful solicitude for the weal
of Christendom. We feel assured that our first fruits
will be enhanced in value if it be approved by the wholesome judgment of your Blessedness. May you live long
and happily! From our royal palace at Greenwich,
the twenty-first day of May, 1521. Your Holiness'
most devoted and humble son, Henry, by the grace of
God King of England and France, and Lord of Ireland.

christiani officii suique splendoris meminisse, pestiferumque hunc hominem, unâ cum facinorosis hæreticisque libellis, postquam ad Deum amplius redire spernit, radicitùs vellent extirpare, studiose rogavimus. Sed nostro in Christianam rempublicam ardori, in catholicam fidem zelo, et in apostolicam sedem devotioni non satis adhuc fecisse existimantes, propriis quoque nostris scriptis quo animo sumus in Lutherum, quodve de improbis ejus libellis nostrum sit judicium, innuere voluimus, omnibusque apertius demonstrare, nos sanctam Romanam Ecclesiam non solum vi et armis, sed etiam ingenii opibus., christianisque officiis in omne tempus defensuros ac tutaturos esse. Primam ideo ingenii nostræque mediocris eruditionis feturam nemini magis quàm Vestræ Sanctitati dicandam consecrandamque esse duximus; tum ob filialem nostram in eam observantiam, tum etiam ob solicitam ipsius christianæ reipublicæ curam. Hujusmodi autem primitiis nostris plurimum accessum iri judicabimus, si sano vestræ beatitudinis judicio quæ comprobentur dignæ habitæ fuerint. Et felicissime ac diutissime valeat! E regia nostra Greenwici, die XXI. Maii, 1521. E. V. Sanctitatis. Devotissimus atque obsequentissimus filius Dei gratia Angliæ et Franciæ rex ac Dominus Hiberniæ, Henricus.

The Oration of Mr. John Clark,

Orator for Henry VIII. King of England, France and Ireland, Defender of the Faith; on his exhibiting this Royal Book, in the Consistory at Rome, to Pope Leo X.

Most Holy Father:

What great Troubles have been stirred up, by the pernicious Opinions of *Martin Luther;* which of late Years first sprung out of the lurking Holes of the *Hussitanian* Heresy, in the School of *Wittenberg* in *Germany;* from thence spreading themselves over most Parts of the *Christian World;* how many unthinking Souls they have deceived, and how many Admirers and Adherents they have met with; because these are all Things very well known; and because, in this Place, a *Medium* is more requisite, than Prolixity; I care not for relating. Truly, although many of *Luther's* Works are most impiously, by his *Libels,* spread abroad in the World: Yet none of them seems more execrable, more venomous, and more pernicious to Mankind, than That, entituled, *The Babylonian Captivity of the Church;* in refuting which, many grave and learned Men have diligently laboured.

My most serene and invincible Prince, *Henry* VIII. King of *England, France* and *Ireland,* and most affectionate Son of Your Holiness, and of the sacred *Roman Church,* hath written a *Book* against this *Work* of *Luther's,* which he has dedicated to Your Holiness; and hath commanded me to offer, and deliver the same;

which I here present: But before You receive it, most
holy Father, may it please You, that I speak Somewhat
of the Devotion and Veneration of my King towards
Your Holiness, and this most holy See; as also, of the
other Reasons which moved him to publish this Work.
Nor is it amiss to take Notice, in this Place, of this
horrid and furious Monster; as also of his Stings and
Poisons, whereby he intends to infect the whole World,
and to delineate him before Your Holiness in his own
proper Colours; that the more formidable the Enemy is,
and the greater the Danger appears, the more glorious
may the Triumph shew when that is overcome, and this
removed. But, O immortal God! what bitter Language!
what so hot and inflamed Force of Speaking can be invented, sufficient to declare the Crimes of that most
filthy Villain, who has undertaken to cut in Pieces the
seamless Coat of Christ, and to disturb the quiet State
of the *Church* of God! When, like an excellent
Esteemer of Things, he attributes to Your Holiness no
more Power in the Church of God, than to any of the
least Priests amongst the People; but, like a third
Cato, fallen from Heaven, most unseasonably condemns
the Behaviour of all the *Ministers* in the *Church;* calls
Rome a Sinner, wretched, an Adulteress; and lastly,
Babylon itself! He accuses Your Holiness of *Heresy,*
and makes himself (thrice *Apostate*) as often as there
is Question in the Explication of the *Christian Faith;*
equal in Authority to St. *Peter,* Prince of the *Apostles!*
And that he may the better demonstrate himself as great
an Enemy to Religion, as to *Manners,* his most impure
Hands have burnt the *Decrees* and most *holy Statutes*
of the *Fathers,* in which were contained the true Discipline of a good Life. And, as one most audacious, leaving Nothing unattempted; he at last publishes this *Book*
of the *Babylonian Captivity.* In which, good God!

what and how prodigious Poison, what deadly Bane,
how much consuming and mortal Venom this poisonous
Serpent has spewed out, not only against the wicked
Manners of our Age, which in some Manner might have
been borne with; not only against *Your Holiness,* but
also against *Your Office;* against *ecclesiastical Hierarchy,* this *See,* and against that *Rock* established by
God himself: finally, against the whole Body of the
Church of God! Here, the Bond of *Chastity* is broken,
*holy Fasts, religious Vows, Rites, Ceremonies, Worship
of God, Solemnity at Mass,* &c. are abolished, and ex-
terminated, by the strangest Perfidiousness that ever
was heard of. This Man institutes *Sacraments* after his
own Fancy, reducing them to three, to two, to one; and
that One he handles so pitifully, that he seems to be
about the reducing of it at last to Nothing at all. O
Height of Impiety! O most abominable and most execrable Villainy of Man! What intolerable Blasphemies,
from an Heap of Calumnies and Lyes, without any
Law, Method, or *Order,* does he utter against God, and
his Servants, in this Book! *Socrates,* a Man judged by
Apollo's Oracle, to be the wisest of Men, was by the
Athenians poisoned for disputing against the commonly-
received Opinion they had of God, and against that
Religion which was at that Time taught to be the best
on Earth. Could this Destroyer of *Christian Religion*
expect any better from true *Christians,* for his extreme
Wickedness against God? But indeed he did not look
on it; who, when dreading Punishment (which he well
deserved) fled, with a Mischief, into his perpetual lurking Holes in *Bohemia,* the Mother and Nurse of his
Heresies. If he had remained, and had not by *Your
Holiness* been prohibited the free dispersing abroad of
his Errors; what Danger, what devouring Conflagration
this *Plague* had brought to all *Christendom;* let the

Hussitanian Heresy evince; which though, contented at
first with small Beginnings, yet, through the Neglect of
Superiors, increased to such a Height, that at last it
turned, not only Cities, and People, but also that most
populous Kingdom of *Bohemia,* from the *Christian
Faith;* reducing it to that Misery, under which it now
languishes. What can we think would be the End of
this raging Mischief, which is carried on with such
Violence and unbridled Fury, in his *Prœludiums,* as he
calls them; as if some *Erynnis* were sent from Hell in a
Trice to confound all before it, and so rapidly transported, as if it would seem to leave Nothing whereon to
exercise future Fury? which, tracing the Steps of the
Hussites, has added so much Poison to them, that now
the Enemy appears more formidable, by how much
more he equalizes all *Arch-heretics* in his Doctrine, and
surpasses them in his malicious and wicked Intentions:
Indeed the Danger is also so much the greater, as it is
easier to add worse Proceedings to bad Beginnings, than
to begin Ill; and to increase Inventions, than to invent.
But *Your Holiness,* most blessed Father, has circum-
spectly taken Care of your Flock; and meeting the
Smoak, ready to break into open Conflagration and
Flame, omitted Nothing that might avail to the preventing so great Evils; or at first to the Reconciliation of
their Author; afterwards to his Punishment and Ex-
termination. The great Indignity of this Matter, as also
Your Holiness's, and the King my Master's Letters,
moved the Emperor to send this Man, swelled with Contumelies, into Exile. Learned Men, on all Sides, have
in their Works opposed themselves, as so many *Buck-
lers,* for the *Christian Faith,* against the Darts of this
pernicious Reprobate.

Let others speak of other Nations, certainly my
Britainy (called *England* by our modern Cosmogra-

phers) situated in the furthermost End of the World,
and separated from the *Continent* by the *Ocean;* as it
hath never been behind in the Worship of God, and true
Christian Faith, and due Obedience to the *Roman
Church;* either to *Spain, France, Germany,* or *Italy;*
nay, to *Rome* itself; so likewise, there is no Nation
which more impugns this Monster, and the *Heresies*
broached by him, and which more condemns, and detests
them. In which Sort of most excellent Praise, I can
prefer none to him, whom I have now recorded, King
Henry, Your Holiness's most devoted Son; who, as soon
as he understood, that the Dignity of that Government,
illustrated by Your Integrity and Virtue, and enlarged
by Your great Actions; was, together with the Universal
Church, so bitterly inveighed against, by this Son of
Perdition; not only undertook this pious Work himself,
whereby he has learnedly confuted the Errors of this
impious Man; but likewise the most learned Clergy of
this Realm, have, to the utmost of their Powers, endeavoured, with all Diligence, to remove from the
Hearts of the People all Doubts, Fears and Scruples,
that might in any wise happen to possess, or trouble the
Minds of the weaker Sort; so that, amongst us, the
Church of God is in great Tranquillity; no Differences,
no Disputes, no ambiguous Words, Murmurings or Complaints, are heard amongst the People: All Troubles of
Mind, all Renovations in the World, all vain Horror of
Antichrist's Reign, are now vanished.

But now, lest my Discourse may seem too prolix, or
tedious to the diligent Attention Your Holiness is
pleased to give; I shall presently come to a Conclusion.

Only first be pleased, that I declare the Reason that
moved my most serene King to undertake this Work.
For I believe it will cause Admiration in several, that a
Prince, so much busied with the Cares of his own King-

dom, both at home and abroad; and whose Affairs afford him so little Respite, should undertake such Things, as, according to the common Saying, might require to employ wholly all the Thoughts of a Man, and indeed, of such a one, as is no Novice neither; but rather for his whole Time experienced in the Studies of Learning: Yet, notwithstanding all this, he that considers his great Actions done for the Faith of Christ, and his accustomed Reverence towards this holy See, will not think it so strange that he, who, with his Forces and revenged Sword, has formerly defended the Church of *Rome,* when in greatest Dangers and Calamities of Wars; should now, for the Glory of God, and Tranquillity of the *Roman Church,* by his Ingenuity and Pen, put a Stop to *Heresies,* which so endanger the *Catholic Faith.*

If no sincere *Christian* could suffer so great Evils to creep into the Church, without opposing all his Forces and Studies against them; what ought not a Prince to do, and such a Prince, as, by divine Providence, is advanced to that Honour and Dignity, as it were, for that very Cause, that he might protect the *Catholic Faith,* and maintain the *Christian Religion* inviolable from all pestilential Endeavours?

Shall we admire, that Piety should extort from him (being both a *Christian* and a *Prince,*) what is but the Duty of every Christian? These, most holy Father, are the chief Reasons of his entering upon this Work; his accustomed Veneration to *Your Holiness; Christian* Piety in the Cause of God; and a royal Grief and Indignation of seeing Religion trodden under Foot. I confess the Desire of Glory might have been able to have induced him to these Things; that as he, who, under the Charge of the best Tutors, and a Father none of the most indulgent, having passed his younger Days in good Learning, and afterwards so well versed in *Holy Scrip-*

tures, that confiding in his own Abilities, he often, (not
without great Glory) disputed with the most Learned
in *Britain;* might now also, for Glory's Sake, fight in
the Field of Learning against *Martin Luther;* a Man
indeed not illiterate.

Nor do I see in what else he could, with more Glory
and Applause, have employed this Treasure of Knowledge; a Talent, doubtless, given him by God himself for
this very End. But yet the pious Prince himself does
modestly acknowledge, in his Preface, how little he attributes to the Force of his own Wit, which is so much
esteemed by others: For, excusing his Insufficiency in
Learning, in that Preface, he arrogates no more to himself, than to confess that this Task might have been
much better performed by many others; and that he
himself, (much unfit, confiding only in the Assistance
of the divine Goodness) had, through the Instigation of
Piety, and Grief of seeing Religion so much abused, attempted to discover, by Reason, the *Lutheran Heresies:*
Not that he thought it honourable to contend with
Luther, who is so much despised, hissed at, and cried
down over the whole World; but that, amongst other
Things, he might testify to the World what his Opinion
was of this prodigious Monster, and his Followers;
thinking himself concerned to publish that in Writing,
not so much, lest Scruples of Conscience should follow
his Silence, as, by his Example, to induce others to the
like Undertakings, who had received a richer Gift of
Science from the Giver of Light. I confess what the
Godly Prince has writ against the Errors of *Luther*
might compel *Luther* himself (if he had the least Spark
of Christian Piety in him) to recant his *Heresies,* and
recall again the straying and almost forlorn Flock, not
only from Errors, but from Hell itself, where it miser-
ably runs head-long. But what can be done, where

Pharaoh's Heart is hardened; where the Wound stinks with Putrefaction; where Wickedness, *Lying to itself,* is become miserable? being unwilling to hear that it should understand, or to understand that it should do well. The Change of his Mind, and altering his Councils to better, must be a great Miracle of Almighty God; for what learned Men have writ against him as yet, does but only irritate him to grow every Day worse and worse. Truly, my most serene King is so far from expecting any Good from this Idol and vain *Phantom,* that he rather thinks this raging and mad Dog is not to be dealt with by Words, there being no Hopes of his Conversion, but with drawn Swords, Cannons, and other Habiliments of War; (such as he would use against the *Turks* themselves; if Time permitted,) that, being constrained by due Punishment, he might be reduced, if not to Amendment, at least to Fear. And because, most Holy Father, the King could not revenge with the Sword, God's Cause and Yours; He takes other Arms, and enters the Field of Learning; not in this Kind of Combat, like another *Hercules,* to fight against this *Hydra;* but because this Viper's Madness rages nowhere more to the Dishonour of God, than in his Book of the *Babylonian Captivity;* nor seems he, any where else, by his deceitful Arguments, more to endanger weaker Judgments. Having therefore begun to batter down this Work, he assaults it with the Force and Engines of his Arguments; therein performing the Office of a pious, magnanimous General, whose Duty in military Discipline, is to supply his Soldiers with most Auxiliaries, where the Enemy presses on with greatest force. Which Work of his, though it had the Approbation of the most Learned of his Kingdom; yet he resolved not to publish until Your Holiness (from whom we ought to receive the Sense of the Gospel, by Your quick and most sub-

lime Judgment) deem it worthy to pass through the
Hands of Men.   May therefore Your Holiness take in
good Part, and graciously accept this little Book, sent
and submitted to Your Examination: In which, the
pious, and Your most devoted Prince, has, with all his
Power, endeavoured to procure, in some Manner, that
weaker Understandings should not be drawn out of the
Way, by the most wicked Works of this perverse Man;
and hopes so to have acquitted himself, as at least he
may appear to have demonstrated his Veneration
towards the Christian Religion, and towards Your Holiness.

The Most Holy Bishop Answered in These Words

WE receive this *Book* with great Joy: Truly it is such, as nothing could have been sent more acceptable to Us, and our venerable Brethren. But, indeed, we know not whether more to *praise,* or to *admire,* that most *potent, prudent* and *truly* most *Christian King;* who, with his Sword, has totally subdued the Enemies of *Christ's Church,* Enemies, who like the Heads of the *Hydra,* often cut off, and forthwith growing up again;) have often endeavoured to tear in Pieces the *seamless Coat* of *Christ;* and, at Length, the Enemies being vanquished, hath settled in *Peace* the *Church of God,* and this *Holy See.* And now, his Majesty having the Knowledge, Will, and Ability of composing *This excellent Book* against this terrible *Monster,* has rendered himself no less admirable to the whole World, by the Eloquence of his *Style,* than by his great Wisdom. We render immortal Thanks to our *Creator,* who has raised up such a Prince, to defend *His Church* and this *Holy See;* most humbly beseeching Him bountifully to bestow on this *Great Prince,* a most happy Life, and all other good Things that he can wish for; and after his Exit from this transitory Life, to crown him in his cœlestial Kingdom, with a Crown of *Eternal Glory.* We, to our Power, by God's Assistance, shall not be wanting in the Performance of any Thing, that may tend to the Honour and Dignity of his Majesty, and to His and his Kingdom's Glory.

The Pope's Bull

Leo, X. Bishop and Servant of the Servants of God: To our most dear Son in Christ, Henry, the illustrious King of England, and Defender of the Faith, sends Greeting, and gives his Benediction.

By the good Pleasure and Will of Almighty God, presiding in the Government of the *Universal Church,* though unworthy so great Charge. We daily employ all our Thoughts, both at home and abroad, for the continual Propagation of the *Holy Catholic Faith,* without which none can be saved. And that the Methods which are taken for repressing of such as labour to overthrow the *Church,* or pervert, and stain her by wicked Glosses, and malicious Lies; may be carried on with continual Profit, as is ordered by the sound Doctrine of the Faithful, and especially of such as shine in the regal Dignity: We employ with all our Power, our Endeavours, and all the Parts of our Ministry.

And as the other *Roman Bishops,* our Predecessors, have been accustomed to bestow some particular Favours upon *Catholic Princes,* as the Exigencies of Affairs and Times required, especially on those who, in tempestuous Times, and whilst the rapid Perfidiousness of *Schismatics* and *Heretics* raged, not only persevered constantly in the true *Faith,* and unspotted Devotion of the holy *Roman Catholic Church;* but also as the Legitimate Sons and stoutest Champions of the same, have opposed themselves, both spiritually and temporally, against the mad Fury of *Schismatics* and *Heretics:* So also, We, for your Majesty's most excellent Works, and

Bulla pro Titulo Defensoris Fidei*

Leo Episcopus Servus Servorum Dei, Carissimo in Christo Filio, Henrico Angliæ Regi, Fidei Defensori, Salutem et Apostolicam Benedictionem.

Ex supernæ dispositionis arbitrio, licet imparibus meritis, Universalis Ecclesiæ Regimini Præsidentes, ad hoc cordis nostri longe lateque diffundimus cogitatus, ut Fides Catholica, sine qua nemo proficit ad Salutem, continuum suscipiat Incrementum, et ut ea, quæ pro cohibendis conatibus Illum deprimere aut pravis mendacibusque comentis pervertere et denigrare molientium, sana Christi Fidelium, præsertim Dignitate Regali Fulgentium, Doctrina sunt disposita, continuis perficiant Incrementis, Partes nostri Ministerii et Operam impendimus efficaces.

Et, sicut alii Romani Pontifices, Prædecessores nostri, Catholicos Principes (prout Rerum et Temporum qualitas exigebat) specialibus favoribus prosequi consueverunt, illos præsertim, qui procellosis temporibus, et rapida Scismaticorum et Hæreticorum fervente perfidia, non solum in Fidei Serenitate et Devotione illibata Sacrosanctæ Romanæ Ecclesiæ immobiles perstiterunt verum etiam, tanquam ipsius Ecclesiæ legitimi Filii, ac fortissimi Athletæ, Scismaticorum et Hæreticorum insanis Furoribus spiritualiter et temporaliter se opposuerunt; ita etiam nos *Majestatem tuam,* propter Excelsa et Immortalia ejus erga Nos et hanc Sanctam Sedem, in qua, Permissione Divina, sedemus, opera et

*Rymeri Fœdera, Tom. VI., par. I., p. 199.

worthy Actions done for Us, and this Holy See, in
which by divine Permission we preside; do desire to
confer upon your Majesty, with Honour and immortal
Praises, *That,* which may enable and engage you carefully to drive away from our Lord's Flock the *Wolves;*
and cut off with the material Sword, the rotten Members
that infect the mystical Body of Jesus Christ, and confirm the Hearts of the almost discomforted Faithful in
the Solidity of *Faith.* Truly when our beloved Son
John Clark, your Majesty's Orator, did lately in our
Consistory, in presence of our venerable Brethren, *Cardinals* of the *sacred Roman Church,* and divers others
holy *Prelates;* present unto Us, a Book, which Your
Majesty, moved by your Charity, (which effects every
Thing readily and well,) and enflamed with Zeal to the
holy *Catholic Faith,* and Fervour of Devotion towards
Us, and this Holy *See;* did compose, as a most noble
and wholesome Antidote against the Errors of divers
Heretics, often condemned by this Holy *See,* and now
again revived by *Martin Luther:* When, I say, he offered
this Book to Us, to be examined, and approved by Our
Authority; and also declared, in a very eloquent Discourse, *That, as Your Majesty, had by true Reasons,
and the Undeniable Authority of Scripture, and
holy Fathers, confuted the notorious Errors of* LUTHER;
*so you are likewise ready, and resolved to prose-
cute, with all the Forces of your Kingdom, those
who shall presume to follow, or defend them;* having
found in this *Book* most admirable Doctrine, sprinkled
with the Dew of Divine Grace; We rendered infinite
Thanks to Almighty God, from whom every good Thing,
and every perfect Gift proceeds, for being pleased to
fill with his Grace, and to inspire your most excellent
Mind, inclined to all Good, to defend, by your Writings,
his *Holy Faith,* against the new Broacher of those con-

gesta, condignis et immortalibus præconiis et laudibus efferre desideramus, ac ea sibi concedere propter quæ invigilare debeat a Grege Dominico Lupos arcere, et putida membra, quæ Mysticum Christi Corpus inficiunt, ferro et materiali gladio abscindere, et nutantium corda Fidelium in Fidei soliditate confirmare.

Sane cum nuper Dilectus Filius *Johannes Clerk,* Majestatis tuæ apud Nos Orator, in Consistorio nostro, coram Venerabilibus Fratribus nostris Sanctæ Romanæ Ecclesiæ Cardinalibus, et compluribus aliis Romanæ Curiæ Prælatis, *Librum,* quem *Majestas tua,* charitate quæ omnia sedulo et nihil perperam agit, Fideique Catholicæ zelo accensa, ac Devotionis erga Nos et hanc Sanctam Sedem fervore inflammata, contra Errores diversorum Hæreticorum, sæpius ab hac Sancta Sede Damnatos, nuperque per *Martinum Lutherum* suscitatos et innovatos, tanquam nobile ac salutare quoddam antidotum, composuit, Nobis examinandum, et deinde Auctoritate nostra approbandum, obtulisset, ac luculenta Oratione sua exposuisset, *Majestatem tuam* paratam ac dispositam esse ut, quemadmodum veris Rationibus ac irrefragabilibus Sacræ Scripturæ et Sanctorum Patrum Auctoritatibus notorios Errores ejusdem *Martini* confutaverat, ita etiam omnes eos sequi et defensare præsumentes totius Regni sui viribus et armis persequatur:

Nosque ejus *Libri* admirabilem quandam et cœlestis Gratiæ rore conspersam, Doctrinam diligenter accurateque introspeximus, Omnipotenti Deo, a quo omne Datum optimum et omne Donum perfectum est, immensas Gratias egimus, qui optimam et ad omne bonum inclinatam mentem tuam inspirare, eique tantam Gratiam superne infundere dignatus fuit, ut ea scriberes quibus Sanctam ejus Fidem contra novum Errorum Damnatorum hujusmodi Suscitatorem defen-

demned Errors; and to invite all other *Christians,* by your Example, to assist and favour, with all their Power, the *orthodox Faith,* and *evangelical Truth,* now under so great Peril and Danger.

Considering that it is but *Just,* that those, who undertake pious Labours, in Defence of the Faith of Christ, should be extolled with all Praise and Honour; and being willing, not only to magnify with deserved Praise, and approve with our Authority, what your Majesty has with Learning and Eloquence writ against *Luther;* but also to Honour your Majesty with such a *Title,* as shall give all *Christians* to understand, as well in our Times, as in succeeding Ages, how acceptable and welcome Your *Gift* was to *Us,* especially in this Juncture of Time: We, the true Successor of St. *Peter,* (whom *Christ,* before his Ascension, left as his Vicar upon Earth, and to whom he committed the Care of his Flock) presiding in this Holy *See,* from whence all *Dignity* and *Titles* have their Source; have with our Brethren maturely deliberated on these Things; and with one Consent unanimously decreed to bestow on your Majesty this Title, *viz. Defender of the Faith.* And, as we have by this *Title* honoured you; we likewise command all *Christians,* that they *name* your *Majesty* by this *Title;* and that in their Writings to your Majesty, immediately after the Word *KING,* they add, *DEFENDER OF THE FAITH.* Having thus weighed, and diligently considered your singular Merits, we could not have invented a more congruous *Name,* nor more worthy Your Majesty, than this worthy and most excellent *Title;* which, as often as you hear, or read, you shall remember your own Merits and Virtues: Nor will you, by this *Title,* exalt yourself, or become proud, but, according to your accustomed Prudence, rather more humble in the Faith of Christ; and more

deres, ac reliquos Reges et Principes Christianos tuo exemplo invitares ut ipsi etiam Orthodoxæ Fidei et Evangelicæ Veritati, in periculum et discrimen adductæ, omni ope sua adesse opportuneque favere vellent; æquum autem esse censentes eos, qui pro Fidei Christi hujusmodi Defensione pios Labores susceperunt, omni Laude et Honore afficere; Volentesque non solum ea, quæ *Majestas* tua contra eundem *Martinum Lutherum* absolutissima Doctrina nec minori Eloquentia scripsit, condignis laudibus extollere ac magnificare, Auctoritateque nostra approbare et confirmare, sed etiam *Majestatem ipsam* tali Honore et Titulo decorare, ut nostris ac perpetuis futuris temporibus Christi Fideles omnes intelligant quam gratum acceptumque Nobis fuerit *Majestatis tuæ* munus, hoc præsertim tempore nobis oblatum;

Nos qui Petri, quem Christus, in cœlum ascensurus, Vicarium suum in Terris reliquit, et cui curam Gregis sui commisit, veri Successores sumus, et in hac Sancta Sede, a qua omnes Dignitates ac Tituli emanant, sedemus, habita super his cum eisdem Fratribus nostris matura Deliberatione, de eorum unanimi Consilio et Assensu, *Majestati tuæ* Titulum hunc (videlicet) Fidei Defensorem donare decrevimus, prout Te tali Titulo per Præsentes insignimus; Mandantes omnibus Christi Fidelibus ut *Majestatem tuam* hoc Titulo nominent, et cum ad eam scribent, post Dictionem Regi adjungant Fidei Defensori.

Et profecto, hujus Tituli excellentia et dignitate ac singularibus Meritis tuis diligenter perpensis et consideratis, nullum neque dignius neque *Majestati tuæ* convenientius nomen excogitare potuissemus, quod quotiens audies aut leges, totiens propriæ Virtutis optimique Meriti tui recordaberis; nec hujusmodi Titulo intumesces vel in Superbiam elevaberis, sed solita tua

strong and constant in your Devotion to this *Holy See,* by which you were exalted. And you shall rejoice in our Lord, who is the Giver of all good Things, for leaving such a perpetual and everlasting Monument of your Glory to Posterity, and shewing the Way to others, that if they also covet to be invested with such a Title, they may study to do such Actions, and to follow the Steps of your most excellent Majesty; Whom, with your Wife, Children, and all who shall spring from you, We bless with a bountiful and liberal Hand; in the Name of Him from whom the Power of Benediction is given to Us, *and by whom Kings reign, and Princes govern; and in whose Hands are the Hearts of Kings:*

Praying, and beseeching the most High, to confirm your Majesty in your most holy Purposes, and to augment your Devotion; and for your most excellent Deeds in Defence of his *Holy Faith,* to render your Majesty so illustrious and famous to the whole World, as that our Judgment in adorning you with so remarkable a *Title,* may not be thought vain, or light, by any Person whatsoever; and finally, after you have finished your Course in this Life, that he may make you Partaker of his eternal Glory. It shall not be lawful for any Person whatsoever, to infringe, or by any rash Presumption to act contrary to *This Letter* of Subscribing, and Command. But, if any one shall presume to make such Attempt; let him know, that he shall thereby incur the Indignation of Almighty God, and of the holy Apostles, *Peter* and *Paul.*

Given at St. Peter's *in* Rome, *the fifth of the* Ides *of* October; *In the Year of our Lord's Incarnation* 1521, *and in the ninth Year of our* Papacy.

Prudentia humilior, et in Fide Christi ac Devotione hujus Sanctæ Sedis, a qua exaltatus fueris, fortior et constantior evades, ac in Domino bonorum omnium Largitore lætaberis perpetuum hoc et immortale Gloriæ tuæ Monumentum Posteris tuis relinquere, illisque viam ostendere ut, si tali Titulo ipsi quoque insigniri optabunt, talia etiam Opera efficere, præclaraque *Majestatis tuæ* Vestigia sequi studeant, quam, prout de Nobis et dicta Sede optime merita est, una cum Uxore et Filiis, ac omnibus qui a Te et ab Illis nascentur, nostra Benedictione, in Nomine illius, a quo illam concedendi Potestas Nobis data est, larga et liberali Manu Benedicentes, Altissimum illum, qui dixit, *per Me Reges regnant et Principes imperant, et in cujus manu Corda sunt Regum,* rogamus et obsecramus ut eam in suo Sancto Proposito confirmet ejusque Devotionem multiplicet, ac præclaris pro Sancta Fide gestis ita illustret, ac toti Orbi Terrarum conspicuam reddat ut Judicium, quod de ipsa fecimus, eam tam insigni Titulo decorantes, a nemine falsum aut vanum judicari possit; Demum, mortalis hujus Vitæ finito Curriculo, sempiternæ illius Gloriæ consortem atque participem reddat.

Dat. *Romæ* apud Sanctum Petrum, Anno Incarnationis Dominicæ Millesimo, Quingentesimo, Vigesimo Primo, Quinto Idus Octobris Pontificatus nostri anno Nono.

Ego Leo Decimus, *Catholicæ Ecclesiæ Episcopus.*
Locus Signi.

Letter from Leo X. to Henry VIII. respecting the "Defence of the Seven Sacraments"

In Acknowledgment of the Book Written by the King against Luther

Most dear Son in Christ, Health and Apostolic Bene-diction:

Some days ago, when the envoy of Your Serenity, Our beloved Son, John Clark, Dean of the Chapel Royal, publicly in Consistory presented us the book which Your Serenity has published against the impious teachings and sect of Martin Luther, and in a brilliant address, exceedingly appropriate to the occasion, de-clared, in the presence of a number of Prelates of the Roman Court, your readiness to aid Us and the Holy See with sword and pen, our soul was filled with joy. Not We alone, but all Our venerable brethren rejoiced, as though deeming that Luther's impiety had, not with-out the divine permission, assailed the Church of Christ, so that to her greater glory she might be fortu-nate enough to find such a champion and defender.

Hence We have resolved, and all agree in Our de-cision, that your exceptional virtue and piety should be made memorable by some mark of Our love and appre-ciation. For if it has often been, most dear Son, a source of honour to great monarchs to take up arms to safeguard the liberty and tranquillity of the Holy Apos-tolic See, how much more glory and reverence should accrue from employing the weapons of the Spirit of God and of heavenly science to remove from the faith

Letter from Leo X. to Henry VIIII. respecting the "Assertio Septem Sacramentorum"

De Gratiis pro Libro per Regem Contra Lutherum Scripto

Charissime in Christo fili noster, salutem et apostolicam benedictionem. His præteritis diebus, cùm tuæ serenitatis Orator dilectus Filius Johannes Clerke Capellæ regiæ Decanus in Consistorio nostro palàm librum eum nobis obtulisset, quem serenitas tua contra impiam Martini Lutheri et mentem et sectam edidit, atque ipse luculentâ maximèque tempori et loco accommodatâ oratione, præsentibus etiàm pluribus romanæ Curiæ Prælatis promptum animum tuum ad nos sanctamque sedem hanc armis pariter et literis juvandam exposuisset, summâ animæ lætitiâ fuimus affecti; neque nos solùm sed omnes venerabiles fratres nostri, quasi reputantes non sine permissu divino erupisse adversùs Christi Ecclesiam Luterianam hanc impietatam, ut ipsâ majore sua eum gloriâ talem propugnatorem ac defensorem sortiri possit.

Visum itaque fuit cunctis, nobisque ità decernentibus ab omnibus est assensum singularem hanc tuam et virtutem et pietatem aliquo et amoris nostri et grati animi monumento esse illustrandam. Etenim, charissime fili noster, si arma sumere ut sanctæ sedis apostolicæ status in sua libertate et tranquilitate permaneret tùtus, magnis sæpè Principibus honori summo fuit, quantò magis arma spiritus Dei cœlestisque scientiæ capere, ut êa fide Christi tanta labes depellatur, sacramentaque ea

of Christ so great a stain, and to preserve inviolate those sacraments by which the salvation of souls is secured.

These two functions, which hitherto We have always found separate, have been united in you alone, a mighty sovereign, in a most eminent degree; for you have both vindicated the liberty of the Church with your arms, and you have evinced your desire to fortify the Christian faith against impious heresy by the treasures of your piety and learning. The one is an evidence of invincible and lofty courage, the other of a spirit and sense of religion tender, devout, and orthodox.

In what words, then, or by what manner of eulogy shall we praise this piety, this plenitude of doctrine, overflowing as though from a celestial fountain? What fit return can we make for your kindness in dedicating to us so noble a product of your intellect? Both considerations exceed the powers of language, or even of thought; nor can we reflect on your services and deserts without being overcome.

What love, what zeal is yours for the defence of Christian faith! What benevolence in Our regard! And in the book itself, what solidity of matter, clearness of method, force of eloquence, wherein the Holy Spirit Himself shows visibly! It is thoroughly judicious, wise, and pious; charitable in instruction, gentle in admonition, correct in argument. If there be any of your opponents who have not fallen entirely into the power of the Prince of Darkness, they must be drawn by your writings to a saner condition of mind, if any chance for sanity be left.

These are distinguished and admirable achievements; and as they have been wrought in a new fashion, by a princely favour, for Almighty God and the Holy See, we render you, Defender of the Faith, unbounded thanks. The Apostolic See thanks you; all who worship Christ

quibus animarum salus, inviolata serventur, et laudem
afferre debet et celebritatem.

Quamquàm hæc duo, quæ duximus anteà semper
divisa, in te uno maximo rege præstantissima fuerunt
conjuncta; idem enim tu et libertatem ecclesiasticam
tuis armis vindicasti, et tu idem fidem christianam
thesauris tuæ et pietatis et scientiæ adversùs impias
hæreses munitam esse voluisti, quorum alterum invictæ
et excelsæ animi fortitudinis, alterum piæ et sanctæ et
veræ mentis ac religionis fuit; sed nos quibus tandem
verbis, quo laudum genere, vel hanc pietatem tuam, hanc
uberrimam velut ex cœlesti fonte doctrinæ copiam com-
mendabimus; vel tuæ ergà nos voluntati, qui nobis ipsis
tam nobilem partum ingenii tui dicasti, gratias agemus?
superat hoc utrumque non solùm verba sed etiàm cogitationes nostras nec verò de tuis officiis ac meritis tantùm
possumus animo concipere, quin à re vincamur ipsâ.
Qui enim in te amor, quod studium defendendæ christianæ fidei? Quanta ergà nos ipsos benevolentia? quæ
denique operis ipsius gravitas? qui ordo? quanta vis
eloquentiæ ut sanctum affuisse spiritum appareat;
omnia plena judicii, plena sapientiæ, plena pietatis; in
docendo charitas, in admonendo mansuetudo, in redar-
guendo veritas; ut si homines sint qui à te refelluntur,
ac non omnino in pessimi Dæmonis potestatem abierunt,
tuis scriptis ad sanitatem debeant reduci, si modò ullus
relictus est sanitatis locus.

Sunt hæc præclara omninò et admirabilia, quæ quoniam à te novà ratione, magnifico munere, Deo maximo
et huic sanctæ sedi elaborata sunt, agimus Majestati
tuæ infinitas gratias, o fidei defensor! Agit sedes apostolica, agunt omnes qui Christum colunt et in ejus fide
consentur.

Et nos quidem titulum hunc defensoris fidei, de
eorumdem venerabilium fratrum nostrorum assensu,

and unite in His faith thank you. We, for Our part, with the concurrence of Our venerable brothers, bestow on you, in other letters sealed with lead, as you will find from their perusal, this title of *Defender of the Faith.* For your part, most dear Son, however you may consider great and desirable these honours which the Holy Apostolic See grants you as a reward of eminent virtue and a mark of its grateful appreciation, realize that greater and more glorious compensation is prepared for you in heaven by Our Lord and Saviour. In upholding His cause and His spouse by every means of defence you have displayed your spirit and your virtue; and while you review those titles which you have acquired on earth and in heaven, remember by what claims you have gained them. Show yourself hereafter such as you have been heretofore. Let your later deeds be equal to your sublime and glorious beginnings. Let the Apostolic See, once defended by your arms, and the Christian faith, now fortified by the shield of your doctrine against the criminal frenzy of heretics, find and prove you ever a helper in all their perils, so that this extraordinary and unspeakable glory which Your Majesty has most mightily merited by your great efforts may continue to the last day of your life and endure to all future time as a theme of eulogy.

Given at Rome, at St. Peter's, under the seal of the Fisherman, the fourth day of November, 1521, the ninth year of Our Pontificate.

On the back:

SADOLETUS

To Our Most Christian Son in Christ, Henry, King of England, Illustrious Defender of the Faith.

tibi per alias nostras sub plumbo literas contulimus, ut
ex ipsis potuisti cognoscere; sed tu, charissime fili, ita
hos honores quos tibi in præmium tuæ præclarissimæ
virtutis, in signum suæ ergà te gratæ voluntatis, sancta
sedes defert apostolica, et magnos et expetendos esse
puta, ut tamen illis longè majora et præstantiora arbit-
rere tibi in cœlo à Domino et Salvatore nostro parata
præmia, ejus tu causam et sponsam defendendo omni
genere tutelæ et animum et virtutem tuam adhibuisti;
ut dùm hos in terris quos adeptus es, titulos recensebis,
et cœlestia illa cogitabis, tecum ipse recordere quibus es
meritis ista consecutus, talemque te imposterùm qualem
antea præstes, ac principiis sublimibus et gloriosis pares
sint exitus, ipsaque sedes apostolica quæ olim tuis de-
fensa armis, fides quoque christiana quæ nunc doctrinæ
tuæ clypeo adversùs sceleratas hæreticorum insanias
communita est, sentiant te eundem semper experian-
turque adjutorem in periculis suis omnibus, ut istam
singularem et inenarrabilem gloriam quam majestas
tua, maximis suis operibus jure optimo promerita est
ad extremum usque hujus vitæ diem et producere possis,
et eam in omni posteritate prædicandam relinquere.

Datum Romæ, apud Sanctum Petrum, sub annulo
piscatoris, die quartà novembris, millesimo quingentesimo vicesimo primo, pontificatus nostri anno nono.

Dorso:

SADOLETUS

Charissimo in Christo filio nostro Henrico Angliæ
regi, illustri fidei defensori.

The Epistle Dedicatory

To our most Holy Lord Leo, X. chief Bishop, Henry, King of England, France, and Ireland, wisheth perpetual happiness.

Most Holy Father:

Perhaps it may appear strange to Your Holiness, that Part of our Youth being spent in martial Affairs, and Part in the Studies of Things belonging to the Common-wealth; we should now undertake the Task of a Man, that ought to have employed all his Time in the Studies of Learning; in opposing Ourself against this growing *Heresy.* But Your Holiness (I suppose) will the less admire, when You consider the Reasons that obliged Us to take upon Us this Charge of Writing. We have seen Tares cast into our Lord's Harvest;* *Sects* do spring up, and *Heresies* increase so much as almost, to overthrow the Faith of Christ: And such Seeds of Discord are sown abroad in the World, that no sincere Christian, can suffer, or endure any longer their spreading Mischiefs, without an Obligation of employing all his Studies and Forces to oppose them. Your Holiness ought not therefore to wonder, if We (not the greatest in Ability, yet in Faith and Good-will inferior to none,) have proposed to Ourself, to employ our Force and Power in a Work so necessary, and so profitable, that it cannot lightly be omitted by any, without Offence; also to declare Our great Respect towards Your Holiness, Our Endeavours for the Propagation of the Faith of Christ, and Our Obedience to the Service of Almighty

*Matt. xiii. 25.

Regis ad Summum Pontificem Epistola

Sanctissimo Domino Nostro, Domino Leoni X, Pontifici Maximo, Henricus, Dei gratia rex Angliæ ac Dominus Hiberniæ, perpetuam felicitatem.

Beatissime Pater:

QUUM partim bellicis, partim aliis longe diversis studiis reipublicæ causa adolescentiam nostram insueverimus, miraturum te, Beatissime Pater, non dubitamus, quod ejus nunc hominis partes nobis sumpserimus, qui omnem potius ætatem consumpsisset in litteris, ut gravem scilicet hæresim pullulantem comprimamus. Sed desinet, opinor, Tua Sanctitudo mirari, postquam causas expenderit, quæ nos subegerunt ut hoc scribendi onus, quanquam non ignari quam sumus impares, subierimus. Vidimus siquidem in messem Domini jacta zizaniæ semina pullulare sectas, hæreses in fide succrescere, et tantam per orbem totum Christianum seminatam discordiæ materiam, ut nemo, qui sincera mente Christianus sit, hæc tanta mala, tam late serpentia, ferre diutius possit, quin et studium cogatur, et vires, qualescumque possit, opponere.

Mirum igitur videri non debet, si nos quoque, tametsi potestate non maximi, fide tamen ac voluntate nemini secundi in opus tam pium, tam utile, tam necessarium, ut a nemine ferme possit absque piaculo prætermitti, et nostram erga Tuam Sanctitatem observantiam, et erga religionem Christi studium, erga Dei cultum obsequium nostrum declarare constituimus: maxime fidentes, etsi eruditio nostra sit tam exigua, ut propemodum nulla, gratiam tamen Dei sic cooperaturam nobiscum, ut,

God: Greatly confiding, that although our Learning is
not much, nay in Comparison, even Nothing; yet His
Grace will so co-operate with Us, that what we are not
able thereby to effect, He, by his Benignity and Power,
may more fully perform, and by his Strength supply
Our Weakness therein. Though we know very well,
that there are every-where several more expert, especially in Holy Writ, who could have more commodiously
undertaken this Great Work, and performed it much
better than We: Yet are We not altogether so ignorant,
as not to esteem it Our Duty, to employ, with all Our
Might, Our Wit and Pen in the *common Cause*. For
having, by long Experience, found, that Religion bears
the greatest Sway in the Administration of Public Affairs, and is likewise of no small Importance in the
Commonwealth; We have employed no little Time, especially since We came to Years of Discretion, in the Contemplation thereof; wherein We have always taken
great Delight: And though not ignorant of Our small
Progress therein made; yet, at least, it is so much, as,
We hope, (especially with the Help, or rather Instigation of such Things as can instruct the most Ignorant,
viz. *Piety, and the Grief of seeing Religion abused,*)
will suffice for Reasons to discover the Subtilties of
Luther's Heresy. We have therefore, (confiding in
those Things,) entered upon this Work; dedicating to
Your Holiness what We have meditated therein; that,
under Your Protection, *who are Christ's Vicar upon
Earth,* it may pass the public Censure. For we are persuaded that this *Heresy,* having for some Time exercised its Rage amongst *Christians;* and being by Your
most weighty and wholesome *Sentence* condemned, and,
as it were, by Force plucked out of Men's Hands, if any
Thing remains hidden in the Bowels of it, fed by Flattery and fair Promises; it is to be rooted out by just

quod doctrina nequivimus perficere, id ipse pro sua
benignitate summaque potentia plenius absolvat,
ac nostram in litteris imbecillitatem suo vigore sup-
pleat.

Quanquam in litteris quoque, præsertim sacris, etsi
certo sciamus nusquam non esse multos, qui hoc scribendi munus et obire commodius, et præstare potuissent
uberius, tamen non usque adeo rudes sumus, ut in communi causa dedeceat nos quoque, pro nostra virili,
calamo quid possemus, quantulum id cumque fuerit, ex-
periri.

Postquam enim in administranda republica maximam semper vim, maximumque momentum religionem
habere multo usu advertimus, ut primum maturiores
annos attigimus, cœpimus ejus contemplationi non nihil
studii impendere. Plurimum profecto, postquam cœpimus, in eo delectati; consecuti tamen, non nos latet,
quam exiguum, tantum tamen, ut speramus, quantum,
adjuvantibus præsertim, vel potius instigantibus iis,
quæ vel admodum rudem abunde reddere instructum
possent, pietate scilicet, et læsæ religionis dolore, ad
Lutheranæ hæresis fraudes rationibus detegendas sit
satis.

Itaque etiam hac fiducia rem tentavimus, et quæ in
ea meditati sumus, Sanctitati Tuæ dedicavimus, ut sub
Tuo nomine, qui Christi vicem in terris geris, publicum
judicium subeant. Sic enim nobis persuasimus, quum
ea hæresis aliquandiu inter Christianos grassata gravis-
simæ saluberrimæque sententiæ tuæ vi e manibus
hominum sit excussa, si quid ejus in pectoribus vel
captione aliqua deceptis, vel blandis pollicitationibus
inescatis, adhuc resedit, id esse justis rationibus ex-
imendum. Sic enim futurum, ut quum duci quam
trahi se ingenia libentius patiantur, non desit his
mitioris quoque remedii ratio; in qua promoverimus-ne

Reasons, and Arguments; that, as Men's Wits suffer themselves more willingly to be led than drawn; so Reason also may supply these with the mildest Remedies. Whether or no any Thing is effectually done in this, shall rest to Your Holiness's Judgment: If We have erred in any Thing, We offer it to be corrected as may please Your Holiness.

nos quicquam, an non, Beatitudinis Tuæ judicium erit.
Cujus etiam arbitrio, si quid est a nobis erratum, corri-
gendum offerimus.

To the Reader

ALTHOUGH I do not rank myself amongst the most Learned and Eloquent; yet (shunning the Stain of Ingratitude, and moved by *Fidelity* and *Piety;*) I cannot but think myself obliged, (would to God my Ability to do it, were equal to my good Will!) to defend my Mother, the *Spouse of Christ:* Which, though it be a Subject more copiously handled by others; nevertheless I account it as much my own Duty, as his who is the most learned, by my utmost Endeavours, to defend the *Church,* and to oppose myself to the poisonous Shafts of the Enemy that fights against her: Which this Juncture of Time, and the present State of Things, require at my Hand. For *before,* when none did *assault,* it was not necessary to *resist;* but *now* when the Enemy, (and the most wicked Enemy imaginable,) is risen up, who, by the Instigation of the Devil, under Pretext of Charity, and stimulated by Anger and Hatred, spews out the Poison of Vipers against the *Church,* and *Catholic Faith;* it is necessary that every Servant of Christ, of what Age, Sex, or Order soever, should rise against this common Enemy of the *Christian Faith;* that those, whose Power avails not, yet may testify their good Will by their cheerful Endeavours.

It is now therefore convenient, that we arm ourselves with a two-fold Armour: the one *Celestial,* and the other *Terrestrial.* With a *celestial* Armour; That he, who, by a feigned and dissembled Charity, destroys others, and perishes himself, being gained by true Charity, may also gain others; and that he who fights by a *false*

Ad Lectores

Motus quidem fidelitate ac pietate, quanquam mihi nec eloquentia sit, nec scientiæ copia, cogor tamen, ne ingratitudine maculer, matrem meam, Christi sponsam, utinam tanta facultate, quanta cum voluntate defendere. Quod licet alii præstare possint uberius ac copiosius, mei tamen officii esse duxi, ut ipse quoque, quantumvis tenuiter eruditus, quibus rationibus possem, Ecclesiam tuerer, meque adversus venenata jacula hostis eam oppugnantis objicerem.

Quod ut faciam, tempus ipsum, et præsens rerum status efflagitat: nam antea quum nemo oppugnaret, nemini propugnare necesse erat. At quum jam hostis exortus sit, quo nullus potuit exoriri malignior, qui dæmonis instinctu charitatem prætexens, ira atque odio stimulatus, et contra Ecclesiam, et contra catholicam fidem vipereum virus evomuit, necesse est adversus hostem communem Christianæ fidei omnis Christi servus, omnis ætas, omnis sexus, omnis ordo consurgat: ut qui viribus non valent, officium saltem alacri testentur affectu.

Nunc itaque convenit ut duplici armatura muniamur, cœlesti scilicet ac terrestri. Cœlesti, ut qui ficta charitate et alios perdit, et perit ipse, vera charitate lucrifactus, alios lucrifaciat, et qui falsa doctrina depugnat, doctrina vera vincatur. Terrestri vero, ut si tam obstinatæ malitiæ sit, ut consilia sancta spernat, et corruptionem piam contemnat, merito coerceatur supplicio: ut qui bene facere non vult, desinat male facere, et qui nocuit verbo malitiæ, supplicii prosit exemplo.

Doctrine, may be conquered by *true Doctrine:* With a *terrestrial;* that, if he be so obstinately malicious, as to neglect holy Councils, and despise God's Reproofs, he may be constrained by due Punishments; that he who will not do Good, may leave off doing Mischief;* and he that did Harm by the Word of Malice, may do Good by the Example, of his Punishments. What *Plague* so pernicious did ever invade the *Flock of Christ?* What *Serpent* so venemous has crept in, as he who writ of the *Babylonian Captivity of the Church;* who wrests Holy *Scripture* by his own Sense, against the *Sacraments of Christ;* abolishes the *ecclesiastical Rites and Ceremonies* left by the *Fathers;* undervalues the holy and antient Interpreters of Scripture, unless they concur with his Sentiments; calls the most Holy See of *Rome, Babylon,* and the *Pope's* Authority, *Tyranny;* esteems the most wholesome Decrees of the *Universal Church* to be *Captivity;* and turns the Name of the most Holy Bishop of *Rome,* to that of *Antichrist?* O that detestable Trumpeter of *Pride, Calumnies* and *Schisms!* What an *infernal Wolf* is he, who seeks to disperse the Flock of Christ?† What a great Member of the Devil is he,‡ who endeavours to tear the Christian Members of Christ from their Head?

How infectious is his Soul, who revives these detestable *Opinions* and buried *Schisms;* adds new ones to the old, brings to Light (*Cerberus*-like, from Hell) the *Heresies* which ought to lie in eternal Darkness; and esteems himself worthy to govern all Things by his own Word, opposed against the Judgments of all the Antients; nay also to ruin the *Church of God!* Of whose Malice I know not what to say. For I think neither Tongue nor Pen can express the Greatness of it. Wherefore, before I exhort, pray, and beseech, through

*Rom. xiii. 3, 4.   †Matt. vii. 15.   ‡John viii. 44.

Quæ pestis unquam tam perniciosa invasit gregem Christi? Quis serpens unquam tam venenatus irrepsit, quam is, qui de Babylonica Captivitate Ecclesiæ scripsit, qui Scripturam sacram ex suo sensu contra Christi sacramenta detorquet, traditos ab antiquis Patribus ecclesiasticos ritus eludit, sanctissimos viros, vetustissimos sacrarum litterarum interpretes, nisi quatenus ipsius sensui conveniunt et consentiunt, nihili pendit, sacrosanctam sedem Romanam Babylonem appellat, summum Pontificium vocat tyrannidem, totius Ecclesiæ decreta saluberrima captivitatem censet, sanctissimi Pontificis nomen in Antichristum convertit. O detestabilis arrogantiæ, contumeliæ, ac schismatis buccinator! Quantus inferorum lupus est iste, qui Christi gregem dispergere quærit! Quantum diaboli membrum, qui Christianos Christi membra quærit a capite suo decerpere! Quam putris hujus animus, quam execrabile propositum, qui et sepulta ressuscitat schismata, et vetustis adjicit nova, et hæreses æternis abdendas tenebris velut Cerberum ex inferis producit in lucem, dignumque ducit se, cujus unius verbo, posthabitis antiquis omnibus, universa regatur, imo subvertatur Ecclesia! De cujus ego malitia quid dicam, nescio: quam tantam censeo, quantam neque lingua cujusquam, neque calamus exprimere possit.

Quamobrem vos omnes Christi fideles hortor, oro, et per Christi nomen, quod professi sumus, obtestor, ut qui Lutheri opera (si modo is Babylonicæ Captivitatis sit auctor) omnino velint inspicere, caute illud, et cum judicio faciant, ut, quemadmodum Virgilius aurum se colligere dixit e stercore Ennii, sic e mediis malis colligant bona. Nec ita, si quid arridet ipsis, afficiantur, ut cum melle simul imbibant venenum. Multo enim satius fuerit utroque carere, quam utrumque glutire.

the Name of Christ (which we will profess) all Christians, who are willing to look upon, and read *Luther*'s Works, especially the *Babylonian Captivity,* (if he be Author of it) to do it warily, and very judicially; that, as *Virgil* said, *he gathered Gold out of the Dross of* Ennius; so they may also gather good Things out of Evil: And if any Thing please them, let them not be so taken with it, as to suck the Poison with the Honey; for it is better to want both, than to swallow *both.* To hinder which, I wish the Author may *Repent, be converted, and live;** aud, in Imitation of St. *Augustine,* (whose Rule he professed) correct his Books, filled with Malice, and revoke his Errors. If *Luther* refuses this, it will shortly come to pass, if Christian Princes do their Duty, that these Errors, and himself, if he perseveres therein, may be burned in the Fire. In the mean while, we thought it fit to discover to the *Readers* some chief Heads or Chapters in the *Babylonian Captivity,* which have the most Venom in them, by which it will appear, very clearly, with what exulcerated Mind he began this Work; *pretending* the public Good, but writing Nothing but malicious Inventions.

We need not seek any foreign Testimonies for proving what we have said; for *Luther* (fearing that any one should go up and down in Search of such,) discovers himself, and his Mind, of his own Accord, in his very Beginning. For who should doubt of what he aimed at, when he reads this one Sentence of his?

*Ezech. xxxiii. 11.

Quod ne accidat, utinam auctor aliquando resipiscat, *ut convertatur, et vivat!* ac suos libros omni malitia refertos, exemplo Augustini, cujus regulam profitetur, retractet, erroresque revocet! Quod si recuset Lutherus, brevi certe fiet, si Christiani principes suum officium fecerint, ut errores ejus, eumque ipsum, si in errore perstiterit, ignis exurat. Interea nobis visum est in Captivitate Babylonica quædam loca commonstrare lectoribus, in quibus præcipuum latet venenum. Ex quibus aperte satis constabit quam exulcerato animo agressus sit opus, qui, quum publicum bonum prætendat, nihil præter malitiam ad scribendum afferat.

Ut hæc doceamus, quæ diximus, haud longe nobis petendæ probationes sunt: nam ne quis ob eam rem sursum deorsum cursitet, Lutherus ultro sese atque animum suum primo statim principio prodit. Quis enim dubitet quo tendat, quo se proripiat is, cujus vel hunc unum versum legerit?

CHAP. I

Of Indulgences, and the Pope's Authority

Indulgentiæ sunt adulatorum Romanorum *nequitiæ.*

As every living Creature is known chiefly by its Face, so by this first Proposition it evidently appears, how corrupt and rotten his Heart was, whose Mouth, being filled with Bitterness, broke out into such a Corruption; for what he said of INDULGENCES in Times past, seemed to many, not only to detract much of the *Roman* Bishop's Power, but also to lessen the good Hope and holy Consolation of the Faithful, and mightily to excite Men to confide in the Riches of their own Penitence, and despise the Treasures of the *Holy Church,* and the Bounty of God: And yet what he then writ, was favourably interpreted, because he only disputed many of them, but did not affirm them; desiring to be taught, and promising to obey him that would instruct him better. But what this new Saint, (who refers all Things to the Holy Spirit, which cannot brook any Thing of Falsehood,) did then write with a simple Intention, is easily discovered: For as soon as he had any Thing of wholesome Advice given him, he immediately vomited his Malediction against those, who endeavoured his Good, reviling them with Reproaches and Quarrels; for which it is worth our While to see what Height of Folly he is come to at last. He confessed before that *Indulgences* were good, at least to absolve us, besides the *Crime,* from the Punishments also which should be enjoined us by the Order of the *Church,* or

CAP. I

Indulgentiæ

Sunt adulatorum Romanorum nequitiæ.

QUEMADMODUM animal omne potissimum ex facie dignoscitur, ita ex hac quoque prima propositione clarescit quam suppuratum ac putridum is habeat cor, cujus os, amaritudine plenum, tali exundat sanie. Nam quæ de Indulgentiis olim disseruit, ea plærisque multum videbantur adimere non modo de potestate Pontificis, verum etiam de bona spe ac sancta consolatione fidelium, hominesque vehementer animare, ut in pœnitentiæ suæ confisi divitiis, Ecclesiæ thesaurum, et ultroneam Dei benignitatem contemnerent: et tamen ea, quæ tum scripsit, omnia, idcirco mitius accepta sunt, quia plæraque disserebat duntaxat, non asserebat, subinde etiam petens doceri, seseque pollicens meliora docenti pariturum. Verum istud quam simplice scripsit animo homo sanctulus, et omnia referens ad spiritum, qui fictum effugit, hinc facile deprehenditur, quod simul atque a quoquam salubriter est admonitus, ilicet pro benefacto regessit maledictum, conviciis et contumeliis insaniens: quibus operæ pretium est videre, quo vesaniæ tandem provectus est. Ante fassus est Indulgentias hactenus saltem valere, ut præter culpam etiam a pœnis absolverent, quascumque videlicet vel Ecclesia statuerat, vel suus cuique sacerdos injunxerat. Nunc vero non eruditione, ut ipse inquit, sed malitia tantum profecit, ut sibi ipsi contrarius, Indulgentias in universum condemnet, ac nihil aliud eas dicat esse, quam meras im-

by our particular *Priest:* But now it was not by Learning, (as he says himself,) but by mere Malice that he wrought; and, contradicting himself, he condemns *Indulgences;* and says, *That they are nothing but mere Impostures, fit only to destroy People's Money, and God's Faith.* Every Man may see how wickedly and furiously he rails in this Matter: For, if *Indulgences,* as he says, are but mere *Impostures,* and good for Nothing, then it follows, that not only our *Chief Bishop, LEO* X. (whose innocent, unspotted Life, and most holy Conversation are well known through the World, as *Luther* himself confesses in a Letter of his to the *Pope*) is an *Impostor;* but also all *Roman Bishops* in so many past Ages, are so, who, as *Luther* himself says, did use to give *Indulgences; some a Year's Remission; some three Years; some to forgive a Lent's Penance; some a certain Part of the whole Penance, as the Third, or one Half; at least Something, as to plenary, or full Remission of the Sin and Punishment.*

Then were they all *Impostors,* if *Luther* be true: But how much more Reason is there to believe, that this little Brother is a scabbed Sheep, than that so many Pastors were treacherous, and unfaithful? For *Luther,* as is said above, shews what Kind of Man he is, and how uncharitable, when he blushes not, to lay such a Crime against so great, and so holy Bishops. If God (in *Leviticus*) says to all, *Thou shalt not be an Accuser, or Backbiter amongst the People;** what may we think of *Luther,* who casts such a foul Scandal, not only on one Man, but on so many, and so *venerable Prelates?* And this he whispers, not only in one City, but publishes to the whole World. If he be accursed (as in *Deuteronomy*) *who shall privately smite his Neighbour;†* with how great a Curse shall he be strucken, who

*Levit. xix. 16.   †Deut. xxvii. 24.

posturas, ad nihil omnino valere, præterquam ad per-
dendam hominum pecuniam, ac Dei fidem.

Qua in re quam non scelerate modo, verum etiam
furiose bacchatur, nemo est qui non videt. Nam si nihil
omnino valent Indulgentiæ, sed meræ sunt, ut Lutherus
ait, imposturæ, tunc necesse est impostores fuerint, non
hic tantum Pontifex Leo decimus, cujus innocens et in-
culpata vita moresque sanctissimi ab ineunte ætate per
orbem totum satis explorati sunt, quemadmodum in
epistola quadam ad Pontificem Lutherus etiam ipse
fatetur, verum etiam tot retro sæculis omnes Romani
Pontifices, qui, quod Lutherus ipse commemorat, in-
dulgere solebant, alius remissionem annuam, alius
triennem, quidam aliquot condonare quadragesimas,
nonnulli certam totius pœnitentiæ partem, tertiam puta,
vel dimidiam: aliqui demum remissionem indulserunt
et pœnæ, et culpæ plenariam. Omnes ergo, si vera dicit
Lutherus, fuerunt impostores.

At quanta magis cum ratione creditur hunc unum
fraterculum morbidam esse ovem, quam tot olim Pontifices perfidos fuisse pastores? Nam Lutherus, ut dixi,
cujusmodi vir sit, quam nihil omnino charitatis habeat,
evidentissime declarat, quum non vereatur tot summis,
tot sanctis Pontificibus tantum crimen impingere. Si
Deus in Levitico dicit omnibus: *"Non eris criminator,
nec susurro in populis,"* quid de Luthero censendum
est? qui tam immane crimen non in unum aliquem
hominem, sed in tam multos, tam venerandos spargit
antistites, idemque non in una quapiam urbe susurrat,
sed per totum buccinat orbem? Si maledictus in
Deuteronomio dicitur, qui clam percusserit proxi-
mum, quanta maledictione percutitur, qui palam
tantis opprobriis insultat in præpositos? Denique
si *"homicida est,"* ut ait evangelista, *"nec vitam
habet æternam, qui odit fratrem,"* annon hic æterna

insults over his Governors with such Reproaches? Finally, *If,* (as the Gospel says) *he be a Murtherer, and has not Life everlasting, who hates his Brother;** does not this *Parricide* deserve *everlasting Death,* who, with *Hatred pursues his Father?* Seeing he is come to that Pass, as to deny *Indulgences* to be profitable in this Life; it would be in vain for me to dispute what great Benefits the Souls in *Purgatory* receive by them: Moreover, what would it avail us to discourse with him of the great Helps, whereby we are relieved from *Purgatory* itself? Not able to endure to hear of the *Pope's* delivering any Person out of it, he presumes to leave none there himself.

What Profit is there to dispute, or fight against him, who fights against himself? What should my Arguments avail me, though I force him to confess what he before denied, since he now denies what before he confessed? But admit the *Pope's Indulgences* were disputable; yet it is necessary that the Words of *Christ* remain firm, by which he gave the Keys of the Church to St. *Peter,* when he said, *Whatsoever thou shalt bind on Earth, shall be bound in Heaven; and whatsoever thou shalt loose on Earth, shall be loosed in Heaven:†* Likewise, *Whose Sins ye forgive, shall be forgiven unto them, and whosoever Sins ye retain, shall be retained.‡* By which Words, if it is manifest that any *Priest* has Power to absolve Men from Sins, and take away eternal Punishment due thereunto; who will not judge it ridiculous, that the Prince of all *Priests* should be denied the taking away of temporal Punishment?

But perhaps some may say, that *Luther* will not admit that any *Priest* has Power of binding, or loosing any Thing; or that the Chief Bishop has any greater Power than other *Bishops* or *Priests:* But what con-

*I. John iii. 15.   †Matt. xvi. 19.   ‡John xx. 22.

dignus morte parricida est, qui odio prosequitur
patrem ?

Qui quum eousque progreditur, ut neget Indulgentias
quicquam valere in terris, frustra cum eo disputem
quantum valeant in purgatorio. Præterea quid profuerit cum illo loqui quibus subsidiis liberemur a purgatorio, qui totum ferme tollit purgatorium? Unde quum
pati non possit ut Pontifex quemquam eximat, ipse sibi
tantum sumit, ut neminem ibi relinquat. Quid attinet
cum eo pugnare, qui pugnat ipse secum ? Quid argu-
mentis promoveam si cum eo agam, ut donet quod
ante negavit, qui nunc id ipsum negat, quod ante dona-
verat ?

Verum, quantumvis disputentur Indulgentiæ Pontificis, necesse est inconcussa maneant verba Christi,
quibus Petro claves commisit Ecclesiæ, quum dixit:
"Quidquid ligaveris super terram, erit ligatum et in
cælo; et quidquid solveris super terram, erit solutum et
in cælo." Item: *"Quorum remiseritis peccata, remit-*
tentur; et quorum retinueritis peccata, retinebuntur."
Quibus verbis si satis constat sacerdotem quemlibet
habere potestatem a mortalibus absolvendi criminibus,
et æternitatem pœnæ tollendi, cui non videatur absurdum sacerdotum omnium principem nihil habere juris
in pœnam temporariam?

Verum aliquis fortasse dicet: "Lutherus ista non ad-
mittet, sacerdotem ullum quicquam ligare, vel solvere,
aut Pontificem summum plus habere potestatis, quam
alium quemvis episcopum, imo quam quemlibet sacerdotem." At quid id mea, quid admittat, aut quid non
admittat is, qui quorum nihil admittat nunc, eorum
plæraque paulo prius admisit, quique omnia nunc rejicit solus, quæ tota tot sæculis admisit Ecclesia? Nam,
ut cætera taceam, quæ novus iste Momus reprehendit,
certe Indulgentias, si Pontifices peccavere, qui conces-

cerns it me, what that Man admits, or denies, who granted many Things a while ago, which now he denies, and who, alone, rejects all Things which the *Holy Church* has held during so many Ages? For (to omit other Things which this new *Momus,* or feigned *Deity* censures) certainly if the *Popes* have erred, who granted *Indulgences;* the whole *Congregation of the Faithful* were not free from Sin, who received them for so long a Time, and with so great Content: In whose *Judgment,* and in the Custom observed by the *Saints,* I doubt not but we may rather acquiesce, than in *Luther* alone, who furiously condemns the *whole Church,* whose *Chief Bishops,* he not only loads with mad Reproaches, but also fears not to publish, that this *Supremacy of the Pope* is but a vain Name, and is effectually Nothing but the Kingdom of *Babylon,* and the Power of *Nimrod,* that strong Hunter; and desires his *Readers,* and the *Book-binders,* that (burning whatsoever he first writ of *Papacy,*) they may reserve this one Proposition, *&c.*

serunt, immunis a peccato non erat tota congregatio
fidelium, qui eas tamdiu tanto consensu susceperunt:
quorum ego judicio, et observatæ sanctorum consuetu-
dini non dubito potius acquiescendum, quam Luthero
soli, qui totam Ecclesiam tam furiose condemnat. Qui
non modo summum Pontificem conviciis insanis in-
cessit, verum etiam proclamare non veretur: *Ponti-*
ficium ipsum inane prorsus nomen esse, nec re quicquam
aliud esse censendum, quam regnum Babylonis, et
potentiam Nemrod robusti venatoris: eoque lectores
orat, orat librarios, ut omnibus, quæ prius de Pa-
patu scripsit, exustis, hanc unam propositionem
teneant.

CHAP. II

Of the Pope's Authority

Papatus est robusta Venatio Romani Pontificis.

INDEED it is no ridiculous Desire in him, to wish the
Things he writ before should be burned; because many
of them deserved it; yet much more this *Proposition,*
which he desires may be preserved after the rest are
burned, as if worthy of Eternity. What Man, if he had
not known his Malice, but would have admired his Inconstancy in this Place? For first, he denied the *Pope's
Supremacy* to be of *divine Right,* or *Law,* but allowed
it to be of *human Right:* But now, (contrary to himself) he affirms it to be of neither of them; but that the
Papacy, by mere Force has assumed, and usurped
Tyranny. Formerly he was of Opinion, That Power
was given to *Roman Bishops* over the *Universal Church*
by human Consent, and for the public Good: And so
much was he of that Opinion, that he detested the
Schism of the *Bohemians,* who denied any Obedience to
the See of *Rome;* saying, *That they sinned damnably
who did not obey the* Pope: Having written these
Things so little Time before, he now embraces what then
he detested. The like Stability he has in this: That
after he preached, in a Sermon to the People, *That Excommunication is a Medicine, and to be suffered with
Patience and Obedience;* he himself, being (for every
good Cause,) a while after *excommunicated,* was so impatient of that *Sentence,* that (mad with Rage) he
breaks forth into insupportable Contumelies, Re-

CAP. II

Papatus

Est robusta venatio Romani Pontificis.

ILLUD, hercle, non absurdum votum est, quod quæ ante scripsit, flammis optat absumi. Erant enim pleraque flammis digna: sed multo tamen ipsa propositio dignior, quam, exustis illis, jubet velut dignam æternitate substitui.

Quanquam, quis non hic quoque, nisi qui malitiam norit, miretur inconstantiam? Nam prius Papatum negaverat esse divini juris, sed humani juris esse concesserat. Nunc vero, secum dissidens, neutrius juris esse confirmat, sed Pontificem sibi mera vi sumpsisse atque usurpasse tyrannidem. Sentiebat ergo pridem, humano saltem consensu, propter bonum publicum Romano Pontifici super Ecclesiam catholicam delatam esse potestatem. Idque usque adeo sentiebat, ut Boemorum quoque schisma detestaretur, quod se ab obedientia Romanæ Sedis abscinderent; pronuncians eos peccare damnabiliter, quicumque Papæ non obtemperarent. Hæc quum haud ita pridem scripserit, nunc in idem quod tum detestabatur, incidit.

Quin istud quoque similis est constantiæ: quod quum in concione quadam ad populum excommunicationem doceat esse medicinam, et obedienter patienterque ferendam, paulo post excommunicatus ipse, idque meritissimo jure, sententiam tamen tam impotenter tulit, ut rabie quadam furibundus in contumelias, convicia, blasphemias, supra quam ullæ possint aures ferre,

proaches and Blasphemies: So that by his Fury, *it*
plainly appears, that those who are driven from the
Bosom of their *Holy Mother the Church,* are immediately seized, and possessed with *Furies,* and tormented
by *Devils.* But I ask this; he that saw these Things so
short a while since, how is it that he becomes of Opinion,
that then he saw Nothing at all? What new Eyes has
he got? Is his Sight more sharp, after he has joined
Anger to his wonted *Pride,* and has added *Hatred* to
both? Does he see farther with these so excellent
Spectacles?

I will not wrong the Bishop of *Rome* so much, as
troublesomely, or carefully to dispute his Right, as if
it were a Matter doubtful; it is sufficient for my present
Task, that the Enemy is so much led by Fury, that he
destroys his own Credit, and makes clearly appear, that
by mere Malice he is so blinded, that he neither sees,
nor knows what he says himself. For he cannot deny,
but that all the Faithful honour and acknowledge the
sacred *Roman* See for their Mother and Supreme, nor
does Distance of Place or Dangers in the Way hinder
Access thereunto. For if those who come hither from
the *Indies* tell us Truth, the *Indians* themselves (separated from us by such a vast Distance, both of Land and
Sea,) do submit to the See of *Rome.* If the Bishop of
Rome has got this large Power, neither by Command of
God, nor the Will of Man, but by main Force; I would
fain know of *Luther,* when the *Pope* rushed into the
Possession of so great Riches? for so vast a Power, (especially if it begun in the Memory of Man,) cannot
have an obscure Origin. But perhaps he will say, it is
above one or two Ages since; let him then point out the
Time by Histories: Otherwise, if it be so antient that
the Beginning of so great a Thing is quite forgot; let
him know, that, by all Laws, we are forbidden to think

proruperit sic, ut suo furore plane perspicuum fecerit
eos qui pelluntur gremio matris Ecclesiæ statim Furiis
corripi, atque agitari dæmonibus.

Sed istud rogo: qui illa tam nuper vidit, unde nunc
subito videt nihil se tunc vidisse? Quos novos oculos
induit? An acutiore cernit obtutu, postquam ad superbiam solitam ira quoque supervenit, et odium? Et
longius videlicet prospicit, usus tam præclaris con-
spiciliis?

Non tam injurius ero Pontifici, ut anxie ac sollicite
de ejus jure disceptem, tanquam res haberetur pro
dubia. Satis est ad præsens negotium, quod inimicus
ejus ita furore provehitur, ut sibi fidem deroget ipse, ac
dilucide se ostendat præ malitia neque constare secum,
neque videre quid dicat. Nam negare non potest quin
omnis Ecclesia fidelium sacrosanctam Sedem Romanam
velut matrem primatemque recognoscat ac veneretur,
quæcumque saltem neque locorum distantia, neque periculis interjacentibus prohibetur accessu. Quanquam,
si vera dicunt qui ex India quoque veniunt huc, Indi
etiam ipsi, tot terrarum, tot marium, tot solitu-
dinum plagis disjuncti, Romano tamen se Pontifici
submittunt.

Ergo si tantam ac tam late fusam potestatem, neque
Dei jussu Pontifex, neque hominum voluntate consecutus est, sed sua sibi vi vendicavit, dicat velim Lutherus quando in tantæ ditionis irrupit possessionem.
Non potest obscurum initium esse tam immensæ poten-
tiæ, præsertim si intra memoriam hominum nata
sit. Quod si rem dixerit unam fortassis aut duas
ætates superare, in memoriam nobis rem redigat ex
historiis.

Alioqui, si tam vetusta sit, ut rei etiam tantæ oblit-
erata sit origo, legibus omnibus cautum esse cognoscit,
ut cujus jus omnem hominum memoriam ita super-

otherwise, than that Thing had a lawful Beginning, which so far surpasses the Memory of Man, that its Origin cannot be known. It is certain, that, by the unanimous Consent of all Nations, it is forbidden to change, or move the Things which have been for a long Time immoveable. Truly, if any will look upon antient Monuments, or read the Histories of former Times, he may easily find, that since the Conversion of the World, all Churches in the Christian World have been obedient to the See of *Rome.* We find, that, though the Empire was translated to the *Grecians,* yet did they still own, and obey the *Supremacy* of the Church, and See of *Rome,* except when they were in any turbulent *Schism.*

St. *Hierome* excellently well demonstrates his good Esteem for the *Roman* See, when he openly declares, (*though he was no* Roman *himself,*) *that it was sufficient for him that the Pope of* Rome *did but approve his Faith, whoever else should disapprove it.*

When *Luther* so impudently asserts, (and that against his former Sentence,) *That the Pope has no Kind of Right over the* Catholic Church; *no, not so much as human; but has by mere Force tyrannically usurped it;* I cannot but admire, that he should expect his Readers should be so easily induced to believe his Words; or so blockish, as to think that a *Priest,* without any Weapon, or Company to defend him, (as doubtless he was, before he enjoyed that which *Luther* says he usurped,) could ever expect or hope, without any Right or Title, to obtain so great a Command over so many *Bishops,* his Fellows, in so many different, and divers Nations. How could he expect, I say, that any Body would believe, (as I know not how he could desire they should,) that all Nations, Cities, nay Kingdoms and Provinces, should be so prodigal of their Rights and Liberties, as to acknowledge the Superiority of a strange

greditur, ut sciri non possit cujusmodi habuerit initium, censeatur habuisse legitimum; vetitumque esse constat omnium consensu gentium, ne, quæ diu manserunt immota, moveantur.

Certe si quis rerum gestarum monumenta revolvat, inveniet jam olim, protinus post pacatum orbem, plerasque omnes Christiani orbis Ecclesias obtemperasse Romanæ. Quin Græciam ipsam, quanquam ad ipsos commigrasset imperium, reperiemus tamen, quod ad Ecclesiæ primatum pertinebat, præterquam dum schismate laborabat, Ecclesiæ Romanæ cessisse. Beatus vero Hieronymus quantum Romanæ Sedi censeat deferendum vel inde luculenter ostendit, quod quum Romanus ipse non esset, tamen aperte fatetur sibi satis esse, si suam fidem, quibusvis improbantibus aliis, comprobaret Papa Romanus.

Cui quum Lutherus tam impudenter pronunciet, idque contra suam pridem sententiam, nihil omnino juris in Ecclesiam catholicam, ne humano quidem jure, competere, sed Papam mera vi meram occupasse tyrannidem, vehementer admiror quod aut tam faciles, aut tam stupidos speret esse lectores, ut sacerdotem credant inermem, solum, nullo septum satellitio, qualem fuisse eum necesse est, priusquam eo potiretur, quod eum Lutherus ait invasisse, vel in spem venire unquam potuisse, ut nullo jure fultus, nullo fretus titulo, in tot ubique pares episcopos, apud tam diversas, tam procul disjectas gentes, tantum obtineret imperium. Nedum ut credat quisquam populos omnes, urbes, regna, provincias, suarum rerum, juris, libertatis fuisse tam prodigos, ut externo sacerdoti, cui nihil deberent, tantum in sese potestatis darent, quantum ipse vix esset ausus optare.

Sed quid refert quid in hac re Lutherus sentiat, qui præ ira atque invidia non sentit ipse quid sentiat, sed

Priest, to whom they should owe no Subjection? But
what signifies it to know the Opinion of *Luther* in this
Case, when (through Anger and Malice,) he himself is
ignorant of his own Opinion, or what he thinks? But
he manifestly discovers the Darkness of his Understanding and Knowledge, and the Folly and Blindness of his
Heart, abandoned to a reprobate Sense, in doing and
saying Things so inconsistent. How true is that saying of
the Apostle? *Though I have Prophecy, and understand
all Mysteries, and all Knowledge; and though I have
all Faith, so as to remove Mountains, and have not
Charity, I am Nothing.** Of which Charity *Luther* not
only shews how void he is, by perishing himself through
Fury; but much more by endeavouring to draw all
others with him into Destruction, whilst he strives to
dissuade them from their Obedience to the Chief
Bishop, whom, in a three-fold Manner, he himself is
bound to obey, *viz.* as a *Christian,* as a *Priest,* and as a
religious Brother; his Disobedience also deserving to be
punished in a treble Manner: He remembers not *how
much* Obedience is better than Sacrifice;† not does he
consider how it is ordained in *Deuteronomy, That the
Man that will do presumptuously, and will not hearken
unto the Priest, (that stands to minister there before
the Lord thy God,) or unto the Judge, even that Man
shall die:‡* He considers not, I say, what cruel Punishment he deserves, that will not obey the chief *Priest*
and supreme Judge upon Earth. For this poor Brother,
being cited to appear before the *Pope,* with Offers to pay
his Expences, and Promise of safe Conduct; he refuses
to go without a Guard; troubling the whole Church as
much as he could, and exciting the whole Body to rebel
against the Head; which to do, *is as the Sin of Witch-
craft;* and in whom to acquiesce, *is as the Sin of Idol-*

*I. Cor. xiii. 2. †I. Kings xv. 22. ‡Deut. xvii. 12.

bene declarat *offuscatam scientiam suam, et cor ipsius insipiens obscuratum, traditumque in reprobum sensum, ut faciat ac dicat ea quæ non conveniunt.* Quam verum est illud Apostoli : *"Si habuero prophetiam, et noverim omnia mysteria, et omnem scientiam, et si habuero omnem fidem, ita ut montes transferam, charitatem autem non habuero, nihil sum !"* A qua quam longe abest iste, non illud tantum ostendit, quod præ furore perit ipse, sed istud multo magis, quod universos secum trahere conatur in perditionem, dum omnes ab obedientia summi Pontificis laborat avertere : cui ipse triplici vinculo tenetur astrictus, utpote Christianus, sacerdos, et postremo fraterculus, tripliciter a Deo vicissim puniendus.

Neque meminit quicquam, quanto *melior est obedientia quam victimæ.* Neque considerat, si in Deuteronomio cavetur ut *qui superbierit, nolens obedire sacerdotis imperio, qui pro tempore ministrat Domino Deo suo, et decreto judicis, moriatur,* quam atroci sit supplicio dignus is, qui sacerdoti omnium summo, eidemque supremo in terris judici non paruerit. Nam et quum vocaretur ad Pontificem, oblatis expensis, et data fide, venire tamen fraterculus, nisi munitus præsidio, contempsit ; et jam, quoad potest, totam perturbat Ecclesiam, corpusque totum sollicitat ad rebellandum capiti, *cui quasi peccatum ariolandi est repugnare, et quasi scelus idolatriæ nolle acquiescere.*

Quamobrem quum Lutherus, odio provectus, se præcipitet in perniciem, et legi Dei recuset esse subjectus, suam nimirum quærens constituere, nos vicissim Chris-

*atry.** Seeing therefore that *Luther,* (moved by Hatred)
runs head-long on to Destruction, and refuses to submit
to the Law of God, but desires to establish a Law of his
own; *it behoves all Christians to beware, lest* (as the
Apostle says) *through the Disobedience of one, many be
made Sinners;*† but on the contrary, by hating and de-
testing his Wickedness, we may sing with the Prophet,
I hated the wicked, and loved your Law.‡

*I. Kings xv. 23.   †Rom. v. 19.   ‡Ps. cxviii. 113.

ticolæ caveamus ne, quod Apostolus ait, *"per inobedi-
entiam unius hominis peccatores constituti simus
multi;"* sed illius iniquitatem perosi, Domino cum
propheta canamus: *"Iniquos odio habui, legem autem
tuam dilexi."*

CHAP. III

The Defence of the Seven Sacraments

But these two Chapters, (of abrogating *Indulgences,* and taking away all Authority of the chief Bishop,) of which we have already given our Opinion; tho' they are wicked, yet are they but the Flourishings or first Essays of *Luther,* who now begins to murder and destroy the *Sacraments,* which in his Book he goes about to do; all which whole Book, he confesses to be but a Flourish, to I know not what Work: I suppose it is some Work, in which he intends to fight more seriously against our most holy *Faith,* yet I much admire he should think to compose any Thing whatsoever, more stuffed with Venom, than is this whole Preface, or Flourish of his: In which of *seven Sacraments,* he leaves us but *three,* nor them neither, unless for a Time; giving us to understand, that he shall soon also take *them* from us; for of the three, he takes away one immediately after in the same Book; whereby he plainly shews us what he intends to do with the rest.

To which Undertaking it seems he prepares the Way, when he says, *That if he would speak according to Scripture, he would leave but one Sacrament and three Sacramental Signs.* If any one do but diligently examine how he handles these three *Sacraments,* (which, for the present, he puts as three *Sacraments,* or under three Signs) he may perceive that he treats of them in such a Manner, as that none should doubt, but that when he sees his own Time, and at his own Pleasure, he intends wholly to deprive us of them all.

CAP. III.

De Sacramentis

At ista duo capita de tollendis prorsus Indulgentiis, et auferenda potestate summi Pontificis, de quibus quid nobis videtur exposuimus, quantumvis impia sint, Lutheri tamen non nisi præludia sunt ad Sacramenta perimenda, quod toto agit libro. Quem librum totum fatetur præludium, ad operis, opinor, quippiam, in quo decrevit serio moliri totius expugnationem fidei. Quanquam vehementer admiror, si quicquam edet unquam tam serium, ut plus tumere veneno queat, quam totum hoc turget præludium. In quo protinus, ex sacramentis septem, tantum relinquit tria, nec ea tamen, nisi pro tempore, nimirum significans illa etiam ipsa propediem sese sublaturum: nam e tribus unum aufert paulo post eodem libro, quo plane declaret quid proponet in reliquis.

Quam in rem viam etiam videtur præstruere, quum ait se, si Scripturarum more loqui velit, non nisi unum sacramentum, et tria signa sacramentalia positurum. Quod si quis diligenter inspiciat quo pacto tractet hæc tria sacramenta, quæ, seu tria, seu, tribus sub signis, unum ponit pro tempore, videbit ea sic ab illo tractata, ut nemini relinquat dubium id illum in animo moliri, ut omnia tria possit suo rursus tempore prorsus amoliri.

Let the *Reader* diligently observe his Steps, and look to his own, that he may discover the Subtilties of this Serpent; and let him not, with too much Security, thrust himself amongst these Thorns, Brambles, and Dens, but warily walk round his Caverns, fearing lest he should secretly strike his mortal Sting into his Heel: This hideous Monster being caught, will become benumbed, and pine away by his own Venom.

CHAP. IV

The Sacrament of the Altar

LET us therefore begin where he began himself, with the adorable *Sacrament* of *Christ's Body.* The changing of the Name thereof, calling it, *The Sacrament of Bread,* shews that this Man cannot well endure, that we should be put in Mind of *Christ's Body,* by the Name of the *Blessed Sacrament;* and that, if under any fair Pretext, it were possible for him, he would give it a worse Name. How much differs the Judgment of St. *Ambrose* from this Man's, when he says, *Though the* Form *of the* Bread *and* Wine *is seen upon the Altar, yet we must believe, that there is Nothing else but the* Body *and* Blood *of Christ:* By which Words it clearly appears, that St. *Ambrose* confesses no other Substance to remain with the *Body and Blood of Christ in the Sacrament,* when he says, *That which is seen under the Form of* Bread *and* Wine, *is Nothing else but the* Body *and* Blood *of Christ.* If St. *Ambrose* had only said *Flesh* and *Blood,* without adding any Thing more, perhaps *Luther* would have said, that the *Bread* and *Wine* were there also; as *Luther* himself says, *That the Substance of the* Flesh *is with the* Bread, *and the Substance of the*

Quas colubri istius astucias quo facilius, lector, possis deprehendere, observa diligenter singula vestigia ejus, et suspende gressus tuos, neque nimium securus inter vepres ac tribulos, latebras et speluncas ejus obambula, ne, ex occulto insidiatus, calcaneo tuo exitiale virus instillet. Deprehensus enim torpebit ignavus, et suo ipse veneno tabescet.

CAP. IV

De Sacramento Eucharistiæ

INCIPIAMUS ergo, unde ipse incepit, a venerabili sacramento corporis Christi. Cujus primo quod nomen mutet, ac vocari velit sacramentum panis, indicat hominem non valde bene ferre, quod ipso sacramenti nomine admoneamur corporis Christi, et sicubi reperire colorem potuisset, quo nomen dare potuisset deterius, libenter fuisse daturum. Cujus ab animo perquam longe dissidet ac dissentit beatus Ambrosius, quum dicit: "Licet figura panis et vini in altari videatur, nihil tamen aliud, quam caro et sanguis Christi, credenda est." Ex quibus verbis evidentissime clarescit Ambrosium fateri nullam aliam substantiam cum Christi corpore manere permixtam, quum dicat nihil aliud esse quam corpus et sanguinem Christi id quod figura panis videtur, et vini. Si tantum dixisset Ambrosius: caro et sanguis, potuisset fortasse Lutherus dicere quod Ambrosius, fatendo esse carnem et sanguinem, non negaret tamen panem simul esse ac vinum; quemadmodum Lutherus ipse dicit carnis substantiam cum pane, et sanguinis una cum vino subsistere. Sed quum Ambrosius dicat nihil esse aliud, quam carnem et sanguinem, aperte contradicit Luthero,

Blood *along with the* Wine: But seeing St. *Ambrose* says, *That there is Nothing else but the Flesh and Blood,* it appears that he is manifestly against *Luther,* who affirms, *That the* Bread *is with the* Flesh, *and the* Wine *with the* Blood.

And though this which *Luther* says, were as true as it is false, *viz. That the* Bread *should remain mingled with the* Body *of Christ;* yet was it not necessary for him to blot the Name of the *Body of Christ* out of the *Sacrament,* in which he confesses that the *true* Body *of Christ is.* For if the Substance of *Bread* should be with the *Body of Christ,* (as he contends,) yet there is no Reason that the inferior Substance should take away the Name from the more worthy: Because, though the Apostle, (conforming himself to the Understanding of the Auditors, then ignorant People,) called it *Bread;* yet now, after the Faith has been so long established, it was not fit or convenient to change this so adorable a Name, (which represents to the Hearers, the Thing in the *Sacrament,*) into such a Name as would have turned their Minds from the *Body* to the *Bread;* neither would *Luther,* without Doubt, have changed it, if he had not determined with himself to draw the People to worship the *Bread,* and leave out *Christ's Body;* from which he himself is divided; concerning which, I shall presently speak more fully.

The Sacrament of the Eucharist under One Form only Administered to the Laity

In the mean while, let us truly examine how subtilely, under Pretence of favouring the *Laity,* he endeavours to stir them up to an Hatred against the *Clergy:* For when he resolved to render the Church's Faith suspicious, that its Authority should be of no Consequence against him; (and so, by opening that Gap, he might

qui simul cum carne dicit esse panem, et simul cum sanguine vinum.

Quanquam si id, quod Lutherus dicit, tam verum esset quam falsum est, pane cum Christi carne simul manere permixtum, tamen ne sic quidem necesse fuit Luthero delere nomen corporis Christi ex sacramento in quo fatetur verum Christi corpus esse. Nam si panis etiam substantia simul cum Christi corpore adesset, quemadmodum iste contendit, non est tamen ratio cur inferior substantia nomen præripiat digniori. Nam etsi rudibus adhuc populis, ad auditorum captum se demittens Apostolus panem vocavit, nunc tamen tamdiu stabilita fide, nomen tam venerabile, quod rem sacramenti repræsentet audientibus, in id nomen, quod auditorum animos a corpore in panem averteret, non oportebat immutari. Nec immutasset haud dubie Lutherus, nisi secum statuisset populum paulatim a Christi corpore, a quo ipse jam præcisus est, in panis venerationem traducere, qua de re paulo post dicemus uberius.

De Sacramento Eucharistiæ sub Una Tantum Specie Laicis Ministrato

INTERIM vero libet excutere quam fraudulenter per speciem favoris in laicos conetur eorum odium concitare in sacerdotes. Nam quum decrevisset Ecclesiæ fidem suspectam reddere, ne quid ponderis ejus haberet auctoritas, atque ita facta via, præcipua quæque Christianæ religionis evertere, ab ea re sumpsit initium, cui popu-

destroy the chiefest Mysteries of Christianity,) he began with that Thing, which he foresaw would be praised and applauded by the People: For he touched the old Sore, by which *Bohemia* had been formerly blistered, *viz. That the Laity ought to receive the* Eucharist *under both Kinds.* When first he began to handle this Point, he only said, *That the* Pope *would do well, to have it ordained by a general Council, that the* Laity *should receive the* Sacrament *under both Kinds;* but that being by some disputed with him, and denied, he contented not himself to stop there, but grew to such a perverse Height, that he condemned the whole *Clergy* of Wickedness, *for not doing it without staying for any Council.* For my Part, I do not dispute the first: And though to me, no Reason appear why the Church should not ordain, that the *Sacrament* should be administered to the *Laity,* under both Kinds; yet doubt I not, but what was done in Times past, in omitting it, and also in hindering it to be so administered now, is very convenient. Nor can I believe the whole Clergy, (during so many Ages,) to have been so void of Sense, as to incur eternal Punishment for a Thing by which they could reap no temporal Good. It further appears not to be a Thing of any such Danger; because God, not only bestowed Heaven upon those Men, who did this Thing themselves, and writ that it ought to be done; but likewise would have them honoured on Earth, by those by whom he is adored himself: Amongst whom (to omit others,) was that most learned and holy Man *Thomas Aquinas,* whom I the more willingly name here; because the Wickedness of *Luther* cannot endure the Sanctity of this Man, but reviles with his foul Lips, him whom all *Christians* honour. There are very many, though not canonized, who are contrary to *Luther's* Opinion in this; and to whom, in Piety and Learning, *Luther* is in no wise comparable:

lum sperabat alacriter applausurum. Tetigit enim
vetus ulcus, quo pridem ulcerata est Boemia, *quod laici
sub utraque specie non recipiant Eucharistiam.* Eam
rem quum prius ita tractasset, ut duntaxat diceret recte
facturum Pontificem, si curaret communi concilio statu-
endum ut sub utraque specie laici communicarent, post,
ubi nescio quis illud ei negavit, non contentus in eo
manere, quod dixerat, sic profecit in pejus, ut totum
clerum condemnet impietatis, quod istud non faciant,
non expectato concilio.

Ego de primo non disputo. Cæterum, etiam si causas
non viderem, cur non decernat Ecclesia ut utraque
species ministretur laicis, tamen dubitare non possem
quin sint idoneæ quæ et olim fecerunt ut id omitteretur,
et nunc quoque faciunt ne redintegretur. Nec plane
assentior totum clerum per tot sæcula fuisse tam stolidum, ut se obstrinxerit æterno supplicio propter eam
rem, unde nihil reportaret commodi temporalis: imo
vero, quam nihil sit talis periculi, vel hoc evidenter
ostendit, quod eos qui non tantum istud fecerunt, verum
etiam qui scripserunt esse faciendum, Deus non modo
suscepit in cœlum, verum etiam voluit esse venerandos
in terris, et ab hominibus honorari, a quibus honoratur
ipse. Inter quos fuit (ut de aliis interim taceam) vir
eruditissimus, et idem sanctissimus divus Thomas
Aquinas, quem ideo libentius commemoro, quoniam ejus
viri sanctitatem Lutheri ferre non potest impietas, sed
quem omnes Christiani venerantur, pollutis labiis
ubique blasphemat. Quanquam sunt permulti, qui,
etiam si pro sanctis recepti non sunt, tamen, sive doctrina, sive pietate spectentur, tales sunt, ut Lutherus eis
comparari non possit, qui hac in re contrarium Luthero

Among whom are the Master of the *Sentences, Nicholas de Lyra,* and many others; to each of whom it behoves all Christians to give more Credit, than to *Luther.*

But pray observe how *Luther* staggers, and contradicts himself: In one Place, he says, *That Christ, in his last Supper, not only said to all the Faithful, as permitting, but as commanding, Drink ye all of this:** Yet afterwards, (fearing to offend the Laity, whom he flatters, with a View to stir up their Hatred against the Priests,) he adds these Words, *not that they, who use but one Kind do sin against Christ, seeing Christ did not command to use any Kind, but left it to every Man's Discretion, saying,* As often as ye do this, do it in Remembrance of me: *But,* says he, *they sin who forbid to give both Kinds to such as are willing to receive them: The Blame,* says he, *lies on the* Clergy, *and not on the* Laity. You see how clearly he first holds it for a Command, and then says, it is no Commandment, but a Thing left to every Man's Discretion. What need we contradict him, who so often contradicts himself?

And yet before, when he speaks of all, in general, he does not defend the *Laity* well, if any Body would urge the Matter: And he proves no Sin to be in the *Priests,* whom he accuses most bitterly: *For,* he says, *the Sin consists in the* Priest's *taking the Liberty of one Kind from the* Laity: If any Body should ask him here, how he knows that Custom to have been practised against the People's Will? I believe he cannot tell it. Why then does he condemn the whole *Clergy,* for having taken the *Laity's* Right from them by Force, seeing he cannot by any Testimony prove that this was forcibly done? How much more reasonable should it be, to say, that the Consent of the People did concur with this Custom for so

*Matt. xxvi. 27.

sentiunt. Inter quos sunt Magister sententiarum, et Nicolaus de Lira, et complures alii, quorum cuilibet magis expedit Christianos omnes, quam Luthero, credere.

At vide, quæso, quam vacillat ac sibi repugnat Lutherus. Uno loco dicit Christum in Cœna omnibus omnino fidelibus, non permittendo, sed præcipiendo dixisse: *"Bibite ex eo omnes."* Postea vero timens ne laicos, quibus in sacerdotum odium adulatur, offenderet, hæc verba subjungit: "Non quod peccent in Christum qui una specie utuntur, quum Christus non præceperit ulla uti, sed arbitrio cujuslibet reliquerit, dicens: *Quotiescunque hæc feceritis, in mei memoriam facietis;* sed quod illi peccant, qui hoc arbitrio volentibus uti prohibent utramque dari, culpa non est in laicis, sed in sacerdotibus." Videtis aperte, quod primo dixit esse præceptum, hic dicit non esse præceptum, sed cujuslibet arbitrio relictum. Quid opus est ergo nos illi contradicere, qui sibi toties contradicit ipse?

Et tamen quum dixit omnia, laicos non satis defendit, si quis rem urgeret, et in sacerdotibus, quos tam atrociter accusat, nihil probat esse peccati. Nam in eo dicit totum esse peccatum, quod sacerdotes alterius speciei laicis invitis adimerent libertatem. Hic igitur si quis eum percontetur qui sciat istum ritum inolevisse renitente populo, non potest, opinor, docere. Cur ergo totum condemnat clerum, quod laicis invitis ademerit suum jus, quum id invitis esse factum nullo possit documento probare? Quanto fuit æquius, si, nisi volentibus illis, recte nequivit institui, pro nunciare, pro tot sæculorum consuetudine, plebis intervenisse consensum? Ego certe, qui video quas res a plebe clerus obtinere non potest, ne tantum quidem, quin ferme sub ipso altari

many Ages, if it could not be justly established but with their Pleasure? For my Part, when I see what Things the *Clergy* cannot obtain from the *Laity*, (not even an Exemption from burying their Dead almost under their *Altars*) I cannot easily believe that they should suffer themselves to be injuriously, and by Force, deprived of any such great Part of their Rights; but that rather this was instituted for some reasonable Causes, and with the Consent of the *Laity*.

What I most admire, is, that *Luther* should be so angry and passionate, for having one Kind taken away from the *Laity* in the *Communion;* but is Nothing at all moved that Children should be debarred from both: For he cannot deny, but that Children, in the primitive Times, did receive the *Communion:* Which Custom, if it was justly omitted, (though Christ said, *Drink ye all of this,**) and that, without Doubt, for very good Reasons, (though no Body can now remember them) why should we not think that it was for good and just Reasons, unknown at this Time, the primitive Custom of the *Laity*'s receiving the *Sacrament* in both Kinds, (which perhaps continued not for any considerable Time,) was taken away?

Moreover, if he examines the strict Form of the *Evangelical Narration,* and leaves Nothing in this Matter to the Church; why does he not command the *Sacrament* to be always received at Supper-time, or rather after it?

Finally, it should not be esteemed less inconvenient to do any Thing in the Manner of receiving this *Sacrament,* which ought not to be done. If therefore the Custom of the whole Church does not well, in denying to the *Laity* the *Communion* under the Form of *Wine,* by what Reason durst *Luther* put *Water* into the *Wine?*

*Matt. xxvi. 27.

suorum condant cadavera, non facile credo populum
fuisse passurum ut inviti per contumeliam, in tanta
re, ab ulla juris sui parte pellerentur, sed causis
aliquot idoneis, e laicorum quoque voluntate, consti-
tutum.

At istud miror, tam vehementer indignari Lutherum
laicis ademptam alteram, quum nihil eum permoveat,
quod utraque species adimatur infantibus: nam illos
olim communicasse nec ipse negare potest. Qui mos si
recte fuit omissus, quanquam Christus dicat: *"Bibite
ex hoc omnes,"* nec quisquam dubitat quin causæ fuerint
magnæ, etiam si nunc earum nemo meminisset, cur non
etiam cogitemus bonis justisque rationibus, quantumvis
nunc ignoratis, abolitam esse consuetudinem qua laici
olim, nec id fortasse diu, sub utraque specie solebant
recipere sacramentum ?

Præterea, si eam rem ad exactam evangelicæ narra-
tionis formam revocat, neque quicquam prorsus per-
mittit Ecclesiæ, cur Eucharistiam non jubet semper in
cœna recipi, imo vero post cœnam ?

Denique non minus incommodi fuerit in hoc sacramento facere, si quid fecisse non debeas, quam si quid
non facias, quod fecisse debueras. Ergo si totius Ecclesiæ consuetudo rectum non facit ut in laicis omittatur
species vini, qua ratione aquam in vinum audet Lutherus infundere ? Neque enim tam audacem puto, ut
sine aqua consecret, quam tamen ut admisceret, neque
exemplum habet ex Cœna dominica, neque ex Apostoli

for I do not think that he is so bold as to consecrate without *Water;* yet has he no Example in our *Lord's Supper,* nor any certain one, of the *Apostles Tradition,* of mingling the *Wine* with *Water:* But he learned it only by the Custom of the Church; to which, if he thinks himself obliged to be obedient in this Part, why does he so arrogantly oppose it in the other?

Whatever *Luther* chatters concerning this Matter; for my Part I judge it more safe, to believe that the *Laity* do rightly *communicate,* though under one Kind; than that the *Clergy,* for so many Ages, were damned, for omitting both, (as he disputes;) for he calls them all wicked, *and so wicked, that they all were guilty of the Crime of* Evangelical Treason, *If* (says he) *we must name them that are* Heretics *and* Schismatics; *it is not the* Bohemians, *or* Græcians, *(for they endeavour to follow the* Gospel) *but the* Romans *who are the* Heretics *and* Schismatics, *and, by their Fictions, presume against the evident Truth of Scripture.*

If *Luther* admits Nothing else, but the evident and plain Text of Scripture, why does he not (as I said) command the *Eucharist* to be received at *Supper-time?* For the *Scriptures* mention that Christ did so. How much better should *Luther* believe, that this Institution of the Church, in giving the *Communion* to the *Laity* under one Kind, was done by the Authority of God, not by any human Invention, as it was by God's Authority instituted that it should be received when the People are fasting: For as St. *Augustin* says, *It has pleased the Holy Ghost, that the Body of our Lord, which, by the Apostles, was received after other Meats, should, in the Church, be received fasting, before any other Meats?* It is very probable, that the *Holy Ghost,* which governs the Church of Christ, as he has changed the Time of receiving the *Sacrament,* from *Supper,* to the *Morning,*

traditione compertum, sed sola Ecclesiæ consuetudine didicit : cui si putat hac in parte parendum, cur eam in altera tam arroganter oppugnat ?

Qua de re, quicquid Lutherus obgannit, ego certe tutius opinor credere laicos recte sub altera tantum specie communicatos, quam per tot sæcula totum clerum, quod iste disputat, hac una de causa fuisse damnatum. Nam omnes appellat impios, et tales ut in crimen inciderint læsæ majestatis evangelicæ. "Quod si utri sint," inquit, "hæretici et schismatici nominandi, non Boemi, non Græci, quia evangeliis nituntur, sed vos, Romani, estis hæretici et impii schismatici, qui solo vestro figmento præsumitis contra evidentes Dei Scripturas."

Si Lutherus nihil admittit aliud quam evidentes Dei Scripturas, cur non jubet Eucharistiam, uti dixi, sumi a cœnantibus ? Nam sic factum a Christo Scriptura commemorat. Quanto melius crederet Lutherus, non humano figmento, sed eodem auctore Deo factum in Ecclesia ne laici sub utraque specie reciperent Eucharistiam, quo auctore factum est ut reciperetur a jejunis ? "Placuit enim," ut ait beatus Augustinus, "Spiritui sancto, ut corpus Domini, quod post alios cibos ab apostolis in Cœna receptum est, ante alios cibos a jejunis reciperetur in Ecclesia." Videtur ergo verisimile quod Spiritus sanctus, qui Christi regit Ecclesiam, sicut Eucharistiæ sacramentum mutavit a cœnantibus ad jejunos, ita laicos ab utraque specie deduxit in alteram.

fasting, has also changed the *Laity's* receiving under both, to the *communicating* under one Kind: For he that could change the one, why could he not also alter the other.

Luther shews plainly in this Place, that his Intention is to flatter the *Bohemians,* whose Perfidiousness he before detested: For none of those, whom he calls *Papists,* and *Flatterers* of the *Pope,* do so much flatter the *Roman* Prelates, as *Luther* flatters the very Scum of the *Bohemian* Commonalty; and not without Reason indeed; for he foresees that the *Germans,* (whom he formerly deceived under the Form of a simple Sheep,) would reject him, as soon as they should perceive him to be a devouring Wolf. And therefore he insinuates himself into the Esteem of the *Bohemians,* and makes himself Friends of the *Mammon* of Iniquity* (as much as he is able,) that when he is banished his own Country, he may pass into that of those, into whose Errors he has already entered.

And that some remarkable Action may render him more commendable to them when he goes, he endeavours to extinguish all the Force and Authority of *Ecclesiastical Customs,* and so, in the Conclusion, to ruin all, if his Designs should take; which God forbid!

He aims at greater Things than he can expect to accomplish; and therefore pleads for the *Laity,* though his Thoughts are quite contrary to what he pretends; for though he sweetly offers them *Bread* in the one Hand, yet he holds a *Scourge*† for them in the other. In the first Place, he is altogether for the *Laity's* being admitted to receive under both Kinds: (And who would not think, that he thereby endeavours to increase their Devotion towards the *Sacrament?*) But look a little further what he drives at: For at last he brings his Business so far, as

*Lu. xvi. 9.　　　　　　　†Lu. xi. 11.

Nam qui alterum mutare potuit, cur non alterare potuerit et alterum ?

Hoc loco plane se ostendit Lutherus, quid agitet in animo, quum Boemos, quorum perfidiam pridem exe-crabatur, nunc tam blande vicissim demulceat. Neque enim quisquam eorum quos ille papistas appellat, et adulatores Pontificis, ita Romano blanditur antistiti, quomodo Lutherus etiam fæci Boemicæ plebis adulatur. Nec id tamen ab re: videt enim brevi fore ut Germani, quibus pridem per speciem ovinæ simplicitatis imposuit, agnitum tandem lupum sint ejecturi; atque ideo Boemis ante se insinuat, ac sibi, quoad potest, *amicos facit de mammona iniquitatis,* ut in quorum immigravit errores, extorris aliquando sua, illorum immigrare sinatur in patriam. Ad quos ut ob facinus aliquod insigne veniat commendatior, conatur interim ecclesiasticæ consuetu-dinis omnem vim atque auctoritatem extinguere; post, si id (quod omen avertant Superi!) feliciter ei cesserit, concussurus omnia.

Longius enim destinat, quam quo putatur tendere; atque ita causam agit laicorum, ut longe meditetur aliud, quam præ se fert: quibus quantumvis blande por-rigat altera manu panem, altera tamen gestat scor-pionem. Nam multis primum verbis agit ut laici per-mittantur utramque speciem sumere. Et quis nunc non credet hoc eum conari, ut laicorum cultum erga sacra-mentum adaugeat? Verum paulisper observa quo tendat: nam tandem sic rem totam claudit, ut id quoque permitti postulet, ne laici communicare cogantur in Paschate, neve ullum eis sumendæ Eucharistiæ tempus indicatur, sed liber quisque suo relinquatur arbitrio; imo vero, ut ne sæpius in tota vita quisquam sumat, quam semel, idque non ante extremum vitæ diem, qui et

to desire, that they may not be obliged to receive at *Easter;* and that no Time may be appointed them for receiving, but that every Man may be left to his own Discretion; nay further, *That none should receive more than once, in his whole Life, and that at the Day of his Death;* which is uncertain, and at which many are not able to receive. So, he that pretended to stand for the *communicating* under both Kinds, recommends the quite Contrary, to wit, *That it may be lawful for them never to receive under* any Kind; and he esteems it an excellent Liberty, that the People may be altogether freed from receiving the *Sacrament at all.*

Wherefore, though this *Serpent* seems to flatter you with an amiable Aspect; yet that venomous Tail of his seeks to sting you: For he makes it plainly appear, that he is more concerned for the People's receiving under one Kind, than for their abstaining from both. And even as the old *Serpent,* being cast out of Heaven, envyed Man's Happiness in *Paradise;* so *Luther,* being fallen, by his own Sin, under the Penalty of *Excommunication,* (and thereby deprived of the wholesome and life-giving *Communion* under both Kinds,) endeavours to entrap all others in the same Snare; in Order, that, being freed from the Obligation of receiving under both Kinds, they may, by little and little, bring themselves under no Kind at all. And the further you advance in reading his Libel, the more you will discover this detestable Fetch of his.

About Transubstantiation

He makes it a second Captivity, that any Man should be forbidden to believe, that the true *Bread* and true *Wine* remain after Consecration: So that in this, (con-

incertus est, et quum ad eum ventum est, sumere
plerique non sustinent. Ita, qui videbatur id agere, ut
laici recipere sinerentur utrumque, id oblique procurat,
ut impune liceat ne speciem unquam quisquam sumat
ullam; et hanc præclaram libertatem ducit, ut populus
in toto a suscipiendo sacramento liberetur!

Quamobrem utcumque serpens amico blandiatur
aspectu, certe venenata ista cauda spiculum quærit in-
figere, facitque perspicuum hoc magis illum torquere,
quod populus alteram speciem recipiat, quam quod
altera abstineat. Nam quemadmodum serpens antiquus,
ejectus e cœlo, invidit homini Paradisum, ita Lutherus
quoque, postquam sua culpa sic in excommunicationis
incidit laqueum, ut utriusque speciei salubri communione privetur, reliquos omnes eodem laqueo cupit
implicare, ut utriusque recipiendæ vinculo soluti, neutram paulatim assuescant recipere. Quod illius ex-
secrandum propositum, quo magis in libello progrederis,
eo magis magisque pellucet.

De Transsubstantiatione

Nam secundam Captivitatem facit, quod quisquam
vetetur credere verum panem verumque vinum restare
post consecrationem. Qua in re contra quam totus jam

trary to the Belief of the whole Christian World, both
now, and for so many Ages past,) he endeavours to per-
suade, that the *Body* and *Blood* of Christ are after such
a Manner in the *Eucharist,* that the Substance of true
Bread and true *Wine* remains still after Consecration.
I suppose, afterwards, when it pleases him, he will deny
the Substance of the *Body* and *Blood* to be there, when
he has a Mind to change his Opinion, as he has three
Times done already; and yet he feigns that he teaches
those Things, *as being moved with Pity towards the
Captivity of the* Israelites, *in which they are kept Slaves
to* Babylon. Thus he calls the whole Church, *Babylon,*
and the Faith of Christ, *Slavery:* And this merciful
Man offers Liberty to all those, who will divide themselves from the Church, and become corrupted with the
Infection of this rotten and separated Member: But it
is worth our While to know by what Means he invites
People to this more than servile Liberty.

He esteems this to be his greatest and chiefest Reason,
to wit, *That Scripture is not to be forced, either by Men
or Angels; but to be kept in the most simple Signification that can be: And* (says he) *unless for some manifest Circumstances requiring, it is not to be taken otherwise than in its proper and grammatical Sense; lest
Occasion should be given to the Adversaries to under-
value the whole Scriptures: But* (says he) *the Divine
Words are forced, if that which* Christ *called* Bread, *be
taken for the Accidents of* Bread; *and what he called*
Wine, *for the Form of* Wine: *Therefore, by all Means,
the true* Bread *and true* Wine *remain upon the Altar,
lest Violence be done to* Christ's *Words, if the* Species
be taken for the Substance. *For,* (says he) *seeing that
the* Evangelists *so plainly write, that* Christ *took* Bread,
and blessed it; and, afterwards, in the Book of the
Acts, *and by* Paul, *it is called* Bread, *we ought to take*

credit Christianus orbis, ac multis retro sæculis credidit, persuadere conatur Lutherus in Eucharistia sic esse Christi corpus et sanguinem, ut tamen substantia veri panis verique vini remaneat; posthac, opinor, quum libebit, corporis aliquando substantiam sanguinisque negaturus, tanquam post in melius mutata sententia, quemadmodum ter ante jam fecit, nempe in Indulgentiis, in potestate Pontificis, et communione laicorum. Interea se fingit ista docere, motum videlicet misericordia captivitatis, qua populus Israeliticus serviat Babyloni. Ita totam Ecclesiam appellat Babylonem; Ecclesiæ fidem vocat servitutem, et homo misericors offert libertatem omnibus qui velint ab Ecclesia separari, et istius putridi et abscisi membri contagione corrumpi. At quibus modis invitat in hanc plus quam servilem libertatem, operæ pretium est cognoscere.

Magnam censet ac primariam rationem, quod verbis divinis non est ulla facienda vis neque per hominem, neque per angelum, "sed quantum fieri potest," inquit, "in simplicissima significatione servanda sunt, et, nisi manifesta circumstantia cogat extra grammaticam et propriam, accipienda non sunt, ne detur adversariis occasio universam Scripturam eludendi. At vis," inquit, "fit verbis divinis, si, quod Christus ipse vocat panem, hoc nos dicamus intelligi panis accidentia, et, quod ille vinum vocat, hoc nos dicamus esse tantum vini speciem. Omnibus ergo modis verus panis, ac verum vinum restat in altari, ne verbis Christi fiat vis, si species sumatur pro substantia. Nam quum evangelistæ clare scribant," inquit, "Christum accepisse panem, ac benedixisse, et Actuum liber, et Paulus panem deinceps appellent, verum oportet intelligi panem verumque vinum, sicut

it for true Bread, *and true* Wine, *as a true Chalice.
For they do not say themselves, that the Chalice is
transubstantiated.*

This is *Luther*'s great, and (as he says) his chief
Reason; which I hope so to handle, as to give all Men
to understand, of how little Consequence it is. For in
the first Place, though the *Evangelists* had plainly said,
what he says they did; yet that does not prove any Thing
clearly for him; but on the Contrary, they say nothing
in any Place that may seem to favour his Side. *Do not
they write* (says he) *that he took* Bread, *and blessed it?*
And what does that argue? We confess he took Bread,
and blessed it; *But that he gave* Bread *to his Disciples,
after he had made it his Body,* we flatly deny; and the
Evangelists do not say he did: That this may more evidently appear, and that there may be less Room left for
Wrangling; let us hear the *Evangelists* themselves:

St. *Mathew*'s Words are these, *While they were at Supper, Jesus took* Bread *and blessed it, and brake it, and
gave it to his Disciples, saying, take, and eat, this is my*
Body: *And taking the Chalice, he gave Thanks, and
gave it to them, saying, drink ye all of this; This is my*
Blood *of the New Testament, which is shed for many,
for the Remission of Sins.** But St. *Mark*'s Words are
these, *And while they were eating, Jesus took* Bread,
*and blessed and brake it, and gave to them, and said,
take, eat, This is my* Body: *And when he had taken the
Chalice, and given Thanks, he gave it to them; and
they all drank of it: And he said unto them, This is my*
Blood *of the new Testament which is shed for many.*†
St. *Luke* has it after this Manner, *And he took* Bread,
*and gave Thanks, and brake it, and gave unto them,
saying, This is my* Body *which is given for you: This
do in Remembrance of me; likewise also the Chalice,*

*Matt. xxvi. 26-29.   †Mk. xiv. 22-24.

verum calicem. Non enim calicem transsubstantiari etiam ipsi dicunt."

Hæc est ergo magna, et, quemadmodum ait ipse, primaria Lutheri ratio, quam ego me spero facturum ut omnes quam primum intelligant nihil magni habere momenti. Nam primum id, quod ait evangelistas clare dicere, quantumvis clare dicant, pro Luthero tamen nihil clare probat; contra vero, quod pro illo probaret, hoc nusquam dicunt. "An non scribunt," inquit, "accepisse panem, et benedixisse?" Quid tum postea? Accepisse panem et benedixisse etiam nos fatemur; panem vero dedisse discipulis, postquam inde suum corpus confecerat, hoc et nos instanter negamus, et evangelistæ non dicunt.

Quæ res quo fiat apertior, et tergiversandi minus pateat locus, evangelistas ipsos audiamus. Matthæus ergo sic narrat: *"Cœnantibus autem eis, accepit Jesus panem, et benedixit, ac fregit, deditque discipulis, et ait: Accipite, et comedite, hoc est corpus meum. Et accipiens calicem, gratias egit, et dedit illis dicens: Bibite ex hoc omnes; hic est sanguis meus novi testamenti, qui pro multis effundetur in remissionem peccatorum."* Marci vero verba sunt ista: *"Et manducantibus illis, accepit Jesus panem, et benedicens fregit, et dedit eis, et ait: Sumite, hoc est corpus meum. Et accepto calice, gratias agens dedit eis; et biberunt ex illo omnes, et ait illis: Hic est sanguis meus novi testamenti, qui pro multis effundetur."* Lucas denique narrat hoc pacto: *"Et accepto pane gratias egit, ac fregit, et dedit eis, dicens: Hoc est corpus meum, quod pro vobis tradetur: hoc facite in meam commemorationem. Similiter et calicem, postquam cœnavit, dicens: Hic est*

after Supper, saying, This Chalice is the New Testament of my Blood, *which is shed for you.**

In all these Words of the *Evangelists,* I see none, where, after the Consecration, the *Sacrament* is called *Bread* and *Wine;* but only *Body* and *Blood.* They say, *That Christ took* Bread *in his Hands,* which we all confess; but when the Apostles received it, it was not called *Bread,* but *Body.* Yet *Luther* endeavours to rest the Words of the *Gospel,* by his own Interpretation. *Take, eat; this,* that is, *this Bread,* (says he, which he had taken and broken,) *is my Body.* This is *Luther's* Interpretation; not Christ's Words, nor the Sense of his Words. If he had given to his Disciples the *Bread* which he took, as he took it; without converting it into *Flesh,* before he bad them (in giving it) *take and eat;* it had been rightly said, that he gave what he took in his Hands; for then he had given Nothing else: But seeing he turned the *Bread* into his *Flesh,* before he gave it the Apostles to eat; they now receive, not the *Bread* which he took, but his *Body,* into which he had turned the *Bread;* as if one who had taken Seed, should give to another the Flower sprung thereof: He would not give what he had taken, though the common Course of Nature had made the one of the other. So likewise, much less did Christ give the Apostles what he took in his Hand, when, by so great a Miracle, he turned the *Bread* which he took, into his own *Body;* unless, perhaps, some will say, because *Aaron* took a Rod in his Hand, and cast a Rod from him,† that the Substance of the Rod remained with the *Serpent,* and the Serpent's Substance with the Rod, when it was restored again: If the Rod could not remain with the *Serpent,* how much less can the *Bread* remain with the *Flesh* of Christ, that incomparable Substance?

*Lu. xxii. 19, 20.   †Ex vii. 12.

calix novum testamentum in sanguine meo, qui pro vobis fundetur."

Ex omnibus his evangelistarum verbis nullum video locum, in quo post consecrationem sacramentum vocetur panis aut vinum, sed tantum corpus et sanguis. Dicunt in manus Christum sumpsisse panem, id quod etiam nunc fatemur omnes; at quum reciperent apostoli, non panis nominatur, sed corpus. At Lutherus evangelistæ verba in suam partem conatur interpretatione torquere: *"Accipite, manducate, hoc,"* id est, hic panis, inquit is, quem acceperat et fregerat, *"est corpus meum."* Sed hæc est interpretatio Lutheri, non verba Christi, neque verborum sensus. Si panem quem accepit, quemadmodum accepit, sic tradidisset discipulis, nec ante convertisset in carnem, ac porrigendo dixisset: *Accipite, et manducate,* recte diceretur porrexisse quod in manus acceperat: nihil enim fuisset aliud, quod porrigeretur. At quum, priusquam daret Apostolis manducandum, panem convertit in carnem, non jam accipiunt panem, quem ille susceperat, sed corpus ejus, in quod panem converterat. Quemadmodum si quis, quum semen accepisset, alii daret inde natum florem, non id dedisset, quod acceperat, quanquam naturæ communis ordo alterum fecisset ex altero, ita multo minus porrexit apostolis id quod in manus acceperat Christus, quum panem susceptum in suam ipse carnem tanto vertisset miraculo: nisi quis contendat, quoniam Aaron virgam sumpsit in manum, et virgam projecit e manu, ideo cum colubro quoque virgæ restitisse substantiam, aut colubri denuo cum recepta virgula. Quod si cum colubro virga restare non potuit, quanto minus restare potest panis cum carne Christi tam incomparabili substantia?

As for what *Luther* argues, or rather trifles, to shew the Simplicity of his own Faith; when of the *Wine,* Christ does not say, *Hoc, est Sanguis meus,* but, *Hic, est Sanguis meus:* I wonder why it should enter into any Man's Mind to write thus: For who sees not that this makes Nothing at all for him, nay, rather, does it not make against him? It had seemed more for his Purpose, if Christ had said, *Hoc est Sanguis meus:* For then he might have had some Colour at least, whereby he might have referred the *Article of Demonstrating* to the *Wine.* But now, though *Wine* is of the *neuter Gender;* yet *Christ* did not say *Hoc,* but *Hic est Sanguis meus.* And though *Bread* is of the *masculine Gender,* yet, notwithstanding, he says, *Hoc est Corpus meum,* not *Hic;* that it may appear, by both *Articles,* that he did not mean to give either *Bread* or *Wine,* but his own *Body* and *Blood.* Is it not very ridiculous, that *Luther* should imagine this Pronoun *Hoc,* not to be by Christ's Intention referred to the *Body,* but only for the Conveniency of the *Greek* and *Latin* Tongues; and therefore sends us back to the *Hebrew?* For the *Hebrew,* if it has not the *neuter Gender,* cannot so conveniently declare to what *Christ* has referred this *Article,* as the *Greek* or *Latin* can do.

For though in the *Hebrew,* the *Article* should be of the *masculine Gender,* that is, *Hic est Corpus meum;* nevertheless, the Matter would be left doubtful, because that Speech might seem forced by the Necessity of the Language, which has no *neuter Gender.* But because *Bread* and *Body* are of different *Genders* in the *Latin;* he that translated it from the *Greek* should have joined the *Article* with *Panis,* if he had not found that the *Evangelical* Demonstration was made of the *Body.* Moreover, when *Luther* confesseth that the same Difference of Gender is in the *Greek,* he might easily know

Nam quod argutatur, imo nugatur Lutherus pro suæ simplicitate fidei facere, quum de vino dicat Christus, non: *Hoc* est *sanguis meus,* sed *Hic* est *sanguis meus,* miror quid homini venerit in mentem, quum istud scriberet. Quis enim non videt quam nihil omnino facit pro eo? Imo contra, videretur magis pro eo fecisse si dixisset Christus: *Hoc* est *sanguis meus;* habuisset enim ansam saltem Lutherus, qua demonstrandi articulum referret ad vinum. Nunc vero quum vinum sit neutri generis, Christus ait, non: *Hoc,* sed *Hic* est *sanguis meus;* et quum panis sit generis masculini, ait tamen: *Hoc* est *corpus meum,* non *Hic,* ut uterque ostendat articulus Christum neque panem propinare, neque vinum, sed suum ipsius corpus, et sanguiuem.

Nam quod videri vult Lutherus pronomen *hoc* ad corpus referri, non Christi proposito, sed occasione linguarum, nempe latinæ et græcæ, ac proinde nos remittit ad hebraicam, annon ridiculum est? Nam hebræa lingua si neutrum genus non habet, non potest tam aperte declarare ad utrum Christus retulit articulum, quam latina, vel græca. Nam in hebræa lingua si articulus fuisset masculus, tanquam diceret: *Hic* est *corpus meum,* tamen res relinqueretur ambigua, quia potuisset ea locutio videri coacta necessitate linguæ non habentis neutrum. Sed quum apud Latinos panis et corpus sint diversi generis, is qui transtulit e græca articulum conjunxisset cum pane, nisi apud evangelistam reperisset demonstrationem factam de corpore. Præterea, quum Lutherus fateatur idem generis discrimen esse et

that when the *Evangelists* writ in *Greek*, they would have put in the Article relating to the Bread, if they had not known our Lord's Mind; but they were willing to teach the *Christians*, by the Article relating to the *Body*, that, in the Communion, Christ did not give Bread to his *Disciples*, but his Body.

Wherefore, when *Luther*, to serve his own Turn, interprets the Words of *Christ*, 'take, and eat, this is my Body,' that is, this Bread he had taken; not I, but Christ himself teacheth us to understand the Contrary, to wit, That what was given them, and seemed to be Bread, was not Bread, but his own Body; if the *Evangelists* have rightly delivered us the Words of *Christ*: For otherwise he should say, not *Hoc*, that it might be expounded for *Hic*,) but, more properly, *Hic Panis est Corpus meum*: By which Saying he might teach his *Disciples*, what *Luther* now teaches to the whole Church, to wit, 'That in the Eucharist the Body of *Christ*, and the Bread are together.' But our Saviour spoke after that Manner, that he might plainly manifest, that only his Body is in the Sacrament, and no Bread.

How magnificently *Luther* brings in this for his Argument, 'That Christ speaks of the Chalice, which no body holds to be transubstantiated!' I admire the Man is not ashamed of so unmeasurable a Folly. When Christ says, *This Chalice of the New Testament is my Blood*, what does that make for *Luther*? For what else does it signify, but that what he gave his Disciples to drink, was his own *Blood*? Will *Luther* make appear, by those Words of *Christ*, that the *Substance* of *Wine* remains, because Christ speaks of *Blood*? Or that the *Wine* can-

Græcis, facile potuisset cognoscere evangelistas, qui
scripserunt græce, articulum fuisse posituros, qui refer-
retur ad panem, nisi quod conscii mentis dominicæ,
voluerunt admonere Christianos articulo corporis,
Christum non panem communicasse discipulis, sed
corpus.

Quamobrem quod Lutherus interpretatur in suam
partem verba Christi: *"Accipite et manducate, hoc est
corpus meum,"* id est, *hic panis* quem acceperat, non ego,
sed ipse Christus, contra docet sua verba intelligi, nempe
hoc, quod eis porrigebat, non esse quod ipsis videbatur
panem, sed suum ipsius corpus (si recte Christi verba
recensent evangelistæ). Nam alioqui poterat dicere,
non: *Hoc,* quod exponeretur id est *Hic,* sed aperte
potius: *Hic panis est corpus meum;* quo sermone doce-
rentur discipuli id quod nunc Lutherus docet Ecclesiam,
nempe in Eucharistia pariter et Christi esse corpus, et
panem. Nunc vero sic locutus est, ut ostenderet manifeste corpus duntaxat, non panem.

Item quod tam magnifice transfert ad se Lutherus
quod Christus etiam loquitur de calice, quem nemo dicat
esse transsubstantiatum, miror hominem non pudere
tam intemperantis ineptiæ. Quum dicit Christus: *"Hic
calix novi testamenti in meo sanguine,"* quid facit pro
Luthero? Quid enim significat aliud, quam id, quod
discipulis propinabat in calice, suum esse sanguinem?
An ex his Christi verbis ostendet nobis Lutherus manere
vini substantiam, quia Christus loquitur de sanguine,
aut vinum in sanguinem non posse mutari, quia adhuc

not be changed into *Blood,* because the *Chalice* is still
there? I wish he had chosen to himself some other
Matter in which he might have played and sported with
less Danger. For when he so much excuses the *Bohemians* and *Greeks* from *Heresy;* as to call all the *Roman
Catholics* Heretics, he shews himself to be a worse
Heretic than either of those; who not only deny the
Faith which the whole *Church* believes, but also persuades People to believe worse than the *Greeks* or *Bohemians* ever did. I have thus far disputed these Things,
that I might make appear, that what he brags himself
to make out, cannot be shewn by the Words of *Christ,*
and the *Evangelists;* nay in them the quite contrary is
very clear, to wit, that *Bread* is not in the *Eucharist.*

Luther speaks of the Eucharist's being called *Bread,*
in the *Acts* of the *Apostles:* I desire he would shew us
the Place: For my Part, I find none that is not ambiguous, and which seems not rather to speak of a common
Banquet, than the *Sacrament.* Yet I confess the *Apostle*
speaks more than once of *Bread,* following the Custom
of *Scripture* (which sometimes calls a Thing, not by the
Name of what it is, but of what it was before; as when
it says, *the Rod of* Aaron *devoured the Rods of the*
Magicians;* which then were not Rods, but Serpents) or
else perhaps content to call it what in Species it appeared to be; deeming it sufficient to feed the People
with Milk,† who as yet were but inexpert in Faith; and
at first to exact Nothing of them, but even to believe that
the Body of *Christ* was, after any Manner whatsoever,
in the Sacrament; but afterwards, by little and little,
to feed them with more solid Meat, as they gathered
more Strength in *Christ.* He might as well have also
touched, in the *Acts* of the *Apostles,* at that Place where
St. *Peter,* speaking to the people, and insinuating into

*Ex vii. 12.   †Heb. v. 12.

restat calix? Utinam præludium delegisset sibi Lutherus ex alia materia, in qua minore periculo potuisset ludere. Nam quum Boemos et Græcos sic excuset ab hæresi, ut hæreticos clamet omnes esse Romanos, multo magis ostendit se Lutherus hæreticum, qui non solum fidem abnegat, quam tota credit Ecclesia, sed etiam deteriora credi suadet, quam aut crediderunt Græci, aut unquam credidere Boemi.

Hactenus ista disserui duntaxat, ut ostenderem ex ipsius Christi verbis et evangelistarum ostendi non posse quod iste se jactat ostendere, imo contra liquere perspicue in Eucharistia panem non esse.

Quod in Actis apostolorum ait Eucharistiam appellari panem, vellem protulisset locum: ego nullum reperio, qui non sit ambiguus, et potius videatur de communi convivio dicere, quam sacramento. Apostolus tamen, fateor, panem non semel appellat, vel Scripturæ secutus in sermone morem, quæ solet interdum vocare quippiam, non id quod est, sed quod ante fuerat, ut quum ait: *"Virga Aaron devoravit virgas magorum,"* quæ tamen tunc virgæ non erant, sed serpentes; vel contentus fortasse vocare quod specie præ se ferebat, quum satis haberet rudem adhuc in fide populum lacte pascere, nec primum aliud exigere, quam ut quocumque modo crederent in sacramento esse corpus Christi: postea paulatim solidiore cibo pasturus, postquam adolevissent in Domino. Idem potuit et in apostolorum Actis contingere, ubi nec beatus Petrus alloquens populum, et illis Christi fidem insinuans, ausus est adhuc aperte quicquam de ejus divinitate dicere; ita abdita, et populis dubia mysteria non temere proferebant! At Christus apostolos suos, quos tamdiu sua doctrina formaverat, ipso sacramenti instituendi principio docere non dubi-

them the Faith of *Christ;* yet durst not as yet say any
Thing openly of his Divinity: So cautious were they then
of exposing rashly the sacred Mysteries to the People.
But *Christ* made no Difficulty to teach his *Apostles,*
(whom he had for so long Time instructed in his own
Doctrine,) the very first Time he instituted the blessed
Sacrament, that the Substance of Bread and Wine remained no longer in the Sacrament; but that the Forms
of both remaining, the Substance was changed into his
Body and Blood: Which he so plainly taught, that it is
a very strange Thing that any Body should ever after
call in Question a Thing so clear in itself.

For how could he have more properly said, that no
Bread and Wine remain in the Sacrament, than when he
said, *This is my Body?* for he did not say, *my Body is in
this,* or, *with this which you see, is my Body;* as if it
should consist in the Bread, or with the Bread; but *this*
(says he) *is my Body,* manifestly declaring, (to shut the
Mouth of every yelping Fellow) what he then gave, to
be his Body. And though he had called what he gave to
the *Apostles,* by the Name of Bread, (which he did not)
yet, when he should teach them that were present, that
what he called Bread, was no other Thing but his Body,
(into which, by his Will, the Bread was changed) none
could doubt what *Christ* would have us understand by
the Name of Bread. And that very Circumstance (for
Luther admits Circumstances) evidently declares, that
the Word Bread, when the Bread is turned into Flesh,
signifies, (without any Violence to the Text,) the
Species, not the Substance of Bread; unless *Luther* will
stick so closely to the Propriety of Words, as to believe,
that *Christ* was wheaten, or barley Bread in Heaven;
because he says of himself, *I am the Bread which descended from Heaven;** or that he was a Vine laden

*John vi. 41.

tavit, panis vinique non amplius restare substantiam,
sed manente utriusque specie, utrumque tamen, et
panem, et vinum in corpus et sanguinem suum esse conversum. Quod tam aperte docuit, ut plane mirandum
sit exortum quemque postea, qui rem tam claram rursus
vocaret in dubium.

Quomodo enim potuisset apertius dicere nihil illic
remanere panis, quam quum dixit: *"Hoc est corpus
meum?"* Non enim dixit: *In hoc* est corpus meum,
aut: *Cum hoc,* quod videtis, est corpus meum, tanquam
in pane, aut simul cum pane consisteret, sed: *"Hoc est,"*
inquit, *"corpus meum,"* nimirum declarans manifeste,
ut os cujusque gannientis obstrueret, hoc totum, quod
porrigebat, ipsius corpus esse. Quod ita porrectum
apostolis, etiamsi, quod non fecit, nomine panis appellas-
set, tamen, quum simul admoneret audientes idipsum,
quod vocaret panem, nihil aliud esse, quam suum
corpus, in quod totus fuerat, ipso mutante, conversus,
nemo potuisset dubitare quid Christus vellet panis appellatione significare; eoque circumstantia ipsa (nam
circumstantiam Lutherus admittit) declarat evidenter
vocabulum panis, quum panis mutatur in carnem absque
ulla violentia facta verbo divino, panis significare
speciem, non substantiam: nisi Lutherus adeo inhæreat
proprietati verborum, ut Christum credat in cœlis
quoque fuisse panem triticeum, aut hordeaceum, propterea quod ipse dicit de se: *"Ego sum panis, qui de cœlo
descendi;"* aut veris uvis onustam vitem, quia dixit
ipse: *"Ego sum vitis vera et Pater meus agricola est;"*

with real Grapes, because he said, *I am the true Vine,
and my Father is the Husbandman;** or that the Elect
shall be rewarded in Heaven with corporal Pleasures,
because *Christ* said, *I dispose unto you a Kingdom, as
my Father has disposed unto me; that ye may eat and
drink at my Table in my Kingdom.*†

Luther takes a deal of Pains to confute the Arguments
of the *Neoteries,* by which they endeavoured to maintain and prove Transubstantiation, by philosophical
Reasons, out of *Aristotle*'s School; in which he troubles
himself more than is requisite: For the Church does not
believe it, because they dispute it so to be; but because
She believed so from the Beginning, and that none
should stagger about it, decreed that all should so believe.   They therefore exercise their Wit with philosophical Reasons, that they may be able to teach that no
absurd Consequence can follow that Belief; or that the
Change of Bread into a new Substance, does not necessarily leave, but take away the former.

Luther says, 'This Doctrine of Transubstantiation, is
risen in the Church within these three Hundred Years;
whereas before, for above twelve Hundred Years, from
Christ's Birth, the Church had true Faith: Yet all this
while was there not any Mention made of this prodigious (as he calls it) Word Transubstantiation.'   If
he strives thus only about the Word, I suppose none will
trouble him to believe Transubstantiation; if he will
but believe, that the Bread is changed into the Flesh,
and the Wine into the Blood; and that Nothing remains
of the Bread and Wine but the Species; which, in one
Word, is the Meaning of those who put in the Word
Transubstantiation.   But after the Church decreed that
to be true, (though this were the first Time it should
be ordained) yet if the Antients did not believe the Con-

*John xv. 1.   †Lu. xxii. 29, 30.

aut electos denique remunerandos in cœlo voluptate corporea, propterea quod Christus ait: *"Ego dispono vobis,
sicut mihi disposuit Pater meus, regnum, ut edatis et
bibatis super mensam meam in regno meo."*

Lutherus multus est in destruendis Neotericorum ar-
gumentis, quibus defendere nituntur, et probare Transsubstantiationem rationibus petitis ex Aristotelica
schola: qua in re videtur plus laboris insumere quam
res exigat. Neque enim ideo credit Ecclesia, quia sic
illi disputant, sed quia sic Ecclesia jam inde ab initio
credidit, et, ne quis vacillet, ita credendum esse decrevit: ideo illi rationibus etiam philosophicis exercent in-
genium, quibus utcumque docere possint, quod ex tali
fide nihil sequatur absurdum, aut conversio panis in
substantiam novam necessario tollat, ac non relinquat
priorem.

Nam quod Lutherus ait hanc fidem Transsubstantiationis jam intra trecentos annos proximos esse natam,
quum prius a Christo plus annis mille ducentis Ecclesia
recte crediderit, nec interim de Transsubstantiatione
tam portentoso, ut ait ille, vocabulo mentio unquam ulla
sit facta, si de vocabulo tantum litiget, nemo erit,
opinor, illi molestus, ut credat Transsubstantiationem,
modo credat panem sic esse conversum in carnem, et
vinum in sanguinem, ut nihil neque panis remaneat,
neque vini, præter speciem, quod ipsum uno verbo
volunt quicumque ponunt Transsubstantiationem. At
istud postquam Ecclesia verum esse decrevit, etiamsi
nunc primum decerneret, tamen, si veteres non credidere
contrarium, quanquam de ea re nunquam ante quisquam
cogitasset, cur non obtemperaret Lutherus Ecclesiæ
totius præsenti decreto: persuasus id nunc tandem reve-

trary, although none should ever think of that Thing before; why should not *Luther* be obedient to the present
Decree of the whole Church, as persuaded that this is
revealed now at length to the Church, which was hidden
· before? For as the Spirit inspires where he is willing;* so likewise he inspires when he pleases.

But this is no such Thing, as *Luther* feigns, when he
says, 'this Doctrine of Transubstantiation is risen up
within three hundred Years.' Yet let it not vex him to
allow us four hundred Years; for I think it is so many
since *Hugo de Sancta Victore* writ a Book of the Sacraments, in which, though not the Word *Transubstantiation* itself, yet the Sense of his Words you may find to
be of the same Effect. 'Though this Sacrament (says
he) is but one, yet three different Things are proposed
in it; to wit, the visible Form, the real Presence of the
Body, and Virtue of spiritual Grace.' You see how he
puts down the Accidents of Bread, not the Substance;
and the true Substance of the Body, not the Form; and
more plainly a little further: 'For what we see is the
Species of the Bread and Wine; but what we believe to
be under that Form, is the very Body of Christ which
hung on the Cross, and the very Blood which flowed
from his Side.' He is yet clearer in another Place,
where he says, 'by the Word of Sanctification, the true
Substance of Bread and Wine is turned, or changed into
the true Body and Blood of *Christ,* only the Form of
Bread and Wine remaining, and the Substance passing
into another Substance.' By this, then, it appears, that
this Doctrine of *Transubstantiation* is somewhat more
antient than *Luther* pretends it to be. But, for the better Confirmation of this, we will shew, that what he
thinks to be risen within three hundred Years, was the
Faith of the holy Fathers above a thousand Years ago:

*John iii. 8.

latum Ecclesiæ, quod ante latuisset? *Spiritus* enim, sicut *ubi vult spirat,* ita spirat et quando vult.

Nunc vero non est istud tam novum, quam fingit Lutherus: qui quum hanc Transsubstantiationis fidem natam esse dicat ab annis hinc trecentis, ne gravetur, quæso, concedere saltem quadringentos; totidem enim opinor effluxisse post editum ab Hugone de Sancto-Victore librum de sacramentis, in quo Transsubstantiationis, etsi non verbum, rem certe, et sententiam reperias. Ait enim hoc pacto: "Jam quum unum sit sacramentum, tria ibi discreta proponuntur, species videlicet visibilis, et veritas corporis, et virtus gratiæ spiritualis." Vides ut speciem ponat panis, non veritatem, veritatem corporis, non speciem. Et paulo post apertius: "Quod enim videmus, species est panis et vini; quod autem sub specie illa credimus, verum corpus Christi est, et verus sanguis Jesu Christi, quod pependit in cruce, et qui fluxit de latere." Item alio loco multo adhuc manifestius, quum ait: "Verbo sanctificationis vera panis, et vera vini substantia in verum corpus et sanguinem Christi convertitur, sola specie panis et vini remanente, et substantia in substantiam transeunte."

Clarum est igitur hanc Transsubstantiationis fidem antiquiorem esse aliquanto, quam fingit Lutherus. At ut eum astringamus fortius, ostendemus quod ille natum videri vult intra annos trecentos, fidem fuisse sanctissimorum Patrum ab annis hinc plus mille. Constat enim ante annos plus mille sic credidisse fideles, ut faterentur totam panis vinique substantiam in Christi corpus et

For it is certain, that the Faithful, for above a thousand Years past, did believe the Substance of Bread and Wine to be truly changed into the Body and Blood of *Jesus Christ:* Which makes me wonder that *Luther* is not ashamed of himself, to say, that this Belief of *Transubstantiation* has not been in the Church above three hundred Years. Who knows not that *Eusebius Emissenus* dyed above six hundred Years since? who, as if dreading the Broaching of such false Opinions said, 'Let all Doubt or Ambiguity of Unfaithfulness be put away: For he that is the Author of the Gift, is also the Witness of the Truth; now the invisible Priest converteth, by his secret Power, the visible Creatures into his own Body and Blood; saying, take and eat, this is my Body.' Does not this holy Man say, most plainly, that the Substance of the Bread and Wine is changed into the Substance of the Body and Blood? What could be said more to the Purpose, than this of St. *Augustine?* 'We honour, (says he) invisible Things, *viz.* the Flesh and Blood in the visible Form of the Bread and Wine:' He does not say, in the Bread and Wine, but in the Form of the Bread and Wine. *Luther* denies that the Form of Bread is to be called Bread; and does he think that St. *Austin* should call that the Form of Bread, which is the true Substance of Bread?

Likewise St. *Gregory Nissenus* says, 'That before the Consecration, it is but Bread; but when it is consecrated by Mystery, it is made, and called the Body of *Christ.*' His saying that it is so, before the Consecration, gives us to understand, that it is not so after the Consecration. *Theophilus* also, expounding the Words, *Hoc est, &c.* This is my Body, *&c.* says, 'This, which now I give, and you receive. For the Bread is not a Figure only of the Body of *Christ,* but is changed into the proper Body of the Flesh and Blood of Christ;' and a while after, 'If we did see, says he, the Flesh and Blood of *Christ,* we

sanguinem veraciter esse conversam. Quo magis miror non pudere Lutherum, quum dicat hanc fidem Transsubstantiationis intra annos natam esse trecentos. Eusebium Emissenum quis nescit ante annos plus sexcentos esse defunctum? Qui quasi veritus olim fore, qui talia molirentur, tot annis jam præteritis clamavit: "Recedat," inquit, "omne infidelitatis ambiguum, quoniam quidem qui auctor est muneris, ipse est etiam testis veritatis. Jam invisibilis sacerdos visibiles creaturas in substantiam corporis et sanguinis sui secreta potestate convertit, ita dicens: *Accipite, et comedite, hoc est corpus meum;* et repetita benedictione: *Accipite et bibite, hic est sanguis meus."* Nonne hic vir sanctissimus aperte dicit panis ac vini substantias in substantias corporis et sanguinis esse conversas? Quid beatus Augustinus, quum ait: "Nos autem in specie panis et vini, quam videmus, res invisibiles, id est carnem et sanguinem, honoramus?" Quid potest apertius dici? Non enim dicit *in pane et vino,* sed *in specie panis et vini.* Lutherus negat panem appellandum esse quod tantum sit species panis, et putat Augustinum fuisse vocaturum speciem panis id quod esset panis vera substantia!

Gregorius item Nyssenus: "Panis," inquit, "est ante consecrationem, sed, ubi consecratur mysterio, fit et dicitur corpus Christi." Quod ait esse ante consecrationem, hoc designat post consecrationem non esse. Quin Theophilus quoque declarans hæc verba: *hoc est corpus meum,* "hoc," inquit, "quod nunc do, et quod nunc sumitis. Non autem panis figura tantum est corporis Christi, sed in proprium Christi corpus transmutatur." Et paulo post ait: "Si carnem et sanguinem cerneremus, sumere non sustineremus: propter hoc Dominus, nostræ infirmitati condescendens, species

could not endure to eat them: Therefore our Lord condescending to our Weakness, preserves the Forms of the Bread and Wine; but changeth the Bread and Wine into his own true Flesh and Blood.' *Luther* is here, by this good and learned Man, twice beaten down: For first he teaches, that *that* Article, *Hoc,* is not to be understood as *Luther* interprets it; *Hoc,* that is, *Hic Panis;* but *Hoc,* that is, This which now I give, and ye take: Secondly, he plainly says, that the Form of the Bread and Wine remains, and that the Substance is changed into the Body and Blood. But what else do they mean, who use the Word *Transubstantiation,* than what *Theophilus* said, not within three hundred Years, for he was dead some hundred Years before the Word *Transubstantiation* was used? What need I mention St. *Cyril,* who not only affirms the same Thing, but almost in the same Words? 'For God, (says he) condescending to our Frailties, lest we should abhor Flesh and Blood on the holy Altars, infuseth the Force of Life into what is offered, by changing them into the Truth of his own proper Flesh.' Moreover, that none should say that the antient Fathers believed the Body of *Christ* in such Manner, to be in the Eucharist, as that the Bread should still remain; not only those Things which I have related, do fully evince, (as plainly they do) but likewise what we have above related out of St. *Ambrose,* when he said, 'that although the Form of Bread and Wine is seen, nevertheless we are to believe that there is nothing else after the Consecration, but the Body and Blood of *Christ.'*

You see how the Holy Father says, 'That it is not only the Body and Blood; but that there is nothing besides them, although the Bread and Wine seem to be there.' And he that speaks this, has not said it within three hundred Years past, in which *Luther* feigns that this Belief of *Transubstantiation* is risen; but he spoke it above a thousand Years ago:

panis et vini conservat; sed panem et vinum in veritatem convertit carnis et sanguinis." Hic vir piissimus,
idemque doctissimus bis premit Lutherum; nam primum illum articulum *hoc* docet, non quomodo Lutherus
docet exponendum, *hoc,* id est *hic panis,* sed *hoc,* id est
id quod nunc ego do, et quod vos sumitis; deinde dicit
aperte panis et vini non nisi species esse conservatas,
substantias ipsas in corpus et sanguinem esse conversas.
At quid aliud volunt, qui ponunt Transsubstantiationem, quam quod hic ait Theophilus, non intra trecentos hos annos proximos, quippe qui defunctus est
aliquod annorum centenariis prius quam Transsubstantiationis vocabulum nasceretur? Quid beatum Cyril-
lum commemorem? Qui non tantum dicit idem, sed
ferme etiam eodem modo? Ait enim: "Ne horreremus
carnem et sanguinem apposita sacris altaribus, condescendens, Deus, fragilitatibus nostris, infundis
oblatis vim vitæ, convertens ea in veritatem propriæ
carnis."

Præterea, ne quis dicat antiquos Patres credidisse
sic in Eucharistia corpus esse Christi, ut tamen remaneat panis, non ista tantum obstant, quæ diximus (quæ
tamen obstant apertissime), sed illud præterea, quod
supra diximus ex Ambrosio, quum ait: "Licet figura
panis et vini videatur, nihil tamen aliud, quam caro
Christi, et sanguis post consecrationem credendum est."

Videtis ut beatissimus Pater dicat non tantum corpus
esse et sanguinem, sed etiam nihil esse præterea, licet
panis et vinum esse videatur. Et istud qui dicit, non
intra trecentos annos proximos hoc dixit, intra quos
hanc Transmutationis fidem exortam esse fingit Lutherus, sed dixit ante annos plus mille.

Neither can I believe that any of the antient Fathers would have approved that fine Comparison of *Luther*'s, viz. of *Iron joined with the Fire*. For none ever said that Iron is so converted into Fire, that the Form only remains, the Substance of the Iron being changed into that of the Fire; which was the Opinion of all the Ancients concerning Bread and the Flesh of *Christ;* or if, perhaps, any one Person was of a contrary Sentiment, *yet one Swallow makes no Summer:* And that Man, who ever he was, is rather to be excused for not perfectly seeing through a Matter, at that Time not in Dispute, than to be imitated, contrary to the Belief of all the rest of the whole Church, and of so many Ages, in a Thing which he, if a good Man, and now alive, without Doubt, would not argue against: For that Man that has so much Esteem for the Body of *Christ,* as he ought to have, will more easily consent that any other two Substances should remain together, than that any other Body remain, mixed with the adorable Body of *Christ;* seeing there is no Substance worthy to be mixed with that Substance which created all Substances.   Moreover, I suppose that the primitive Fathers would as little approve that Comparison of *Luther,* by which he intends to prove, that the Bread remains with the Flesh, as God did remain with Man in the Person of *Christ:* For as the most learned and the most holy of the ancient Fathers confess, in divers Places, that the Bread is changed into Flesh; so none of them were so wicked or ignorant, as to think that the Humanity was changed into the Divinity; unless perhaps *Luther* will devise a new Person, that as God took on him the Nature of Man, so God and Man take the Nature of Bread, and Wine; which if he believes, he shall be accounted an Heretic, by all those who are not Heretics.

Nec ego certe veterum fere sanctorum Patrum quemquam puto fuisse probaturum concinnam istam Lutheri
similitudinem ferri cum igne conjuncti; nam nemo unquam dixit ferrum sic in ignem converti, ut tantum
ferri species relinquatur, substantia ferri in ignis
mutata substantiam, quod de pane et Christi carne
veteres senserunt omnes. Aut si quis unus forte sensit
aliter, tamen neque una hirundo facit ver; et ille, quisquis fuerit, potius excusandus est, quod in re tum non
satis excussa parum perviderit, quam contra cæterorum
omnium, contra totius Ecclesiæ, contra tot ætatum
fidem sequendus, in quam ipse quoque, quisquis fuerit,
modo bonus fuerit, si nunc viveret, dubio procul fuerat
concessurus. Nam quisquis beatissimum Christi corpus
sic, ut debet, existimat, facilius assentietur quascumque
duas substantias simul manere conjunctas, quam ullum
corpus aliud manere commixtum cum venerando corpore
Christi. Neque enim ulla substantia digna est, quæ
cum ea misceatur substantia, quæ substantias omnes
condidit.

Præterea olim Patribus opinor multo adhuc minus
fuisse placituram illam Lutheri collationem, qua sic
vult panem simul restare cum carne, sicut restabat in
una Christi persona Deus cum homine. Nam ut passim
veterum quisque Patrum doctissimus atque sanctissimus fatetur panem mutari in carnem, ita nemo tam
impius erat, aut inscius, ut humanitatem converti
senserit in divinitatem: nisi forte novam nobis per-
sonam fingat Lutherus, ut, quomodo Deus assumpsit
hominem, ita Deus et homo assumant panem et vinum;
quod si credat, habebitur, opinor, hæreticus apud omnes
qui non sunt hæretici.

Wherefore, (to conclude this Discourse of *Transubstantiation*) it evidently appears by *Christ's* Words, and by the Judgment of the holy Fathers, that the Faith of the Church, at this present, is true, by which it is believed, that the Substance of Bread or Wine doth not remain in the Eucharist; whence it follows, that *Luther's* Opinion, in teaching the Contrary, is false and heretical: From which Persuasion, I admire what Profit he promises the People: Is it, as *Luther* says, 'That no Body should esteem himself an Heretic, if perhaps he should be of his Opinion?' But he himself confesses, that there is no Harm in believing this, as the *Catholic* Church now believes; but on the Contrary, the whole Church takes him to be an Heretic, who is of *Luther's* Opinion: He, therefore, ought not to move any one whom he wishes well, to be of his Judgment, which is condemned by the whole Church; but rather advise those he loves, to join themselves to those whom he himself witnesses to be in no Danger. That Opinion of *Luther* is therefore false, as it is against the public Faith, not only of this Time, but also of all Ages: Nor does he free from Captivity those who believe him; but, drawing them from the Liberty of Faith, that is, from a safe Hold, (as he himself confesses) he captivates them, leading them into a Precipice, into inaccessible, uncertain, doubtful and dangerous Ways: *And he that loves Danger, shall perish therein.**

The Mass is a Good Work

AFTER this Man, who is free from any Evil, has escaped these two Captivities, which he imagines to himself; that he may not captivate his Mind to the Obedience of God, he overcomes (as he pretends) a third Captivity; and proposes a Liberty by which he may capti-

*Ecclus. iii. 27.

Quamobrem, ut aliquando finem de Transsubstantiatione faciam, ex ipsis Christi verbis et sanctorum viro-
rum sententiis evidenter liquet hanc, quam nunc tenet
Ecclesia, veram esse fidem, qua creditur panis aut vini
substantiam in Eucharistia non manere; ex qua et illud
sequitur, hoc Lutheri dogma, quod contra docet, falsum
esse prorsus et hæreticum: quo ex dogmate miror quid
fructus populo spondeat. An, quod ait ipse, ne quis
propterea semet credat hæreticum, quod fors ita cum
Luthero sentiat? At Lutherus ipse fatetur nihil esse
periculi, si quis hac in re sentiat quod tota jam sentit
Ecclesia. At contra tota Ecclesia censet hæreticum esse
eum, qui sentiat cum Luthero. Non debet ergo Lutherus
animare quemquam, cui bene cupit, ut secum sentiat,
cujus sententiam tota condemnat Ecclesia, sed debet his
suadere, quos amat, ut accedant illis, quos ipse quoque
indicat in nullo versari periculo.

Falsa est ergo ista Lutheri via contra publicam fidem,
non hujus modo temporis, sed etiam ætatum omnium,
nec liberat captivitate credentes ei, sed educens e libertate fidei, hoc est e loco tuto, quod Lutherus ipse fatetur,
captivat in errorem, ducens in præcipitium, et vias in-
vias, incertas, dubias, eoque plenas periculi; et *"qui
amat periculum, perit in illo."*

Quod Missa sit Opus Bonum

Postquam duas illas, quas ipse sibi fingit, Captivi-
tates homo in malum liber evasit, ne mentem in Dei
captivet obsequium, expugnat, ut simulat, Captivitatem
tertiam, et libertatem proponit, qua totam captivet Ecclesiam, utpote cujus lucidissimam nubem dispergere,
columnam ignis exstinguere, arcam violare fœderis,

vate the whole Church. This, worse than sacrilegious
Caitif, endeavours to scatter abroad the Church's most
splendid Congregation; to extinguish its Pillar of Fire;
to violate the Ark of the Covenant; and to destroy the
Chief and only Sacrifice which reconciles us to God,
and which is always offered for the Sins of the People:
For, as much as in him lies, he robs the *Mass* of all the
Benefits that flow from it to the People; denying it to
be a good Work, or to bring to them any Kind of Profit.
In which Thing I know not whether more to admire his
Wickedness, or his foolish Hope; or rather his mad
Pride; who, seeing so many Obstructions before him, as
he himself mentions, brings Nothing with him, whereby
to remove the least; but seems as if he would go about
to pierce a Rock with a Reed. For he sees, and confesses himself, that the Opinions of the holy Fathers
are against him, as also the Canon of the *Mass,* with the
Custom of the universal Church, confirmed by the Usage
of so many Ages, and the Consent of so many People.
What Defence then does he oppose against so innumer-
able, so powerful, and so invincible Armies? His accustomed Force rages; he strives to breed Discord, and
move Seditions, to excite the Commonalty against the
Nobility: And that he may the more easily stir them up
to a Revolt; he, by his foolish and weak Policy, falsely
pretends that he has *Christ* for Captain of the whole
Army in the Camp; and that the Trumpet of the Gospel
sounds only for him; which is the most ridiculous
Stratagem that ever was invented. For what Man living is so wicked or blockish, as to think that the Church,
which is the mystical Body of *Christ* should be in such
Manner delacerated, as that the Head should be severed
from the rest of the Members, joined together amongst
themselves; or that *Christ,* who never abandoned the
Flesh which once he took, should have cast off the

summum, atque unicum sacrificium Dei propitiatorium,
quod assidue pro populi peccatis offertur, homo plus-
quam sacrilegus conatur auferre. Nam Missam omni
fructu qui ex ea promanat in populum, pro sua virili
despoliat, quum Missam negat bonum opus esse, aut
populo quicquam prodesse. Qua in re nescio magisne
impietatem hominis admirer, an stultissimam spem, vel
potius insanam superbiam: qui quum tam multas ipse
commemoret sibi objectas obices, nihil affert secum, quo
revellat ullam, sed perinde agit, ac si rupes foret arun-
dine perfossurus.

Videt enim et fatetur obstare sibi sanctorum Patrum
sententias, Missæ canonem, totam denique totius Ecclesiæ consuetudinem, tot sæculorum usu, tot populorum consensu corroboratam. Quid ergo præsidii adversus tot acies, tam validas, tam invictas opponit?
Usitata via grassatur, laborat seminare discordiam, et
serere seditiones, plebem in patres excitare, et quo
vulgus ad defectionem provocet stultissima solertia, et
facillime coarguenda, mentitur totius exercitus ducem
Christum in suis sese castris habere, et evangelii tubam
pro se simulata canere. Quo stratagemate nullum unquam fuit excogitatum stultius. Nam quis usquam
vivit, aut tam impius, aut tam omnino stupidus, qui
Ecclesiam, corpus Christi mysticum, sic laceratam censeat, ut ubi membrorum omnium compago sit, illinc
caput putet esse divulsum? ut is qui carnem, quam
sumpsit, nunquam deseruit, Ecclesiam, propter quam
sumpsit carnem, deseruerit, et cum qua se promisit ad
finem usque sæculi permansurum, ab ea prorsus tot jam
sæculis abfuerit, atque ad Lutherum tandem, conjura-
tissimum ejus hostem, transfugerit.

Church, for whose Sake he took that Flesh; and that he should, for so many Ages, absent himself from her, with whom he promised to remain to the End of the World, and should now pass to *Luther's* Side, who is her professed Enemy? But pray let us see by what Enchantment he makes it appear for Truth, that *Christ* is on his Side, as he brags. After many idle Circumstances, he goes about to define what the *Mass* is; afterward he separates the Ceremonies of the *Mass,* from the *Mass* itself; he examines the Lord's Supper, and ponders the Words which *Christ* used in the Institution of the Sacrament of the *Mass:* And, having found in them the Word Testament, (as if a Thing very obscure,) he begins to triumph, as though he had conquered his Enemies: He beautifies with Words this his new found Mystery; (as he calls it) and with great Gravity, as if it was never heard of before, teaches us what a Testament is. He bawls aloud, 'that it is to be marked and taken notice of, that a Testament is the Promise of a dying Person, by which he bequeaths the Inheritance, and institutes Heirs: Therefore (says he) this Sacrament of the *Mass,* is no other Thing than the Testament of *Christ;* and the Testament is Nothing but the Promise of the eternal Heritage giving his Body and Blood to us Christians, whom he appointed for his Heirs, as a Sign for the ratifying his Promise:' This he repeats over and over again; he inculcates, and fixes it; intending to make it his immoveable Foundation whereon to build Wood, Hay and Stubble;* For, in laying this Ground-work, *That* Mass *is the Testament of* Christ, he boasts, 'that he will destroy all the Wickedness that impious Men (as he says) have conveyed into the Sacrament; and that he will clearly prove we ought to receive the Communion with Faith alone, without much regard to any Manner

*I. Cor. iii. 12.

Verum videamus, obsecro, quid afferat præstigii, quo faciat verum videri, quod dicit, Christum pro se stare. Post longas ambages diffinit Missam; deinde separat a Missa Missæ cærimonias, excutit Cœnam dominicam, et verba Christi trutinat, quibus usus est, quum institueret Missæ sacramentum. Ibi quum testamenti verbum, rem videlicet tam abstrusam, reperisset, jam tanquam profligatis hostibus cœpit ingeminare victoriam; verbis adornat inventum, ut jactat, suum, et tanquam mysterium hactenus inauditum magno supercilio docet quid sit testamentum. Notandum esse clamat, ac memoria tenendum, testamentum esse morituri promissionem, qua nuncupat hæreditatem, et instituit hæredes. "Hoc igitur sacramentum," inquit, "Missæ, nihil est aliud, quam testamentum Christi, testamentum vero, nihil aliud est, quam promissio hæreditatis æternæ nobis Christianis, quos suos hæredes instituit, corpus et sanguinem suum, velut signum ratæ promissionis, adjiciens."

Hoc igitur decies repetit, inculcat, infigit, utpote quod haberi vult immobile fundamentum, super quod ædificet *ligna, fœnum, stipulam.* Nam hoc fundamento jacto, quod Missa Christi sit testamentum, omnem sese jactat impietatem eversurum, quam impii, ut ait, homines invexerunt in hoc sacramentum, et se dilucide probaturum ad communionem recipiendam sola fide veniendum esse; de operibus cujusmodi sint, non admodum esse curandum; conscientia quanto magis erronea sit, ac peccatorum vel morsu, vel titil-

of Good-works whatsoever; and by how much the more
erroneous our Consciences are, and the more moved with
the Sting or Titillation of our Sins, the more holy is our
State for approaching the Communion: But the more
clear, pure and free from the Stain of Sin our Consciences are, in the worse Capacity are we to receive.
Further (he says) that *Mass* is no Sacrifice; that it is
only profitable to the Priest, not to the People; that it
is nothing available, either to the Dead, or to the Living;
that to sing Mass for Sins, for any Necessity, or for
the Dead, is an impious Error; that Fraternities, as also
the annual Commemorations for the Dead, are vain and
wicked Things; that our voluntary maintaining of
Priests, Monks, Canons, Brothers, and whatsoever we
call religious, is to be abolished.' These, therefore, with
many other great good Things, he glories to have found
out by this Discovery, of the blessed Sacrament being
the Testament of *Christ*. And now he inveighs against
the sententious Doctors, as he calls them: He exclaims
against all such as preach to the People; 'Those for
writing, These for preaching so much in the Defence of
the blessed Sacrament of the Eucharist; and neither of
them saying any Thing of the Testament, but most impiously concealing that most incomparable Good from
the People, which so long since might have been profitably known. The Laity, (he says) neither alive, nor
after Death, will ever receive any Benefit by the *Mass:*'
For the Ignorance of which Matter, he denounces all
Priests and Monks at this Day in the World, with their
Bishops and Superiors, to be Idolators, and in a very
dangerous Condition.

I do not therefore discuss how true that Mystery of
Luther is, from which he attributes so much Glory to
himself, in applying so accurately his Definition of the
Testament to the Sacrament; yet at the same Time, I

latione moveatur, tanto sanctius accedi; quanto
serenior, purior, et errore purgatior, tanto sumi deterius.

Ad hæc Missam bonum opus non esse. Missam non
esse sacrificium. Missa sacerdoti tantum, non autem
populo prodesse. Nihil prodesse defunctis, nihil cuiquam viventium. Impium esse errorem, si Missa cana-
tur pro peccatis, si pro cujusquam necessitate, si pro
mortuis. Inanem esse rem et impiam fraternitates, et
annuas defunctorum memorias, abolendam esse talem
omnem sacerdotum, monachorum, canonicorum, fratrum, religiosorum denique, quos vocamus, omnium ali-
moniam. Hæc igitur tot et tam immensa bona se
reperisse gloriatur, in eo solo, quod hoc sacrosanctum
sacramentum comperit esse Christi testamentum.
Jamque in sententiarios protinus, quos vocat, doctores
invehitur; exclamat in omnes qui declamant apud populum, quod quum illi tam multa scribant, hi tam multa
loquantur et prædicent de Eucharistiæ sacramento,
neutri tamen attingant quidquam de testamento, sed
impie celent populum bonum illud incomparabile, quod
tamen jam olim scisse profuisset, ex Missa nihil unquam boni laicos, neque vivos, neque defunctos, esse
consequuturos. Ob cujus rei ignorantiam, denunciat
universos hodie sacerdotes et monachos cum episcopis, et
omnibus suis majoribus idolatras esse, atque in statu
periculosissimo versari.

Igitur illud Lutheri mysterium, e quo tantas efflat
glorias, quod definitionem testamenti tam accurate ad
sacramentum applicat, quam verum sit, non excutio;
sed interim certe video, cur hoc inventum, tanquam

do not see why he should brag so much of this new Invention of his. I do not know indeed who he hears preach, where he is; but here, I am sure, we have heard Preachers, over and over again, not only treat of those Things, which *Luther* brings out for so new and exquisite, *viz.* 'That *Christ* is a Testator; that he made his Testament in the last Supper; that he promised an Inheritance, which he declared to be the Kingdom of Heaven; that he instituted the Faithful for his Heirs; that the Sacrament is a holy Sign, exhibited for a Seal;' not only these, and such like, but also 'the Number of Witnesses, the Bill, and other Rites of Testaments, they unfolded to us out of the deepest Secrets of both Laws, and applied all of them exactly to the Sacrament.' And this they did more consciously, and truly, than *Luther:* For they referred to the same Testament, not only what *Christ* did at his last Supper, but also what he suffered on the Cross; only in this differing from *Luther,* that they did not find out the admirable and hitherto unheard-of Benefits of the *Mass,* by which the Clergy should lose all the Fruits of it in this Life, and the Laity in the Life to come: For the People would not maintain the Clergy to say *Mass,* if they should be persuaded they could reap no spiritual Good thereby.

But it is worth our While to see from what Tree *Luther* gathers this Fruit. After he has very often repeated, that the Sacrament of the Eucharist is the Sign of the Testament, and the Testament is nothing else but the Promise of Inheritance; he thinks that it consequently follows, that the Mass cannot be a good Work, or a Sacrifice. To which, if any one consents, he must immediately admit that Catalogue of Plagues, by which he endeavours to confound the whole Face of the Church: But if you deny it, then can he do nothing with so monstrous a Design: For I am almost ashamed of

novum, tam magnifice jactet prosuo. Nescio quos illic
concionantes audiat, hic certe, non semel audivimus,
eam similitudinem ad tædium usque tractantes frater-
culos, ut qui non ea duntaxat afferrent, quæ nunc pro
novis et exquisitis affert Lutherus, Christum esse testa-
torem, testamentum in Cœna condidisse, hæreditatem
promisisse, eamdem nuncupasse regnum cœlorum, hæredes instituisse fidelium cœtum, sacramentum hoc
sacrum esse signum, quod sit adhibitum pro sigillo: non
hæc, inquam, tantum, sed et testium numerum, et syn-
grapham, et alios testamentorum ritus, ex intimis utriusque juris erutos penetralibus explicarent, atque ada-
mussim omnia applicarent ad sacramentum. Hoc
aliquando concinnius, ac verius quoque, quam Lutherus,
quod ad idem testamentum referebant, non tantum, quæ
Christus fecit in Cœna, sed etiam quæ passus est in
cruce; hoc uno tantum impares Luthero, quod mira-
biles, et hactenus inauditos Missæ fructus non invene-
runt, quibus et clerus præsentis vitæ fructum omnem, et
populus futuræ perderet. Neque enim sacerdotibus
quidquam laici temporalis boni conferrent ob Missam,
e qua persuaderentur nihil se spiritualis boni referre.
Sed operæ pretium est videre qua ex arbore tam salubres
fructus colligat Lutherus.

Postquam ergo sæpius inculcavit Eucharistiæ sacramentum signum esse testamenti, testamentum vero
nihil esse aliud, quam promissionem hæreditatis, inde
continuo censet consequi, ut Missa neque bonum opus
esse possit, neque sacrificium: quod quisquis ei concesserit, jam illi statim admittendus erit totus ille pestium
catalogus, quo totam Ecclesiæ faciem confundit. At
quisquis negaverit illi, jam tam magno molimine nihil
egerit. Nam argumenta, quibus docere præ se fert,
pudet propemodum recensere, ita sunt in re tantæ majestatis nugacia prorsus ac frivola. Sic enim colligit

the Arguments, by which he pretends to teach these Things; they are so trifling and frivolous, in a Matter of so great Majesty. Thus he concludes; (for I will give you his own Words) 'You have heard that Mass is nothing else but the divine Promise, or Testament of *Christ,* commended by the Sacrament of his Body and Blood; which, if it be true, you understand, that by any Means it cannot be a Work; nor is it to be used after any other Manner, than by Faith alone; and Faith is not a Work, but the Mistress and Life of Works.' It is a strange Thing, that, after so much Pains-taking, he vents nothing but mere Wind: Which, though he would have us believe it to be of Strength to overturn Mountains; yet truly to me, it seems not of Force enough to shake a Reed. For if you withdraw the Coverings of his Words, with which (like an Ape in Purple) he decks this ridiculous Matter; if you take away the Exclamations, whereby he so often rails, and insults, as a Conqueror; (though not as yet entered the Battle against the Church;) or if he had clearly proved the Thing, you will find that nothing remains, but a naked, and miserable Piece of Sophistry. For what else has he said by all that Heap of Words, but that Mass is a Promise, and therefore no Work? Who would but pity this Man, that is so blockish, as not to perceive his own Impertinency; or, if he understands himself, who would but take it heinously from him, that thinks all Christians so dull, as not to discover or comprehend so manifest Follies? I shall not dispute with him about the Testament or Promise, or the whole Definition, or Application thereof to the Sacrament. I will not trouble him so much; he may perhaps find others who will ruin the best Part of his Foundation, by saying, 'That the Testament is the Promise of the Evangelical Law, as the Old Testament was of the Law of *Moses;* and by

(nam ipsius verba recitabo): "Audisti Missam nihil
aliud esse, quam promissionem divinam, seu testamentum Christi, sacramento corporis et sanguinis sui
commendatum." Quod si verum est, intelligis eam non
posse opus esse ullo modo, nec alio studio a quoquam
tractari, quam sola fide: fides autem non est opus, sed
magistra, et vita operum. Mirum est, quanto nixu par-
turiens, quam nihil peperit, nisi merum ventum, quem
quum ipse tam validum velit videri, ut montes posset
evertere, mihi profecto videtur tam languidus, ut agi-
tare non possit arundinem. Nam si verborum tollas
involucra, quibus rem absurdam, velut simiam purpura,
vestit, si tollas exclamationes illas, quibus jam velut re
delucide probata, toties in totam bacchatur Ecclesiam,
et nondum collata manu, tanquam ferox victor insultat,
nihil aliud restare videbis, quam nudum et miserum
sophisma. Quid enim aliud dicit tanto verborum am-
bitu, quam Missa est promissio; ergo non potest esse
opus? Quem non misereat hominis, si tam stupidus sit,
ut ineptiam suam non sentiat? Aut quis non indigne-
tur, si sibi conscius, tam stupidos tamen omnes æstimet
Christianos, ut tam manifestas insanias nequeant deprehendere?

Non contendam cum eo de testamento et promissione,
et tota illa diffinitione, et applicatione testamenti ad
sacramentum. Non ero tam molestus ei, quam alios
fortassis inveniet, si qui bonam ei partem istius fundamenti subruerint, qui et testamentum novum dicant
promissionem esse legis evangelicæ, quemadmodum
vetus fuit mosaicæ, et testamentum istud negent a Lu-

denying it to be rightly handled by *Luther.'* For neither
was the Testator particularly to name what he should
leave to the Heir, whom he had appointed over all in
general; nor is the Remission of Sins, which *Luther*
says, *is bequeathed for an Inheritance,* the same with
the Kingdom of Heaven, but rather the Way to Heaven.
If any one should urge and press *Luther* in these, and
such-like Sayings, he might, perhaps, by fastening these
Engines in any Part of his Structure, shake the whole
Frame thereof; but I shall leave that to such as shall be
willing to do it: And because he desires his Foundation
should remain unshaken, I shall not go about to move
it; I will only shew, that the House he has built upon
it, falls of itself. And to shew this more plainly, let us
consider a little the Original of the Matter, and examine
the Mass by its first Pattern.

Christ, in his most holy Supper, in which he instituted this Sacrament, made of Bread and Wine, his
own Body and Blood, and gave to his Disciples to be
eaten and drunk: A few Hours afterwards, he offered
the same Body and Blood on the Altar of the Cross, a
Sacrifice to his Father for the Sins of the People; which
Sacrifice being finished, the Testament was consummated. Being now near his Death, he did (as some
dying Persons are wont to do) declare his Will concerning what he desired should be done afterwards in Commemoration of him. Wherefore, instituting the Sacrament, when he gave his Body and Blood to his Disciples, he said, *Do this in Commemoration of me.* He who
diligently examines this, will find *Christ* to be the eternal Priest, who, in Place of all the Sacrifices which were
offered by the temporary Priesthood of *Moses's* Law,
(whereof many were but the Types and Figures of this
holy Sacrifice) has instituted one Sacrifice, the greatest
of all, the Plenitude of all, as the Sum of all others,

thero satis scite tractari; neque enim testatori nuncupandum esse nominatim, quid relinquat hæredi, quem
ex asse instituat, neque remissionem peccatorum, quam
pro hæreditate nuncupatam Lutherus ait, idem esse
quod regnum cœlorum, sed viam potius ad cœlum.
Quas res, atque alias item aliquot quisquis urgere volet,
ac premere, posset fortassis fundamenti Lutheriani
structuram machinis alicunde concutere. Verum istud
eis permittam, qui volent. Ego istud ei fundamentum,
quod immobile postulat esse, non movebo; tantum ostendam ædificium, quod superstruxit, facile per se corruere.
Quod quo liquidius appareat, consideremus paulisper
originem rei, Missamque ad primum ejus exemplar examinemus.

Christus igitur in illa Cœna sanctissima, qua sacramentum illud instituit, corpus suum et sanguinem ex
pane et vino confecit, ac tradidit manducandum bibendumque discipulis, tunc intra paucas horas idem corpus,
eumdem sanguinem in ara crucis obtulit in sacrificium
Patri pro peccatis populi: quo sacrificio peracto, testamentum consummatum est. In Cœna jam morti proximus, quemadmodum solent morientes, testamento
quodam testatus est mentem suam, quid se defuncto
fieret in memoriam sui.

Instituens igitur sacramentum, quum suum corpus
ac sanguinem exhibuisset discipulis, ait illis: *"Hoc
facite in meam commemorationem."* Hoc si quis expendat diligenter, videbit Christum sacerdotem æternum, loco sacrificiorum omnium, quæ temporarium
mosaicæ legis sacerdotium offerebat (quorum etiam
pleraque sacrosancti hujus sacrificii typum gerebant)
unum sacrificium, omnium summum, omnium plenitudinem, et quamdam veluti summam instituisse, quod et

that it might be offered to God, and given for Food to
the People: In which Thing, as *Christ* was the Priest,
so his Disciples did for that Time represent the People,
who themselves did not consecrate, but received, from
the Hands of their Priest, the consecrated Sacrament.
But God did shortly after elect and institute them
Priests, that they might consecrate the same Sacrament,
in Commemoration of him.

And what else then is this, but that they should consecrate, and not only receive it themselves, but likewise
give it to the People, and offer it to God? For, if
Luther should argue that the Priest cannot offer, because
Christ did not offer in his Supper, let him remember
his own Words, *That a Testament involves in it the
Death of the Testator;* therefore has no Force or Power,
nor is in its full Perfection; till the Testator be dead.
Wherefore, not only those Things which *Christ* did first
at his Supper, do belong to the Testament, but also his
Oblation on the Cross: For on the Cross he consummated the Sacrifice which he began in the Supper: And
therefore the Commemoration of the whole Thing, to
wit, of the Consecration in the Supper, and the Oblation
on the Cross, is celebrated, and represented together in
the Sacrament of the Mass; so that it is, the Death that
is more truly represented than the Supper. And therefore, the Apostle, when writing to the *Corinthians,* in
these Words, *As often as ye shall eat this Bread, and
drink this Cup,* adds, *not the Supper of our Lord, but
ye shall declare our Lord's Death.**

Let us now come to *Luther*'s chief Reasons, by which
he proves *Mass* to be neither good Work, nor Sacrifice.
And though it were better first to treat of Sacrifice; yet
because he has first moved concerning Work, we will
follow him. When therefore he thus argues, *Mass is a*

*I. Cor. xi. 26.

offerretur Deo, et in cibum daretur populo. Qua in re, ut Christus sacerdos erat, ita discipuli eatenus repræsentabant populum, qui non consecrabant ipsi, sed consecratum de manu sacerdotis sui sumebant; sed eos statim Deus in sacerdotes elegit, atque instituit, ut ipsi idem sacramentum facerent in commemorationem ejus.

Quod quid aliud est, quam ut consecrarent, nec sibi tantum sumerent, sed et exhiberent populo, et offerrent Deo? Nam si ibi nobis instet Lutherus, sacerdotem offerre non posse, quia Christus in Cœna non obtulit, recordetur eorum quæ dixit ipse, testamentum involvere mortem testatoris, nec ante vires et robur sumere, et tota perfectione compleri, quam eo moriente, qui testatus est. Quamobrem non ea solum pertinent ad testamentum, quæ prius fecit in Cœna, sed etiam oblatio ejus in cruce; nam in cruce consummavit sacrificium, quod inchoavit in Cœna, eoque totius rei commemoratio, nempe consecrationis in Cœna, et oblationis in cruce, uno celebratur ac repræsentatur sacramento missæ; atque adeo verius mors repræsentatur, quam Cœna. Apostolus enim quum Corinthiis scriberet: *"Quotiescumque panem hunc comederitis, et calicem biberitis,"* adjecit, non Cœnam Domini, sed *"mortem Domini annuntiabitis."*

Veniamus ergo nunc ad præclaras istas Lutheri rationes, quibus probat Missam neque bonum opus esse, neque sacrificium; et quanquam præstaret prius tractare de sacrificio, tamen quoniam ille primam quæstionem fecit de opere, sequemur illum. Quum igitur ita colligit: "Missa est promissio, ergo non est bonum

Promise, therefore no good Work, because no Promise is a Work; we answer, that the Mass, which the Priest celebrates, cannot more properly be called a Promise, than the Consecration of *Christ* was: And all under one we will demand of him, if *Christ* did not do a Work, when he consecrated? which if he deny, we shall certainly begin to admire that there should be some Work done by him who cuts an Image out of Wood, and not by *Christ,* when he made his own Flesh of Bread! And if *Christ* did any Work, I am certain none will doubt of its being a good Work: For if the Woman, who poured the Ointment upon his Head,* wrought a good Work in that, who doubts of his performing a good Work, when he gave his Body for our Nourishment, and offered it in Sacrifice to God? If this cannot be denied, unless by him who intends to trifle in so serious a Matter, neither can it also be denied that the Priest worketh a good Work in the Mass; seeing that in the Mass he does nothing else but what *Christ* did in his last Supper, and on the Cross; for this is declared in *Christ's own Words, Do this in Commemoration of me.* By which Words, what was he willing they should represent, and do in the Mass, but what he had done himself in his last Supper, and on the Cross? For he instituted, and began the Sacrament at his last Supper, which he perfected on the Cross. And from this Reason especially it seems, was taken the Occasion of mingling Water with the Wine, according to the Custom of the Church; because Water and Blood did flow from the Side of *Christ,* dying on the Cross.

Since it cannot be denied that *Christ* wrought a good Work in his last Supper, and on the Cross; neither can it be denied, that the Priest represents, and performs the same Things in the Mass: How can it then

*Matt. xxvi. 7-10.

opus, quia nulla promissio est opus," dicemus Missam, quam sacerdos celebrat, non verius esse promissionem, quam fuit consecratio Christi; et simul quæremus ab eo, an non aliquod opus tum fecerit Christus: quod si neget, mirabimur profecto, si quum is opus faciat, qui imaginem facit ex ligno, Christus nullum prorsus opus fecerit, quum carnem suam fecerit ex pane. Quod si ullum opus fecerit, quin id bonum fuerit, nemo, opinor, dubitabit: nam si bonum opus fecit mulier, quæ caput ejus perfudit unguento, quis potest ambigere an bonum opus fecerit Christus, quum corpus proprium et in cibum exhiberet hominibus, et in sacrificium offerret Deo? Quod si negari non potest nisi ab eo, qui in re maxime seria valde velit nugari, bonum opus fecisse Christum, nec istud etiam negari potest, in Missa bonum opus facere sacerdotem, quippe qui non aliud facit in Missa quam Christus in Cœna fecit, et cruce. Hoc enim declarant verba Christi: *"Hoc facite in meam commemorationem,"* quibus verbis quid aliud volebat, ut in Missa repræsentarent ac facerent, quam quod ipse faciebat in Cœna et cruce? Instituebat enim, et inchoabat in Cœna sacramentum, quod in cruce perfecit: nam hac ratione potissimum nata esse videtur occasio, ut aqua ex Ecclesiæ ritu uno misceretur in calice, quia aqua cum sanguine de latere morientis effluxit in cruce.

Quum ergo negari non possit, quin bonum opus et in Cœna, et in cruce fecerit Christus, neque etiam quod sacerdos eadem repræsentat ac facit in Missa, quomodo tum fingi potest Missam bonum opus non esse.

be feigned that the Mass is not a good Work? Wherefore, since *Luther* so handles the Matter, as to say, 'That, because the Communion of one Layman does not profit another of the Laity, so neither does the Mass of the Priest profit the People;' how dim of Sight is he himself, and how much does he endeavour to spread his Darkness over the Eyes of others, when he sees not that there is this Difference in the Case, That now the Laity receives out of the Priest's Hand, as the Apostles did first from *Christ*'s; and the priest performs what *Christ* did then perform; for he offers to God the same Body that was offered by *Christ?*

From whence also it appears how cold an Argument is *Luther*'s Comparison of the Mass, with the Sacrament of Baptism or Marriage; endeavouring to prove, that, because one Layman cannot be baptized for another, nor marry a Wife for another Man; so a Priest cannot celebrate Mass for any other Person! For he openly puts Marriage out of the Number of the Sacraments, and Baptism too, under a Colour; when he says, *That really there is but one Sacrament:* Why then does he now compare Baptism and Marriage with the Sacrament of the Mass, if he does not hold them to be Sacraments?

And although he should confess them both to be Sacraments, (as indeed they are) yet is neither of them to be compared to this of the Mass; but in such Manner as this Sacrament, which is the proper Body of him who is Lord of all Sacraments, may have a Prerogative above all other, which he himself made; since it is manifest, that the Priest, in administering all other Sacraments, does Good to all those who receive them; so in this, while he offers it in the Mass, he is profitable, and communicates Good to all.

Otherwise, if *Luther* exact with such Severity, that

Quamobrem etiam quum Lutherus ita rem tractet, ut quia laici communio alteri non prodest laico, ideo nec sacerdotis Missa prosit populo, vehementer ipse cœcutit, dum tenebras aliis conatur effundere, quum non videat hoc interesse, quod laicus nunc recipit tantum e manu sacerdotis, sicut primo receperunt apostoli e manu Christi, sacerdos vero facit quod tum fecit Christus, nam idem corpus offert Deo, quod obtulit Christus. Qua ex re et illud patet, quam frigidum argumentum sit, quo Missam comparat cum sacramento Baptismi, aut Conjugii, contendens efficere ut, quoniam laicus baptizari non potest pro alio, aut pro alio uxorem ducere, ideo nec sacerdos Missam pro alio possit celebrare: nam Conjugium plane sustulit e sacramentis, et recte etiam Baptismum, quum dicit non esse vere, nisi unum sacramentum. Cur ergo nunc Baptismum comparat, et Conjugium cum sacramento Missæ, si illa non habet pro sacramentis? Quanquam etiam si utrumque fateretur esse sacramentum (quod revera sunt), tamen neutrum erat sic comparandum huic sacramento Missæ, quin hoc sacramentum, quod est proprium corpus ipsius, qui Dominus est sacramentorum omnium, sacramenta reliqua possit, quæ fecit ipse, singulari aliqua prærogativa præcellere, quum clare constet quod, quemadmodum in omnibus aliis sacramentis sacerdos prodest ministrando singulis, sic in hoc sacramento, dum offert in Missa, prodest, et bonum communicat universis.

Alioqui si tam severe Lutherus exigat ut omnia sacra-

all Sacraments should be alike, and no Difference amongst them; and that, in the Sacrament of the Eucharist, the Priest's Condition is no better than that of the Laity; why compels he not the Priest to receive the Communion from the Hands of another, and not suffer him to take it himself, though he can consecrate it; even as he cannot absolve himself, though he has the Keys of Penance?

And what he says of Faith, which he believes all Men are to have in their own Persons, and that not the Priest's, but every Man's own Faith, is that which profits him, even (says he) *as* Abraham *has not believed for all the Jews.* I allow it to be very true; yet it proves no more than what it proposes: For neither has *Christ* himself, offered by himself on the Cross, saved the People, without every Man's particular Faith; that none may think the Mass of any Priest should do it; yet the Mass of every Priest helps those to Salvation, who, by their Faith, have deserved to be Partakers of the greatest Good communicated in the Mass to many.

It may likewise be sometimes advantageous to the procuring the Infusion of Faith into the Unfaithful, as it is procured by the Death and Passion of *Christ,* that Grace should be given to the *Gentiles;* by which, through the Hearing of the Word, they might come to the Understanding of the Faith of Christ.

The Sacrifice of the Mass

But *Luther* easily perceives, that it is no hard Matter to destroy what he himself has built, if Mass can be a Sacrifice or Offering, which may be offered to God; he therefore promises to remove this Obstacle, which, that he may the more easily seem to do, he objects against himself such Things, as he perceives to stand in his Way. 'And now, (says he) another, the greatest and most spacious

menta sint inter se similia, et in Eucharistiæ sacramento nihilo potior sit sacerdotis conditio, quam laicorum, quare non cogit ut sacerdos alterius manu semper
communicet, nec sinatur sibi sacramentum sumere,
quanquam potest conficere, quemadmodum, licet claves
habeat Pœnitentiæ, semet non potest absolvere ? Nam
quod affert de fide, quam a singulis censet oportere
præstari, et suam cuique fidem prodesse, non sacerdotis,
quemadmodum nec Abraham, ut ait, pro omnibus
Judæis credidit, istud quidem verum dicit, at nihil
tamen magis id probat, quod proponit: nam neque
Christus ipse a semet oblatus in cruce sine sua cujusque
fide servavit populum, ne quis id Missam putet cujusque
sacerdotis efficere, quæ tamen Missa cujuslibet sacerdotis illis prodest ad salutem, quorum propria fides
meruit ut boni, quod tam immensum Missa communicat
multis, possint esse participes. Quanquam potest et ad
hoc valere nonnunquam, ut incredulo quoque fidem procuret infundi, quemadmodum Christi mors et Passio
procuravit ut gratia daretur Gentibus, qua per auditum
verbi venirent in fidem Christi.

De Sacrificio Missæ

SED Lutherus satis sentit ipse facile destrui quicquid
astruxerat, si Missa possit esse sacrificium, aut oblatio,
quæ offeratur Deo. Hanc igitur obicem se pollicetur
amoturum, quod quo fidelius facere videatur, et efficacius, objicit sibi ipse prius quædam, quæ sibi sentit obstare. "Jam et alterum," inquit, "scandalum amoven-
dum est, quod multo grandius est, et speciosissimum, id

of all Scandals, is to be taken away, that is, Mass believed every where to be a Sacrifice offered to God;' which Opinion the Words of the Canon seem to favour, where it is said *these Gifts, these Presents, and these holy Sacrifices; and below that, this Offering.* He likewise complains, that it is taken for a Sacrifice, &c. From thence Christ is called *the Host of the Altar.* To this may be added the Words of the holy Fathers, so many Examples, and the constant Custom observed over the whole World.

You see, gentle Reader, what Blocks he himself finds standing in his Way: Take Notice now with what *Herculean* Strength he undertakes to remove them: *But to all these, (says he) are constantly to be opposed the Words and Example of* Christ. But pray what Words of Christ are these, which have been unknown to so many holy Fathers in Times past, and to the whole Church of Christ, during so many Ages, and now, by *Luther,* like a new *Esdras,* found out? This he declares himself, when he says, 'For unless we bring it to pass, that Mass be accounted a Promise or Testament, as the Words, clearly make out; we lose the whole Gospel, and all Comfort:' These are his Words: It now remains that we see his Example. *'Christ,* says he, at his last Supper, when he instituted this Sacrament, and bequeathed the Testament, offered it not to God the Father, and has not performed it as a good Work for others; but sitting at the Table, he proposed the same Testament, and exhibited a Sign to every one of them.' Those are therefore the Words of Christ! This is the Example, by which, now at last, only *Luther* himself clearly sees Mass neither to be a Sacrifice, nor Offering! It is a Wonder that, of so many holy Fathers, of so many Eyes which have read the Gospel in the Church for so many Ages, none was ever so quick-sighted, as

est, quod Missa creditur passim esse sacrificium, quod
offertur Deo. In quam opinionem et verba Canonis
sonare videntur, ubi dicitur: *hæc dona, hæc munera,
hæc sancta sacrificia,* et infra: *hanc oblationem;* item
clarissime postulatur ut acceptum sit sacrificium, sicut
sacrificium Abel, etc. Inde Christus hostia altaris
dicitur. Accedunt his dicta sanctorum Patrum, tot exempla, tantusque usus per orbem constanter obser-
vatus."

Audisti, lector, quas obices ipse sibi sentit objectas;
audi nunc vicissim quam Herculeis viribus aggreditur
amovere. "His omnibus," inquit, "oportet constantis-
sime opponere verbum et exemplum Christi." At quæ
sunt igitur illa verba Christi, quæ tot olim sanctis
Patribus, ac toti Christi Ecclesiæ tot ignorata sæculis,
velut novus Esdras nobis Lutherus invenit? Hoc declarat ipse, quum dicit: "Nisi enim Missam obtinueri-
mus esse promissionem, seu testamentum, ut verba clare
sonant, totum evangelium, et universum solatium amit-
timus." Verba nunc audivimus; restat ut videamus
exemplum: exemplum ergo subjungit. "Christus," inquit, "in Cœna novissima, quum institueret hoc sacramentum, et condidit testamentum, non obtulit ipsum
Deo Patri, aut ut opus bonum pro aliis perfecit, sed in
mensa sedens singulis idem testamentum proposuit, et
signum exhibuit." Ista sunt ergo verba Christi, istud
est exemplum, e quibus nunc demum Lutherus unus
perspicue videt Missam non esse sacrificium, nec oblationem. Mirum est igitur ex tot sanctis Patribus, ex
tot oculis, quot in Ecclesia tam multis sæculis idem
legerunt evangelium, nullum fuisse unquam tam per-
spicacem, ut rem tam apertam deprehenderet, imo
omnes etiamnum tam cæcos esse, ut ne adhuc quidem
queant id quod cernere se Lutherus jactat, quanquam

to perceive a Thing so apparent; and that at this present Time they are all so blind, as not to discern what *Luther* (though he points it out with his Finger,) brags so clearly to see himself! Is not *Luther* rather mistaken, and thinks himself to see something, which in Reality he sees not, or endeavours to shew us with his Finger, that which is no-where to be found? For pray what Sort of Proof is that where he undertakes to teach *'that* Mass *is no Sacrifice, because it is a Promise;'* as if Promise and Sacrifice were as repugnant together as Heat and Cold? Which Reason of his is altogether so weak, that it seems not worthy an Answer. For the so many Sacrifices of *Moses*'s Laws, though all Figures of Things to come, yet were they Promises in themselves, promising the Things for which they were done; not only the Future, of which they were Figures, but also Deliverances, Expiations, Purgations and Purifications, of the People then present, for whom they were solemnly offered every Year. Which Thing being so apparent, that it leaves no Plea for Ignorance, makes *Luther*'s Dissimulation appear altogether ridiculous; when arguing that this Thing cannot be done; which not only he himself, but all the People know to have been so often performed.

Now come we to the Example of *Christ,* by which *Luther* thinks he so vehemently oppresses us; because *Christ,* in his last Supper, did not use the Sacrament for a Sacrifice, nor has he offered it to his Father: Out of which he goes about to prove, 'That the *Mass,* which ought to agree with the Example of *Christ,* by whom it was instituted, cannot be a Sacrifice or Offering.'

If *Luther* so rigidly summons us to the Example of our Lord's Supper, as not to permit the Priest to do any Thing that we do not read Christ to have done in it; then must they never receive themselves in the Sac-

ipso monstrante, perspicere. Annon Lutherus halluci-
natur potius, et aliquid se videre putat, quod non videt,
et digito conatur ostendere, quod nusquam est?

Nam, obsecro, qualis est ista probatio, quum docere
nititur Missam non esse sacrificium ex eo quod sit
promissio? quasi promissio et sacrificium ita sibi mutuo
pugnarent, quemadmodum frigus et calor? Quæ Lutheri ratio adeo prorsus friget, ut nec responso digna
videatur. Nam legis Mosaicæ tam multa sacrificia,
quanquam essent figuræ omnia futurarum rerum, tamen
promissiones erant et ipsa: promittebant enim ea,
propter quæ fiebant, non modo futura quondam illa,
quorum erant figuræ, sed etiam liberationes, expia-
tiones, purgationes, purificationes populi tunc præsentis, pro quo more solemni quotannis offerebantur.
Quæ res quum tam aperta sit, ut nemo prorsus eam
possit ignorare, ridicula plane dissimulatio est ista Lutheri, quum nunc argumentetur fieri id non posse, quod
non ipse tantum, sed populus quoque novit tam sæpe
factum.

Nunc veniamus ad exemplum Christi, quo nos arbi-
tratur Lutherus vehementer opprimi, propterea quod
Christus in Cœna sacramento non usus est pro sacrificio,
nec obtulit Patri: ex quo probare conatur quod Missa,
quæ respondere debet exemplo Christi quo fuit instituta, non potest esse sacrificium, nec oblatio.

Si Lutherus tam rigide nos revocet ad exemplum
Cœnæ dominicæ, ut nihil sacerdotes permittat facere,
quod ibi Christus fecisse non legitur, sacramentum,
quod consecrant, nunquam ipsi recipient. Suum enim

rament which they consecrate: For we do not read in
the Gospel, where it mentions the last Supper of our
Lord, that our Lord himself received his own Body:
and though some Doctors, and the whole Church, do
hold that he did receive it: yet that makes nothing for
Luther, who discredits not only all the Doctors, but the
Faith of the whole Church; and thinks not any Thing
to be believed, but what is confirmed by Scriptures, and
that clearly to; (for so he writes in the Sacrament of
Orders.) In which Sort of Scripture, I am of Opinion,
he will not find that *Christ* received his own Body at
his last Supper. Whence it will follow, as I have said,
that the Priests ought not to take what they consecrate
themselves, if he binds us so strictly to the Example of
the last Supper. But if then he allows that the Priests
are to receive, because the Apostles did so; and that he
holds they are commanded to do what the Apostles did
then, not what *Christ* has done; then must they never
consecrate; for *Christ,* and not the Apostles, did then
consecrate. The Matter itself shews, that, in this, the
Priests do not only perform what *Christ* did in his last
Supper, but also what he has afterwards done on the
Cross; the Apostles leaving us some Things by Tradition, which *Christ* either never did, or which we do not
read that he had done; as the Ceremonies and Signs
used in the Consecration, of which I believe most are
delivered down to us from the Apostles themselves.
Furthermore, they repeat some Words in the Canon of
the *Mass,* as if spoken by *Christ* himself, which are not
read in Scripture; and yet there is no Doubt but he
spoke them; for many Things were said and done by
Christ, which are not recorded by any of the Evangelists, but by the fresh Memory of those who were
present: delivered afterwards, as it were, from Hand
to Hand, from the very Times of the Apostles, down to

corpus Christus in evangelio non legitur, ubi Cœna scribitur, ipse recepisse. Nam quod Doctores aliquot eum recepisse tradunt, et quod idem canit Ecclesia, nihil potest pro Luthero facere, quum illi neque Doctores omnes, neque totius Ecclesiæ fides ullam faciat fidem, neque credendum censeat quicquam (nam ita scribit in sacramento Ordinis) nisi firmatum Scripturis, et iisdem etiam claris, cujusmodi certe Scripturis, non opinor, inveniet quod suum corpus in Cœna receperit Christus; ex quo sequetur, ut dixi, nec sacerdotes debere, quod consecrant ipsi, recipere, si tam rigide nos obstringat Lutherus ad exemplum Cœnæ dominicæ. Quod si ideo concedat recipiendum sacerdotibus, quia receperunt apostoli, et eos contendat id jussos facere, quod tunc apostoli fecerunt, non quod Christus, hac ratione nunquam consecrabunt sacerdotes: consecrabat enim Christus, non apostoli. Res ergo docet non id solum sacerdotes in hoc sacramento facere, quod Christus fecit in Cœna, sed etiam quod postea fecit in cruce, quædam etiam tradentibus apostolis, quæ Christus aut nusquam fecit, aut certe non legitur usquam fecisse, cujusmodi sunt gestus et signa quibus utuntur dum consecrant: quorum ego nonnulla credo ab ipsis promanasse apostolis.

Præterea quod in Canone Missæ quædam verba velut a Christo prolata recensent, quæ nusquam in Scriptura sacra leguntur, et tamen non dubitatur, quin dixerit: Multa enim dicta sunt et facta per Christum, quæ nullus evangelistarum complectitur, sed quædam recente memoria eorum, qui interfuerunt, velut per manus deinceps tradita, ab ipso apostolorum tempore ad nos usque pervenerunt. Lutherus non dubitat Christum in

us. *Luther* doubts not, that *Christ* said in his last Supper, *As often as ye shall do this, ye shall do it in Commemoration of me:* And he is so sure that they were *Christ*'s Words, that, from thence he takes his Argument; 'That Nobody is obliged to receive the Sacrament; but that it is left to every Man's Discretion, and that we are only bound, as often as we do it, to do it in Remembrance of *Christ*.' These very Words he does not read in the Evangelists concerning the Supper of our Lord: For no other Thing is read there, but, *do this in Commemoration of me.*

Where then read he these, 'as often as ye shall do these Things?' Whether, not in the Mass? Indeed I believe no where else. For the Apostles Words are not so: Wherefore, seeing he trusts so much in these Words, and uses them, because he finds them in the Canon; why does he not give so much Credit to that Part of the same Canon, in which Mass is called an Offering, and Sacrifice?

Wherefore, if he confess that the Priests do rightly receive what they consecrate in the Mass, though no clear Scripture (which only he admits of,) testifies *Christ* to have done it at his last Supper, nor in any other Place; he ought not to wonder if the Priest offers *Christ* to his Father; which *Christ* himself has done on the Cross, as it is witnessed by clear Scripture in several Places: For *Luther*'s own Arguments demonstrate, that the Cross belongs to the Testament made at the Supper, when he says, 'That the Testament involves the Death of the Testator, by which alone it can be made perfect.' Moreover, it seems, as is said, that the mingling of Water with the Wine, had its Beginning from no other Place; which Thing is not said by Scripture to be done at the last Supper, but on the Cross. Let *Luther,* therefore, forbear to oppose his trifling

Cœna dixisse: *"Hæc quotiescunque feceritis, in mei memoriam facietis,"* atque hæc usque adeo pro comperto habet Christi verba fuisse, ut inde sumat argumentum, neminem cogi ad recipiendum sacramentum, sed rem cujusque relictam arbitrio, tantum ad hoc adstringi, ut, quoties facimus, faciamus in memoriam Christi. Hæc ergo verba non legit apud evangelistas in Cœna Domini: nam illic nihil aliud legitur, quam: *"Hoc facite in mei commemorationem."* Ubi ergo legit illa verba: *"Hæc quotiescunque feceritis,"* annon in Missa? Opinor certe non alibi: nam apud Apostolum alia sunt. Igitur qui tantum fidit, et utitur illis verbis, quia reperit in Canone, cur non pari fide suscipit ejusdem verba Canonis, quibus Missa oblatio dicitur, et sacrificium?

Quamobrem si sacerdotes in Missa fatetur recte recipere quod consecrant, quanquam nulla Scriptura clara (cujusmodi solam recipit Lutherus) Christum testetur illud nec in Cœna fecisse, non usquam, non debet mirum videri Luthero, si sacerdos offerat Christum Patri, quod non uno loco, clara testante Scriptura, Christus ipse fecit in cruce; nam crucem etiam ad testamentum in Cœna factum pertinere Lutheri quoque ratio demonstrat, quum testamentum dicit mortem testatoris involvere, utpote qua sola perficitur. Præterea non aliunde, quod dixi, videtur et id institutum, ut aqua vino misceretur in sacramento: quæ res non in Cœna legitur esse facta, sed cruce. Desinat ergo Lutherus argumentum nugax opponere, ut, quia Christus in Cœna sese non obtulit, ideo sacerdos non offerre credatur in Missa, in qua non solum repræsentat quod in

Argument, 'That, because *Christ* at his last Supper did not offer himself, therefore the Priest must not be believed to offer him in the Mass:' In which he not only represents what *Christ* performed in his last Supper, but also what he did on the Cross, on which he consummated what he began in the Supper.

But now come we to the last of *Luther's* Arguments; by which, as by a sacred Anchor, his Ship is sustained: And this is the most frivolous of all the rest. 'How can it be, (says he) that the Priest should offer to God what he takes himself? It is not likely (says he) Mass should be a Sacrifice, when we receive it ourselves. The same Thing cannot be received and offered at one and the same Time, nor given and received by one and the same Person.' *Luther* deters us every-where from philosophical Reasonings, when he, in so sacred a Thing, endeavours to sustain himself by the merest Sophistry in the World. For pray was there ever a Sacrifice in *Moses's* Law, which was not taken by those who offered it? Or did God himself eat what they offered him? *Shall I eat the Flesh of Bulls, or drink the Blood of Goats, saith the Lord?** Besides, if Christ was both Priest and Sacrifice; why could he not institute that the Priest, who should supply the same Sacrifice, might both offer and receive the Victim himself? But lest I may seem, in this Case, to imitate *Luther,* who has nothing to say for himself, but what issues out of his own idle Brain; I will lay before you what St. *Ambrose* says to the Mass, 'O Lord God, (says he) with how great Contrition of Heart, with what Fountains of Tears, with how great Reverence and Fear, with what Chastity and Purity of Mind that divine and cælestial Mystery is to be celebrated: Where thy Flesh is truly received; where thy Blood is truly

*Ps. xlix. 13.

Cœna fecit Christus, sed etiam quod in cruce, in qua
consummavit Christus quod inchoavit in Cœna.

At postremum argumentum Lutheri, quo velut an-
chora sacra sustinetur navis, omnium est nugacissimum.
"Quomodo," inquit, "fieri potest ut sacerdos offerat Deo
quod ipse sumit? Repugnat," inquit, "Missam esse
sacrificium, quum illam recipiamus: idem simul recipi
et offerri non potest, nec ab eodem simul dari et accipi."
Deterret nos ubique Lutherus a rationibus philosophicis, quum ipse in re tam sacra se firmet in meracissimo
sophismate: nam quod unquam fuit sacrificium in lege
Mosaica, quod non sumebant qui offerebant? An quod
Deo offerebatur, ipse comedebat? *"Numquid ego man-*
ducabo carnes taurorum, aut sanguinem," inquit Deus,
"hircorum potabo?"

Præterea si Christus et sacerdos fuit, et sacrificium,
cur non potuit Christus instituere ut sacerdos, qui idem
sacrificium repræsentaret, victimam et offerret, et
sumeret? Sed hac in re, ne Lutherum videar imitari,
qui nihil habet pro se, nisi quod e suo fingit capite, afferemus quod dicit beatus Ambrosius de Missa: "Quanta," inquit, "cordis contritione, et lacrymarum fonte,
quanta reverentia et tremore, quanta corporis castitate
atque animi puritate istud divinum et cœleste mysterium est celebrandum, Domine Deus: ubi caro tua in
veritate sumitur, ubi sanguis tuus in veritate bibitur,
ubi summis ima, humanis divina junguntur: ubi adest
sanctorum præsentia, et angelorum: ubi tu es sacerdos
et sacrificium mirabiliter et ineffabiliter! Quis digne

drank; where the lowest is joined to the highest; and
divine Things with human: Where the Saints and
Angels are present; where, after an admirable and unspeakable Manner, thyself are both Priest and Sacrifice! Who shall be able to celebrate this Mystery
worthily, if then Almighty God do not render him
worthy that offers ?' You see how the holy Father, in
this Place, calls Mass an Oblation, and says that Christ
himself is both Priest and Sacrifice in it, even as he was
on the Cross. Let *Luther* see how much he attributes
to this Man's Authority; but St. *Gregory* makes appear
how much he had him in Esteem, when, in this Manner,
he imitated him in his Writings:—'Which of the Faithful (says he) can doubt, but that in the very Time of
the Immolation, the Heavens are opened to the Words
of the Priest, in that Mystery of Christ: That Choirs
of Angels are present; that the lowest Things are associated to the highest: That Earth is joined with
Heaven; and that of Visible and Invisible is made one
Thing ?' And in another Place, 'For this singular
Victim, which renews to us the Death of the only Begotten, does loose our Souls from eternal Death.' Nor
speaks he less to the Purpose, when he says, 'Hence
therefore let us ponder with ourselves, how much that
Sacrifice stands us in stead, which always imitates the
Passion of the only begotten Son.' We see, that not
only St. *Ambrose,* but also St. *Gregory,* calls Mass an
Immolation and Sacrifice; and confesses, that, not only
the last Supper of *Christ,* (as *Luther* holds) but also his
Passion is represented in it.

But these Fathers alone were not of that Judgment,
for St. *Augustine* confesses the same Thing, in divers
Places, who says thus of the Mass, 'The Oblation is
every Day renewed, though Christ has but once suffered: Because we daily fall, therefore is Christ daily

hoc potest celebrare mysterium, nisi tu, Deus omni-
potens, offerentem feceris dignum?"

Videtis ut hic beatissimus Pater et oblationem appellat Missam, et in eadem Christum ipsum dicat et sacerdotem esse, et sacrificium, quemadmodum fuit in cruce.
Cujus auctoritati quantum Lutherus tribuat, viderit
ipse: quantum vero tribuerit beatus Gregorius, facile
declaravit, quum illum imitatus ita scriberet: "Quis
fidelium dubitare possit in ipsa immolationis hora ad
sacerdotis vocem cœlos aperiri, in illo Christi mysterio
angelorum choros adesse, summis ima sociari, terram
cœlestibus jungi, unum quid ex visibilibus et invisibili-
bus fieri?" Et alibi: "Hæc namque singularis victima
ab æterno interitu animas solvit, quæ illam nobis mortem Unigeniti reparat." Nec minus aperte quum dicit:
"Hinc ergo pensemus quale sit pro nobis istud sacrificium, quod unigeniti Filii Passionem semper imita-
tur." Videmus ut non solum divus Ambrosius, sed et
beatus Gregorius immolationem appellat Missam, et
sacrificium, ac fatetur in ea non ultimam tantum
Christi Cœnam, quod Lutherus ait, sed et Passionem
ejus repræsentari. Nec tamen istud soli censuerunt
illi: nam et Augustinus non semel idem fatetur. Ait
enim de Missa: "Iteratur quotidie hæc oblatio, licet
Christus semel passus sit; quia quotidie labimur, Christus pro nobis quotidie immolatur." Item: "Eucharistia
est oblatio benedicta, per quam benedicimur, adscripta,
per quam omnes in cœlum adscribimur, rata, per quam
in visceribus Christi censemur."

offered for us. Also the Eucharist is a blessed Offering by which we are blessed; an Enrollment, by which we all are enrolled in Heaven; a Ratification, whereby we are mustered in the Bowels of Christ.'

Seeing, therefore, that Mass is by so holy and learned Men called an Offering, and a Sacrifice; and that they are of Opinion, that not only the last Supper of Christ, but also his Passion is by it commemorated; that they confess so immense and great Advantages to proceed from it; and that the Church, agreeing with them, sings the same in the whole Mass: I much admire with what Face *Luther* dares to cry out, on the Contrary, that Mass is no Sacrifice or Offering; and that it brings no Profit to the People; deriding the Authority of so many holy Fathers, or rather of the whole Church, by his most vain Device; as if they were all Things, which were understood of the Reliques of the Jewish Ceremonies, (in which he says, 'the Priest did heave up what was offered by the People.') Which Comment of *Luther*'s did seem so foolish and absurd, even to himself, that he doubted whether he should withstand the Sentiments of the holy Fathers, and the Customs of the whole Church, by such a babbling Argument, or rather openly despise them: 'For, says he, what shall we say to the Canons and Authorities of the Fathers?' 'I answer, says he, that if we have nothing at all to say against them; it is more safe to deny all Things, than to confess that Mass is a Work or Sacrifice, lest we deny the Words of Christ, corrupting them together with the Mass. Nevertheless, that we may agree with them also, we will say that all these Things were the Reliques of Jewish Ceremonies.' Lest, therefore, there should be nothing said, this civil Man, tendering the Repute of the holy Fathers, and the Honour of the whole Church, (lest they might be thought to speak foolishly) will seem

Quum igitur viri tam eruditi, tam sancti, Missam dicant oblationem, et sacrificium, quum per eam non Cœnam tantum sentiant, sed etiam Passionem Christi commemorari, quum inde tam immensa bona provenire fateantur, quum iisdem consentiens, eadem in Missa tota decantet Ecclesia, vehementer admiror qua fronte Lutherus audeat clamare contrarium, Missam non esse sacrificium, non esse oblationem, non prodesse populo, eludens auctoritatem tot sanctorum Patrum, imo totius Ecclesiæ vanissimo figmento suo, quasi omnia quæ de oblatione et sacrificio fiunt, et dicuntur in Missa, intelligerentur de reliquiis judaici ritus, quo levasse dicit sacerdotem ea quæ offerebantur a populo. Quod Lutheri commentum tam ineptum visum est et tam absurdum etiam ipsi Luthero, ut dubitaverit an sanctorum Patrum sententias, et Ecclesiæ totius consuetudinem tam futili ratione defenderet, an potius ex professo contemneret. Nam: "Quid dicemus," inquit, "ad Canones, et auctoritates Patrum? Respondeo," inquit, "si nihil habetur, quod dicatur, tutius est omnia negare, quam Missam concedere opus, aut sacrificium esse, ne verbum Christi negemus, simul cum Missa pessumdantes: tamen quo servemus et eos, dicemus illa omnia reliquias esse ritus judaici."

Ergo ne nihil dicatur, homo civilis, et honori sanctorum Patrum parcens, et honori totius Ecclesiæ, tanquam officii gratia, ne stulte loqui viderentur, præ clarum illud figmentum suum de reliquiis judaici ritus

to oblige them, by covering their Shame with the Veil of his most excellent Devices, concerning the Reliques of the Jewish Rites; which, if any Body remove, it will be to their Danger. For *Luther* does not ingeniously apprehend, that if any one urge him more narrowly, he would rather blow away all the Testimonies of the holy Fathers, and the Customs of the Church, than that he should allow Mass to be a good Work, or a Sacrifice; that is, rather than allow that to be true which is true: 'For in that (he says) they deny Christ's Words, and corrupt Faith with Mass, who affirm Mass to be a Sacrifice:' I suppose that none will believe him, unless he first shews that he has read another Gospel different from that the holy Fathers ever read, or that in reading the same, he has been more diligent than they, or has better understood it; or finally, that he is more careful about Faith, than ever any Man before him was.

But I believe he will not prefer any other Gospel unto us; nor, if he do, will it be admitted, though an Angel from Heaven should descend with it. And that which he proffers, has not been more diligently examined, nor more narrowly pryed into by him, than it has been tryed and searched into by others heretofore; of whom none ever said, that they found in it what he boasts himself to have found, viz. 'That Mass is not a good Work; that it is not an Oblation, nor a Sacrifice.' Lastly, if any one diligently considers what has been written by the one and the other, he cannot be ignorant what Difference has been in their Care about Faith: Those holy antient Fathers have observed, that, as this is the chiefest of all Sacraments, as containing in it the Lord of Sacraments; so is it the only Sacrifice, which alone remains, instead of so many Sacrifices of the Old Law; and lastly, of all the Works that can be done for the Salvation of the People, this, without Comparison,

pro velamento dignatus est eorum pudendis prætexere;
quod si quis admoveat, illorum periculo fecerit: nam
Lutherus ingenue non veretur, si quis eum stringat
arctius, quicquid unquam fuit sanctorum Patrum, quicquid unquam in Ecclesia moris fuit, exsufflare potius
videlicet, quam concedat Missam bonum opus esse, vel
sacrificium, hoc est, potius quam concedat verum esse,
quod verum est. Nam quod ait eos negare verbum
Christi, ac fidem simul cum Missa pessumdare, quicumque dicunt Missam esse sacrificium, nemo est,
opinor, qui credat hac in parte Luthero, nisi primum
doceat aut aliud evangelium legisse se, quam sancti illi
Patres legerunt, aut illud idem vel legisse diligentius,
vel intellexisse melius, aut sibi denique majorem esse
curam fidei, quam ulli unquam hactenus mortalium
fuerit. At evangelium, credo, non proferet nobis aliud;
neque, si proferet, audietur, etiamsi angelus cum eo de
cœlo descenderit. Illud vero, quod profert, neque diligentius excussit, neque perspicit acutius, quam olim et
excussum est, et perspectum ab illis, quorum nemo se
reperisse dixit illic, quod nunc iste jactat reperisse sese,
Missam bonum opus non esse, non esse oblationem,
non esse sacrificium; denique fidei cura cujusmodi
fuit utrique, non potest cuiquam esse obscurum,
qui quid utrinque scriptum sit, non oscitanter expenderit.

Veteres illi viri sanctissimi viderunt sicut sacramentorum omnium hoc esse summum, quod ipsum
sacramentorum Dominum complectatur, ita sacrificiorum omnium hoc esse unicum, quod solum in loco tot
olim sacrificiorum restiterit, postremo operum omnium,
quæ pro salute populi fieri possunt, longe lateque salu-

is the best and most wholesome. For when other Sacraments are only profitable to particular Persons receiving them: This, in the Mass, is beneficial to all, in general. And when Prayers made to God by one Man for another, may not only be hindered, but also rendered ineffectual, through the Fault of Men; the merciful Bounty of God has instituted Mass for the Salvation of the Faithful; in which his own Body should be offered a Sacrifice so wholesome, that the Wickedness of the Minister, be it never so great, is not able to lessen, or avert the Benefit of it from the People.

The most holy Fathers seeing these Things, took all possible Care, and used their utmost Endeavours, that the greatest Faith imaginable should be had towards this most propitiatory Sacrament; and that it should be worshipped with the greatest Honour possible: And for that Cause, amongst many other Things, they, with great Care, delivered us this also; *That the Bread and Wine do not remain in the Eucharist, but is truly changed into the Body and Blood of Christ.* They taught Mass to be a Sacrifice, in which Christ himself is truly offered for the Sins of Christian People: And so far as it was lawful for Mortals, they adorned this immortal Mystery with venerable Worship, and mystical Rites: They commanded the People to be present in Adoration of it, whilst it is celebrated, for the procuring of their Salvation. Finally, lest the Laity, by forbearing to receive the Sacrament, should, by little and little, omit it for-good-and-all; they have established an Obligation that every Man shall receive at least once in a Year. By those Things, and many of the like Nature, the holy Fathers of the Church, in several Ages, have demonstrated their Care for the Faith and Veneration of this adorable Sacrament. *Luther* ought

berrimum. Nam quum cætera sacramenta prosint singulis, solum hoc in Missa prodest universis; et quum omnes orationes, quibus alius pro alio intercedit apud Deum, non impediri tantum, sed et frustra fieri possint hominum vitio, misericors Dei clementia Missam institit pro salute fidelium, in qua suum ipsius corpus offerretur tam salubre sacrificium, ut ejus fructum nullius ministri quantavis iniquitas a populo suo vel avertere possit, vel imminuere.

Hæc Patres illi sanctissimi quum vidissent, summam habuerunt curam, summam adhibuere diligentiam, ut propitiatorium hoc sacramentum et fide quam maxima posset, haberetur, et honore quam posset maximo, coleretur; eoque quum alia multa, tum hoc quoque sedulo tradiderunt, panem et vinum in Eucharistia non manere, sed in carnem et sanguinem Christi veraciter esse conversa. Missam sacrificium esse docuerunt, in quo Christus ipse pro populi Christiani peccatis immolatur. Tum, quoad mortalibus licet, immortale mysterium venerando cultu, et mysticis ornarunt ritibus; populum, dum celebratur, in suæ salutis procuratione venerabundum adesse jusserunt. Denique, ne laici desuetudine recipiendi sacramenti paulatim ex toto desinerent, sanxerunt ut semel saltem quotannis Eucharistiam quisque susciperet. His igitur, atque aliis ejusmodi multis sancti Patres Ecclesiæ aliis alii temporibus sollicitudinem suam circa sacramenti hujus reverendi fidem venerationemque declararunt. Ideo jactare non debet Lutherus (id quod jactat tamen) eos, qui Missam dicunt esse sacrificium, aut alii quam sumenti prodesse, verbum Christi, fidemque, ac Missam ipsam pessum-

not therefore to boast (what nevertheless he does) that they who call Mass a Sacrifice, or say that it is profitable to any, but to him who receives the Sacrament in it, does corrupt the Word of Christ, Faith, and Mass itself.

But it will not be amiss, to consider after what Manner *Luther* sustains upon his Shoulders the Word of Christ, Faith, and Mass itself, that they may not become corrupted, or fall. First of all, he changes the Name itself of the Sacrament, into a worse; and that which was, for so many Ages, called the Eucharist, or the Sacrament of *Christ's* Body, lest the Name of it should put the Auditors in Mind of the Majesty of it, he commands to be called Bread: Afterwards the Bread and Wine, which the Antients held to be turned into the Body and Blood of our Lord, are by *Luther* taught to remain entire; that so, by little and little, he may traduce the Honour from Christ to the Bread. After this, though he does not condemn the Church for having adorned and amplified Mass, with Rites and Ceremonies; yet he thinks it should be more Christian-like, if the Pomp of Vestments, Singing, Gestures and other Ceremonies were laid aside; that so it might be more like and near to the first Mass of all, which *Christ* celebrated in his last Supper with his Apostles; or rather, that nothing may be left that might move the simple Minds of the vulgar Sort, and bring them to the Worship of this invisible Deity, through the Majesty of visible Honour. Moreover, he teacheth, and as much as in him lies, inculcates, that Mass is not a good Work, not a Sacrifice, not an Oblation, nor profitable to any of the People. To what Purpose pray is this so evangelical a Lecture? It is, that all the People, leaving Mass to the Priest, (to whom alone they must be persuaded that it is profitable) may themselves neglect it,

dare. At Lutherus Christi verbum, fidemque, ac Missam ipsam, ne pessumdentur et corruant, quo pacto suis humeris sustinet, id vero vicissim considerare profuerit.

Initio nomen ipsum sacramenti demutat in deterius, et quum tot sæculis appellatum sit Eucharistia, vel sacramentum corporis Christi, ille, ne nomen audientes admoneat majestatis rei, jubet vocari panem. Deinde panem et vinum, quæ veteres conversa fatentur in corpus et sanguinem Domini, Lutherus adhuc manere docet integra, ut ordine paulatim honorem a Christo traducat in panem. Tum licet non damnet Ecclesiam, quæ ritibus et cærimoniis ornavit, et ampliavit Missam, tamen censet quod Missa foret multo christianior, si vestium, cantuum, gestuum et cæterarum cærimoniarum omnium pompa tolleretur, ut esset vicinior et similior primæ omnium Missæ, quam Christus in Cœna cele-bravit cum apostolis, imo vero, ut quam minimum supersit eorum quæ simplices animos plebeculæ com-moveant, et in venerationem numinis invisibilis visibilis honoris majestate convertant. Ad hæc docet, et om-nibus modis inculcat Missam bonum opus non esse, sac-rificium non esse, oblationem non esse, nemini prorsus e populo prodesse. Quorsum hæc tam sancta et evan-gelica lectio? Nempe ut populus totus, Missa relicta sacerdoti, cui soli prodesse persuasum habeant, negli-gant ipsi, et suum officium rei sibi inutili subducant: denique ut ipsi, quando communicantur, tantum fidem afferant testamenti se fore compotes, qualescumque con-scientias attulerint, imo quo magis erroneas attulerint, et peccatorum vel morsu, vel titillatione turbatas, tanto

and pay no Duty to a Thing unprofitable to them.
Lastly, that when they communicate, if they only have
but Faith, that they are about to receive the Testament;
whatsoever Consciences they bring; nay, the more erroneous they are, and the more troubled with the Sting
and Concupiscence of Sin, the more are they to assure
themselves that they are Partakers of the divine Promises; especially, because this Sacrament is the Medicine
of Sins past, present, and to come; which would find no
Room for itself in those who should purge themselves
with greatest Anxiety from the Diseases of Sin; and,
according to the Precept of the Apostle, proving themselves,* they may approach our Lord's Table with as
pure and sincere a Conscience as may be possible; that
seeing they cannot say we are justified, at least they may
say we are guilty of nothing to ourselves. After *Luther,*
therefore, has taught this short and compendious Preparation for receiving the Eucharist, to wit, *in the Faith
alone of the Promise; without any good Works, and a
light Examination of Conscience;* he, that nothing be
wanting to the absolute Sanctity of receiving the Sacrament; shews his Desire concerning what Time, and
how often he is willing the People should be obliged to
receive; and that is, in no Time at all. And why so?
What? Is there any one so blind, as not to see what
this so palpable a Matter drives at? Certainly nothing
else, but that the People may, by Degrees, quite give
over communicating at all; who at first changed the
daily receiving, into a Seventh-day communicating; and
after, to a longer Time; and at last would forsake it
altogether; if the Fathers, fearing that should happen,
had not decreed, that every Man should receive thrice
in a Year; threatening, that he who would not obey,
should not be accounted a Christian: Yet nevertheless

*I. Cor. xi. 28.

magis se noverint divinæ promissionis esse participes;
præsertim quum sacramentum hoc sit medicina peccatorum præteritorum, præsentium et futurorum, quæ
nullum sibi locum reperiret, scilicet in eo, qui nimis
anxie semet prius ideo a peccati morbo purgaverit, ut
secundum Apostoli præceptum probans semetipsum,
conscientia quam maxime potest pura et sincera discum-
bat in mensa Domini, ut quum dicere non possit:
Justificatus sum, illud saltem possit: Nullius mihi conscius sum.

Lutherus ergo, posteaquam præparationem istam
docuit brevem et compendiariam ad suscipiendam
Eucharistiam, nempe in sola fide promissionis, nullis
operibus bonis, levissima disquisitione conscientiæ, postremo, ne quicquam desit absolutæ sanctimoniæ ad sus-
cipiendum sacramentum, suum votum aperit quoties, et
quibus anni temporibus potissimum velit cogi populum
communionem sumere, nempe prorsus nullo. Quid ita?
quid? An quisquam tam cæcus est, ut non videat quorsum hæc tam putida tendant? Certe non aliorsum,
quam ut populus sensim a communione sacramenti
desciscat in totum, qui primum a quotidiana communione deflexit in septimum quemque diem, post in
longius distulit: tandem destituturus videbatur omnino,
nisi Patres illud veriti sanxissent, ut ter in anno
quisque communicaret, interminati non habendum pro
Christiano, qui non obtemperaset: at nec id tamen diu
potuit obtineri. Quamobrem adultimum eo descensum
est, ut inferius descendi non possit, nisi ferme prorsus
ad inferos, nempe ut semel saltem in anno communi-

that Custom could they not continue long; so that, at last, the Matter fell so low, that it could descend no lower; for now we are obliged to receive but once in a Year: Which Custom, if *Luther* could demolish, as he endeavours, the World would e'er long (through the Decay of the Fervour of Faith) be reduced to what it should have come to long ago, if it had not been prevented by this solemn Custom of receiving every Year; that at last there would scarce remain the least Foot-step of the Communion amongst the People, nor perhaps, among the Clergy neither, if *Luther* could bring it about that Mass should be so spoiled, not only of its Preparation and Ceremonies, but also of the People's Resort, Hope and Veneration to it. These are the excellent Promises of *Luther;* this is that spacious Liberty he promises to all those who forsake the Catholic Church to follow him, *viz.* That they may be freed at last from the Use and Faith of the Sacrament! Wherefore, I forbear to speak any more of this Thing, as being so clear in itself, that it needs no further Dispute. And seeing we have discovered the crafty Winding of the subtil Serpent; which being now seen, (as without Doubt they are by all who are not quite blind) it is not necessary to exhort any Body to shun such apparent Evils. I believe none are so mad, as to forsake the Church of God, for the Synagogue of Satan. That, shunning the Service of *Christ,* (to serve whom is to reign) he may list himself into the Liberty proposed by *Luther;* where, under the Name of Liberty, he should wilfully, and to his own Knowledge put his Foot into the Snare of the Devil. But rather let all the Faithful of *Christ* say with the Psalmist, *We will not decline from thy Judgments, because thou hast appointed us a Law.**

*Ps. cxviii. 102.

cemus: quam consuetudinem si Lutherus, ut optat,
posset amoliri, mundus, refrigescente in dies fervore
fidei, propediem profecto redigeretur eo, quo jam
pridem pervenisset, nisi hoc solemni quotannis communicandi ritu fuisset retentus, ut aliquando nullum
ferme remaneat in populo communicandi vestigium,
fortasse nec in clero quidem, si Lutherus obtinere
possit, ut Missa non apparatu tantum, et cærimoniis,
sed populi quoque frequentia, spe ac veneratione spoli-
etur.

Hæc sunt ergo præclara illa promissa Lutheri. Hæc
est speciosa illa libertas, quam pollicetur ex Ecclesia
catholica venientibus ad se, nempe ut liberentur aliquando ab usu et fide sacramenti. Quamobrem ego hac
de re amplius disputare supersedeo, utpote re magis ex
se perspicua, quam ut cuiquam disputari debuerit. Tantum indicasse non oberit astutissimas versuti serpentis
insidias, quibus jam perspectis (perspicit enim, non
dubito, quisquis non plane cæcus est), non erit opus
hortari quemquam ut prævisa mala devitet. Nemo erit,
opinor, tam vecors, ut ex Ecclesia Dei desciscat in syna-
gogam Satanæ, e Christi servitute fugiens, cui servire
regnare est, asserat se in libertatem propositam a Luthero, ubi solo libertatis nomine, sciens prudensque in
præmonstratas diaboli pedicas injiciat pedes. Sed una
cum psalmista omnes Christi fideles hunc versum
clament: *"A judiciis tuis non declinavimus, quia tu
legem posuisti nobis."*

CHAP. V

Of Baptism

As for the rest of the Sacraments, it is not necessary to stand long upon them; most of them he takes quite away from us: And the Sacrament of the Eucharist, (being almost the only one he vouchsafed to leave us) has by him been handled in such a Manner, as we have already shewn you; so that none can doubt but he devised by little and little, to demolish this also: Nor does he praise any one of the Sacraments, unless to the Prejudice of another; for he so much extols *Baptism,* that he depresses *Penance:* Though he has treated of *Baptism* itself after such a Manner, that it had been better he had not touched it at all. For first of all, that he might seem to treat with a great deal of Sanctity in a Matter so holy, he, by a long Discourse, teaches that the divine Promise is to be believed, by which he promises Salvation to them who believe, and are baptized. He is angry, and reproaches the Church for not teaching this Faith to the Christians; as if in any Place they were so ignorant of Christian Faith, as not to understand this: And yet *Luther* proposes it for a new Thing, almost never before heard of, to the Reproach of all the Doctors.

But this is no new Method of his Proceedings, to trifle in Things known, as though they had before never been heard of. And having in many Words shewn what this Faith is, he afterwards extols the Riches of Faith, to the End he may render us poor of good Works, without which (as St. *James* saith*) *Faith is altogether dead.*

*James ii. 17-26.

CAP. V

De Sacramento Baptismi

Reliquis ergo sacramentis nihil opus est immorari,
quorum pleraque omnia tollit, quum Eucharistiæ sacramentum, quod unicum ferme relinquere videbatur,
tamen, ut ostendimus, ita tractarit, ut nemini relinquat
dubium quin et illud quoque paulatim machinetur
amoliri; nec ullum sane sacramentum laudat, nisi in
alterius injuriam. Nam sic et Baptismum effert, ut
deprimat Pœnitentiam. Quamquam Baptismum etiam
ipsum tractavit sic, ut satius multo fuerit non attigisse.
Nam primum, quo videretur sancte rem sanctam tracta-
turus, multis verbis docet fidem habendam promissioni
divinæ, qua salutem promittit credentibus et baptizatis.
Irascitur, et insectatur Ecclesiam, quod Christiani non
docentur hanc fidem, quasi quisquam sit usquam tam
rudis Christianæ fidei, ut hoc sit docendus; et tamen
tanquam rem novam et inauditam ferme Lutherus hoc
proponit, cum insigni contumelia doctorum omnium.
Sed hoc non est ei novum in rebus notis, tanquam novis,
nugari.

Qui postquam hanc fidem verbis multis ostendit,
deinde fidei divitias in hoc extollit, ut nos reddat
pauperes bonorum operum, sine quibus, ut beatus
Jacobus ait, *"fides omnino mortua est."* At Lutherus
sic fidem nobis commendat, ut non solum permittat

But *Luther* so much commends Faith to us, as not only to permit us to abstain from good Works; but also encourages us to commit any Kind of Action, how bad soever: 'For (says he) you see now how rich the baptized Man is, who cannot lose his Salvation, though willing to do it, by any Sin whatsoever, except Infidelity: For no Sins can damn him, but only Incredulity.' O most impious Doctrine, and Mistress of all Impiety! so hateful in itself to pious Ears, that there is no need to confute it: Adultery will not damn then! Murder will not damn! Perjury will not damn! Is not Parricide damnable neither, if every one believe that he shall be saved, through the Virtue of the Promise alone in Baptism? For this he openly asserts; nor do the Words, which he presently adds, correct this Sentence in any wise; but rather add to the Force of it: For he saith, 'That all other Things, if Faith return, or stand in the divine Promise made by the Baptized, are swallowed in a Moment in the same Faith; rather by the Truth of God, for he cannot deny himself, if you confess him, and stick faithfully to his Promise:' By which Words, what else does he say, but what he has said before, that, 'Infidelity excepted, all other Crimes are in a Moment swallowed up by Faith alone; if you confess Christ, and stick faithfully to his Promise;' that is, if you firmly believe that you are to be saved by Faith, whatsoever you do notwithstanding. And that you may the less doubt what he aims at, 'Contrition (says he) and Confession of Sins, as also Satisfaction, and all these human Inventions, will forsake you, and leave you the more unhappy, if you busy yourselves with them, forgetting this divine Truth.' What Truth Pray? 'This that no Sins can damn thee, but Infidelity only.' What Christian Ears can with Patience hear the pestilentious Hissing of this Serpent, by which he extols *Bap-*

nobis vacationem ab operibus bonis, sed etiam suggerat audaciam qualiumcumque facinorum. Ait enim: "Jam vides quam dives sit homo Christianus, sive baptizatus, qui etiam volens non potest perdere salutem suam quantiscumque peccatis, nisi nolit credere. Nulla enim peccata eum possunt damnare, nisi sola incredulitas." O vocem impiam, et omnis impietatis magistram, ita per se exosam piis auribus, ut non sit opus eam redarguere! Ergo non damnabit adulterium? non damnabit homicidium? non perjurium? non parricidium? si tantum credat se quisquam salvandum fore per virtutem promissionis in Baptismate? Nam hoc dicit apertissime, neque quicquam corrigunt hanc sententiam verba quæ statim subjungit; imo verius augent. Ait enim: "Cætera omnia, si redeat vel stet fides in promissionem divinam baptizato factam, in momento absorbentur per eamdem fidem, imo veritatem Dei, quia seipsum negare non potest, si tu eum confessus fueris, et promittenti fideliter adhæseris." Quibus verbis, quid aliud dicit, quam quod dixit prius? si absit incredulitas, cætera flagitia omnia in momento absorberi in sola fide si confessus fueris Christum, et ejus promissioni fideliter adhæseris, hoc est firmiter credideris te salvandum per fidem, quicquid feceris. Et quo minus dubites quo tendat: "Contritio," inquit, "et peccatorum Confessio, deinde et Satisfactio, et omnia illa hominum excogitata studia subito te deserent, et infeliciorem reddent, si in ipsis tete distenderis, oblitus veritatis hujus divinæ." Cujus veritatis? nempe hujus, quod nulla peccata possunt te damnare, nisi sola incredulitas.

Quæ Christianæ ferent aures pestilens hoc serpentis sibilum, quo Baptismum non in aliud levat, quam ut premat Pœnitentiam, et Baptismatis gratiam statuat

tism, for no other End, but to depress *Penance,* and
establish the Grace of Baptism for a free Liberty of
Sinning? Contrary to which, is that Sentence of St.
Hierom, which says, *that Penance is the Table after
Ship-wreck:* But this agrees not with *Luther;* for he
denies Sin to be the Ship-wreck of Faith, and disputes
it, as if that only Word should totally destroy all the
Strength of Faith. But beside *Luther,* who is ignorant
that a Sinner not only is not saved by the only Faith
of Baptism, but also that the Baptism will add to his
Damnation? And indeed deservedly; because he has
offended God, from whom he had the whole Grace of
Baptism, and God exacts the more from him to whom
he has given the more: Therefore since Faith becomes
dead by wicked Works, why can it not be said, that he
suffers Ship-wreck who falls from the Grace of God,
into the Hands of the Devil? From which, without
Penance, he cannot escape, or be renewed to such a
Condition that Baptism may be profitable to him. Has
St. *Hierom* written wickedly in this? Does the whole
Church follow an impious Opinion, for not believing
Luther, that Christians are safe enough by Faith alone,
in the midst of their Sins, without Penance? Moreover, he is so taken up with the Faith of the Sacrament,
that he cares not much for the Form of Words; though,
nevertheless, the Word, by which the Water is signified,
ought to be of no less Moment, than the Water itself;
in which, if he thinks that any Care is to be taken, that
it may be pure and elementary; ought not some true
Form also be carefully instituted, and used, as is approved, and now observed in the Church, and was formerly in Use amongst the Antients?

After this, he so magnifies Faith, that he seems almost to intimate, that Faith alone is sufficient without
the Sacrament. For in the mean While, he deprives

impune peccandi licentiam? In quam sententiam et
istud facit, quod ei non placet illud beati Hieronymi
Pœnitentiam esse secundam tabulam post naufragium;
negat peccatum fidei esse naufragium, et sic disputat,
tanquam illud verbum prorsus interimat omne robur
fidei. At quis nescit, nisi Lutherus, peccatorem non
solum non salvari per solam fidem Baptismi, sed etiam
illum ipsum Baptismum ei cessurum in cumulum
damnationis? Et merito quia læsit Deum, a quo totam
acceperat Baptismi gratiam, et cui plus a Deo datur, ab
illo vicissim plus exigitur. Igitur, quum fidem per
opera mala peremerit, cur dici non potest fecisse
naufragium, qui e Dei gratia decidit in manus dæ-
monum, e quibus absque Pœnitentia non reponitur in
eum statum, ut Baptismum ei rursus prodesse possit?
Num hic impie scripsit Hieronymus? Num impie tota
sensit Ecclesia, quæ non credit Luthero, sine Pœnitentia, per solam fidem Christianos esse tutos in mediis
sceleribus?

Præterea sic totus est in fide sacramenti, ut non admodum curet de forma verborum, quum verbum tamen
per quod significatur aqua, non minoris esse momenti
debeat quam aqua ipsa, in qua, si putat ullam adhiben-
dam esse curam, ut pura sit et elementaris, nullam-ne
decet adhiberi ad inquirendam et exercendam veram aliquam verborum formam, quam certum sit et nunc
observari per Ecclesiam, et olim in usu fuisse
veteribus.

Post hæc ita magnificat fidem, ut propemodum videatur innuere solam fidem sine sacramento sufficere. Nam
interim sacramentum privat gratia; dicit sacramentum

the Sacrament of Grace; he says, 'that the Sacrament it self profits nothing;' denies that the Sacraments confer any Grace; or that they are effectual Signs of Grace; or that the Sacraments of the Evangelical Law differ in any Kind from those of the Mosaical Law, as touching the Efficacy of Grace: Which Matter I shall not much dispute: But yet, it seems to me, that as all Things were but Figures with the Jews, (the Truth of which we have in the Christian Law) it may not be absurd to believe, that the Sacraments which the Church uses, do so far excel those of the Synagogues, as the new Law surpasses the old; that is, as much as the Body is more excellent than the Shadow: Nor am I the first, or only Man of this Opinion. For *Hugo de Sancto Victore,* whom none esteems other than a good and learned Man, has spoken thus; 'We say, that all Sacraments are certain Signs, and spiritual Graces which by them are conferred. Moreover, that the Signs of spiritual Graces, according to the Process of Time, ought to be framed more evident and plain, that the Knowledge of Truth might increase with the Effect of Salvation.' And a little further, 'Because Circumcision could only lop off exterior Enormities, but not cleanse the inward Filth of Pollutions, a washing Font of Water succeeded Circumcision, which purgeth the whole, that perfect Justice may be signified.' I hope no body will deny, that this Doctor is of Opinion, That the Sacrament of Baptism cleanses internally, and more efficaciously signifies perfect Justice, than ever Circumcision did. In which Matter *Luther* takes Notice of two Opinions, and refutes both: The first is, 'Of many who have supposed some secret and hidden Virtue to be in the Word and Water, which should work the Grace of God in the Soul of the Baptized:' The other is, 'Of those who attribute no Virtue to the Sacraments, but were of Opinion, That

ipsum nihil prodesse; negat sacramenta gratiam con-
ferre, aut gratiæ efficacia signa esse, aut omnino quoad
efficaciam significationis, sacramenta legis evangelicæ
differre quicquam a sacramentis legis mosaicæ. Qua
in re non multum disputabo, sed tamen videtur mihi,
quum omnia in figuris contigerint Judæis, quarum
veritas est in lege Christiana, nihil absurdi consecu-
turum, si quis credat sacramenta, quibus utitur Ecclesia, tantum præcellere synagogæ sacramentis, quantum lex nova veterem legem antecellit, hoc est, quantum
corpus umbram superat. Quod ego tamen neque primus
cogito, neque solus. Hugo de Sancto-Victore, quem
nemo non habet et pro viro docto et bono: "Dicimus,"
inquit, "sacramenta omnia signa esse quædam ejus, quæ
per illa datur, gratiæ spiritualis. Oportere autem, ut
secundum processum temporum, spiritualium gratia-
rum signa magis ac magis semper evidentia ac declara-
tiva formarentur, ut cum effectu salutis cresceret cogni-
tio veritatis." Et Paulo post: "Quia Circumcisio eas
tantum, quæ foris sunt, enormitates amputare potest,
eas vero, quæ intrinsecus sunt, pollutionum sordes mun-
dare non potest, venit post Circumcisionem lavacrum
aquæ, totum purgans, ut perfecta justitia significare-
tur." Nemo negabit, opinor, hunc saltem Doctorem
sentire sacramentum Baptismi et interius purgare, et
efficacius perfectam significasse justitiam, quam fecerit
Circumcisio.

Qua in re Lutherus duas vias commemorat, et utramque refutat, alteram, qua arbitrati sunt plurimi esse
aliquam virtutem occultam, spiritalem in verbo et aqua,
quæ operetur in animo recipientis gratiam Dei; alteram
eorum qui nihil virtutis tribuerunt sacramentis, sed
gratiam censuerunt a solo Deo dari, qui assistit ex pacto
sacramentis a se institutis: sed quoniam utrique in hoc

Grace was conferred by God alone, who, according to his
Covenant, is present to the Sacraments instituted by
himself.' But because all agree in this, That Sacraments are efficacious Signs of Grace, *Luther* rejects the
one as well as the other : For my Part, as I do not know
which of the Opinions is the truest, so neither dare I
be so bold as to contemn either of them. For that very
Opinion which now is the less assented to, to wit, 'That
the Water, by Virtue of the Word, has an occult Power
of purging the Soul;' seems not to be altogether absurd.
For if we believe, that Fire has any Influence over the
Soul, either to punish or purge Sins ; what hinders, that
Water should, by the Power of God, (by whom also the
other Thing is done) penetrate to wash away the Uncleanness of the Soul? Which Opinion seems to be
much confirmed by the Words of St. *Augustine,* when
he says, 'The Water of Baptism toucheth the Body, and
washes the Heart;' and also that of St. *Beda,* who says,
'That *Christ,* by the Touch of his most pure Flesh, has
given the Water a regenerate Power.' Likewise that of
the Prophet *Ezekiel* seems to incline towards this, 'I
washed thee with Water, and cleansed thy Blood from
thee :'* Which Words, though they were spoken in Times
past, before Baptism was instituted, are, notwithstanding, (according to the Custom of the Prophets) understood of the future. Neither speaks he only of the washing of the Body, in which nothing is worthy the Præ-
dication of a Prophet; nor was ever any other Washing
which washed the Crimes of the Soul, but the Sacrament of Baptism, of which *Ezekiel* seems to have spoken
in the Person of God; prophesying, that there should be
a future Cleansing in the Sacrament of Baptism, by the
washing Font of Water: Which, by the same Prophet
is more plain a little after, when he speaks of the future;

*Ezech. xvi. 9.

consentiunt sacramenta esse efficacia signa gratiæ, utramque viam rejicit Lutherus. Ego ut nescio utra via sit verior, ita neutram audeo plane contemnere.

Nam et illa ipsa via, cui nunc pauciores assentiunt, non omnino videtur absurda, quod aqua ipsa per verbum occultam habeat animæ purgandæ potentiam. Nam si creditur ignis in animam agere, vel ad punienda, vel ad expurganda peccata, quid vetat potestate Dei, per quam et illud fit, aquam quoque ad eluendas animæ sordes posse penetrare. In quam sententiam videntur et Augustini verba facere, quum ait: "Aqua Baptismi corpus tangit, et cor abluit." Et illud Bedæ quoque dicentis, quod Christus tactu mundissimæ carnis suæ vim regenerativam contulit aquis. Præterea videtur illud in idem vergere quod propheta canit Ezechiel: *"Lavi te aqua, et emundavi sanguinem tuum ex te."* Quæ verba, quanquam de præterito loquitur ante Baptismum institutum, tamen, ut mos est prophetarum, de futuro intelliguntur; nec de corpore duntaxat abluendo loquitur, in quo nihil est dignum quod propheta prædiceret, nec alia ablutio unquam abluit animæ crimina, præter sacramentum Baptismi: de illo igitur locutus videtur Ezechiel in persona Dei prædicentis in sacramento Baptismi mundationem futuram esse per aquæ lavacrum. Quod ipsum paulo post idem propheta prosequitur apertius per verbum de futuro: *"Effundam,"* inquit, *"super vos aquam mundam, et mundabimini ab omnibus inquinamentis vestris."* Annon per aquam promittit emundationem? Quanquam multo adhuc apertius rem videtur ostendere Zacharias: *"Exibunt,"* inquit, *"aquæ vivæ de Jerusalem, medium earum ad mare orientale, et medium earum ad mare novissi-*

'I will pour out, saith he, clear Water upon you, and I
will cleanse you from all your Iniquities.'* Whether
does he not here promise a Cleansing by Water? Yet
Zecharias seems to unfold the Matter more apparently,
when he says, 'Living Water shall flow out from *Jerusalem,* the one Half to the Eastern Sea, and the other
Half to the great Sea.'† Does not this Discourse manifest unto us the Figure of Baptism, viz. Water flowing
from the Church, which should purge both original and
actual Sin? which he does not call dead, but living; that
he might demonstrate, as I suppose, That, by the secret
Sanctification of God, the Force of spiritual Life is
infused into a corporeal Element. Although I do not
presume to judge, (as I have said already,) nor am I
curious, after what Manner God infuses Grace by the
Sacraments, because his Ways are inscrutable:‡ Yet I
believe, that by one Way or other, this Water should not
be idle, where he fore-tells so many, and so great
Things, were to be done by Water; especially, since
Water, Salt, and other corporeal Things, do receive
spiritual Force, by the Word of God, without the Sacrament of Faith; unless all those Things should be spoken
in vain; in which Lights, Fire, Water, Salt, Bread, the
Altar, Vestments, and Rings, are either adjured by Ex-
orcisms, or blessed by the Invocation of Grace.

If those Things, I say, receive any Virtue or Presence of the Divinity, without the Sacrament; how much
more credible is it, that the Water flowing from Christ's
Side, does infuse a spiritual Power of Life into the
Fountain of Regeneration? Of which Christ himself
says, *That he, who is not born again of Water, and of
the Holy Ghost, shall not enter into the Kingdom of
Heaven;*§ to which (as the Apostle saith) *we are called*

---

*Ezech. xxxvi. 25.   ‡Rom. xi. 33.
†Zach. xiv. 8.   §John iii. 5.

mum." Hic sermo annon nobis evidenter Baptisma depingit? aquam videlicet de Ecclesia manantem, quæ et originale peccatum purget, et actuale, quam non mortuam appellat, sed vivam, ut ostendat, opinor, per occultam sanctificationem Dei, elemento corporeo vim vitæ spiritualis infusam.

Quanquam, ut dixi, qua via Deus per sacramenta infundat gratiam, neque mihi judicium arrogo, neque valde vestigo, quum sint investigabiles viæ ejus; sed certe aliqua via credo fecisse Deum, ut illic aqua non sit otiosa, ubi tam multa et tam magna prædicat facienda per aquam, præsertim quum et aqua, et sal, et alia quoque corporea, sine sacramento fidei, per verbum Dei recipiant spiritalem vim: nisi prorsus vana sint omnia quibus cerei, ignis, aqua, sal, panis, altare, vestes, annuli, vel adjurantur exorcismis, vel invocatione gratiæ benedicuntur. Quæ si vim ullam recipiunt, aut ullam numinis præsentiam extra sacramentum, quanto magis credibile est aquam e Christi latere manantem, spiritalem vitæ vim fonti regenerationis infundere? De quo Christus ipse pronunciat, quod *nisi quis renatus fuerit ex aqua et Spiritu sancto, non poterit videre regnum Dei,* ad quod, ut ait Apostolus, *"vocamur in Baptismo."*

in Baptism.* In which Baptism, I am not against *Luther,* for having attributed so much to Faith: But, on the other Side, I would not have him attribute so much thereto, as by it to defend an evil Life, or exterminate the Sacraments, which it ought to form. But when he requires that certain and indubitable Faith in the Receiver of the Sacraments; for my Part, I think it is rather to be wished for, than exacted. For I do not doubt, but when St. *Peter* did exhort the People after this Manner, 'Do Penance, and be baptized every one of you, in the Name of Jesus Christ; and receive you the Gift of the Holy Ghost unto the Remission of Sins,'† I doubt not but he was ready to receive all the People to Baptism; yet not so suddenly to have exacted that high, certain and indubitable Faith of *Luther* from them, which none would have been able to have known himself to have attained to: But he promised Remission of Sins, and Grace from the Sacrament itself, to all those who should but only present themselves, and desire it: For an undoubted and certain Faith, is a very great Thing, which happens not always, nor to every Body; no, not perhaps to them who do not doubt but they have it. I indeed shall not doubt to hope, but the Benignity of God assists in his Sacraments, and by Means of visible Signs, infuses invisible Grace; and helps the Tepidity of Believers, by the Fervour of his Sacraments: That many obtain Salvation by the Sacraments, who can promise no more to themselves of their Faith, than he could, who said, 'Lord I believe, help my Unbelief.'‡ In which Thing if any, beside my Adversary, think I attribute too much to the Sacrament; let him know, I define Nothing, I appoint Nothing, in any Case, which may be prejudicial to Faith, from which I derogate Nothing: But as I do not think, that Faith alone, with-

*1. Cor. i.   †Acts ii. 38.   ‡Mk. ix. 23.

Quo in Baptismo, quod Lutherus multum tribuit
fidei, non adversor, modo ne tantum tribuat fidei, ut
fides malam vitam defendat, aut, quæ formare debet,
exterminet sacramenta. At quum certam illam et indubitatam fidem exigit in suscipiente sacramentum, ego
potius optandam quam exigendam puto. Nam et beatus
Petrus, quum ita populum hortaretur: *"Pœnitentiam
agite, et baptizetur unusquisque vestrum in nomine Jesu
Christi in remissionem peccatorum vestrorum, et ac-
cipietis donum Spiritus sancti,"* non dubito quin paratus
fuerit ad Baptismum recipere totum populum; nec
tamen a toto populo repente exegisset illam summam
certam et indubitatam fidem Lutheri, quam nemo se
satis sciret attigisse; sed promittebat ex ipso sacramento
omnibus qui se duntaxat offerrent, et cuperent, remissionem peccatorum, et gratiam. Nam magna quædam
res est, certa et indubitata fides, neque semper, neque
cuique contingit, etiam ex his fortasse, qui sibi contigisse non dubitant. Ego profecto sperare non dubitem,
quin Dei benignitas suis sacramentis assistat, et visibilibus signis invisibilem infundat gratiam, et sacramenti sui fervore teporem credentium adjuvet, multos
per sacramenta consequi salutem, qui de sua fide non
amplius polliceri possunt, quam potuit ille, **qui dixit**:
"Credo, Domine, adjuva incredulitatem meam."

Qua in re, si cui alii præterquam adversario, videar
nimium sacramento tribuere, sciat me nihil definire,
nihil omnino statuere, quod præjudicet fidei, cui ego
nihil derogo; sed ut solam fidem sine sacramento non
puto sufficere in eo qui sacramenti compos esse potest, ita
neque sacramentum sufficere sine fide, sed utrumque

out the Sacrament, is sufficient for him who may receive
it; so neither can the Sacrament suffice him without
Faith; but that both ought to concur and co-operate
with their Power: And I think it more safe to allow
Something to the Sacrament, than, like *Luther,* to attribute so much to Faith, as to leave neither Grace, nor
the Efficacy of a Sign to the Sacrament.

Besides, he makes Faith nothing else but a Cloak for
a wicked Life, as we have before more fully declared:
And that this may the more appear, after he has deprived the Sacraments of Grace, he robs the Church of
all Vows and Laws; nor does it at all move him, that
God said, *Vow, and render to God your Vows.** But
as for Vows, I make no Doubt but some of those, whom
he calls *Vovists* and *Votaries,* will undertake to make
Answer for their own Profession: For at once, he turns
them almost all together, out of the Church.

The Laws of Rulers Are To Be Obeyed

BUT, as for the Laws, I admire, that he could, for
Shame, invent such ridiculous Things; as if Christians
could not sin; but that so great a Multitude of Believers
should be so perfect, that nothing needed to be ordered,
either for the Honour of God, or the avoiding of Wickedness. But by the same Work and Policy he robs Princes
and Prelates, of all Power and Authority; for what
shall a King or a Prelate do, if he cannot appoint any
Law, or execute the Law which was before appointed;
but, even like a Ship without a Rudder, suffer his People to float without Land? Where then is that Saying
of the Apostle, 'Let every Creature be subject to the
higher Powers?'† Where is that other of his, 'If thou
dost Evil, fear the King, it is not without Reason that
he carries the Sword?'‡ Where is also that, 'be obedi-

*Ps. lxxv. 12; Eccles. v. 3.   †Rom. xiii. 1.   ‡Rom. xiii. 4.

oportere concurrere, et utriusque robur cooperari, et tutius opinor aliquid sacramento concedere, quam tantum dare fidei, quantum donat Lutherus, qui sacramento neque gratiam relinquit, neque efficaciam signi.

Praeterea fidem ipsam nihil facit aliud, quam flagitiosae vitae patrocinium, quemadmodum ante uberius declaravimus. Quam rem quo magis adstrueret, postquam sacramenta privavit gratia, Ecclesiam privat et votis omnibus, et legibus. Nec quicquam movet illum, quod Deus ait, *"Vovete, et reddite."* Sed de votis non dubito quin exsurgant ex his quos ille vovistas vocat, et votarios, qui pro sua professione respondeant. Nam illos ex Ecclesia semel ferme prorsus eliminat universos.

Legibus Magistratuum Obediendum Esse

DE legibus vero, demiror hominem prae pudore potuisse tam absurda cogitare, quasi Christiani peccare non possent, sed tam perfecta foret tanta multitudo credentium, ut nihil decerni debeat, vel ad cultum Dei, vel ad vitanda flagitia. Sed eadem opera, et eadem prudentia, tollit omnem potestatem et auctoritatem principum, et praelatorum. Nam quid faciet rex, aut praelatus, si neque legem potest ponere, neque positam exsequi, sed populus absque lege, velut navis absque gubernaculo fluctuet? Ubi est ergo illud Apostoli: *"Omnis creatura potestatibus sublimioribus subjecta sit?"* Ubi illud: *"Si male agis, regem time, non sine causa gladium portat?"* Ubi illud: *"Obedite praepositis vestris, sive regi quasi praecellenti,"* et quae sequuntur? Cur igitur ait Paulus: *"Bona est lex?"* Et alibi: *"Lex est vinculum perfectionis?"* Praeterea, cur ait Augus-

ent to your Governours, whether to the King as excelling?'* And what follows? Why then does St. *Paul* say, 'The Law is good?'† and in another Place, 'The Law is the Bond of Perfection?'‡

Furthermore, why does St. *Augustin* say, 'The Power of the King, the Right of the Owner, the Instruments of the Executioner, the Arms of the Soldier, the Discipline of the Governor, and the Severity of a good Father, were not instituted in vain?' The first have all their Customs, Causes, Reasons, Profits; and when the others are feared, evil Men are restrained from doing Evil, and the Good live quietly amongst the Wicked:

But I forbear to speak of Kings, lest I should seem to plead my own Case. I only ask this, That if none, either Man or Angel, can appoint any Law among Christians, why does the Apostle institute for us so many Laws; as for electing Bishops;§ for Widows;‖ covering the Heads of Women,¶ &c.? Why has he ordained that a Christian Woman should not forsake her Husband, though an Infidel, if she be not by him first abandoned?** Why dares he say, *I myself speak to the rest, not the Lord?*†† Why has he exercised so great Power, as to command the *Incestuous* to be delivered over to *Satan*, to the Destruction of the Flesh?‡‡ Why has St. *Peter* strucken *Ananias* and *Saphira*§§ his Wife with the like Punishment, for reserving to themselves a little of their own Moneys? If the Apostles did, of themselves, beside the especial Command of our Lord, appoint so many Things to be observed by Christians, why may not those who succeed them, do the same for the Good of the People? St. *Ambrose,* Bishop of

---

*Hebr. xiii. 17.
†I. Tim. i. 8; Prov. xiii. 14.
‡Colos. iii. 14.
§I. Tim. iii.; Tit. i. 7.
‖I. Tim. v. 3 fol.

¶I. Cor. xi. 5 fol.
**I. Cor. vii. 12, 13.
††I. Cor. vii. 12.
‡‡I. Cor. v. 4, 5.
§§Acts v.

tinus: "Non frustra sunt instituta potestas regis, et
cognitoris jus, ungula carnificis, arma militis, disciplina
dominantis, severitas etiam boni patris? Habent omnia
ista modos suos, causas suas, rationes, utilitates, et hæc,
quum timentur, et mali coercentur, et boni quieti inter
malos vivunt."

Sed de regibus dicere supersedeo, ne videar meam
causam agere. Istud quæro, si nemo, nec homo, nec angelus potest super hominem Christianum legem ponere,
cur tot leges ponit Apostolus, et de legendis episcopis,
et de viduis, et velandis fœminarum capitibus? cur
statuit ne fidelis conjux ab infideli discedat, nisi desera-
tur? Cur audet dicere: *"Cæteris dico ego, non Dominus?"* Cur exercuit tantam potestatem, ut fornicarium
Satanæ juberet tradi in interitum carnis? Cur Petrus
Ananiam et Saphiram simili pœna percussit, quod e sua
ipsorum pecunia paulum reservassent sibi? Si multa
statuebant apostoli, præter speciale præceptum Domini,
super Christianum populum, cur non idem propter populi commodum faciant hi, qui successerunt in apostolorum locum? Ambrosius Mediolanensis episcopus, vir
sanctus, et nihil arrogans, jubere non dubitavit ut per
suam diocesim conjuges in quadragesima conjugalibus
abstinerent amplexibus, et indignatur Lutherus, si Romanus Pontifex, successor Petri, vicarius Christi, cui
Christus velut apostolorum principi tradidisse creditur
claves Ecclesiæ, ut cæteri per illum et intrarent, et
pellerentur, jejunium indicat aut preculas? Nam quod
suadet, corpore parendum esse, animo retinendam liber-

Millan, a holy Man, (not arrogant) has scrupled, in commanding that married Persons, through his whole Diocese, should abstain from their lawful Pleasures, during the whole Time of Lent. And does *Luther* take it so heinously that the Pope of *Rome,* Successor of St. *Peter,* Christ's Vicar, (to whom, as to the Prince of the Apostles, it is believed that Christ gave the Keys of the Church, that by him the rest should enter, or be kept out) should institute a Fast or Prayers? As for his persuading Men to obey outwardly in Body, but yet to retain to themselves their Liberty in Mind, who is so blind as not to see his Shifts and Quirks? Why carries this simple Man, this Hypocrite, both Water and Fire? Why does he (as it were in the Words of the Apostle) command not to serve Men, not to be subject to the Statutes of Men;* and yet, notwithstanding, command to shew Obedience to the unjust Tyranny of the Pope? Does the Apostle preach after this Manner? Kings have no Right over you, yet suffer you an unjust Empire. Masters have no Right of Power over you, yet suffer an unjust Servitude. If *Luther* is of Opinion, that People ought not to obey; why does he say they must obey? If he thinks they ought to obey, why is not he himself obedient? Why does this Quack juggle thus? Why does he thus reproachfully raise himself against the Bishop of *Rome,* whom he says we ought to obey? Why raises he this Tumult? Why excites he the People against him, whose Tyranny, (as he calls it) he says is to be endured? Indeed I believe, it is for no other End, than to procure to himself the good Esteem of such Malefactors as desire to escape the Punishment due to their Crimes; that so they might choose him for their Head, who now fights for their Liberty; and demolish *Christ's* Church, so long founded upon a firm

*I. Cor. vii. 23.

tatem, quis tam cæcus est, ut strophas istas non videat?
Cur ignem gerit et aquam homo simplex et sanctulus?
Cur jubet velut Apostoli verbis hominum servos non
fieri, hominum statutis non subjici, et tamen parere
jubet Pontificis injustæ tyrannidi! An Apostolus hoc
pacto prædicat: Reges nihil juris habent in vos; injus-
tum feratis imperium? Domini jus non habent in vos;
feratis injustam servitutem? Si Lutherus parendum
esse non putet, cur parendum dicit? Si parendum
censet, cur ipse non paret? Cur homo versipellis talibus
ludit technis? Cur in Pontificem, cui dicit obediendum
esse, convitiis insurgit? Cur tumultum suscitat? Cur
in illum concitat populos, cujus vel tyrannidem, ut
vocat, fatetur esse ferendam? Profecto non ob aliud,
opinor, quam ut favorem sibi conciliet improborum, qui
suorum scelerum impunitatem cuperent, et eum, qui pro
libertate eorum jam decertat, caput ipsis instituerent, et
Ecclesiam Christi tamdiu super firmam petram funda-
tam demolirentur, et Ecclesiam novam ex improbis et
flagitiosis conflatam erigerent contra quam clamat
propheta: *"Odivi Ecclesiam malignantium, et cum impiis non sedebo,"* et una cum illo nostra clamet Ecclesia:
*"Dirige me in veritate tua, quia tu es Deus salvator
meus, et te sustinui tota die."*

Rock; erecting to themselves a new Church, compacted of flagitious and impious Persons, contrary to that Exclamation of the Prophet, *I will have abhorred the Church of Evil-doers, and I not sit with the Impious:** *Direct me in thy Truth; for thou art God my Saviour, and thee have I sustained all the Day long.†*

CHAP. VI

Of the Sacrament of Penance

IT troubles me exceedingly to hear how absurd, how impious, and how contradictory to themselves the Trifles and Babbles are, wherewith *Luther* bespatters the Sacrament of *Penance*. First, after his old Custom, he proposes for a new Thing, what is by every Body commonly known, *viz. That we ought to believe the Promise of God, whereby he promiseth to those who repent, Remission of Sins:* And then he cries out reproachfully against the Church, for not teaching this Faith. Who I pray you, exhorts any one to the Penance of *Judas;* that is, to be sorry for what he has committed, and not expect Pardon? Who should tell us, that we ought to pray for Remission of Sins, if he did not teach Pardon to be promised to the Penitent? What is more frequently preached than the Clemency of Almighty God, which is so great, that he mercifully extends it to all Persons who are willing to reform their wicked Lives? Did no Body, beside *Luther,* ever read, *That at what Time soever a Sinner repents of his Sins, he shall be saved?‡* Has none ever read, that the Adulteress was dismissed?§ That the Prophet was pardoned, who was

*Ps. xxv. 5.   ‡Ezech. xviii. 27.
†Ps. xxiv. 5.   §John viii. 3.

CAP. VI

De Sacramento Pœnitentiæ

De Pœnitentia pœnitet audire quas nugas, quæ somnia, quam absurda, quam impia, quam sibi repugnantia deblateret. Primum suo more, velut novum proponit, quod omnibus est notissimum, fidem habendam promissioni Dei, qua promisit pœnitenti remissionem peccatorum; et jam insectatur Ecclesiam, quod hanc fidem non doceat. Quis est, obsecro, qui hortatur quemquam ad Judæ pœnitentiam, ut doleat quod commisit, nec tamen speret remissionem? Quis doceret orandum pro venia, nisi qui doceret promissam pœnitenti veniam? Quid prædicatur sæpius, quam Dei tam immensa clementia, ut nulli quantumvis scelerato se emendanti claudat misericordiam? Nemo-ne, præter Lutherum, legit unquam: *"Quacumque hora ingemuerit peccator, salvus erit?"* Nemo legit dimissam adulteram, veniam prophetæ datam, non adulterii tantum, sed homicidii quoque, Paradisum latroni datum, et eo datum tempore, quo commissa prius flagitia nulla potuit satisfactione redimere? Tantum abest ut hæc non doceatur fiducia consequendæ veniæ, quam præteritam esse clamat Lutherus, ut potius in eam partem nimii sint qui populos docent: ita per se libenter in hanc fiduciam præcipites, ut magis in alteram partem sint avocandi,

not only guilty of Adultery, but of Murther also?*
That Paradise was given to the Thief on the Cross;†
and at that Time too, when he could not cancel his
Crimes committed, by any Satisfaction? They who instruct the People, are so far from not teaching them this
Hope of obtaining Pardon, which *Luther* cries is past,
that they rather seem to do it too much; the People
being so easily inclined to rely upon this Confidence,
that there is a greater Need of recalling them to the
other Side; whereby they may contemplate the severe
and inflexible Justice of God: For there are ten to be
found, who sin in the too much Confidence of that
Promise; rather than one who despairs of obtaining
Pardon. Let *Luther* then propose that no more for a
Thing so new, and strange to us, which every Body already knows. Let him not any longer complain, that
this is out of Use, than which nothing is more usual.

CHAP. VII

Of Contrition

'HAVING thus blotted out, (says *Luther*) the Promise
and Faith; let us see what they have substituted in their
Place.' 'They allotted (says he) three Parts to Penance,
Contrition, Confession, and *Satisfaction.*' All which
three he so handles, that it appears well enough that
none of them pleaseth him. First of all, he is very
angry with Contrition, and calls the Anger of God insupportable; because Place is given to Attrition, and
God is believed to supply, by the Sacrament, what is
wanting to Man in the Sorrow for his Sins, when it is
less vehement.

*II. Ks. xii.   †Lu. xxiii. 43.

qua contemplentur severam atque inflexibilem Dei justitiam. Decuplo enim plures invenies, qui nimia peccent istius promissionis fiducia, quam desperatione remissionis obtinendæ. Desinat ergo Lutherus eam rem pro nova nobis et admiranda proponere, quam nemo non novit. Desinat quiritari desuetam esse, qua nihil est usitatius.

CAP. VII

De Contritione

"Obliteratis," inquit, "promissione et fide, videamus quid substituerunt in locum earum. Tres," inquit, "partes dederunt Pœnitentiæ: Contritionem, Confessionem, Satisfactionem." Quas omnes tres ita tractat Lutherus, ut satis perspicuum faciat nullam earum satis ei placere. Nam primum in Contritione indignatur, et iram Dei vocat insustentabilem, quod Attritioni fiat locus, et credatur Deus in dolore non satis de se vehementi per sacramentum supplere quod deest homini. Videamus ergo quam præclare tuetur quod dicit, quid ipse contra statuat.

Let us see how well he maintains what he says; what
he brings against himself. He teaches Contrition to be
a great Thing, not easily had: He commands all Men
to be certain that they have it; and to believe undoubtedly, that, through the Words of the Promise, all their
Sins are forgiven them; and that after they are loosed
by the Word of Man here on Earth, they are absolved
by God in Heaven. In which Thing, his own Assertion
will either fall back upon what he has already reprehended, or else will appear much more absurd.

For God has either promised to forgive Sins through
Penance, to those only, who grieve as much for them as
the Nature and Greatness of their Sins require, or to
those who grieve not so much; or, finally, to such as
are in no wise sorry for their Sins. If he has promised
Forgiveness only to those, who are as contrite as the
Greatness of their Crimes requires; then cannot *Luther*
himself, (as he commands all others to be) be assured,
and out of Doubt, that his Sins are forgiven him. For
how will he be certain of his obtaining the Promise,
when he can in no-wise know that he is sufficiently contrite for his Sins? For no mortal Man has ever yet
known, how great Contrition is required for mortal
Sin. If God has promised Pardon to such as are less
contrite, than the Greatness of their Sins requires, then
has he promised it to such as are called *Attrites;* and
by that *Luther* agrees with those he but now reprehended. But if God has promised it to such as have
no Manner of Sorrow for their Sins, he has surely much
more promised it to such as are attrite, that is, to such
as are in some Manner sorry. Wherefore if he admits
but only Contrition, that is, a sufficient Grief, then can
no Body be assured, that he is absolved; and *Luther*'s
certain and undoubted Confidence of Absolution, will
perish, or be false, and erroneous.

Magnam rem docet esse Contritionem, nec facile parabilem. Jubet omnes habere pro certo, et indubitate credere, propter verbum promissionis, omnia sibi peccata esse dimissa, et a Deo se solutos in cœlo, postquam per os hominis soluti sunt in terra. Qua in re ipsius assertio vel in idem recidet, quod reprehendit, vel multo magis erit absurda. Nam Deus aut his duntaxat per Pœnitentiam promisit peccata remittere, qui quantum peccati moles exigit, ante conteruntur, aut his etiam qui minus, aut denique remittit et illis, qui nihil conteruntur omnino. Si non promisit, nisi, quantum poscat peccati magnitudo, contritis, non potest Lutherus, quod omnes jubet, certus esse, et indubius se esse solutum. Nam quomodo scire se potest obtinere promissum, qui se scire non potest satis esse contritum? Nemo enim novit mortalium omnium quantum Contritionis exigat mortale peccatum. Quod si veniam promisit Deus parum (pro sceleris mole) contritis, tunc promisit his, quos isti vocant attritos, et jam cum his consentit Lutherus, quos reprehendit. At si promisit Deus nihil omnino dolentibus, magis promisit attritis, hoc est utcumque dolentibus. Quamobrem, si tantum Contritionem admittit, hoc est sufficientem dolorem, nemo certus esse potest se esse absolutum, et sic Luthero perierit, aut falsa fuerit et erronea absolutionis certa illa et indubitata fiducia.

But if he says, that the Sins of such as do only perform a slack, or luke-warm Penance, are not otherwise forgiven, than by the Sacrament of Penance; by confessing themselves Sinners, and asking and obtaining Pardon by the Mouth of their Brother: What is this different from the Opinion of those whom he reproves, who say, that Attrition, by Means of the Sacrament of Penance, is made Contrition? For what is wanting to Men, is supplyed by the Sacrament; or else *Luther's* Position, *that Man must be certain of Absolution,* is false: Whether he will or no, he must admit, if not the Word Attrition, at least the Thing signified by it; which, if he grants, (as he will do, if he fly not from his own Opinion;) it is a very unseasonable Trifle of him to contend concerning the Word, and to allow the Effect. Again; he sets upon the whole Church with magnificent Words; as though it perversely taught Contrition, in exhorting us to acquire it by the Collection and Aspect of our Sins; when we ought to be first taught, as he says, the Beginnings and Causes of Contrition, *to wit,* the immoveable Truth of divine Threatnings and Promises; as though such Things were not every where taught among the People; many Passages of Scripture for that Opinion being alleged, not less threatning, nor less comfortable; the Causes likewise added to procure Contrition; nor less efficacious, than those which *Luther* exacts and much more holy. For these Causes do almost propose Nothing, but the Fear of Punishment, or the Hopes of Reward; which is a Conversion not so acceptable to God, as a Conversion caused by Love. That may be done, not only by proposing what *Luther* advises, viz. *God's Threatnings, and Promise of Remission;* but also what they teach, whom *Luther* derides; as if they taught Nothing at all, *to wit,* the Bounty of God towards us, and his exceeding great Benefits con-

Sin ei dicat, cujus alioqui tepido ac remisso dolori peccata non remitterentur, per Pœnitentiæ sacramentum remitti omnia, fatenti se peccatorem, et petenti veniam, et per os fratris obtinenti, quid dicit aliud quam sentiunt illi quos insectatur ? Qui dicunt ex Attritione per sacramentum superveniens fieri Contritionem: sacramentum enim supplere quod deest homini. Aut ergo falsa est positio Lutheri, certum esse hominem de absolutione, aut, velit nolit, admittendum est ei, si non verbum Attritionis, certe res quam isti verbo designant; quam si concesserit (concedet autem, nisi velit de sua sententia discedere) hominis est intempestive nugantis re concessa contendere de vocabulo.

Rursus magnificis verbis totam invadit Ecclesiam, tanquam perverse doceat Contritionem, dum ex peccatorum collectu et conspectu docemur parare Contritionem, quum prius doceri deberemus, ut ait ille, principia et causas Contritionis, nempe divinæ comminationis, et promissionis immobilem veritatem: quasi non talia passim dicantur apud populum, prolatis etiam in eamdem sententiam locis multis e Scriptura sacra, neque minus minacibus, neque minus consolantibus, additis præterea causis in procurandam Contritionem, neque minus efficacibus quam sunt istæ, quas Lutherus exigit, et longe sanctioribus. Nam hæ causæ nihil fere proponunt, præter metum pœnæ, et spem præmii, quæ conversio ad Deum non tam grata est, ac si quis convertatur amore, hoc fiet, si non ista quisque tantum proponet sibi, quæ Lutherus affert, comminationem Dei, et remissionis promissionem, sed illa etiam, quæ docent hi, quos Lutherus tanquam nihil docentes irridet, nempe Dei in se benignitatem, et toties in nihil bene merentem, in toties merentem male, ampliter collata beneficia. His

ferred upon us; when, not only undeserving Good, but even demeriting Evil. For the Sinner, having considered these Things, will rather be touched with Sorrow, for having offended so pious a Father, than so potent a Lord; and will less dread his own Punishment, than God's Anger: Neither will he be so desirous of Heaven, as of God's Favour: This Consideration of divine Bounty formeth Contrition; (*Knowest thou, O Man,* says the Apostle, *that the Bounty of God invites thee to Penance?*)* and, as I have said, forms a more holy Contrition, than that which, from the Fear of Punishment, and Hopes of Pardon, is formed by *Luther;* who boasts, that no Body teaches Threatnings but himself; when all Men do teach them, and better too.

CHAP. VIII

Of Confession

HE so treats of Confession, as to hold, 'That in public Crimes, where the Sin is known to all People, without Confession, there (where it is less Matter,) Confession is to be made.' But, in the Confession of secret Sins, he has so uncertain Turnings, that, though he seem not altogether to reject it, yet can it not be known by him whether he admits it as a Thing commanded, or no: For he denies it to be proved by Scripture; and yet says, 'That it pleases him well, and that it is profitable and necessary;' yet he does not say it to be necessary to all; but, as I suppose, only to pacify troubled Consciences; giving it to be understood, that if any Body have a Conscience like his own, which should be either safe

*Rom. ii. 4.

enim rebus sibi a se propositis adducetur peccator, ut
plus doleat offensum tam pium Patrem, quam tam potentem Dominum, et minus pœnam suam timeat, quam iram
Dei, nec tam cœlum cupiat, quam favorem Dei.   Hæc
consideratio bonitatis divinæ format Contritionem.
("*An nescis, homo,*" inquit Apostolus, "*quod Dei benignitas ad Pœnitentiam te invitat?*")   Et format, ut
dixi, sanctiorem quam sit hæc quam ex metu pœnæ et
spe remissionis format Lutherus, qui neminem jactat
illa docere, præter se, quum omnes et eadem doceant, et
meliora.

CAP. VIII

De Confessione

Confessionem ita tractat, ut in publicis criminibus,
quæ sine Confessione nota sunt toti populo, Confessionem exigat ubi minus est opus.   Occultorum vero
Confessionem ita versat lubricus, ut quum non rejiciat
prorsus, tamen relinquat incertum, an pro re jussa et
demandata recipiat.   Nam e Scripturis eam negat probari; tamen placere sibi dicit, et utilem esse, ac necessa-
riam, nec tamen dicit omnibus, sed ad pacandas duntaxat afflictas conscientias: opinor, significans, quod si
quis habeat conscientiam suæ similem, quæ vel de sua
sanctitate secura sit, vel de verbo promissionis divinæ
certa sit, ei non sit opus occultorum Confessione.
Alioqui si quis meticulosus sit, ad pacandam conscientiam confitendum esse.

for his own Sanctity, or assured of the Word of the divine Promise; he need not confess his secret Sins at all, otherwise, if any Man be scrupulous, he may confess himself, to quiet his Conscience. Wherefore, seeing he has so dubiously suspended his Words, I have thought fit to speak something more plainly of the Necessity of Confession: And because he denies Confession of secret Sins to be proved by Scripture, I will, in the first Place, propose that Passage in *Ecclesiasticus,* which seems to many besides me, to comprehend all the three Parts of Penance. 'My Son, (saith he) neglect not thyself in thine Infirmity, but adore our Lord, and he will cure thee; Turn thyself from thy Sins, and lift up thine Hand, and cleanse thy Heart from all Sin.'* For God cures, whilst he looses in Heaven what the Priest has loosed on Earth: We lift up our Hands in a Satisfaction; we turn from our Sins by Contrition; and in Confession, we cleanse our Hearts from Sin; according to that Saying of the Prophet, 'Pour out your Hearts before him.'† St. *Chrysostom* also comprehends the three Parts of Penance, when he says, 'Perfect Penance compels the Sinner to endure all Things willingly;' and further he says, 'Contrition in his Heart, Confession in his Mouth, a perfect Humility in his Works; this is fruitful Penance.' This also makes for Confession; 'Know the Face of your own Cattle:'‡ But how can he know it, if it be not shewn him? What is more clear than that in Numbers the fifth, *The Lord spoke to* Moses, *saying, speak to the Children of* Israel, *when a Man or Woman has committed a Sin, of all the Sins which are wont to happen unto Men; and have through Negligence, transgressed the Commandments of our Lord, and have sinned; they shall confess their Sins.*§

*Ecclus. xxxviii. 9, 10.   ‡Prov. xxvii. 23.
†Ps. lxi. 9.   §Num. v. 5-7.

Quamobrem, quoniam tam dubie verba sua suspendit, mihi visum est afferre quædam, quæ de necessitate Confessionis loquuntur apertius. Et quia ex Scripturis haberi negat occultorum Confessionem, primo loco proponam eum locum ex Ecclesiastico, qui non soli mihi videtur omnes tres Pœnitentiæ partes complecti: *"Fili,"* inquit, *"in tua infirmitate ne despicias teipsum, sed adora Dominum, et ipse curabit te; averte te a delicto, et dirige manus, et ab omni delicto munda cor tuum."*

Curat enim Deus, dum solvit in cœlo, quod sacerdos solvit in terra; dirigimus manus in Satisfactione, avertimus a delicto per Contritionem, cor vero a delicto in Confessione mundamus, juxta illud prophetæ: *"Effundite coram illo corda vestra."* Tres Pœnitentiæ partes complectitur et Chrysostomus, quum ait: "Perfecta Pœnitentia cogit peccatorem omnia libenter sufferre." Et infra: "In corde ejus Contritio, in ore ejus Confessio, in opere tota humilitas: hæc est fructifera Pœnitentia." Pro Confessione facit et illud: *"Cognosce vultum pecoris tui."* Quomodo enim potest cognoscere, si non indicetur? Quid eo manifestius, quod legitur Numeri capite quinto? *"Locutus est Dominus ad Mosen dicens: Loquere ad filios Israel: Vir, sive mulier, quum fecerit ex omnibus peccatis, quæ solent hominibus accidere, et per negligentiam transgressi fuerint mandatum Domini, atque deliquerint, confitebuntur peccatum suum."* Huc et illud pertinet, quod in lege veteri Judæorum, quibus omnia contingebant in figura, populus infectus lepra jussus est se sacerdotibus ostendere. Nam si Deus ideo scripsit in lege: *"Non alligabis os bovi*

To this also belongs that of the Jewish old Law, which had all Things in Figure, the People infected with the Leprosy were commanded to shew themselves to the Priest. For if God has therefore written in the Law, *You shall not bind the Mouth of the Oxen that treads out the Corn;* * that he might admonish us, that it is but just, that he that serves at the Altar, should live by the Altar, (as the Appos, le declares, who says, 'That this is written in the Law, not for the Oxen, but for Men: For what Care, saith he, takes God for Oxen?)' † There is no Reason of Doubt, but that, by this Leprosy of the Body in the carnal Law, was signified that of Sin in the spiritual Law. And that *Christ* might bring us to the Understanding of this, by Degrees, he said to the Lepers which he cleansed, not only from the Leprosy of the Body, but also of the Soul; *Go shew yourselves to the Priest.* ‡ That of St. *James* also, 'confess your Sins to one another:' § Though I am not ignorant of the various Interpretations given by many to this Place; yet I am of Opinion, and many more besides me, that it is commanded of sacramental Confession. Or doth not that manifestly confirm Confession which our Lord saith by *Esais, Declare thou thy Wickedness that thou mayest be justified?* || If the Authority of the Fathers ought to have any Credit, sure it deserves it in this. St. *Ambrose* saith, 'No Man can be justified from Sin, if he do not confess his Sin.' What can be more plainly spoken? Moreover, St. *John Chrysostom* says, 'He cannot receive the Grace of God, unless he be cleansed from all his Sins, by Confession.' Lastly, St. *Augustine,* 'Do Penance, such as is done in the Church; Let no Man say to himself, I do it secretly, because I do it with God:

*Deut. xxv. 4.
†I. Cor. ix. 9.
‡Lu. xvii. 14.
§Jas. v. 16.
||Isai. xliii. 26.

trituranti," ut nos admoneret æquum esse, ut qui altari
servit, de altari viveret, quemadmodum declarat Apostolus, qui illud ait in lege scriptum, non propter boves,
sed propter homines: *"Numquid de bobus,"* inquit,
"cura est Deo?" non est cur quisquam dubitet per
lepram illam corpoream in lege carnali significatam esse
peccatum in lege spirituali: in quam intelligentiam ut
nos' paulatim duceret Christus, ait leprosis, quos dum
irent non a corporis tantum, sed ab animæ quoque lepra
mundavit: *"Ite,"* inquit, *"ostendite vos sacerdotibus."*
Jam illud divi Jacobi: *"Confitemini alterutrum peccata
vestra,"* etiam si non nesciam alios alio trahere, mihi
certe, nec soli, videtur de sacramentali Confessione mandatum. Annon illud quoque facit aperte pro Confessione, quod per Esaiam ait Dominus: *"Tu dic iniqui-
tates tuas, ut justificeris?"*

Quod si quid valere debet auctoritas sanctorum
Patrum, valere debet imprimis quod ait beatus Ambrosius: "Non potest quisquam justificari a peccato, nisi
peccatum ipsum fuerit confessus." Quid dici potest
apertius? Præterea Joannes Chrysostomus: "Non
potest," inquit, "gratiam Dei accipere, nisi purgatus
fuerit ab omni peccato per Confessionem." Denique
beatus Augustinus: "Agite Pœnitentiam, qualis agitur
in Ecclesia. Nemo dicat sibi: Occulte ago, quia apud
Deum ago. Ergo sine causa dictum est: *Quæ solveritis
super terram?* Ergo sine causa claves datæ sunt?"

Therefore, without Reason was it said, What you shall loose on Earth :* Therefore without Reason is it that the Keys were given.' Put the Case, that not one Word was particularly, or figuratively read of Confession, nor any Thing spoken of it by the holy Fathers; yet, when I consider that all People have discovered their Sins to the Priests, for so many Ages; when I consider the Good that continually follows the Practice of it, and no Evil at all; I cannot think, or believe it to be established, or upholded by any human Invention, but by the divine Order of God. For the People could never, by any human Authority, be induced to discover their secret Sins, which they abhor in their Consciences, and which they are so much concerned to conceal, with such Shame, and Confusion, and so undoubtedly to a Man that might, when he pleased, betray them. Neither could it happen, that among such great Numbers of Priests, some good, and some bad, indifferently hearing Confessions, they should all retain them; and that also, when some of them can keep nothing else secret; if God himself, the Author of the Sacrament, did not, by his especial Grace, defend this so wholesome a Thing. For my Part, let *Luther* say what he will, I will believe that Confession was instituted, and is preserved by God himself; not by any Custom of the People, or Institution of the Fathers.

Now *Luther*'s condemning the Reservation of some Sins, by which a particular Priest is restrained from remitting all; but that some are not forgiven, but by the Hand of a Bishop, some by the Hand of the Pope himself; This shews how this popular Man so levels all Things, as that, through the Hatred he bears to the chief Bishop, he casts all other Bishops into the Rank of the lowest Priest; being so blinded with

*Matt. xviii. 18.

Verum de Confessione si verbum nullum neque nominatim, neque in figura legeretur, neque quicquam a
sanctis Patribus diceretur, tamen quum videam totum
populum tot sæculis peccata sua patefacere sacerdotibus,
quum ex ea re tam assidue videam tantum boni proven-
tum, tam nihil enatum mali, aliud neque credere, neque
cogitare possem, quam eam rem non humano consilio,
sed divino plane mandato et constitutam esse, et con-
servatam. Neque enim ulla humana auctoritate populus unquam potuisset adduci, ut occultissima scelera,
quorum tacitam conscientiam horrebant, quæ, ne pro-
dirent in lucem, tanti referebat ipsorum, in alienas aures
(qui posset quum vellet prodere) tanto cum pudore,
tanto cum periculo, tam incunctanter effunderent.
Neque fieri potuisse, quum tam numerosi presbyteri
boni malique promiscue Confessiones audiant, ut audita
continerent, etiam hi, qui alias nihil continent, nisi
Deus ipse, qui sacramentum instituit, rem tam salubrem
speciali gratia defenderet. Mihi ergo, quicquid ait Lutherus, non ex aliqua populi consuetudine, nec ex institutione Patrum, sed ab ipso Deo videtur instituta et
præservata Confessio.

Jam quod Lutherus reservationes peccatorum damnat,
per quas interdicitur ne quilibet sacerdos remittat
omnia, sed quædam episcopi requirant manum, quædam
etiam Papæ, istud spectat, quod homo popularis sic ex-
æquat omnia, ut, summi Pontificis odio, Pontifices
omnes in classem cogat infimorum sacerdotum: tam
cæcus odio, ut jurisdictionem non discernat ab Ordine,
imo vero multo adhuc cæcior, ut qui nec Ordinem videat
ullum, sed omnia plane permisceat, et confundat hor-

Malice, as not to discern Jurisdiction, from Order; nay,
so blind, as not to see any Order at all; but mingles
and confounds all Things with Horror, and reduces
Priests themselves into the Rank of Lay-men. Seeing
that God has formed this his Church-militant to the
Example of the triumphant; why, reading there so
many Degrees, so many Orders, admits he in this
neither Degree, nor Order, nor any Difference at all?
Why then has the Apostle writ so much of Bishops, if a
Bishop has no more Power over his Flock, than any
other Priest, nor than a Lay-man? But we will speak
of the Laity hereafter; let us now speak of Priests.
Every Priest indeed has Orders, but not Authority of
judging, any Thing belonging to him that absolves, before the Care of some Flock be committed unto him:
Yet he is thought a fit Person for it before. If the
Bishop then, who has Care of the whole Diocese, com-
mits any Part of his Care to a Priest; does not Reason
teach us, that this Man can bind or loose no more than
what the other has permitted him, without whose Command, he could not have bound or loosed any Thing at
all amongst the People? for the same Thing is not lawful for the Bishop to do in another Diocese. What
Wonder then, if the Bishop reserves some Things to
himself, whose Care is greater than what might be committed to every Person, though not the least learned,
when it has been for so many Ages observed; fearing
lest the People should fall more pronely into Sin, when
the Power of Remission should be proposed to them in so
easy a Manner? *Luther* now at last, that no Body,
through the Difficulty of Penance, should be deterred
from Sin, commands every Thing to be permitted to
every Person; not to Priests only, but also to the Laity:
Nay, he comes to that Height of Madness, that, though
Women have commonly that bad Esteem of not being

rore, sacerdotesque ipsos prorsus in laicorum classem redigat. Quum Deus ecclesiam hanc militantem ad exemplar triumphantis effinxerit, cur tot gradus, tot ordines legens illic, nullum gradum, nullum ordinem, nullum prorsus discrimen admittit hic ? Quorsum igitur tam multa scripsit Apostolus de episcopis, si nihil juris in gregem suum plus quam sacerdotes reliqui, nihil plus quam laicus quivis haberet episcopus ? Sed de laicis dicemus postea; interim de sacerdote dicemus.

Sacerdos quilibet Ordinem quidem habet, sed auctoritatem judicandi non habet (quæ res ad absolventem pertinet) priusquam ei gregis alicujus cura committitur; idoneus tamen ante reputatur, cui cura tuto possit committi. Episcopus ergo qui curam habet totius diœcesis, si cui sacerdoti partem quampiam suæ curæ commiserit, annon ipsa ratio docet hunc non amplius aut ligare posse, aut solvere, nisi quatenus ille permiserit, sine cujus mandato nihil omnino in illius populo vel ligare quemquam, vel solvere potuisset ? Quippe quod nec ipsi liceat episcopo in aliena diœcesi. Quid ergo miri est, si quædam sibi reservat episcopus, quorum curam putat esse majorem, quam ut cuilibet possit, etiam non imperito, committi ? Quod quum tot sæculis observatum sit, ne populus, nimis facili proposita remissionis facultate, proclivius in scelera prolaberetur, Lutherus nunc demum, ne quisquam difficultate Pœnitentiæ deterreretur a peccando, quidlibet jubet permitti cuilibet non sacerdoti modo, sed etiam laico; in tantum progressus ineptiæ, ut quum vulgo mulieres male audiant, quasi parum probe taceant, si quid audierint secretius, ille mulieres etiam velit viris esse a confessionibus. At mulierem quum docere non permittat Apostolus, non eliget, opinor, in sacerdotem

able to conceal any Thing of a Secret; yet is he willing
Men should have them to hear their Confessions!—But
I suppose, since the Apostle permits not a Woman to
teach, *Luther* will not make her a Priest; because he
denies almost any to be a Priest, who is not a Preacher.
But the Sentiments of the holy Fathers declare, That
we ought to confess our Sins only to Priests, unless
otherwise forced by Necessity: 'Let him come, (saith St.
Augustin) to the Priests, who can administer to him the
Keys of the Church.' He does not say, *Let him come to
Lay-men,* or let him come to Women. The same Thing
he further tells us more plainly, in another Place: 'He
that repents, let him truly repent; let him signify his
Grief by Tears; let him present his Life to God by the
Priest; let him prevent the Judgment of God by Confession. For the Lord commanded them that should be
cleansed, that they should shew themselves to the
Priest:' By this, teaching us, that Sins are to be confessed by a corporal Presence. Likewise Pope *Leo;*
'Christ gave this Power to the Governors of the Church,
that they should give the Satisfaction of Penance to
them that confess.' Further, venerable *Bede;* 'Let us
discover our light and daily Crimes to our Co-equals,
and our grievous Sins to the Priest; and as long as they
have Dominion in us, let us take Care to purge them;
for Sins cannot be forgiven, without Confession.' Moreover, what should Confession avail us, if Absolution did
not follow by the Keys of the Church: 'But this Power
(saith St. *Ambrose*) is given only to Priests.' In another Place, he declares what the Sense of these Words
is, when he says, 'The Words of God remit Sin, the
Priest is Judge.' Likewise St. *Augustine,* in another
Place, writes most plainly, saying, 'He that doth Penance, without the Appointment of the Priest, frustrates
the Keys of the Church.' Now let any one judge of the

Lutherus, qui, nisi prædicantem, negat ferme quemquam esse sacerdotem. At sacerdoti tantum confitendum esse, nisi necessitas ingruat, sanctorum Patrum declarat sententia. "Veniat, inquit Augustinus, ad antistites, per quos illi claves ministrantur Ecclesiæ." Non dicit: Veniat ad laicos, veniat ad mulieres. Item alibi dicit apertius: "Quem pœnitet, omnino pœniteat, et dolorem lacrymis ostendat, repræsentet vitam suam Deo per sacerdotem, præveniat judicium Dei per Confessionem: præcepit enim Dominus mundandis, ut ostenderent ora sacerdotibus, docens corporali præsentia confitenda peccata." Item Leo papa: "Christus hanc præpositis Ecclesiæ tradidit potestatem, ut confitentibus Pœnitentiæ Satisfactionem darent." Denique venerabilis Beda: "Coæqualibus quotidiana et levia, graviora vero sacerdotibus pandamus, et quanto jusserit tempore, purgare curemus, quia sine Confessione peccata nequeunt dimitti."

Præterea quid prodesset Confessio, nisi per claves Ecclesiæ sequeretur absolutio? "At hoc jus," inquit Ambrosius, "solis permissum est sacerdotibus:" quod quomodo velit intelligi, declarat alibi, quum dicit: "Verbum Dei dimittit peccata, sacerdos est judex." Alio item loco scribit Augustinus apertissime: "Frustrat claves Ecclesiæ, qui sine sacerdotis arbitrio Pœnitentiam agit." Nunc igitur judicet quisque quam vere sentit Lutherus, qui contra sanctorum omnium sententiam claves Ecclesiæ trahit ad laicos, trahit ad mulieres, et ait

Truth of *Luther's* Opinion, who, contrary to the Sentiments of all the holy Fathers, draws the Keys of the
Church to the Laity, and to Women; and says, that
these Words of Christ, *Whatsoever you shall bind,* &c.
are spoken not only to Priests, but also to all the Faithful. *Marcus Aemilius Scaurus,* a Man most excellent,
and of known Honesty, being accused at *Rome* to the
People, by *Varius Sucronensis,* a Man of little Sincer-
ity; his Accuser having made a long and tedious Discourse; *Scaurus* confidently relying on the Judgment of
the People, not thinking him worthy of an Answer, said,
Romans, Varius Sucronensis says it, *Aemilius Scaurus*
denies it; which of them do you believe? By which
Words, the People, applauding this honourable Man,
scorned the idle Accusations of his babbling Adversary.
Which Discourse seems not more applicable to them,
than to what we hear state: For *Luther* says, That the
Words of *Christ* concerning the Keys are spoken to the
Laity; St. *Augustine* denies it: Which of them is the
rather to be believed? *Luther* affirms, *Bede* denies;
which of them will you believe? *Luther* affirms, St.
Ambrose denies; which of them has the greatest Credit?
Finally, *Luther* affirms it, and the whole Church deny
it: Which do you think is to be believed? But if any
Body be so mad, as to believe with *Luther,* that he ought
to confess himself to a Woman; perhaps it may not be
amiss for him also to follow the other Opinion of
Luther; in which he persuades us, not to be too careful
in calling to Mind our Sins. For certainly, it is not
altogether convenient to be too solicitous in examining
your Memory for what you are to put into such a Person's Ear, who has so large and passable a Road from
her Ear to her Tongue. Otherwise seeing it may be
done without any such Danger; I shall not scruple to
prefer, before the Council of *Luther,* the Example of the

verba Christi: *"Quæcumque ligaveritis,"* et cætera, non
sacerdotibus tantum, sed omnibus dicta fidelibus M.
Æmilius Scaurus vir clarissimus, et exploratæ probi-
tatis, Romæ quum a Vario Sucronensi homine parum
sincero accusaretur apud populum, et accusator oratione
longa perorasset, ille breviter et sua, et populi fretus
conscientia, non dignatus oratione contendere: "Quiri-
tes," inquit, "Varius Sucronensis ait, Æmilius Scaurus
negat; utri potius credendum censetis ?" Quibus verbis
applaudente populo, vir honoratus hominis nihili fu-
tilem accusationem elusit. Quæ percontatio non illic
magis mihi visa est, quam in præsente quæstione con-
gruere: nam verba Christi de clavibus laicis dicta, Lutherus ait, Augustinus negat; utri magis credendum esse
censetis ? Lutherus ait, negat Beda; utri magis credendum censetis ? Lutherus ait, negat Ambrosius; utri
magis credendum censetis? Denique Lutherus ait,
tota negat Ecclesia; utri magis censetis esse credendum ?

At si quis adeo desipiat, ut, auctore Luthero, mulieri
quoque putet esse confitendum, huic non inutile fortasse
fuerit illud alterum Lutheri dogma suscipere, quo
suadet non adhibendum multum studii ad recogitanda
peccata. Non expedit profecto nimis anxie multa revo-
care in memoriam, ut omnia in ejus infundas aurem,
quæ perviam et patulam viam ab auribus habet ad
linguam. Alioqui quum res fieri potest absque tali periculo, non dubitem Lutheri consilio exemplum prophetæ
præponere, qui dicit: *"Recogitabo tibi omnes annos meos
in amaritudine."* *Omnes,* inquit, *annos meos,* sed *in
amaritudine.* Talis enim Confessio non solum præterita

Prophet; who saith, 'In Bitterness will I reckon over
all my Years unto thee;* all my Years, (says he) and
that in Bitterness:' For such a Confession, not only
cleanses from Sins past, but also begets abundantly new
Grace; according to that of St. *Ambrose,* 'St. *Peter*
became more faithful after he bewailed the Loss of his
Faith; and so he obtained a greater Grace than he had
lost.' St. *Gregory,* following him, says, 'That Life,
which is fervent in Love after Sin, is much more acceptable to God, than Innocency that is sluggish in Security.' When *Luther* calls them idle People, who are of
Opinion that the Circumstances of Sin are to be confessed; see how much in this St. *Augustine* differs from
him, when he says, 'Let him consider the Quality of the
Crime; as to the Place, Time, Perseverance, Distinction
of Persons, and with what Temptation it was done, how
often the Sin was committed? For a Fornicator ought
to repent according to the Excellency of his State, or
Affairs, and according to the Quality of the Person with
whom he has sinned; according to the Crime itself; if
in a sacred Place, in Time of Prayer, as holy Days, and
Times of fasting; he is to consider how long he persisted
in Sin, and let his Sorrow be according to his Perseverance in Sin, and by what Assault he was overcome; for
some there are, who, far from being overcome, do volun-
tarily offer themselves to Sin; nor do they stay for
Temptation, but prevent the Pleasure: Let him consider
with what Pleasure, and how often, he has committed
the Sin: All these Circumstances are to be confessed,
and bewailed; that when he has known his Sin, he may
soon find God propitious to him. In pondering the
Weight of his Offences, let him consider of what Age
he is, of what Understanding, and Order: Let him ponder each of these singly, and examine the Manner of

*Isai. xxxviii. 15.

peccata diluit, sed novam etiam parit ubertim gratiam,
juxta illud Ambrosii: "Fidelior factus est Petrus, postquam fide se perdidisse deflevit, atque ideo majorem
gratiam reperit, quam amisit." Quem secutus Gregorius: "Fit, inquit, plerumque gratior Deo amore
ardens vita post culpam, quam in securitate torpens
innocentia."

Nam quum Lutherus otiosos homines appellet, qui
censuerunt confitendas peccatorum circumstantias,
Augustinus longe censet aliter. "Consideret," inquit
Augustinus, "qualitatem criminis in loco, in tempore, in
perseverentia, in varietate personæ, et quali hoc fecerit
tentatione, an ipsius vitii multiplici exsecutione.
Oportet enim pœnitere fornicantem secundum excellen-
tiam sui status, vel officii, et secundum modum mere-
tricis, et modum operis sui, et qualiter turpitudinem
peregit, si in loco sacrato, si in tempore orationi con-
stituto, ut sunt festivitates et tempora jejunii. Consideret quantum perseveraverit, et doleat, quam per-
severanter peccaverit, et quanta victus fuerit oppugna-
tione. Sunt enim qui non solum non vincuntur, sed
etiam ultro se peccato offerunt, nec exspectant tenta-
tionem, sed præveniunt voluptatem. Et pertractet
secum quam multiplici actione vitii, quam delectabiliter
peccavit. Omnis ista varietas confitenda est, et deflenda,
ut quum cognoverit quod peccatum est, cito inveniat
Deum sibi propitium. In cognoscendo augmentum peccati, inveniat se cujus ætatis fuerit, cujus sapientiæ, et
ordinis. Immoretur in singulis istis, et sentiat modum
criminis, purgans lacrimis omnem qualitatem vitii."
Hactenus Augustinus, quo uno haud scio an reperiat
quemquam Lutherus ex his, quos otiosos vocat, qui dili-

the Crime, purging with Tears every Quality of the Vice.' Hitherto the Words of St. *Augustine:* That *Luther* may not think that Circumstances do not appertain to Confession; who has more diligently reckoned up the Circumstances of Sins, than this Holy Man? I scarce know whether *Luther* will find any one of these he calls idle. But, if the various Circumstances of Sin are so diligently to be called to Mind, how much more are heinous and different Crimes to be collected, and our Conscience diligently to be examined, that, if possible, we may not let one Sin escape our Knowledge? For what *Luther* darts as a keen Shaft, 'That no Body can possibly confess all his Sins, because none can remember them all,' is indeed but a very obtuse one: For who knows not, that none of those who said, *all Sins are to be confessed,* was so stupid as to think that a Man must tell the Priest in his Ear, what came not into his own Memory to confess?

gentius enumerarit peccatorum circumstantias, ne putet Lutherus circumstantiarum nihil quicquam ad Confessionem pertinere.

Quod si ejusdem peccati variæ circumstantiæ sint, quoad possumus in memoriam revocandæ, quanto magis gravia et diversa crimina colligenda sunt, et diligenter excutienda conscientia, ut, si fieri possit, nullum nobis patiamur excidere? Nam quod Lutherus velut acutissimum telum conjicit, neminem posse omnia peccata confiteri, propterea quod nemo potest omnium recordari, telum est obtusissimum: quis enim nescit neminem, qui dixit omnia peccata confitenda fuisse, tam stolidum ut senserit etiam illa sacerdoti narranda in aurem, quæ confitenti non venissent in mentem?

CHAP. IX

Of Satisfaction

I KNOW not how *Luther* will satisfy others concerning *Satisfaction:* For my Part, I think that, rather than he would remain silent, he would chuse to speak many Things of no Signification at all. For first, when he says, 'That the Church so teaches Satisfaction, as that the People can never understand true Satisfaction, which is a Renovation of Life;' who does not see it to be a Calumny? Who taught *Luther,* that the Church does not teach, That we ought to renew our Lives? He has not travelled over the whole Church; he has not been present at all Confessions, to hear this Ignorance of the Priests: He must then have the holy Ghost in his Bosom, or some Devil in his Breast, who has inspired this into him. But what Spirit soever this was, it could not be a good one, that taught him a Lye, but that Spirit, of whom it is said, *The Devil is a Lyar, and the Father of Lyes;*[*] for there is none that knows not that to be false, which *Luther* affirms to be true: For who was ever so doltish, as to enjoin such satisfactory Works for past Sins, as should indulge the future? Who does not continually, when he absolves, pronounce these Words of *Christ, Go, and sin no more?*[†] And that of St. *Paul, As you have exhibited your Members to serve Uncleanness, and Iniquity, unto Iniquity, so now exhibit your Members to serve Justice unto Sanctification.*[‡] Who has not read that of St. *Gregory, We are not able to perform our Penance, as we ought, unless we*

[*]John viii. 44.   [†]John viii. 11.   [‡]Rom. vi. 19.

CAP. IX

De Satisfactione

De Satisfactione nescio an satisfaciat aliis; mihi profecto videtur potius, quam taceret, maluisse multis verbis nihil dicere. Nam primum quod ait Ecclesiam sic docere Satisfactionem, ut populus veram Satisfactionem non intelligat unquam, quæ est innovatio vitæ, quis non videt meram esse calumniam? Quis Lutherum docuit Ecclesiam non docere innovandam esse vitam? Totam non peragravit Ecclesiam, non omnibus interfuit confessionibus, ut hanc audiret inscitiam sacerdotum. Necesse est ergo aut Spiritum sanctum habeat in sinu, aut dæmonem aliquem in pectore, qui istud ei inspiraverit. Sed quisquis hic spiritus fuit, bonus esse non potuit, qui falsitatem docuit: sed spiritus ille de quo dictum est: *"Diabolus mendax est, et Pater ejus."* Nam nemo nescit falsum esse, quod Lutherus affert pro vero. Quis enim unquam adeo stipes fuit, ut sic indiceret opera satisfactoria pro præteritis, ut indulgeret futura? Quis non assidue, quum absolvit, illa Christi verba succinit: *"Vade, et noli amplius peccare?"* Et illud Pauli: *"Sicut exhibuistis membra vestra servire immunditiæ, et iniquitati ad iniquitatem, ita nunc exhibete membra vestra servire justitiæ in sanctificationem?"* Quis non legit illud Gregorii: "Pœnitentiam quippe agere digne non possumus, nisi modum quoque ejusdem Pœnitentiæ cognoscamus. Pœnitentiam quippe agere, est et perpetrata mala plangere, et plangenda non perpetrare: nam qui sic alia deplorat, ut iterum alia committat, adhuc Pœnitentiam agere ignorat, aut dissimulat. Quid enim

know the Manner of the same Penance? For to do Penance, is to bewail our Sins formerly committed, and re-
solve not to do any Thing hereafter that we should have
cause to sorrow for. For he that laments the past, so
as to commit the future, knows not how to perform
Penance, but dissembleth. What avails it to any Body,
to grieve for his Sins of Luxury, and yet to burn with
Covetousness? If there were Nothing of this said; yet
seeing the Priest imposes Penance for Sins committed,
he shews that the Thing itself is not to be again committed, which must again be punished. It is therefore
very evident, that *Luther* has no Regard to what he
says, so he may but say Somewhat that may slander the
Church: Which Thing always appears wheresoever, (as
in some Matter of great Moment) he cries aloud, even
as he does in these Words: 'For what monstrous Things
are we indebted to thee, thou *See* of *Rome!* and to thy
murthering Laws and Rites, whereby thou hast so destroyed the whole World, that People think they can
satisfy God for their Sins, by Works; when Nothing,
but the Faith only of a contrite Heart, can satisfy;
which, by these Tumults, thou not only puttest to
Silence, but even oppressest, only that thy insatiable
Blood-suckers may have People to say to them, bring,
bring, that you may sell Sins!' Who would not think,
by reading these so furious and tragical Words, but
Luther had discovered some great, and abominable
Prodigies in the Roman See? But he that diligently
examines all these Things, will see that *the Mountains
bring forth a ridiculous Mouse:* For first, how ridiculous is that Exclamation of his against the See of *Rome?*
as if Works of Satisfaction were only exacted, and
Penance imposed only at *Rome,* and not through the
whole Church, in all Parts of the World; or, as if many
of the Laws, which he calls murthering Laws, were not

prodest, si peccata luxuriæ quis defleat, et tamen adhuc avaritiæ æstibus anhelat?" Quod si nihil horum diceretur, tamen quum sacerdos indicit Pœnitentiam pro commissis, ipsa redocet non esse rursus committenda quæ rursus sint punienda.

Lutherum ergo manifeste liquet nihil habere pensi quid dicat, modo verborum effutiat aliquid, quo calumnietur Ecclesiam : quæ res maxime semper patet, ubicumque, velut in re maximi momenti, maxima voce declamat, quemadmodum in his verbis facit: "Quæ monstra tibi debemus, Romana Sedes, et tuis homicidis legibus, et ritibus, quibus mundum totum eo perdidisti, ut arbitrentur sese posse Deo per opera pro peccatis satisfacere, cui sola fide cordis contriti satisfit, quam tu his tumultibus non solum taceri facis, sed opprimis etiam tantum, ut habeat sanguissuga tua insatiabilis, quibus dicat: Affer, affer, et peccata vendat?" Quis non arbitretur, quum hæc verba legat tam atrocia, tam tragica, Lutherum in Sede Romana deprehendisse ingentia et abominanda portenta ? At si quis omnia pensiculet diligentius, videbit parturiente monte, natum ridiculum murem : nam primum quam ridiculum est illud, quod exclamat in Romanam Sedem ? quasi Romæ tantum, et non per omnem totius orbis Ecclesiam exigerentur opera Satisfactionis, et injungatur Pœnitentia : aut quasi leges, quas ille vocat homicidas, non sint editæ pleræque a sanctissimis olim Patribus, et publico Christianorum consensu in synodis, ac generalibus conciliis. Denique quum dicit quod per opera non satisfit Deo, sed sola fide, si sentit quod non per sola opera sine fide, stulte baccha-

ordained in former Times by the holy Fathers, and
public Consent of all Christians, in Synods, and general Councils. Finally, when he says, 'That we cannot
satisfy God by Works, but by Faith alone;' if he means,
that by Works alone, without Faith, we cannot do it;
he shews but his Folly, by railing against the See of
Rome; in which none was ever yet so foolish, as to say,
that Works, without Faith, can satisfy; being not ignorant of that of St. *Paul, What is not of Faith is Sin.**
But if he thinks that Works are superfluous, and that
Faith alone is sufficient, whatever the Works be; then
he says Something, and dissents truly from the Roman
Church; which, with St. *James,* believes, *That Faith,
without Works, is dead.*† You see how impertinently
Luther troubles himself, who so furiously inveighs
against the Roman See, as in the mean While thus to in-
volve himself in the Snares of Folly and Impiety. Although indeed, I think it is more probable, that *Luther*
is of Opinion, that Faith without good Works, is always
sufficient to Salvation: For, that he is of that Opinion,
evidently appears; as well by other Passages of his, as
by his saying, 'That God does Nothing regard our
Works, nor has any Need of them: But he has Need that
we should esteem him true in his Promises.' What
Luther meant by these Words, he knows best himself.
For my Part, I believe, that God cares for our Faith
and our Works, and that he stands in Need of neither
our Faith, nor our Works. For though God has no
Want of our Goods, yet has he so much Care of what
we do, that he commands some Things to be done, and
forbids other Things: Without whose Care, not so much
as one Sparrow falls to the Earth, *five of which are sold
for two Farthings.*‡ But because *Luther* urges that a
Penitent ought only to renew his Life, and neglect to

*Rom. xiv. 23.　　　　†Jas. ii. 17, 20.　　　　‡Lu. xii. 6.

tur in Sedem Romanam in qua nemo fuit unquam tam
stultus, qui diceret opera sine fide satisfacere, quum
nemo nesciat illud Pauli: *"Quod non est ex fide, peccatum est."* Sin opera sentit superflua, et fidem solam
sufficere, qualiacumque sint opera, tum dicit aliquid, et
vere dissentit a Sede Romana, quæ credit divino Jacobo,
quod *fides sine operibus mortua est.* Videtis igitur quam
inepte se commovet Lutherus, qui sic invehitur in
Romanam Sedem, ut semet interea vel stultitiæ retibus,
vel impietatis involvat.

Quanquam profecto propinquius opinor vero Lutherum sentire fidem semper absque operibus bonis satis
esse ad salutem: nam id illum sentire, tum ex aliis locis
multis evidenter liquet, tum ex eo, quod dicit: "Opera
Deus nihil curat, nec eis indiget; indiget autem ut verax
in suis promissis a nobis habeatur." Quibus verbis quid
senserit Lutherus, viderit ipse: ego certe Deum credo et
fidem nostram, et opera nostra curare, et neque operibus
nostris egere, neque fide: nam ut bonorum nostrorum
non eget, qui Deus est, ita curam habet omnium, quæ
faciunt homines, qui aliud ab his fieri vetat, aliud jubet,
sine cujus cura, ne unus quidem passer cadit super
terram, *quorum duo veneunt dipondio.* Sed quia videtur
Lutherus eo vergere, ut pœnitens tantum ingrediatur
novam vitam, ac negligat a sacerdote pro commissorum
Satisfactione suscipere Pœnitentiam, audiamus quid in
hac quoque parte scribat sanctissimus Augustinus:
"Non sufficit," inquit, "mores in melius commutare, et
a præteritis malis recedere, nisi etiam de his, quæ facta

undergo any Penance from the Priest, for his past Sins;
let us hear what St. *Augustine* has writ on this Subject:
'It is not sufficient (says he) to change our Manners to
better, and forsake our former Wickedness; unless we
do also satisfy our Lord, for the Sins committed, by the
Sorrow of Penance, by the Sobs of Humility; by the
Sacrifice of a contrite Heart, with the Co-operation of
Alms-deeds, and Fasts.' And in another Place, he saith,
'Let the Penitent deliver himself altogether unto the
Judgment and Power of the Priest;' reserving Nothing
of himself to himself, that he may be ready to do all
Things, as he is commanded, towards recovering the
Life of the Soul; which he should do, to avoid the Death
of the Body. Likewise, in another Place, 'The Priests
do also bind, (says he) while they enjoin the Satisfaction of Penance to those who come to Confession; they
loose when they remit any Thing thereof: For they exercise a Work of Justice towards Sinners, when they bind
them with just Punishment; a Work of Mercy, when
they remit Somewhat of the same Punishment:' I hope
I have plainly made appear how rashly he calumniates
the Church; and through the whole Sacrament of Penance, how impertinent, how impious, and how absurd he
is against the holy Fathers; against Scriptures; against
the public Faith of the Church; against the Consent of
so many Ages and People; even against Common-sense
itself; with all which, he is not yet content; but, after
having held a long Time that Penance is a Sacrament,
he began, in the End of his Book, to repent himself, that
it should contain any Thing of Truth at all; and therefore, as his Custom is, changes his Opinion into a worse,
and wholly denies Penance to be a Sacrament. Yet he
confesses before, 'That he does not doubt, but that whoever, of his own Accord, or moved by Reproofs, has privately confessed himself before any Brother, and de-

sunt, satisfaciat Domino per Pœnitentiæ dolorem, per
humilitatis gemitum, per contriti cordis sacrificium,
cooperantibus eleemosynis, et jejuniis." Et alibi:
"Ponat se pœnitens," inquit, "omnino in judicio et
potestate sacerdotis, nihil sui reservans sibi, ut omnia,
eo jubente, paratus sit facere pro recipienda vita animæ,
quæ faceret pro vitanda corporis morte." Item alibi:
"Ligant quoque," inquit, "sacerdotes, dum Satisfactionem Pœnitentiæ confitentibus imponunt; solvunt quum
de ea aliquid dimittunt: opus enim justitiæ exercent in
peccatores, quum eos justa pœna ligant; opus miseri-
cordiæ, quum de ea aliquid relaxant."

Satis igitur aperte me docuisse confido, quam temere
calumniatur Ecclesiam, et per omnem Pœnitentiæ partem quam inepta, quam impia, et quam absurda contra
sanctos Patres, contra Scripturam sacram, contra publicam Ecclesiæ fidem, contra tot ætatum, tot populorum
consensum, contra sensum ferme communem constituat:
quibus tamen ille non est contentus, sed quum diu fassus
esset Pœnitentiam esse sacramentum, tandem in fine
totius libri pœnitere cœpit eum, quod quicquam omnino
liber haberet veri, eoque mutata, quod solet, in deterius
sententia, Pœnitentiam prorsus negat esse sacramentum.
At idem ante fatetur se non dubitare quin quicumque
coram quovis privatim fratre, vel sponte confessus, vel
correptus veniam petierit, et emendaverit, ab omnibus
occultis absolutus sit. Si ita sentit (quanquam falsum
in hoc sentit, quod ait coram quovis privatim fratre, et

manded Pardon, and amends himself, is absolved from
all his secret Sins.' If that be his Sentiment, though
false indeed; (because he says, 'before any Brother privately, and that indifferently; whether he ask Pardon of
his own Accord, or as forced thereto by Rebukes:') If,
I say, he think such a Penance to be profitable, why
excludes he it from the Number of the Sacraments? not
indeed for any other Intent, but that it may be the less
valued; and, being deprived of the Name of a Sacrament, (which amongst Christians is in great Veneration) it might become despicable: For which Thing he
finds no other Pretext, but that Penance has no visible
Sign; as though the exterior Penance, or the very Act
and Gestures of the Body, when the Priest absolves the
Penitent, could not be a Sign of spiritual Grace, by
which the Penitent obtains Remission. But, in fine, to
conclude the Discourse of Penance, I wish he may at
last repent himself, for having treated of Penance after
so evil a Manner; that he may wholesomely perform all
its Parts, as he endeavours to destroy them all; that he
may be contrite for his Malice, confess publicly his
Errors; and that, submitting himself to the Judgment
of the Church, (which with so many Blasphemies he
has offended) he may recompence for what he has before
committed, with the greatest Satisfaction possible; for
indeed he cannot do it worthily.

in hoc item, quod nihil interesse censet, an confiteatur ultro, an correptus petat veniam), tamen si Pœnitentiam etiam talem censet esse tam utilem, cur Pœnitentiam eximit e numero sacramentorum? Non ob aliud omnino, quam ut haberetur in minore pretio, et viduata nomine sacramenti, quod apud Christianos est in veneratione, vilesceret. Quam in rem non alium reperit prætextum, quam quod Pœnitentia non habeat signum visibile, quasi vel exterior Pœnitentia, vel ille ipse corporeus actus, et gestus, quo sacerdos absolvit pœnitentem, signum esse non possit spiritalis gratiæ, qua pœnitens consequitur remissionem.

Sed ut aliquando finem loquendi faciam de Pœnitentia, utinam aliquando pœniteat ipsum tam male tractatæ Pœnitentiæ; et cujus omnes partes conatur evertere, salubriter olim partes omnes adimpleat: conteratur de malitia, publice confiteatur errores, et Ecclesiæ, quam tot blasphemiis offendit, judicio se subjiciens, quicquid ante commisit, quanta maxima potest (nam digna profecto non potest) Satisfactione recompenset!

CHAP. X

Of Confirmation

LUTHER is so far from admitting *Confirmation* to be a Sacrament, that, on the Contrary, he says, *he admires what the Church's Intention was in making it one.* And this most impertinent Babler trifles thus in so sacred a Thing; asking why the Church does not make three Sacraments of Bread, as having in Scripture some Occasions to do it? The Church has not done any such Thing, because she takes no Occasions, from any Words whatsoever in Scripture, for having any other Sacraments, than those which were instituted by *Christ,* and sanctified by his most holy Blood: Even so it omits none of them which have been given by *Christ* and his Apostles, and transmitted to us, as it were, from Hand to Hand, though Nothing should be writ of them in any Place.

But when he says, that *Confirmation works no Salvation,* and that it is supported by no Promise of *Christ;* he only says this, proving Nothing, but only denying all. But when *Luther* makes Mention of some Passages, from which (though he laugh at it) the Sacrament of Confirmation may probably have its Beginning; why judges he so perversely of the whole Church, as if it should rashly admit a Sacrament; because he reads no Word of Promise in these Places; as if *Christ* had promised, said, or done Nothing, but what the Evangelists mention in the Scriptures! By this Rule, if there was no Gospel but that of St. *John,* he should deny the Institution of the Sacrament of our Lord's

CAP. X

De Sacramento Confirmationis

CONFIRMATIONEM adeo non recipit pro sacramento, ut
etiam mirari se dicat quid Ecclesiæ in mentem venerit,
ut Confirmationem faceret sacramentum, et in re tam
sacra ludit et nugatur homo nugacissimus, quærens cur
non ex pane quoque faciant sacramenta tria, quum ansas
quasdam habeant ex Scripturis. Ideo non facit Ecclesia,
quia non apprehendit ansam ex qualibuscumque Scripturæ verbis alia condendi sacramenta, quam quæ
Christus instituit, et suo sanctificavit sanguine, quemadmodum e diverso nullum eorum omittit, quæ a Christo
et apostolis per manus deinceps tradita sunt, etiamsi
nusquam quicquam de eis scriberetur: nam quod ait
Confirmationem nullam operari salutem, nulla fulciri
promissione Christi, hoc dicit tantum, neque probat
quicquam, duntaxat negat omnia.

At quum loca quædam Lutherus ipse commemorat, e
quibus, quanquam id Lutherus irridet, habere non absurde potuerit sacramentum Confirmationis initium, cur
tam maligne de tota judicat Ecclesia, quasi temere
sacramentum suscipiat, propterea quod in illis locis
nullum legit verbum promissionis? quasi nihil omnino
promiserit, dixerit, fecerit Christus, quod non com-
plectantur evangelistæ. Hac ratione si tantum Joannis
exstaret evangelium, negaret institutionem sacramenti
in Cœna Domini, de qua institutione nihil omnino per-

Supper; of which Institution St. *John* writes Nothing
at all: Many other Things done by *Jesus* have been
omitted by all; which (as the Evangelist himself saith)
are not written in this Book, and which the whole World
could not contain;* of which, some have, by the Mouth
of the Apostles, been delivered to the Faithful, and have
been ever after conserved by the perpetual Faith of the
holy Catholic Church; whom, I think, you ought to believe concerning some Things which are not in the Gospels; when, (as St. *Augustine* says) *You could never
know which is the Scripture itself, but by the Tradition
of the Church.* And though none should have been ever
written, yet the Gospel would have always remained
written in the Hearts of the Faithful, which was more
antient than all the Books of the Evangelists. Let not
Luther think it is a prevailing Argument to prove the
Nullity of the Sacraments, not to find them instituted
in the Scriptures. Otherwise, if he admits Nothing at
all, but what he reads clearly in the Gospel, (that he
may have no Place for Wrangling) how comes he to believe, (if he believes it, for he scarce believes any Thing
at all) the perpetual Virginity of the blessed Virgin
Mary? Of which he is so far from finding any Thing
in Scripture, that *Helvidius* took Occasion by Scripture
itself to prove the Contrary. Neither is any Thing opposed against him, but the Faith of the whole Church,
which is no where greater and stronger than in the Sacraments. For my Part, I do not think that any Person,
who has the least Spark of Faith in him, can be persuaded, that *Christ, who prayed for St.* Peter, *that his
Faith should not fail;†* *who placed his Church on a firm
Rock;* should suffer her, for so many Ages, to be bound
by vain Signs of corporal Things, under an erroneous
Confidence of their being divine Sacraments. If Noth-

*John xxi. 25.   †Lu. xxii. 32.

scribit Joannes, qui eodem Dei consilio non tetigit istud,
quo multa alia præterierunt omnes, quæ fecit Jesus:
"Quæ," ut inquit evangelista, *"non sunt scripta in libro
hoc, et quæ totus mundus non posset capere."* Ex quibus
nonnulla per apostolorum ora fidelibus patefacta sunt, et
perpetua deinceps Ecclesiæ catholicæ fide conservata:
cui quare non debeas de quibusdam credere, quanquam
non legantur in evangeliis, quum, ut Augustinus ait
"nisi tradente Ecclesia scire non posses quæ sint evan-
gelia?" Quorum si nullum unquam scriptum esset,
maneret tamen evangelium scriptum in cordibus fidelium, quod antiquius fuit omnium evangelistarum
codicibus; manerent sacramenta, quæ et ipsa non dubito
evangelistarum libris esse omnibus antiquiora, ne putet
Lutherus efficax argumentum esse frustra suscepti sacramenti, si non reperiat institutum in evangeliis. Alioqui
si nihil omnino recipiat, quod non tam aperte legat in
evangelio, ut tergiversandi non sit locus, quomodo credit
(si modo credit, qui fere nihil credit) perpetuam Mariæ
virginitatem? De qua adeo nihil invenit in Scripturis,
ut Helvidius non aliunde quam ex Scripturarum verbis
arripuerit ansam decernendi contrarium. Nec aliud
opponitur illi, quam totius Ecclesiæ fides, quæ nusquam
major est, aut fortior, quam in sacramentis.

Ego certe neminem esse puto, qui scintillam ullam
habeat fidei, cui persuaderi possit quod Christus qui pro
Petro oravit, ne fides ejus deficeret, qui Ecclesiam suam
supra firmam petram collocavit, pateretur eam tot
sæculis universam corporalium rerum signis inanibus,
erronea fiducia velut divinis sacramentis obstringi. Si
nusquam inde quicquam legeretur, illi tamen verbo
mentem Domini poterant enarrasse, qui præsentes versati

ing should be read of it any where, yet those who were present, and conversed with our Lord, could, by Word of Mouth, tell what his Mind was, of whom himself says, *Ye are Witnesses who have been with me from the Beginning.** What was to be done, might be taught by the Holy Ghost, of whom Christ said, *But when the Paraclite comes, whom I will send you from the Father, the Spirit of Truth which proceedeth from the Father, he shall give Testimony of me.*† And in another Place, *When he shall come, that is, the Spirit of Truth, he shall teach you all Truth, for he shall not speak of himself; but what Things soever he shall hear, he shall speak; and the Things that are to come he shall shew you.*‡ Shall we believe then, that the Church, having so many, and so great Ministers, so many living Evangelists, and that Spirit which inspires Truth, has rashly instituted a Sacrament, and puts her Hope in an empty Sign? Or shall we not rather believe, that it has learned from the Apostles, and from the Spirit of Truth? Certainly, if the Name of this Sacrament, the Minister, and the Virtue promised in it, be considered, it will appear not to be a Thing which we may believe to be unadvisedly used by the Church. For, as *Hugo de St. Victore* saith, *From Chrism is Christ named; from Christ, Christian;* every one ought to have taken Chrism, or Unction, since from it they take their common Name. For we are all an elected Nation, and a royal Priesthood§ in *Christ:* We are not anointed, unless in Case of Necessity, but by the Bishops, that they may seal the Christian, and give him the Holy Ghost: 'Even (says he) as we read that the Apostles only, in the primitive Church, had Power to give the Holy Ghost by Imposition of Hands.' The same Doctor declares also the Fruit of the Sacrament;

*John xv. 27. ‡John xvi. 13.
†John xv. 26. §I. Pet. ii. 9.

sunt cum eo, de quibus ait ipse: *"Vos testes estis, qui mecum ab initio fuistis."* Docere poterat quid debebat fieri, Paracletus ipse, de quo dixit Christus: *"Quum autem venerit Paracletus, quem ego mittam vobis a Patre meo, Spiritus veritatis, qui a Patre procedit, ille testimonium perhibebit de me."* Et rursus: *"Quum venerit ille, qui est Spiritus veritatis, ducet vos in omnem veritatem: non enim loquetur a semetipso, sed quæcumque audierit, loquetur; et quæ futura sunt, annuntiabit vobis."* Ecclesia ergo quum tot et tales habuerit præceptores, tot vivos evangelistas, et Spiritum illum, qui veritatem inspirat, credetur temere instituisse sacramentum, et spem in signo collocare nihili? Non credetur potius ab apostolis, non credetur potius a Spiritu sancto didicisse?

Certe si quis nomen hujus sacramenti, si quis ministrum, si quis virtutem, quam spondet, æstimet, videbit rem non esse talem, quam temere credatur Ecclesia suscepisse. "A chrismate enim," ut inquit Hugo de Sancto-Victore, "Christus dicitur: a Christo, Christianus; cujus ex quo nomen omnes communicare cœperunt, omnes unctionem accipere debuerunt, quia in Christo omnes electum genus sumus, et regale sacerdotium." Nec ungimur, excepta necessitate, nisi per episcopos, ut Christianum consignent, et Spiritum Paracletum tradant, quemadmodum idem ait Hugo, sicut, in primitiva Ecclesia, Spiritum sanctum per impositionem manuum dandi soli apostoli potestatem habuisse leguntur. Fructum quoque sacramenti idem Doctor declarat: "Sicut," inquit, "in Baptismo remissio peccatorum accipitur, ita per manus impositionem Spiritus Paracletus datur. Illic gratia tribuitur ad remissionem

'As the Remission of Sins, (saith he) is received in Baptism; so, by the Imposition of Hands, the Holy Ghost is given: There, Grace is given to the Remission of Sins: Here, Grace is given to Confirmation; for what avails it you to be lifted up from your Fall, if you are not confirmed to stand?' These are *Hugo*'s Words, which are also consonant to Reason. For as in the corporal Life, besides Generation, by which we get Life, another Action is required, by which we may increase, and grow to the Perfection of Strength: So, in the spiritual Life, which is required by Regeneration in Baptism, the Sacrament of Confirmation is necessary, by which the spiritual Life is led to perfect Virtue, and the Holy Ghost is given for perfect Strength. And besides, the Sacrament of Baptism, which helps us to believe, Confirmation is profitable to give us Courage to confess our Faith boldly. For to this it is ordained, that Man may, before the Persecutor, boldly confess his Faith: And this is what *Melchiades* saith; In Baptism we are regenerated to Life, after Baptism we are confirmed for the Combat; for Confirmation arms and instructs us against the Agonies of this World.

Finally, that *Luther* may understand that this Sacrament is no new Thing, or vain Fiction; but that it is so far from being void of Grace, that it confers the Spirit of Grace and Truth: We will here relate what St. *Hierom* has written of this Sacrament of Confirmation. 'If the Bishop impose his Hand, it is on them who have been baptized in the true Faith, who have believed in the Father, Son, and Holy Ghost, three Persons and one Substance. But the *Arian,* who believes in no other (stop your Ears, that you may not be polluted with the Words of such monstrous Impiety,) but in the Father alone, in Jesus Christ as a Creature, in the Holy Ghost as Servant to both; how shall he receive the Holy Ghost

peccatorum, hic gratia datur ad confirmationem. Quid
autem prodest si a lapsu erigeris, nisi ad standum con-
firmeris ?" Hactenus Hugo, cui recta quoque consentit
ratio. Quemadmodum enim in vita corporali præter
generationem, per quam vitam consequimur, alia requi-
ritur actio, per quam et crescimus, et ad perfectionem
virtutis perducimur, ita in spiritali vita, quæ per
generationem Baptismatis acquiritur, opus est sacramento Confirmationis, per quam vita spiritualis ad perfectam virtutem perducitur; et Spiritus sanctus datur
ad perfectum robur. Et præter sacramentum Baptismi,
quod adjuvat ad credendum, Confirmatio prodest in
adjutorium fortitudinis ad audacter confitendum. Ad
hoc enim ordinatur, ut homo coram persecutore fidem
confiteatur audacter; et hoc est, quod ait Melchiades:
"In Baptismo regeneramur ad vitam, post Baptisma
confirmamur ad pugnam:" nam Confirmatio ad hujus
mundi agones armat, et instruit.

Denique ut Lutherus intelligat hoc sacramentum
neque novum esse, neque inane figmentum, sed adeo non
vacare gratia, ut Spiritum etiam gratiæ conferat, ac
veritatis, afferemus in medium quid beatus Hieronymus
de Confirmationis sacramento scripserit. Ait enim:
"Episcopus si imponit manum, his imponit, qui recta
fide baptizati sunt, qui in Patre, et Filio, et Spiritu
sancto, tres personas, et unam substantiam crediderunt.
Arrianus vero, quum nihil aliud crediderit (claudite,
quæso, aures, qui audituri estis, ne tantæ impietatis
vocibus polluamini) nisi in Patre solo vero Deo, et in
Jesu Christo salvatore creatura, et in Spiritu sancto
utriusque servo, quomodo Spiritum sanctum ab Ecclesia

from the Church, who has not as yet obtained Remission of his Sins? For the Holy Ghost inhabits not, but where Faith is pure, nor remains but in that Church which has true Faith for her Guide.'

'If in this Place, you ask why he that is baptized in the Church, receives not the Holy Ghost but by the Hands of the Bishop? Learn, that this Observation is descended from this Authority; because, after our Lord's Ascension, the Holy Ghost descended on the Apostles, and we find the same to have been done in many Places.' Hitherto St. *Hierom.* Which Sentence is also confirmed by divers Passages in the Scripture, and particularly by that in the *Acts,* which shews that the People baptized before in *Samaria,* received the Holy Ghost, when *Peter* and *John* came among them, and laid their Hands upon them.* I therefore admire how it should come into *Luther's* Mind to dispute, that Confirmation is only to be accounted a Rite and a Ceremony, and deny it to be a Sacrament; when it is demonstrated, not only by the Testimony of holy Fathers, and by the Faith of the whole Church, but also by clear Passages of Scripture; that not only Grace, but also, the very Spirit of Grace, is conferred by the visible Sign of the Bishop's Imposition of Hands.

Let *Luther* therefore forbear to contemn any more the Sacrament of Confirmation, which the Dignity of the Minister, the Authority of the Church, and the Profit of the Sacrament itself, commend.

*Acts viii. 14-17

recipiet, qui necdum remissionem peccatorum consecutus est? Spiritus quippe sanctus nisi mundam
fidem non incolit, nec habitator ejus templi efficitur,
quod antistitem non habet veram fidem. Quod si hoc
loco quæras quare in Ecclesia baptizatus nisi per manus
episcopi non accipiat Spiritum sanctum, disce hanc ob-
servationem ex ea auctoritate descendere, quod post
ascensum Domini Spiritus sanctus ad apostolos descendit, et multis in locis idem factitatum reperimus."
Hactenus Hieronymus: cujus sententiæ, quum alia
multa Scripturæ loca subscribunt, tum ille multo clarissime, qui in Actis apostolorum declarat quod populus,
qui ante baptizatus est in Samaria, descendentibus ad
eos Petro ac Joanne, ac manus eis imponentibus, accepit
Spiritum sanctum. Demiror igitur quid in mentem
Luthero venerit, ut Confirmationem pro ritu tantum ac
cærimonia contendat habendam, pro sacramento vero
neget: quæ non solum sanctorum testimonio Doctorum,
et totius Ecclesiæ fide, sed etiam sacræ Scripturæ claris-
simis locis ostenditur visibili signo manus pontificiæ
non gratiam tantum, sed et ipsum gratiæ Spiritum con-
ferre. Desinat ergo Lutherus Confirmationis sacramentum contemnere, quod ministri dignitas, Ecclesiæ
auctoritas, et ipsius sacramenti commendat utilitas.

Of the Sacrament of Marriage

MARRIAGE, the first of all Sacraments, celebrated by the first of Mankind, and honoured with our Saviour's first Miracle, being for so long Time had in a religious Veneration for its very Name of a Sacrament; is now, at last, (that People should not so much regard or value conjugal Faith,) denyed by *Luther* to be any Sacrament at all; and as in other Sacraments, (some of which he takes away, by denying the Sign instituted; others, by denying promised Grace) he denies both of them to be in Marriage; (holding, that Grace has been no where promised thereby) he teaches also, That it has been no where instituted for a Sign: And how knows he this? *Because* (says he) *we read it not.* O strong Reason, and Mother of many Heresies! This was the Fountain, from which *Helvidius* drew his Venom. You admit no Sacrament, unless you read its Institution in a Book! What Book has he ever writ who instituted all? *Concerning some Things,* (says he) *I believe* Christ's *Evangelists:* Why then does he not, in some Things, believe also the Church of *Christ;* which is by Christ himself preferred to all the Evangelists, who have been only Members of the Church? Wherefore, if he confides so much in one, why does he distrust all together? If he attribute so much to a Member, why nothing at all to the whole Body?

The Church believes it to be a Sacrament; that it has been instituted by God; given by Christ; and left to us by his Apostles; delivered afterwards by the Holy

CAP. XI

De Sacramento Matrimonii

MATRIMONIUM sacramentorum omnium primum inter primos homines celebratum, primo Christi miraculo cohonestatum, quod, propter sacramenti nomen, ipsum tandiu tam religiose cultum est, Lutherus nunc demum, ne conjugalem fidem tanti quisquam putet in posterum, negat esse sacramentum ullum. Et quum alia sacramenta sic sustulerit, ut in uno negaret institutum signum, in alio negaret promissam gratiam, in Matrimonio negat utrumque : nam negat usquam promissam esse gratiam ; negat usquam institutum esse pro signo. Unde hæc novit ? "Quia non legitur," inquit. O rationem fortem, et multarum hæresum parentem! Ex hoc fonte venenum hausit Helvidius. Nullum sacramentum admittis, cujus institutionem non legis in libro ? Quem librum unquam scripsit ille, qui instituit omnia ? "De quibusdam," inquit, "credo evangelistis Christi. Cur ergo de quibusdam Christi non credis Ecclesiæ, quam Christus omnibus præponit evangelistis, qui non nisi membra quædam fuerunt Ecclesiæ ? Quamobrem, si fidis uni, cur diffidis omnibus ? Si membro tribuis tantum, cur toti nihil tribuis corpori ? Ecclesia credit esse sacramentum ; Ecclesia credit a Deo institutum, a Christo traditum, traditum ab apostolis, traditum a sanctis Patribus, per manus deinceps pro sacramento traditum ad nos pervenisse, pro sacramento per nos tradendum posteris ad finem usque sæculi, pro sacramento venerandum. Hoc Ecclesia credit, et quod credit, dicit. Hoc, inquam, tibi dicit eadem Ecclesia, quæ tibi

Fathers for a Sacrament, and given as it were, from Hand to Hand down to us; from us also, as a Sacrament, down to Posterity, and to be honoured to the End of the World. The Church believes this; and tells you what it believes too. The same Church that says, *The Evangelists writ the Gospel,* tells you this also. For if the Church had not said, That the Gospel of *John,* is the Gospel of *John,* you should not have known it; for you were not present when he writ it. Why then do you not believe the Church, when she tells you that Christ has done these Things; has instituted these Sacraments; that the Apostles have delivered them; as well as when she says, *That the Evangelists writ such, and such Gospels?*

But *Luther* says, 'Marriage was amongst the antient Patriarchs, and amongst the Gentiles; and that as truly as amongst us, yet was it not a Sacrament with either of them.' As for the Fathers that were under the Law, and before the Law, I do not agree with *Luther;* but am certain, that Marriage was a Sacrament with them as well as Circumcision. But amongst the Gentiles, the Case is otherwise; for their Marriage depended on the Custom and Laws of each People: So that some Marriages were lawful with some of them, which by others were accounted ridiculous: And yet, contrary to *Luther,* we find some of Opinion, that even the Marriages of the Gentiles were a Sacrament amongst them. For St. *Augustine* says, 'That the Sacrament of Marriage is common to all Nations: But the Sanctity of it is only in the City of our God, and in his holy Mountain,' (the Church.) On which Sentiment, let him that pleases read *Hugo de Sancto Victore.* But though the Marriage of the Unfaithful be no Sacrament, yet does it not follow what *Luther* infers, That the Marriage of the Faithful is none either. For the People of God have some-

dicit evangelistas scripsisse Evangelium : nam nisi Ecclesia diceret evangelium Joannis Joannis esse, nescires
esse Joannis : non enim assedisti scribenti. Cur ergo
non credis Ecclesiæ, quum dicit hæc Christum fecisse,
hæc sacramenta instituisse, hæc apostolos tradidisse,
quemadmodum credis ei, quum dicit hæc evangelistam
scripsisse ?

"Matrimonium," inquit Lutherus, "erat apud antiquos Patres, erat apud Gentiles, et tamen apud neutros
Matrimonium erat sacramentum, quum tamen apud
utrosque Matrimonium fuerit æque verum, atque apud
nos. De Patribus, qui sub lege erant, et ante legem, non
accedo Luthero ; imo plane censeo Matrimonium fuisse
illis sacramentum, sicut fuit et Circumcisio. De
Gentibus alia quæstio est, quarum Conjugium totum
pendebat a moribus ac legibus cujusque populi ; eoque
talia erant apud alias legitima conjugia, qualia haberen-
tur alibi perabsurda. Quanquam non desunt, qui contra
Lutherum sentiant etiam Gentium Conjugium sacramentum esse : nam et beatus Augustinus ait quod sacramentum Conjugii omnibus Gentibus commune est,
sanctitas autem sacramenti non est, nisi in civitate Dei
nostri, et monte sancto ejus. In quam sententiam, qui
volet, Hugonem de Sancto-Victore perlegat.

Quanquam si Conjugium infidelium sacramentum
non esset, non sequeretur tamen, quod Lutherus infert,
ut ideo ne fidelium quidem Conjugium sacramentum
sit. Populus enim Dei in Matrimonio quiddam habet

thing more holy in Marriage, and have always had, as
well as its first Institution, as when it was honoured
with Laws given by God. Moreover, the Gentiles, because it was acted as a human Thing amongst them,
were wont, by Compacts and human Laws, to take
Wives, and after to reject them again. *Divorcement*
was not lawful in former Times amongst the People of
God: For though God, by *Moses,* permitted the Bill of
Divorcement among the *Hebrews;* yet *Christ* confesses
that it was indulged them for the Hardness of the People's Hearts: *For, from the Beginning* (saith our Saviour,) *it was not so.* But *Christ* hath restored Christians to pristine Sanctity, consecrating Marriage with
an indesolvable Bond of Society; unless in Case of
Fornication between those, whom no human Error, but
God himself, has joined together. It follows not, therefore, that if Marriage has not been a Sacrament amongst
the Gentiles, it must be none amongst us Christians, or
has not been a Sacrament amongst the antient Patriarchs; amongst Christians, if it was no where read, yet
the Faith of the Church ought to suffice us. And yet
that one Passage of the Apostle, which *Luther* endeavours to put by with a Scoff, does plainly demonstrate,
that Marriage, not only now, but also at the very first
Beginning of Mankind, was instituted a Sacrament:
Which I suppose will not be doubted by any Body who
reads that Part of the Epistle to the Ephesians, and attentively considers it. Which whole Passage we have
here inserted; because, by any Man's Words, it cannot
be more clearly explicated, than it is already by the
Apostle himself, who has so plainly shewn us his Mind
therein, that no Place of Refuge is left to *Luther*'s impertinent Calumnies. For he saith, 'Let Women be subject to their Husbands, as to our Lord: Because the
Man is Head of the Woman, as *Christ* is Head of the

sanctius, habuitque semper, et quum primum instituere-
tur, et quum datis a Deo legibus honestaretur. Porro
apud Gentes, quoniam humana tantum res agebatur,
adsciscere sibi conjuges ac rejicere pactis ac legibus
humanis solebant. In Dei populo junctos Conjugio non
licuit olim divelli. Nam quod per Moysem Deus per-
misit Hebræis libellum repudii, Christus fatetur in-
dultum propter duritiam populi: alioquin uxores animo
suo non satis commodas interfecturi: *"nam ab initio,"*
inquit Christus, *"non erat sic."* Christianos vero
Christus ad pristinam revocavit sanctitatem, consecrans
Matrimonium indissolubili vinculo societatis, excepta
fornicationis causa, inter eos quos non humanus error,
sed Deus rite conjunxit. Non sequitur igitur ut si Conjugium non fuerit sacramentum Gentibus, idcirco sacramentum aut nunc non sit Christianis, aut non fuerit
priscis olim Patribus.

Nam quod ad Christianos pertinet, etiam si nusquam
legeretur, Ecclesiæ fides sufficeret. Et tamen unus ille
locus ex Apostolo, quem Lutherus cavillo conatur
eludere, manifeste docet Matrimonium non nunc tantum, sed et olim quoque in generis humani primordiis
institutum pro sacramento. Quod nemini, opinor,
dubium relinquetur, qui locum illum ex epistola ad
Ephesios perleget et considerabit attentius, quem totum
placuit inserere, propterea quod nullius interpretatione
poterit res elucere clarius, quam ipsis verbis Apostoli,
qui tam aperte quod sensit, explicuit, ut ineptis Lutheri
calumniis nullum reliquerit locum. Ait enim: *"Mu-*
lieres viris suis subditæ sint, sicut Domino: quoniam
vir caput est mulieris, sicut Christus caput est Ecclesiæ,
ipse Salvator corporis ejus. Sed sicut Ecclesia subjecta
est Christo, ita et mulieres viris suis in omnibus. Viri,

Church: Himself the Saviour of his Body. But as the
Church is subject to Christ, so the Women to their Husbands, in all Things. Husbands love your Wives, even
as Christ loved the Church, and delivered himself for it.
That he might sanctify it, cleansing it by the Laver of
Water in the Word; That he might present to himself a
glorious Church, not having Spot or Wrinkle, or any
such Thing; but that it may be holy and unspotted. So
also Men ought to love their Wives as their own Bodies;
he that loveth his Wife, loveth himself. For no Man
ever hated his own Flesh, but he nourishes it and cherishes it, as also Christ the Church; because we are Members of his Body, of his Flesh, and of his Bones: For
this Cause shall a Man leave Father and Mother, and
cleave to his Wife, and they shall be two in one Flesh;
This is a great Sacrament: But I speak in Christ, and
in the Church.'* You see how the blessed Apostle
teacheth every-where, that the Marriage of Man and
Wife is a Sacrament, which represents the Conjunction
of Christ with his Church: For he teacheth, that God
consecrated Matrimony, that it might be the Mystery of
Christ joined with his Church. He tells you, 'That the
Man and Wife make one Body, of which the Man is the
Head; and that Christ and the Church make one Body,
of which Christ is the Head.' He makes the chief Cause
why the Husband ought to love his Wife, no other, than
that he may not be an unlike Sign to Christ, whom he
represents: And this he makes rather the Cause, than
that common Nature of the Male and Female, which of
itself should also excite Love. He, by the same Example, 'exhorts the Wife to fear and respect her Husband;'
that is, because she represents the Church of Christ.
And after he has by many Words inculcated these
Things over and over again; (fearing lest any Body

*Ephes. v. 22 fol.

diligite uxores vestras, sicut et Christus dilexit Eccle-
siam, et semetipsum tradidit pro ea, ut illam sanc-
tificaret, mundans eam lavacro aquœ in verbo vitœ, ut
exhiberet ipse sibi gloriosam Ecclesiam non habentem
maculam, aut rugam, aut aliquid hujusmodi, sed ut sit
sancta, et immaculata. Ita et viri debent diligere
uxores suas, ut corpora sua. Qui suam uxorem diligit,
seipsum diligit. Nemo enim unquam carnem suam odio
habuit, sed nutrit et fovet eam, sicut et Christus Eccle-
siam; quia membra sumus corporis ejus, et de carne
ejus, et de ossibus ejus. Propter hoc relinquet homo
patrem suum, et matrem suam, et adhœrebit uxori suœ:
et erunt duo in carne una. Sacramentum hoc magnum
est, ego autem dico in Christo et Ecclesia."

Videtis ut beatus Apostolus Matrimonium viri et
uxoris docet undique sacramentum esse, quod repræsentat conjunctionem Christi cum Ecclesia. Docet enim
consecratum a Deo Matrimonium, ut esset Christi cum
Ecclesia conjuncti sacramentum, atque ideo virum comparat Christo, uxorem Ecclesiæ. Virum caput esse dicit
ejus corporis, quod unum facit cum fœmina; Christum
caput esse dicit ejus corporis, quod unum facit cum
Ecclesia. Præcipuam causam facit cur vir uxorem
diligat non aliam, quam ne dissimile signum sit Christi,
quem repræsentat; et hanc potiorem causam facit, quam
communem masculi et fœmellæ naturam, quæ et ipsa
potuisset incitare ad diligendum. Mulierem vero, ut
virum timeat ac revereatur, eodem exemplo provocat,
nempe quod illa referat Ecclesiam obedientem Christo.
Quæ quum iterum atque iterum multis verbis inculcas-
set, ne quis hanc viri cum Christo et uxoris cum Ecclesia
collationem putaret similitudinem esse quampiam
duntaxat exhortandi gratia desumptam, ostendit rem

should think this Comparison of the Husband with Christ, and the Wife with the Church, to be some Similitude, used only for the Conveniency of the Exhortation,) he shews it to be a true Matter, a true Sacrament, foretold by the Prophesy of the chiefest and first of all Prophets, when the World was but newly created: For when the Apostle saith, 'He that loves his Wife, loves himself; for no Man ever hated his own Flesh, but loves and cherishes it, even as Christ loveth his Church; because, (says he) we are Members of his Body, of his Flesh, and of his Bones,' This he spoke to remind us of the Words, much like to these, which *Adam* spoke, when *Eve* was first brought into his Sight, 'This is Bone of my Bone, and Flesh of my Flesh.'

And that the Apostle might more clearly shew that the Sacrament of the Conjunction of *Adam* and *Eve* pertains to that Union of *Christ* with his Church, he added *Adam*'s very Words, 'Wherefore a Man shall leave Father and Mother, and cleave to his Wife; and they shall be two in one Flesh.'* This Sacrament, saith the Apostle, is great in Christ and the Church. How could he have more evidently refuted *Luther,* than by these Words, which he so impertinently scoffs at, in contending that the Apostle had taken away the Sacrament from the Marriage of Man and Wife, by saying, 'This Sacrament is great in Christ and his Church'? As if he should, by saying, the Sacrament of Baptism is great in the washing of the Soul, deny the Baptism of the Body to be a Sacrament; or, as if he should, by saying, the Sacrament of the Eucharist is great in the Body of Christ, deny the Species of Bread and Wine to be a Sacrament; or, as if by saying, That the same Sacrament is great in the mystical Body of Christ, he should detract the Sacrament from the Body which he took of the

*Gen. ii. 28.

esse veram, verum esse sacramentum a prophetarum
omnium primo, primoque ejus ipsius vaticinio, orbe jam
tum recens condito, prænunciatum. Nam quum dixisset: *"Qui suam uxorem diligit, seipsum diligit. Nemo*
enim carnem suam odio habuit, sed nutrit, et fovet eam,
sicut et Christus Ecclesiam: quia membra sumus," inquit, *"corporis ejus, et de carne ejus, et de ossibus ejus."*
Quæ verba dixit Apostolus, ut nos in memoriam duceret
eorum verborum quæ verbis istis similia dixit Adam,
quum in conspectu ejus primum adducta est **Eva**: *"Hoc*
nunc os ex ossibus meis, et caro de carne mea." Et ut
evidentius ostenderet Apostolus ad Christi copulam cum
Ecclesia pertinere sacramentum conjunctionis Adæ cum
Eva, Adæ verba ipsa subjunxit: *"Propterea relinquet*
homo patrem et matrem, et adhærebit uxori suæ: et
erunt duo in carne una. Hoc sacramentum," inquit
Apostolus, *"magnum est in Christo et Ecclesia."* Quomodo potuisset Apostolus evidentius refellisse Lutherum, quam his ipsis verbis, quæ Lutherus inepte conatur
eludere? Qui ex eo quod Apostolus dixit sacramentum
hoc magnum esse in Christo et Ecclesia, contendit Apostolum abstulisse sacramentum a Matrimonio viri et
uxoris, tanquam si quis ita loqueretur: Sacramentum
Baptismi magnum est in ablutione animæ, negaret Baptismum corporis esse sacramentum; aut si quis diceret
sacramentum Eucharistiæ magnum esse in ipso Christi
corpore, negaret panis et vini species esse sacramentum;
aut si dicat idem sacramentum esse magnum in Christi
corpore mystico, sacramentum detraheret corpori,
quod sumpsit de Virgine? Quis unquam vidit quemquam tam nugace glossemate, tanta se cum gloria
jactantem?

blessed Virgin. Who has ever seen any Man swell with greater Pride for so frivolous a Gloss? For if the Apostle had been of his Opinion, and willing his Words should be so interpreted, as to shew this Sacrament to be great only in *Christ* and his Church, without any Reference at all to the Marriage of Man and Wife; it would lessen the Force and Weight of all those Things, whereby, in that Comparison of the two Conjunctions, he had before commended Marriage.

It would also, in another Manner prejudice the Matter he undertook, if he should refer these Words of *Adam* only to Christ and his Church, which, of themselves, seem to unite Man and Wife together in mutual Love, so as to teach, that there is in them no Reference to Man and Wife. The Apostle teaches, that those Words of *Adam,* were a Prophecy of *Christ* and his Church; which is confirmed by all the holy Doctors, and very clearly demonstrated by *Adam*'s speaking these Words at the very first Sight of *Eve,* by which he preferred a Wife to Father and Mother; nor as yet any Command of begetting Children, to instruct him, by the Comparison of Parents and Children, what Father and Mother were. Because, if those Words of *Adam* were a Prophecy of Christ and his Church, then it seems they either did not belong to that Marriage which was there performed; or that some Marriage, as a proper Sign of this Conjunction, was then made a Sacrament by God himself, whose Spirit then formed the Words of *Adam,* that the same Words might signify what was then done, and what was prophesied.; that is, the Marriage of Men, and the Conjunction of Christ with the Church; and as one Sacrament comprehends a sacred Thing, and the proper and sacred Sign of the same Thing.

Moreover, that you may the more plainly discern, that

Nam si Apostolus hoc sensisset, et sic voluisset accipi, ut hoc sacramentum magnum esset duntaxat in Christo et Ecclesia, neque pertineret quicquam ad viri et uxoris Matrimonium, imminuisset robur et pondus illorum omnium, quibus illa comparatione duarum conjunctionum commendaverat ante Conjugium. Quin alia quoque ratione nocuisset causæ quam susceperat, si illa Protoplasti verba, quæ per se posita videbantur conjuges in mutuum amorem trahere, sic traxisset ad Christum et Ecclesiam, ut nihil pertinere doceret ad virum et uxorem. Verba illa Adæ fuisse vaticinium de Christo et Ecclesia docet Apostolus, et omnes Doctores sancti confirmant, et ipsa res ostendit. Nam ad primum Evæ conspectum protulit ea verba, quibus patri et matri præferebat uxorem, quum ipse neque patrem habuisset neque matrem, neque adhuc præceptum procreandi liberos, ut parentum et liberorum collatione cognosceret, quid pater esset, aut mater. Quod si illa Protoplasti verba fuerunt vaticinium de Christo et Ecclesia, tunc aut nihil pertinuisse videntur ad Matrimonium quod agebatur, et de quo dici videbantur, aut illud ipsum Matrimonium velut illius conjunctionis idoneum signum, ab ipso Deo, cujus Spiritu formabatur Adæ loquentis os, sacramentum instituebatur : ut eadem verba possent, et in id quod agebatur, et in id etiam quod prænuntiabatur, hoc est in hominum Conjugium, et Christi cum Ecclesia copulam competere, et tanquam unum sacramentum ex re sacratissima, et ejusdem rei sacro et congruente signo, comprehendere.

Præterea, ut liquido patere possit Lutherum nihil

what *Luther* speaks, is to no Purpose; observe, that the Apostle's Business, in that Place, to the *Ephesians,* is not about teaching them how great a Sacrament *Christ* joined with the Church, is; but about exhorting married People how to behave themselves one towards another, so as they might render their Marriage a Sacrament, like, and agreeable to, that so sacred a Thing, of which it is the Sacrament. *Luther,* therefore, in this Place, is either negligent himself, and unadvisedly reads this Passage, or else he most impiously dissembles what Truth he discovers therein; when he says, 'That which we give, (which is the Sense of the whole Church) proceeds from great Idleness, Negligence and inconsiderate Reading thereof.' Does St. *Augustine* therefore carelessly read the Apostle? Has St. *Hierom* negligently understood him? and all Men except *Luther,* by whose Vigilance St. *Paul* himself is discovered to have writ, not a Sacrament, but a Mystery? O this quick-sighted Man! who is able to see that the whole *Latin* Church does wrongfully name that a Sacrament, which the Apostle, writing in *Greek,* calls Mystery, and not Sacrament! as though the Latins had erred by speaking the Word in *Latin,* because St. *Paul* does not use a *Latin* Word in the *Greek* Tongue. If the Interpreter had translated it not a Sacrament, but a Mystery, and had left the Greek Word entire; yet had not this taken away the Argument, whereby Marriage is, from this Place of the Apostle, concluded to be a Sacrament; seeing it is taught so to be, by the Circumstance of the whole Matter. For let him wrest the Word Mystery, as much as he will; yet can he never by it take away, or deny, the Sacrament, though thereby it may not be proved. Neither shall it be said, that he speaks or thinks ill, who says, that the Eucharist is a great Mystery; for there is no Sacrament but what is a Mystery, that is,

dicere, non hoc agit Apostolus in illo loco ad Ephesios,
ut doceret ex illis verbis quam magnum esset sacramentum Christus conjunctus cum Ecclesia, sed ut
moneret conjunctos Matrimonio, ut se sic mutuo gererent, ut ipsorum conjugium rei tam sacræ, cujus sacramentum erat, idoneum et quam simillimum sacramentum redderent. Lutherus igitur hoc in loco, vel oscitat
ipse, atque indiligenter et inconsulte legit illum locum,
aut, quod lectione comperit, impietate dissimulat, quum
hunc intellectum, quem attulimus, et quomodo intelligit
Ecclesia, respondet esse magnæ oscitantiæ, et intelli-
gentis inconsultatæque lectionis. Ergo Augustinus
oscitanter legit Apostolum? Oscitanter legit Hieronymus? Oscitanter omnes, præter unum Lutherum? Qui
vigilantia sua deprehendit Paulum ipsum non scripsisse
sacramentum, sed mysterium? O hominem oculatum,
qui viderit totam Ecclesiam latinam perperam vocare
sacramentum id quod Apostolus, dum græce scriberet,
appellet mysterium, non sacramentum : quasi ideo latini
errarent, qui rem efferant latine, quia Paulus in lingua
græca non utatur latino vocabulo. Quod si non sacramentum, sed mysterium vertisset interpres, et græcam
vocem reliquisset integram, non abstulisset tamen argumentum quo ex eo loco Apostoli concluditur Matrimonium esse sacramentum, quum id ita esse rei totius
doceat circumstantia. Nam ut maxime torqueat mysterii verbum, nunquam tamen efficiet ut, etiamsi non
statuat sacramentum, ideo tollat ac neget sacramentum ;
neque male aut sentire dicetur, aut loqui, qui sic
loquatur : Eucharistia magnum est mysterium. Quamobrem, quum nullum sit e sacramentis, quod non idem
sit mysterium, utpote quod sub visibili signo complectitur arcanam et invisibilem gratiam, interpres animad-
vertens in illis Pauli verbis ad Ephesios totius loci
seriem declarare planissime id mysterii genus Apos-

what contains, under a visible Sign, a secret and invisible Grace; the Interpreter noting in the Words of St. *Paul* to the *Ephesians,* that the whole Passage does most evidently declare the Apostle to write of such a Mystery as is a Sacrament. And if he had not truly translated it, St. *Augustine* and St. *Hierom,* his Readers, were not so careless, but they would have discovered the Errors in the Translation: Nor were they so much inclined to favour Marriage, as to follow an Error, rather than correct it, when once discovered; especially, seeing St. *Augustine* was nothing inferior to *Luther,* in the Knowledge of the *Greek* Tongue: And St. *Hierom,* who, without Doubt, was the most skilled of his Time in that Language, did so favour Virginity, that, by some Persons, he was thought to be almost unjust towards Marriage.

Wherefore, that all Men may the more easily understand, not only these, whom *Luther* in Contempt calls sententious, and now idle Readers; but also the best and most learned of the antient Fathers of the Church; let us here what St. *Augustine* says, 'Not only Fæcundity, (says he) whose Fruit is in the Off-spring; not only in Chastity, whose Bond is Faith,' but also the Sacrament of Marriage, is commended to the Faithful, married People: For which Reason, the Apostle says, 'Husbands love your Wives, even as *Christ* loved his Church:'* St. *Augustine,* then, calls it a Sacrament; and that *Luther* may not say he has read this Passage carelessly, he treats of the same Text, again and again, in divers Works. For in another Place, he says, 'It has been said in Paradise, Man shall leave Father and Mother, and cleave to his Wife;'† which by the Apostle is called a great Sacrament in *Christ* and his Church.

Why does not St. *Augustine* explicate that Mystery of

---

*Ephes. v. 25.   †Gen. ii. 24.

tolum describere, quod vere sit sacramentum, ac præterea videns Ecclesiam totam Matrimonium observare pro sacramento, mysterium illic, ut debuit, vertit sacramentum. Qui si verbum non recte vertisset, neque tam oscitantes erant lectores aut Hieronymus, aut Augustinus, ut vertentis errorem non deprehenderent, neque tam proni fautores Conjugii, ut deprehensum sequerentur potius, quam castigarent, præsertim quum Augustinus græcarum litterarum peritia non cederet Luthero, et Hieronymus ejus linguæ sine controversia doctissimus, adeo virginitati faverit, ut apud multos Matrimonio parum æquus fuisse videretur.

Quamobrem, ut omnes facilius intelligant non eos tantum, quos per contemptum vocat sententiarios, a Luthero nunc appellari lectores oscitantes, sed veteres etiam Ecclesiæ Patres optimos et doctissimos, audiamus quid ait beatissimus Augustinus: "Non tantum," inquit, "fœcunditas, cujus fructus in prole est, nec tantum pudicitia, cujus vinculum est fides, verum etiam sacramentum nuptiarum commendatur fidelibus conjugatis. Unde dicit Apostolus: *Viri, diligite uxores vestras, sicut et Christus dilexit Ecclesiam.*" Augustinus igitur sacramentum vocat, quem ne dicat Lutherus oscitanter et indiligenter legisse locum; iterum atque iterum, aliis atque aliis operibus in eamdem sententiam eumdem locum tractat. Ait enim alibi: "Dictum est in Paradiso: *Relinquet homo patrem et matrem, et adhærebit uxori suæ.* Quod magnum sacramentum dicit Apostolus in Christo et Ecclesia." Cur hic non explicat Augustinus illud Lutheri mysterium, errorem esse, quod latini vocant sacramentum? quoniam græce Paulus ap-

Luther to be an Error, which the *Latins* call a Sacrament; seeing that in the *Greek* Text St. *Paul* calls it Mystery, not Sacrament? St. *Augustine,* above a thousand Times, calls it the Sacrament of Marriage; as in that Place where he says, *That Off-spring, Faith, and Sacrament, which are all the Goodness of Marriage, is fulfilled in the Parents, of Christ himself.* Why has he not here admonished us, that it is not a Sacrament, but a Mystery? For if what *Luther* says, be true, to wit, That it is not a Sacrament, but concern Christ and his Church; then is it not true which St. *Augustine* says: For that which *Luther* takes for only a Mystery, is not the good Sacrament of Marriage, nor has it been fulfilled in the Marriage of the Virgin *Mary.*

And in another Place, St. *Augustine,* treating of the same Words of the Apostle, says, *What is great in Christ and the Church, is very little in Man and Wife; and yet it is an inseparable Sacrament of Conjunction.*

If *Luther* holds that it is not called a Sacrament, unless in Christ and his Church; the Apostle's very Words, if diligently examined only by a *Grammarian,* shall convince him; as when the Apostle says, *This Sacrament is great; but I say in Christ and the Church.* What Sacrament is that, that is great in Christ and the Church? Christ and the Church cannot be a Sacrament in Christ and the Church: For none speaks after this Manner. It is therefore a necessary Consequence, that this Sacrament, which he says is great in Christ and the Church, is that Conjunction of Man and Wife which he has spoken of. There is Nothing else but this spoken here by the Apostle, viz. *This Conjunction of Man and Woman, is a great Sacrament in Christ and the Church, as a sacred Sign in a most sacred Thing.* Lastly, if *Luther* still obstinately deny, that (by these Words of the Apostle) Marriage should be called a Sacrament;

pellat mysterium, non sacramentum. Augustinus plus
millies appellat sacramentum connubii, et sacramentum
nuptiarum : quemadmodum et illic, ubi dicit, quod omne
nuptiarum bonum impletum est in ipsis Christi parenti-
bus, proles, fides, sacramentum. Cur hic non admonuit
nos non esse sacramentum, sed mysterium ? Præterea,
si verum dicit Lutherus sacramentum non esse, nisi in
Christo et Ecclesia, verum non dicit Augustinus. Nam
neque illud sacramentum bonum est nuptiarum, præsertim ut accepit Lutherus, qui dicit duntaxat esse mysterium, neque in Mariæ nuptiis impletum est.

Et iterum super eadem Apostoli verba dicit Augustinus : Quod in Christo et Ecclesia est magnum, hoc in
singulis quibusque viris et uxoribus est minimum, sed
tamen conjunctionis inseparabile sacramentum. Quod
si Lutherus dicat non vocari sacramentum, nisi in
Christo et Ecclesia, revincetur etiam ipsis Apostoli
verbis, si diligenter expendantur vel a grammatico.
Nam quum Apostolus dicat : *"Sacramentum hoc magnum est, ego autem dico in Christo et Ecclesia,"* quod
est illud sacramentum, quod magnum est in Christo et
Ecclesia ? Christus et Ecclesia non potest esse sacramentum in Christo et Ecclesia : nemo enim sic loquitur.
Necesse est igitur ut id sacramentum, quod dicit esse
magnum in Christo et Ecclesia, sit illa conjunctio viri
cum conjuge, de qua dixerat. Non aliud igitur dicit
Apostolus, quam hoc, id est illa conjunctio viri et mulieris, magnum est sacramentum in Christo et Ecclesia,
tanquam sacrum signum in re sacerrima.

Denique si pertinaciter neget Lutherus in illis Apostoli verbis Conjugium vocari sacramentum, sed tantum
Christi copulam cum Ecclesia, saltem non negabit istud,

but merely the Conjunction of Christ with the Church:
Yet surely he will not deny Conjunction of Man and
Wife to be at least a Sign of that sacred Conjunction of
Christ and his Church, and that too by God's own Institution; not by human Invention, seeing our first Parents
were joined by God himself. But if he denies all this
that has been said; the Apostle's Words will, however,
manifest his Impudence: For it is so often, and so
plainly repeated, that he who should not see it, must undoubtedly confess himself to be blind.

If therefore it shall evidently appear, that Grace is
conferred by Marriage, which is a Sign of so sacred a
Thing; *Luther* will be compelled, whether he will or no,
to admit Marriage as a Sacrament, or else to reject all
Sacraments; seeing that, by his own Confession, a Sacrament consists in the *Sign of a sacred Thing, and the
Promise of Grace*. Let us see then, if it can be evidently made out, that Grace is infused after any Manner by Marriage; for *Luther* flatly denies it.

'We read in no Place, (says he) that he who marries
a Wife shall receive any Grace from God.' *Marriage*
(says the Apostle) *is honourable in all, and a Bed undefiled:** The Bed could not be undefiled, if the Marriage wanted Grace; neither has Marriage any Thing
else to confer, *but a Bed unspotted*. But because God,
whose Bounty has provided, that no necessary Thing
should be wanting, even to irrational Creatures, according to their several Natures and Capacities; nay, even
to Things wanting Sense; has, by the like bountiful
Providence, joined Grace to Marriage, by which, he that
does not slight it, but keeps his Faith inviolate to his
Wife, shall not only not contract any Blemish by the
carnal Act, (whose filthy Concupiscence would otherwise stain him) but shall, on the Contrary, be advanced

*Hebr. xiii. 4.

quin illa conjunctio viri et mulieris signum saltem sit
sacræ illius conjunctionis, qua Christus conjungitur cum
Ecclesia, idque ex institutione Dei, quum primi
parentes, Deo ipso copulante, conjuncti sunt, non autem
humano ingenio inventum postea. Istud saltem, quod
dixi, Lutherus si neget ex Apostoli verbis patere, negabit
impudentissime: nam hoc in eo loco tam sæpe, tam
aperte dicitur, ut qui non id videat, cæcum se fateatur
oportet. Igitur si Conjugio, quod rem tam sacram
significat, constabit etiam conferri gratiam, tunc, velit,
nolit, cogetur Lutherus aut Conjugium pro sacramento
suscipere, aut omnia prorsus sacramenta rejicere, quum,
ipso fatente, signum rei sacræ cum promissione gratiæ
faciant sacramentum.

Videamus igitur an aliquo modo liquere possit infundi Conjugio gratiam; nam id aperte negat Lutherus:
"Nusquam," inquit, "legitur aliquid gratiæ Dei acceptu-
rum, quisquis uxorem duxerit." *"Honorabile Conjugium,"* inquit Apostolus, *"in omnibus, et thorus im-
maculatus;"* thorus macula carere non posset, si Conjugium careret gratia. Nec aliunde habet Conjugium,
ut thorum servet immaculatum, quam quod Deus, cujus
providit bonitas, ut nec rebus his, quæ naturali feruntur
ordine, etiamsi non ratione tantum, sed etiam sensu
careant, quicquam deesset eorum, quæ pro cujusque
captu sint necessaria, simili benignitate curavit ut Conjugio gratiam jungeret, qua quisquis eam nollet ab-
jicere, et fidem debitam servaret Conjugii, et ex com-
mixtione carnali, cujus alioqui fœda concupiscentia
macularetur, non solum non contraheret labem, sed
etiam proveheretur ad gloriam. Conjugium enim non
haberet thorum immaculatum, nisi quia gratia, quæ
infunditur Conjugio, verteret illud in bonum, quod alias

to Grace. For Marriage should not have an immaculate Bed, if the Grace, which is infused by it, did not turn that unto Good, which should be otherwise a Sin. Which, in another Passage of St. *Paul,* where he treats of the Woman's Duty, is more plainly demonstrated; *She* (saith he) *shall be saved, through the Generation of Children:** But if you take away Marriage, what else shall Generation be, (by which, as the Apostle saith, *there is no Salvation in Marriage*) *but Death and eternal Damnation?* For, *Take away Marriage,* (says St. *Bernard*) *and an undefiled Bed from the Church, and do you not then fill it with Adulteries, Incests, Sodomy, and all Sorts of Uncleanness?* If all Generation, out of Wedlock, is damnable, the Grace of Marriage must needs be great, by which that Act, (which of its own Nature defiles to Punishment) is not only purged, to take away the Blemish; but is so much sanctified, that, as the Apostle testifies, it becomes meritorious. Neither has it that Privilege of Grace, but by Virtue of the Sacrament, consecrated for that Purpose by God himself; that Man, at his first Creation, might, by the Use thereof, both perform his Duty of Propagation, and have also a Remedy of Concupiscence, when restored: Yet what should the conjugal Act itself be, but Concupiscence, if God had not made it the Remedy thereof? Which now the holy Grace of the Sacrament has so made a Remedy of Concupiscence, as that the paternal Substance may not be negligently consumed, (as the prodigal Son had done) forbidding not only, not to thirst after stolen Waters of other Men's Cisterns, but also not to inebriate ourselves with our own; but make our sober Draughts so wholesome, that they may profit to Life everlasting. The Apostle, in the same Place, though he exhorted as much as possible to Continency and Virginity, (Virtues

*I. Tim. ii. 15.

esset peccatum. Quod ipsum et alibi quoque, quum de mulieris agit officio, Paulus designat apertius: *"Salvabitur,"* inquit, *"per filiorum generationem."* At si tollas Conjugium, quid aliud fuerit generatio, per quam, ut Apostolus ait, salvabitur in Conjugio, quam mors et æterna damnatio? "Nam tolle, inquit beatus Bernardus, de Ecclesia honorabile connubium, et thorum immaculatum, nonne reples eam concubinariis, incestuosis, seminifluis, mollibus masculorum concubitoribus, et omni denique genere immundorum." Si igitur extra Conjugium omnis generatio damnabilis est, magna videtur gratia Matrimonii, qui eumdem actum (si naturam respicis) ex quo maculareris in pœnam, non solum ita purgat, ut eluat labem, sed etiam sic sanctificat, ut Apostolo teste, reportet præmium. Nec istud habet privilegium gratiæ, nisi virtute sacramenti ab ipso Deo in id consecrati, ut homini ipsius cultori foret et in propagationis officium, quum creatus est, et in remedium concupiscentiæ, quum restitutus est. Quanquam ille ipse conjugalis actus quid esset aliud, quam concupiscentia, nisi Deus illum faceret remedium concupiscentiæ? Quem nunc sancta sacramenti gratia sic fecit concupiscentiæ remedium, ut eos, qui gratiæ paternæ substantiam, quam Deus infundit Conjugio, negligenter nolit, ut filius prodigus fecit, effundere, non solum defendat, ne quid aquæ furtivæ sitiant e cisternis alienis, sed etiam ne se inebrient suis, et sobrios haustus efficiant tam salubres, ut in vitam proficiant æternam.

Nam et Apostolus in illo etiam loco, ubi, quantum potuit, hortabatur ad continentiam et virginitatem, contrariam conjugali generationi virtutem, tamen Matri-

contrary to conjugal Generation) yet confesses, that Marriage is the Gift of God; and one of those Gifts, of which it is said, *Every good and perfect Gift is from above, descending from the Father of Lights.** And certainly the Gift of God, (which is so given, that he who receives it, may continue in that State of Life, in which he ought to remain, and not fall into the State of Destruction) doth it not shew that it hath in itself preservative Grace?

Moreover, when the Apostle saith, *If any Brother have a Wife, an Infidel, and she consent to live with him, let him not put her away: And if any Woman have an Husband, an Infidel, and he consent to dwell with her, let her not put away her Husband: For the Man, an Infidel, is sanctified by the faithful Woman; and the Woman, an Infidel, is sanctified by the faithful Husband; otherwise, your Children should be unclean; but now they are holy.*† Do not these Words of the Apostle shew, that, in Marriage (which is an entire Thing of itself, after one of the Parties is converted to the Faith) the Sanctity of the Sacrament sanctifies the whole Marriage, which before was altogether unclean? But why should that Marriage be now more holy than before, (as being a Marriage) if, for one of the Parties converted, sacramental Grace were not added to it, which, before Baptism, (the Door of all the Sacraments) could not enter to the Marriage of the Unfaithful?

But, to pass by the Apostle; let us consider God, the Consecrator of this Sacrament. Has he not consecrated Marriage with his Blessing, when he joined together our first Parents? For the Scripture saith, *God blessed them; saying, increase, and multiply:*‡ Whose Blessing, having operated in all other living Creatures, according to their several Capacities; who should doubt

*Jas. i. 17.   †I. Cor. vii. 12.   ‡Gen. i. 28.

monium etiam Dei donum fatetur, nimirum ex illis, de quibus dicitur: *"Omne datum optimum, omne donum perfectum desursum est, descendens a Patre luminum."* Et certe donum Dei, quod ideo datur, ut qui accipit, in eo vitæ statu sit, in quo servari debeat, ne in eum decidat statum, in quem si cadit, pereat, annon habere se docet adjunctam præservatricem gratiam? Ad hæc quum ita dicat Apostolus: *"Si quis frater uxorem habet infidelem, et hæc consentit habitare cum illo, non dimittat illam. Et si qua mulier fidelis habet virum infidelem, et hic consentit habitare cum illa, non dimittat virum. Sanctificatus est enim vir infidelis per mulierem fidelem, et sanctificata est mulier infidelis per virum fidelem. Alioqui enim filii vestri immundi essent, nunc autem sancti sunt,"* annon his verbis ostendit Apostolus, quod quum integra quædam res sit Conjugium, postquam alterutra pars ad fidem conversa est, sanctitas sacramenti totum sanctificat Conjugium, quod prius totum fuit immundum? At cur istud Conjugium plus haberet sancti, quam prius, quatenus Conjugium est, nisi, propter alterius accedentem fidem, accederet Conjugio sacramentalis gratia quæ, ante Baptismum, qui sacramentorum omnium janua est, ad infidelium Conjugium non potuit ingredi?

Sed prætereamus Apostolum. Consideremus hujus sacramenti consecratorem Deum. Annon ille, quum primos parentes conjungeret, Conjugium benedictione sacravit? Ait enim Scriptura: *"Benedixit illis Deus, ac dixit: Crescite et multiplicamini."* Cujus benedictio, quum in reliquis animantibus ad corporis robur pro cujusque captu sit operata, quis dubitet in homine rationis capace vim gratiæ spiritalis infudisse spiritui:

but that he has infused the Force of spiritual Grace into the Spirit of Man, who alone is capable of Reason, unless he did believe, that God, (being so bountiful to the meanest of Beasts, as to give them largely, according to their Natures, what was necessary) should be so sparing of his Blessings to Man, whom he created after his own Image; that having only Regard to his Body, he should omit the Soul, *that Breath of Life,* which he himself has breathed, and by which he was most represented, without imparting any Part of that great Blessing to it?

Further; when Christ, God and Man, conversing amongst Men, not only honoured Marriage with his own Presence, but also adorned it with his first Miracle; has he not taught, *That Marriage is to be honoured?* And without Grace, I do not find any Thing in it deserving Honour. Nor do I think he would have been present at it, if Marriage had not already some Grace, which might render it acceptable to Christ; or else he conferred Grace to it himself: But I see, the Miracle that he wrought,* admonishes us that the insipid Water of carnal Concupiscence, by the secret Grace of God, is changed to Wine of the best Taste. But why search we so many Proofs in so clear a Thing? especially, when that only Text is sufficient for all, where Christ says, *Whom God has joined together, let no Man put asunder.*† O the admirable Word! which none could have spoken, but the Word that was made Flesh! who thinks it not to have been abundantly sufficient, that God has joined the first of Mankind; and that the Bounty of so great a God is to be admired by all Men? But now we are taught from Truth itself, that those who are lawfully married, are not rashly joined together; not by the Ceremonies of Men only, but by the invisible Presence

*John ii.   †Matt. xix. 6.

nisi quis Deum credat, quum infimis quibusque bestiolis
fuisset tam benignus, ut pro sua cuique natura largitus
sit affluenter, homini, quem ad ipsius condidisset imaginem, tam parce manum in benedictione restringeret, ut,
corporis duntaxat habita ratione, animam, illud vitæ
spiraculum, quod ipse inspiraverat, et qua maxime
repræsentabatur, tanta benedictione præteriret intac-
tam.

Iterum, quum Christus homo et idem Deus versatus
inter homines, nuptias non solum sua honoravit præsentia, sed etiam nobilitavit miraculo, annon docuit
honorandum esse Connubium? Quod ego certe non
video quid honore dignum habere possit absque gratia.
Neque illum puto ad nuptias fuisse venturum, nisi vel
jam tum haberet aliquid gratiæ Conjugium, quod ipsum
Christo faceret gratum, vel ut Conjugio gratiam ipse
conferret. Quin et miraculum, quod operabatur, nos admonere video insipidam concupiscentiæ carnalis aquam,
per occultam Dei gratiam, in optimi saporis vinum esse
conversam.

Sed quid opus est in re tam clara tot probamenta con-
quirere? Præsertim quum vel unus ille locus abunde
sufficiat, quo Christus ait: *"Quos Deus conjunxit, homo
non separet."* O verbum admirabile, et quod nemo
potuisset effari, præter Verbum quod caro factum est!
Quis non putasset abunde satis esse, quod primos
homines, initium generis, conjunxisset Deus? Atque id
ipsum fuerat, in tanta Deitatis majestate, nulli non
admiranda benignitas. At nunc, Veritate referente
didicimus quicunque legitimo Conjugio copulantur, eos
non temere neque mortalium duntaxat cærimoniis, sed
ipso Deo invisibiliter assistente, et insensibiliter co-

and insensible Co-operation of God himself: And therefore is it forbidden, that any should separate those whom
God has joined together. O Word as full of Joy and
Fears as it is of Admiration! Who should not rejoice,
that God has so much Care over his Marriage, as to
vouchsafe, not only to be present at it, but also to preside in it? Who should not tremble, whilst he is in
Doubt how to use his Wife, whom he is not only bound
to love, but also to live with, in such a Manner, as that
he may be able to render her pure and immaculate to
God, from whom he has received her?

Wherefore, seeing that God himself, as he says, *joins
all married People together;* who believes not that he
infuses Grace by Marriage? Does he join always, and
give his Blessing but once? Why reassumes he the
Office of joining, if we believe him not also to reassume
that of Blessing? Or can we imagine, that the most
holy Spirit, *which is to be adored in Spirit and in
Truth,* should always exercise the Office of joining married People, for Care of carnal Copulation only? Indeed, as for that Matter, it should be sufficient that God
leaves Man, like other Animals, to his own natural and
corrupt Inclinations. There must be understood Something sure more holy than the Care of propagating the
Flesh, which God performs in Marriage; and that, without all Doubt, is Grace; which is by the Prelate of all
Sacraments infused into married People in consecrating
Marriage.

Seeing therefore, we have, by so many Reasons,
proved Grace to be conferred in Marriage; and that
Marriage, which (as appears by the Words of the Apostle) is a Sign of a sacred Thing, (which Sign, is joined
with Grace, as is already said) cannot be a bare Figure
only; it follows then, that, in Despite of *Luther,* Mar-

operante conjungi. Atque ideo vetitum ne, quos Deus
junxit, ullo separentur ab homine. O verbum non ad-
miratione magis, quam gaudio pariter et timore plenum! Quis non lætetur Deo tantæ curæ esse suum Conjugium, ut non solum interesse, sed etiam præesse
dignetur? Quis non inhorrescat, dum dubitet quomodo
debeat tractare conjugem, quam non solum tene-
atur amare, sed etiam sic convivere, ut puram et sine
macula possit Deo, quo tradente recepit, reposcenti
reddere?

Igitur quum Deus, ut dicit ipse, conjungat omnes,
quis ab illo credet Conjugio non infundi gratiam? An
qui semper copulat, semel duntaxat benedixit? Cur
jungendi resumit officium, nisi credatur et benedicendi
repetere? An sanctissimum illum Spiritum, quem in
spiritu et veritate oportet adorare, putandum est assidue
subire ministerium copulandorum conjugum, copulæ
tantum cura carnalis? Certe, quod ad eam rem attinet,
sufficeret Deo si genus humanum, quemadmodum cætera
animalia, naturæ ab ipso inditæ, et hominis vitio cor-
ruptæ relinqueret. Sanctius igitur aliquid subesse oportet, ultra carnis propagandæ curam, quod augustum
illud Dei numen in Conjugio peragat, id est haud dubie,
quod Antistes sacramentorum omnium conjugibus infundit in Conjugio consecrando gratiam.

Ergo, quum tot modis probavimus conferri in Conjugio gratiam, Conjugium vero sacræ rei signum esse
patet et ex Apostolo, quod signum, quum gratiam, sicut
ostendimus, adjunctam habeat, figura duntaxat esse non
possit, consequens est ut, invito Luthero, Conjugium
sacramentum sit, etiamsi sacramenti nomine, quod

riage is a Sacrament; though it had not, (as it is) been so called by the Apostle.

But has any one, either Antient or Modern, doubted to call Marriage a Sacrament, without being hissed at by the Church? In which alone, as *Hugo de Sancto Victore* mentions, is found a two-fold Sign: 'For Marriage itself is the Sacrament of the Society, which is in the Spirit between God and Man; but the Duty of Marriage is the Sacrament of that Society, which in the Flesh is between Christ and the Church. For if that (says he) which is in the Flesh, is great, much more that which is in the Spirit: And if God is rightly called in Scripture, a Bridegroom, and the Soul of Man the Bride, there is certainly Something betwixt God and the Soul; of which, what consists in Marriage betwixt Man and Woman, is the Sacrament, and Image. But perhaps, (to speak more expressly) that Society, which is exteriorly observed, according to the Contract in Marriage, is the Sacrament; and the mutual Love of the Souls, which is kept by an interchangeable Bond of conjugal Society and Alliance, is the Matter of the Sacrament.' And again; 'this same Love, by which Male and Female are spiritually united in the Sanctity of Wedlock, is the Sacrament and Sign of that Love, by which God is interiorly joined to the rational Soul, by Infusion of his Grace, and Participation of his Spirit.' Thus far the Words of *Hugo.*

Wherefore, seeing that not only the public Faith of the Church, for so many Ages before us, and the antient Fathers, remarkable for their virtuous Lives and Knowledge in Scripture; but also the blessed Apostle, St. *Paul,* Doctor of the *Gentiles,* have esteemed Marriage as a Sacrament, (which makes Wedlock honourable, and does by Grace, not only conserve the Bed unspotted from Adultery; but also washes away the Stains

tamen facit, non appellaret Apostolus. Sed quis unquam aut veterum, aut novorum, nisi quos explosit Ecclesia, Matrimonium dubitavit appellare sacramentum?
"In quo uno," quod Hugo de Sancto-Victore commemorat, "duplex invenere signum : nam et Conjugium
ipsum sacramentum est illius societatis quæ in Spiritu
est inter Deum et animam, officium vero Conjugii sacramentum est illius societatis, quæ in carne est inter
Christum et Ecclesiam. Nam si magnum est," inquit,
"quod in carne est, multo magis utique est, quod in
spiritu est. Et si recte per Scripturam sanctam Deus
Sponsus dicitur, et anima rationalis Sponsa vocatur,
aliquid profecto inter Deum et animam est, cujus id
quod in Conjugio inter masculum et fœminam constat,
sacramentum et imago est. Sed forte, ut expressius
dicam, ipsa societas, quæ exterius in Conjugio pacto
fœderis servatur, sacramentum est, et ipsius sacramenti
res est dilectio mutua animorum, quæ ad invicem societatis et fœderis conjugalis vinculo custoditur. Et hæc
rursus ipsa dilectio, qua masculus et fœmina in sanctitate Conjugii animis uniuntur, sacramentum est, et
signum illius dilectionis, qua Deus animæ rationali intus
per infusionem gratiæ suæ, et Spiritus sui participa-
tionem, conjungitur." Hactenus Hugo. Quamobrem,
quum non solum publica fides Ecclesiæ tot ante nos
sæculis, ac vetusti Patres Scripturarum scientia et vitæ
meritis insignes, sed ipse etiam beatus Apostolus et
Doctor Gentium Paulus Matrimonium habuerint pro
sacramento, quod honorabile faciat connubium, et
thorum per gratiam non solum servet immaculatum ab
adulterio, sed et abluat immunditiam libidinis, et aquam
convertat in vinum, sanctamque procuret voluntatem a
licitis nonnunquam abstinendi complexibus, non video
quid contra Lutherus possit afferre nisi quod "hæretici,"
ut beatus ait Bernardus, "pro libitu quisque suo sacra-

of Lust, turns Water into Wine, and procures a holy
Pleasure of abstaining, even from lawful Pleasures.)
I do not perceive what *Luther* can say to the Contrary;
unless it is because Hereticks (as St. *Bernard* saith) *do
still, according to their own Fancies, strive who shall
exceed others, in endeavouring, with their viperous
Teeth, to tear in Pieces the Sacrament of the Church,
as the Bowels of their Mother.*

CHAP. XII

❦f the Sacrament of ❦rders

In the Sacrament of *Orders, Luther* keeps no Manner
of Order; but gathering together from here and there
all the Treasuries of his Malice, he pours them out
against it.

He shews how well his Mind is composed for Evil,
if his Power were answerable thereto: He proposes
many Things, and asserts and affirms the worst: But,
satisfying himself by only saying, thus, and thus, he
confirms Nothing at all, by any Manner of Reason. In
which Proceeding his great Impudence appears, who,
not vouchsafing to believe the whole Church, (without
having Reasons for its Faith) does unreasonably require
that he himself should be credited, without shewing any
Reason at all; and that in Matters of such Nature, as
he cannot tell what is to be believed, unless the Church
teach him: And yet he desires to be believed, and that
in such Sort, as to do it, is to confound and trample
under Foot the whole Church: For what else aims he at,
by endeavouring to take away the *Holy Sacrament of*

menta Ecclesiæ, tanquam matris viscera, dente vipereo
certatim inter se dilacerare contendunt."

CAP. XII

De Sacramento Ordinis

In sacramento Ordinis nullo procedit ordine; sed
hinc atque inde colligens omnes malitiæ suæ thesauros
effundit, animum ostendit egregie versum ad nocendum,
si respondeant vires, proponit multa, asserit atque af-
firmat pessima, sed omnia sat habens dicere, nihil
prorsus ulla ratione confirmat. Qua ex re videre licet
insignem hominis impudentiam, qui quum toti credere
non dignetur Ecclesiæ, nisi rationem reddenti suæ fidei,
sibi ut credatur uni sine ratione postulet, idque de rebus
ejusmodi, de quibus quid credat cognoscere, nisi Ecclesia docente, non potest. Et tamen sic postulat sibi
credi, quomodo, si quis credat, non aliud agat, quam ut
totam confundat atque pessumdet Ecclesiam. Nam quid
aliud molitur, qui conatur tollere sacrosanctum sacramentum Ordinis, quam ut, postquam mysteriorum ministri viluerint, incipiant utpote etiam, quæ per viles minis-
trentur, vilescere sacramenta? quem unum scopum toto
petit opusculo. De Ordine igitur, quia nullo procedit
ordine, colligemus hinc inde Lutheri dogmata, ut acer-

Orders, than, by rendering the Ministers of the Church contemptible, he may procure, that the Sacraments of the Church may be also despised, and undervalued, as being ministered by the Hands of vile and unworthy Ministers: Which is the only Drift of his whole Work.

And because *Luther* proceeds with no Order, in treating of Order; we will gather his Opinions here and there, that the Reader may have under one View that Heap of Evils; which being looked over, we need not take any great Pains, I suppose, to convince him, whose wicked Doctrine all Men may see tends directly to the Destruction of the Faith of *Christ,* by Infidelity. For what designs he else, who disputes that there is no Difference of Priesthood between the Laity, and Priest? that all Men are Priests alike: That all Men have the same Power, in what Sacrament soever: That the Ministry of the Sacraments is not given to the Priests, but by Consent of the Laity: That the Sacrament of Orders is Nothing else but the Custom of electing a Preacher in the Church: That he is not a Priest, who is not a Preacher, unless it be equivocally, as a painted Man, may be called a Man: That a Priest may be made a Layman again, when he pleases; because his priestly Character is Nothing: Moreover, that Order itself, which as a Sacrament, ordains some to be Clergymen, is merely and altogether a Fiction invented by Men, who understand Nothing of ecclesiastical Matters, of Priesthood, of the Ministry, of the Word, or of a Sacrament? Finally, this holy Priest, (whereby you may conjecture how chaste he himself is) makes it the greatest Error, and greatest Blindness imaginable, that Priests should undertake to lead a single Life. And when *Christ* praises those who have made themselves Eunuchs for the Kingdom of Heaven; this most filthy *Antichrist* compares them to the old idolatrous gelded

vum illum malorum lector semel habeat sub oculis, quo
conspecto non erit, opinor, multum insumendum operæ
ut illum coarguamus, cujus impiam doctrinam videbunt
omnes eo recta contendere, ut omnem Christi fidem
possit infidelitate pervertere.

Quid enim destinat aliud, qui decernit inter laicos
et sacerdotes nullum esse discrimen sacerdotii, omnes
ex æquo presbyteros esse, omnes eamdem habere potestatem in quocumque sacramento? Sacerdotibus sacramentorum ministerium non nisi laicorum consensu
committi? Sacramentum Ordinis nihil aliud esse posse,
quam ritum quemdam eligendi concionatoris in Ecclesia? Quicumque non prædicat, eum non esse sacerdotem, nisi æquivoce, quemadmodum homo pictus est
homo, qui sacerdos est, rursus fieri posse laicum:
characterem enim nihil esse. Ordinem denique ipsum
(qui velut sacramentum homines in clericos ordinat, qui
prædicare nesciunt) esse vere mere omninoque figmentum ex hominibus natum nihil de re ecclesiastica, de
sacerdotio, de ministerio verbi, de sacramento intelli-
gentibus. Postremo sanctus iste sacerdos, ut quam
castus ipse sit, conjecturam præbeat, tanquam errorem
summum, et summam cæcitatem ponit, et Captivitatem
maximam, quod sibi sacerdotes indixerint cœlibem casti-
tatem. Et quum Christus eos laudet eximie, qui se
castraverunt ob regnum cœlorum, Antichristus iste
spurcissimus eosdem comparat eviratis olim Cybelis deæ
sacerdotibus idolatris. Jamdudum scio, aures pii lec-
toris exhorrent impium hunc dogmatum perniciosorum

Priests of the *Heathen Sybils.* I know that this Catalogue of pernicious Opinions has long since wearied the
Ears of the pious Reader; every one of which Opinions
is more stuffed with Heresies, than the *Trojan's* Horse
is reported to have been with armed Men.

But his denying Orders to be a Sacrament, is as it
were the Fountain to all the rest; which, being once
stopped up, the other small Springs must of Necessity
become dry of themselves. 'This Sacrament (says he)
is not known to the Church of *Christ,* but has been invented by the Church of the *Pope.'* In these few
Words, are contained a great Heap of Absurdities and
Lyes: For he makes Distinction between *Christ's*
Church, and the *Pope's;* whereas the Pope is Christ's
Vicar, in that, over which Christ is the Head. He says
the Church has invented; when it has received it as
already instituted, and therefore has not invented it.
'This Sacrament (he says) is unknown to the Church
of *Christ:'* Whereas it is most certain, that all Parts of
the World, which have the true Faith of *Christ,* have
Orders for a Sacrament: For if he could find some ob-
scure Corner, (which I doubt he cannot) in which this
Sacrament of Orders should not be known; yet ought not
that Corner to be compared to the rest of the whole
Church; which not only is subject to *Christ,* but also,
for *Christ's* Sake, to *Christ's* only Vicar the *Pope* of
Rome, and believes Orders to be a Sacrament.

Otherwise, if *Luther* persists in his Distinction of the
Pope's Church, from *Christ's;* and in saying that the
one has Orders for a Sacrament, the other not; let him
shew us the Church of *Christ,* which, contrary to the
Faith of the Papal Church, (as he calls it) knows not
the Sacrament of Order. In the mean while, it appears
evidently, that, by asserting this Sacrament to be unknown to the Church of *Christ,* and that they are not

catalogum, quorum fere quodvis magis fœtum est hæresibus, quam fuisse fertur equus ille Trojanus armatis.
Sed omnium veluti quidam fons est, quod Ordinem
negat esse sacramentum, quo obstructo cæteros necesse
est rivulos exarescere.

"Hoc sacramentum," inquit, "Ecclesia Christi ignorat, inventumque est ab Ecclesia Papæ." Hæc pauca
verba non parvum habent et falsitatis et absurditatis
acervum: nam et Ecclesiam Papæ discernit ab Ecclesia
Christi, quum Papa sit ejusdem Ecclesiæ Pontifex,
cujus et Christus. Ait Ecclesiam invenisse quod non
invenit, sed accepit institutum. Ait Ecclesiam Christi
hoc ignorare sacramentum, quum satis constet nullam
fere mundi plagam esse, quæ rite profitetur fidem
Christi, quin Ordinem habeat pro sacramento. Nam si
posset obscurum aliquem angulum reperire (quod,
opinor, non potest) in quo nesciatur sacramentum
Ordinis, tamen angulus ille non esset cum reliqua com-
parandus Ecclesia, quæ non Christo solum subest, sed et
propter Christum unico Christi vicario Papæ Romano,
et Ordinem credit esse sacramentum. Alioqui si perstet
in eo Lutherus, ut Ecclesiam Papæ discernat ab Ecclesia Christi, et apud alteram dicat Ordinem haberi
pro sacramento, non haberi apud alteram, proferat illam
Ecclesiam Christi, quæ contra fidem papalis, ut vocat,
Ecclesiæ, ignorat sacramentum Ordinis. Interim certe
perspicuum est, quum dicat hoc sacramentum ignorari
ab Ecclesia Christi, et de Christi Ecclesia dicat eos,
quibus præsidet Papa, non esse, utraque ratione ab
Ecclesia Christi eum segregare non Romam tantum, sed
Italiam totam, Germaniam, Hispanias, Gallias, Britan-
nias, reliquasque gentes omnes quæcumque Romano

of *Christ*'s Church who are governed by the *Pope;* he separates, by both these Reasons, from *Christ*'s Church, not only *Rome,* but also all *Italy, Germany, Spain, France, Britain,* and all other Nations, which obey the *See* of *Rome;* or have Orders for a Sacrament. Which People, being by him taken from the Church of *Christ;* it consequently follows, that he must either confess *Christ*'s Church to be in no Place at all, or else, like the *Donatists,* he must reduce the *Catholic* Church to two or three *Heretics* whispering in a Corner.

But he draws out of his Shaft, as an inevitable Dart, 'That Grace is in no Place promised to this Sacrament; and that the New Testament makes not the least Mention of it:' He says, 'That it is a ridiculous Thing to assert that for the Sacrament of God, which cannot any where be demonstrated to have been instituted by God.' 'Nor is it lawful (says he) to assert any Thing to be of Divine Institution, which is not of Divine Ordinance; but we ought (says he) to endeavour to have all Things confirmed to us from clear Scripture.'

We will see, by and by, whether no Mention is made at all of this Sacrament in the New Testament: For by the same Dart he expects to wound all the rest of the Sacraments; against which Dart, I will take the same Buckler or Shield which *Luther* himself confesses to be impenetrable.

His own Words are these: 'Truly the Church has this Faculty, That it can discern the Word of God, from the Word of Men;' even as St. *Augustine* confesses, 'That he has believed the Gospel by the Motion of the Church's Authority; which told him that it was the Gospel.' Wherefore, seeing that the Church, as *Luther* confesses, *can discern the Word of God, from the Word of Men;* it is certain it has not that Power, but from God; nor for any other Cause, than that it may not err

Pontifici parent, aut Ordinem pro sacramento recipiunt. Quos populos omnes quum de Christi tollat Ecclesia, necesse est ut aut Ecclesiam Christi fateatur esse nusquam, aut, more Donatistarum, Ecclesiam Christi catholicam ad duos aut tres hæreticos redigat de Christo susurrantes in angulo.

Sed velut inevitabile telum promit, quod hoc sacramentum nullam habeat promissionem gratiæ ullibi, ut inquit, positam: cujus sacramenti vel verbo meminisse negat totum Novum Testamentum, et ridiculum ait asserere pro sacramento Dei quod a Deo institutum nusquam potest monstrari; "nec licet," inquit, "adstruere aliquod divinitus ordinatum, quod divinitus ordinatum non est, sed conandum est ut omnia nobis claris," inquit, "Scripturis sint firmata." Utrum in Novo Testamento nulla prorsus fiat hujus sacramenti mentio, post excutiemus. Interim sic agam cum illo, tanquam nulla prorsus mentio fieret: nam eodem telo se sperat omnia ferme sacramenta perfodere; adversus quod telum ego in scutum mihi idipsum ferrum conjiciam, quod Lutherus ipse fatetur impenetrabile. Sic enim se habent ipsius verba: "Hoc sane habet Ecclesia, quod potest discernere verbum Dei a verbis hominum, sicut Augustinus confitetur se evangelio credidisse, motum auctoritate Ecclesiæ, quæ hoc esse evangelium prædicabat." Igitur quum istud habeat, ut Lutherus fatetur, Ecclesia, quod verbum Dei discernere potest a verbis hominum, certum est istud non aliunde haberi, quam a Deo, nec ob aliam causam, quam ne in his erraret Ecclesia, in quibus non erratum esse oporteat. Sequitur igitur ex hoc fundamento, quod nobis substravit Luthe-

in those Things, in which there ought to be no Error. It follows then, out of this Foundation he has laid for us, that the Church has from God, not only the Power of discerning God's Word from that of Mens, (which he allows) but also the Faculty of discerning betwixt divine and human Sense of Scripture. Otherwise, what should it avail the Church to know, by God's Teaching, the true Scripture from that which is false, if it could not distinguish between the false and true Sense of true Scripture? Finally, it follows, by the same Reason, that God instructs his Church, even in Things which are not written; lest it might, through Errors, embrace false Things for true ones: For that is no less dangerous than that it might admit the Writings of Men, for the Words of God, or draw a false Sense out of the Word of God; especially if it should take false Sacraments for true ones, and human Traditions for divine; nay, not only the Traditions of Men, but the Inventions of the Devil; if the Church of *Christ,* should, as Inchanters do, place its Hope in feigned and vain Signs of corporal Things. It appears, therefore, by *Luther*'s confessing the Church to have a Faculty of discerning the Words of God from the Words of Men, that it has no less Power to discern betwixt divine Institutions, and the Traditions of Men. For, otherwise, the Error which we are to avoid, might as well arise from the one Side, as from the other. And *Christ*'s Care, is not, that his Church may not err, after this or that Manner; but that it may not err in any Manner whatsoever. But it could by no Error commit a greater Injury to *Christ,* than in putting its Trust, which it ought to have in him alone, in Signs not supported by any Grace, but empty and void of all the Advantages of Faith. Therefore, the Church cannot err about the Sacraments of Faith; no more, I say, than in admitting Scripture, (in which

rus, ut Ecclesia habeat a Deo non id solum quod concedit Lutherus, discretionem verborum Dei a verbis hominum, sed etiam discernendi facultatem, qua in Scripturis divinis divinum sensum ab humano discriminet. Alioqui enim quid profuerit si Ecclesia, Deo docente, Scripturam veram discernat a falsa, et in Scriptura vera falsum sensum non discernat a vero? Denique eadem ratione et istud sequitur, ut et in his quæ non scribuntur, Ecclesiam suam doceat Deus, ne per errorem possit falsa pro veris amplecti, quum ex ea re non minus impendeat periculi, quam si vel Scripturas hominum teneat pro verbis Dei, vel e veris Dei verbis falsum eliciat sensum: præsertim si falsa suscipiat sacramenta pro veris, et traditiones hominum pro traditionibus Dei, imo non traditiones hominum, sed figmenta diaboli, si suam spem in fictis ac vanis corporalium rerum signis, quemadmodum magi faciunt, Ecclesia Christi velut in Christi sacramentis collocet.

Liquet ergo manifeste ex eo quod fatetur Lutherus Ecclesiam hoc habere, ut verba Dei discernat a verbis hominum, hoc quoque non minus habere, ut traditiones Dei discernat a traditionibus hominum, quum alioqui utrobique possit ex æquo vitandus error exoriri, nec id agat Christus, ne Ecclesia sua hoc aut illo erret modo, sed ne erret ullo. Errare vero majore cum injuria Christi non possit, quam si fiduciam in illo ponendam solo ponat in signis nulla prorsus fultis gratia, sed omni bono fidei vacuis atque inanibus. Non igitur errare potest Ecclesia in suscipiendis sacramentis fidei, non magis, inquam, quam errare potest in suscipiendis (qua in re Ecclesiam errare non posse fatetur Lutherus ipse) Scripturis. Quæ res si se haberet aliter, multa sequerentur absurda, sed hoc imprimis, quo nihil esse potest

Luther confesses her infallible) which, if it were otherwise, many Absurdities should follow; and especially
this, that almost all Opinions of the Church, in Matters
of Faith, established these many past Ages, may be disputed after the Fancy of every new-fangled Heretic;
which were the most ridiculous Thing imaginable. For,
if Nothing must be certainly believed, but what is confirmed by Scripture; and that (as he says) by clear
Testimonies of Scripture too; we must not only, not
assert the perpetual Virginity of the blessed Virgin
Mary, but also an inexhausted *Materia* will be furnished for battering the Church, at the Pleasure of every
one who is minded to stir up new *Sects,* or renew the
old one: For, there have been at any Time few or no
Heretics, who would not pretend to Scripture, every one
disputing their new-broached Opinions to be confirmed
by Scripture; or, (however agreeable to Scripture, because the contrary was not therein defined) disputing,
that what was alledged against their *Sects,* was otherwise to be understood, than as the orthodox *Church* understood it: And lest it might be clearly brought against
them, they either forged another Sense, or preferred
some other Passages of Scripture, which seemed contrary to the former; troubling all Things in such Manner, as to make them seem ambiguous. If the public
Faith of the Church had not withstood *Arrius,* the
Heretic, I know not if he should ever have wanted a
Subject of Dispute out of Scripture.

Now, seeing we have proved, by *Luther's* own Funda-
mentals, that the Sacraments believed by the Church
could not be instituted but by God himself, though Nothing were read thereof in Scripture: Let us see whether
Scripture makes not some Mention of this Sacrament.
All Men do unanimously confess, (*Luther* only excepted) that the Apostles were by our Saviour ordained

absurdius, quod pleraque omnia fidei Christianæ dogmata, tot stabilita sæculis, ad succrescentium hæreticorum libidinem denuo revocarentur in dubium. Nam
si nihil haberi pro certo debet, nisi quod Scripturis et
iisdem, ut Lutherus ait, claris firmatum est, non solum
non asseremus divæ Mariæ virginitatem perpetuam, sed
et inexhausta suggeretur fidei oppugnandæ materia, si
cui unquam libeat aut novas excitare sectas, aut ressus-
citare sepultas. Nam paucissimi fuerunt hæretici, qui
non receperint Scripturas; sed omnes fere ex eo sua
statuebant dogmata, quod aut ea contenderent esse firmata Scripturis, aut, quum illis viderentur rationi con-
sentanea, contrarium non definiri Scripturis: quoniam
ea, quæ proponebantur adversus suam sectam, aliter con-
tendebant intelligi, quam orthodoxa intelligebat Ecclesia, et, ne clara dici possent, aut alio excogitato sensu,
aut prolatis aliunde ex eadem Scriptura locis, in
speciem valde contrariis, omnia sic turbarunt, ut
viderentur ambigua. Itaque adversus Arium, nisi publica stetisset fides Ecclesiæ, haud scio an defuisset unquam de Scripturis disputandi materia.

Nunc, quoniam ex ipsius Lutheri fundamento probavimus sacramenta, quæ credit Ecclesia, non aliunde
quam a Deo potuisse constitui, etiamsi nihil inde prorsus
in Scriptura legeretur, videamus an Scriptura tam nullam omnino mentionem faciat hujus sacramenti.
Omnes una voce fatentur Apostolos in Cœna Domini
ordinatos in sacerdotes. Solus istud Lutherus negat,

Priests, at his last Supper; where it plainly appears, that Power was given them to consecrate the Body of *Christ,* which Power the Priest alone hath. 'But, says *Luther,* it is not a Sacrament, because there is no Grace promised therein.' But pray, how, or whence has he this Knowledge? 'Because (says he) it is not read in Scripture!' This is his usual Consequence: 'It is not written in the Gospels, therefore has it not been done by *Christ.*' Which Form of reasoning the Evangelist overthrows, when he says, *Many Things were done, which are not written in this Book.** But let us touch *Luther* yet a little closer. He confesses that the Eucharist is a Sacrament; and he were mad, if he did not; but where, pray, does he find in Scripture, that Grace is promised in that Sacrament? For he admits Nothing but Scripture, and that clear Scripture too. Let him read the Passages that treat of our Lord's Supper, and see if he can find in any of the Evangelists, that Grace is promised in the receiving of the *Blessed Sacrament.* We read that *Christ* said, *This is my Blood, which shall be shed for many, to the Remission of Sins;*† whereby he signified, that he should redeem Mankind by his Passion upon the Cross. But when he said, *This do in Remembrance of me:*‡ He promises no Grace, or Remission of Sins, to him that does this; that is, to the consecrated Priests, or to him that receives the Eucharist. Nor doth the Apostle, in his Epistle to the *Corinthians,* when he threatens Judgment to them that unworthily receive, make Mention of any Grace to him that receives it worthily. If any Thing in the 6th of St. *John* promise Grace to him that receives the Sacrament of our Lord's *Body and Blood;* yet can that make Nothing for *Luther,* because he denies the whole Chapter to have any Reference at all to the Eucharist: You

*John xxii. 25.   †Matt. xxvi. 28.   ‡I. Cor. xi. 24.

quum plane constet illic datam potestatem conficiendi corporis Christi, quod solus conficere sacerdos potest. "At non est," inquit ille, "sacramentum, quia non fuit illis ulla promissa gratia." Unde id novit Lutherus? "Quia non legitur," inquit. Familiaris est ista Luthero consequentia: Non est in Evangelio scriptum; ergo non est a Christo factum: quam colligendi formam infirmat Evangelista, quum dicit: *"Multa sunt facta, quæ non sunt scripta in libro hoc."* Sed tangemus tamen Lutherum aliquando propius. Eucharistiam concedit esse sacramentum: quod nisi fateretur, insaniret. At ubi reperit in Scriptura promissam in illo sacramento gratiam? Nam ille nihil recipit, nisi Scripturas, et easdem claras. Legatur locus de Cœna dominica: non reperiet apud ullum evangelistarum in susceptione sacramenti promissam gratiam. Legitur a Christo dictum: *"Hic est sanguis meus novi testamenti, qui pro multis effundetur in remissionem peccatorum:"* quibus verbis significavit semet in cruce per Passionem redempturum genus humanum. Sed quum dixit ante: *"Hoc facite in meam commemorationem,"* nullam hoc facienti, id est sacerdoti consecranti, aut Eucharistiam recipienti gratiam ibi promittit, nullam peccatorum remissionem. At nec Apostolus in epistola ad Corinthios, quum interminetur male manducantibus judicium, ullam mentionem facit de gratia bene manducantium. Quod si quid, ex capite sexto Joannis, gratiam promittat suscipienti sacramentum carnis et sanguinis Domini, ne id quidem quicquam juvare Lutherum potest, quippe qui totum illud caput negat ad Eucharistiam quicquam pertinere.

Videtis ergo ut istam promissionem gratiæ, quam pro totius sacramenti fundamento magnifice nobis in toto

see here, very plainly, that he cannot maintain that Promise of Grace, which he so fairly promised us, in his whole Work, as the sole Basis of the Sacrament, and in that only Sacrament which he admits; unless, besides the Words of Scripture, he has recourse (as it is necessary for him) to the Faith of the Church.

Wherefore; as it is sufficient for us to read in the Gospel, that the Power of consecrating the Sacrament, was given them to whom the Priests succeed; so is it likewise enough, that we read the Council of the Apostle to *Timothy,* 'That he impose not Hands rashly upon any one.' Which Passage plainly demonstrates, that the Ordination of Priests is not performed by the Consent of the Laity, (by which alone *Luther* affirms, that a Priest may be ordained,) but by the Ordination of a Bishop only: and that by a certain Imposition of Hands; in which God, through the exterior Sign, should infuse an interior Grace. Concerning which Grace, why should we not believe the Church of the Living God? which is, as the Apostle saith, *The Ground and Pillar of Truth;** for *Luther* himself must certainly believe her concerning the Grace promised in the Eucharist; as the Promise of that Grace, or the giving of it without any Promise, is known in this Faith of the Church.

Indeed I admire that any one should be so distracted as to doubt, whether Grace is given by the Sacrament of Orders to the Priest of the Gospel; whereas we may read many Places, that seem to signify that Grace was conferred on the Priests of the old Law; and that God saith, *You shall anoint and sanctify* Aaron *and his Sons, that they may exercise to me the Office of Priesthood.*† Otherwise, what should this exterior Sanctification have signified for the Honour of God, if God had not likewise

*I. Tim. iii. 15.   †Exod. xxviii. 1.

promisit opere, non potest in eo tueri sacramento, quod
fere solum relinquit, nisi, quod necesse habet, præter
Scripturæ verba recurrat ad Ecclesiæ fidem. Igitur
quemadmodum satis est nobis quod in Evangelio legimus conficiendi sacramenti potestatem commissam his
in quorum locum succedunt sacerdotes, ita satis est quod
ab Apostolo legimus consilium datum Timotheo, ut
nemini cito manum imponeret: quæ loca plane signifi-
cant ordinationem sacerdotum, non consensu communitatis, quo solo interveniente fieri sacerdotum posse
Lutherus ait, sed sola ordinatione episcopi, idque certa
impositione manuum, in qua per exterius signum Deus
infunderet interiorem gratiam: de qua gratia quid obstat
quominus credamus Ecclesiæ Dei vivi, quæ *"est,"* ut
ait Apostolus, *"columna et firmamentum veritatis,"*
quando eidem Ecclesiæ necesse est ipse credat Lutherus
de gratia promissa in sacramento Eucharistiæ. Nam in
hac fide cognoscitur, aut illius gratiæ promissio, aut
certe sine promissione donatio.

Demiror profecto tam vecordem esse quemquam ut
dubitet an sacerdotibus evangelicis in Ordine conferatur
gratia, quum passim legantur plurima quæ significare
videntur etiam veteris legis sacerdotibus gratiam esse
collatam. Nam: *"Aaron,"* inquit Deus, *"et filios ejus
unges; sanctificabis eos, ut sacerdotio fungantur mihi."*
Alioqui enim, quid profuisset exterior sanctificatio in
cultum Dei, nisi Deus pariter infudisset gratiam, qua
sanctificarentur interius? atque id quoque per Christum, cujus venturi fides robur et vim potuit indidisse

infused Grace, by which they should be likewise interiorly sanctified; and that also through Christ; the
Faith of whose coming, gave Force and Strength to
precedent Sacraments, even as it made the *Jews* capable
of obtaining eternal Salvation?

But if any one will not admit, that Grace was conferred to the Priesthood of the Old Law; yet has he no
Reason to deny the Infusion of Grace into the Priests
of the Evangelical Law: Because now, through the Passion of Christ the Fullness of Grace is come. In the
Acts of the Apostles, when St. *Paul* and *Barnabas* were
set apart for that Work, to which the Holy Ghost has
called them,* they were not sent away, before they were
first ordained by Imposition of Hands. But pray, why
did the Apostles lay Hands on them? Was it to touch
their Bodies in a vain Manner, without profiting their
Souls by spiritual Grace? How then dares *Luther* affirm, that this Sacrament was unknown to the Church of
Christ, which was used by the Apostles? 'But (says
he) it was never called a Sacrament by any of the
antient Doctors, except *Dyonisius;* for we read nothing
at all in the other Fathers, of these Sacraments, neither
did they think on the Name of Sacrament, whenever
they spoke of these Things; for the Invention of Sacraments is new,' (says he.) An excellent Reason of *Lu-*
ther's I must confess, yet altogether false; and if it was
true, yet could it avail nothing for his Purpose. For if
the Antients had not writ at all, of a Thing perhaps
never disputed amongst them; or if, when they did
write of it, they should signify it by its proper Name, and
not by that common Name of Sacrament; should it then
follow, as a necessary Consequence, that there has been
no Order at all, or that it was not a Sacrament? For
if any Body should call Baptism by the proper Name

*Acts xiii.

sacramentis præcedentibus, sicut capacem fecit populum
judaicum consequendæ aliquando salutis æternæ?
Verum si quis id non admittat, veteris legis sacerdotio
collatam gratiam, certe non est cur gravetur tamen admittere gratiam sacerdotibus evangelicæ legis infundi, quia jam per Christi Passionem venit plenitudo
gratiæ.

In Actis apostolorum, quum Barnabas ac Paulus
segregarentur in opus in quod eos Spiritus sanctus
accersivit, non ante dimissi sunt, quam impositis manibus ordinati sunt. At cur, obsecro, manus eis imposue-
runt apostoli? An ut corpus inani tactu pulsarent, nulla
spiritali gratia prodessent animæ? Quomodo potest
ergo Lutherus hoc sacramentum dicere Ecclesiæ Christi
esse incognitum, quo nulla natio Christiana non utitur?
Quomodo potest appellare novum quod instituit Christus, quod in usu habebant apostoli? "At nunquam,"
inquit, "appellatum est sacramentum apud veteres Doctores usquam, excepto Dionysio. Nihil enim prorsus in
reliquis Patribus de istis sacramentis legimus," inquit,
"nec sacramenti nomine censuerunt, quoties de his rebus
locuti sunt. Recens enim est inventio sacramentorum."
Egregia sane ratio est ista Lutheri, quæ et manifeste
falsa est, et, si foret vera, nihil tamen efficeret: nam si
veteres de re fortassis olim non controversa nihil scrip-
sissent omnino, aut si, quum scriberent aliquid, rem
proprio tamen, non communi sacramentorum nomine
designassent, non necessario colligeretur ex eo aut Ordinem non fuisse prorsus, aut non fuisse sacramentum.
Nam si quis Baptismum vocet Baptismum, nec addat
sacramentum, dicetur ideo non habuisse Baptismum pro
sacramento?

of Baptism, and should not add the Word Sacrament;
shall it be therefore said, that he does not think Baptism to be a Sacrament? Moreover, if *Dyonisius* only,
amongst all the holy Fathers, should write Orders to be
a Sacrament, that alone should be sufficient to destroy
Luther's Objection; by which he intends to make People
believe, that the Invention of Sacraments is new; for
this Novelty is contradicted by his confessing it to be
written by him, whom he acknowledges to be antient:
And this would be true, though St. *Dyonisius* were such
a Man, as sacrilegious *Luther* feigns him to be, saying,
'That he had almost no solid Learning in him: That
none of the Things he writ in his ecclesiastical Hierarchy, are proved by Authority, or Reason; but that
they are all his own Inventions, and much like Dreams:
That in his mystical Divinity, which some ignorant
Divines (says *Luther*) so much extoll; he is pernicious;
more like a Platonist than a Christian: In which (says
he) you will not only, not learn who is *Christ;* but if
you had known it before, you should lose your Belief
of him: I speak (says he) by Experience; (By the Ex-
periment, I suppose, of losing *Christ* there himself.)'
And further; 'Pray what performs he in his ecclesiastical Hierarchy, but only describes allegorically some
ecclesiastical Rites?' Finally, that he might shew in
how light a Matter St. *Dyonisius* lost his Labour, 'Do
you think (says he) it should be difficult for me to sport
with Allegories in whatsoever is credited? It should
not be any hard Work for me to write a better Hierarchy
than that of *Dyonisius* is.' Who can patiently endure
to see the pious Labours of the holy Man so much abused
by this Jangler, as if he were raging against some
Heretic like himself? For he calls him illiterate and
foolish, and one that writes not only Dreams, but also
pernicious Doctrines, destroying *Christ!* All which Re-

Præterea si solus ex antiquis Patribus Dionysius Ordinem scriberet esse sacramentum, vel satis esset ad evertendam Lutheri objectionem, qua videri vult inventionem sacramentorum novam esse: repugnat enim esse novum quod ab illo fatetur scriptis comprehensum, quem fatetur antiquum. Atque istud quidem verum esset etiam, si talis esset sacer Dionysius, qualem eum depingit sacrilegus Lutherus, qui ferme nihil in eo dicit esse solidæ eruditionis, nihil eorum quæ scribit, aut auctoritate quicquam, aut ratione probari, sed omnia esse illius meditata ac prope somniis simillima quæcumque in cœlesti scribit Hierarchia. "In Theologia mystica, quam sic inflant," inquit, "ignorantissimi quidam theologistæ, est," inquit, "etiam perniciosissimus, plus platonizans, quam christianizans. In qua," inquit, "Christum adeo non disces, ut, etiamsi scias, amittas.

"Expertus," inquit, "loquor:" hoc est, ut opinor, expertus est ibi se Christum perdidisse. "Demum in ecclesiastica Hierarchia quid facit," inquit, "nisi quod ritus quosdam ecclesiasticos describit, ludens allegoriis?" Denique ut ostenderet in re quam levi divus Dionysius luderet operam: "An mihi putas," inquit, "difficile esse in qualibet re creata allegoriis ludere? Mihi non fuerit operosum meliorem Hierarchiam scribere quam Dionysii sit." Quis patienter ferat in viri sancti pios labores sic debacchantem rabulam, quæ vere meritoque in sui similem baccharetur hæreticum?

Nam et indoctum vocat, et ludicrum, et scribentem non tantum somnia, sed etiam perniciosa, et Christum destruentia dogmata. Quæ tamen omnia convitia sancto viro cedunt in gloriam, cujus opera omnia vel hoc abunde demonstrat esse bona, quod viro malo displiceant. Nam quæ consortia luci cum tenebris, Christo

proaches, are, notwithstanding, to the Glory of the holy Man, whose Works are all sufficiently demonstrated to be good, by their displeasing only a Man so wicked as this. For what Agreement can there be betwixt Light and Darkness, between *Christ* and *Belial?* His own wicked Brain was the Cause that he gained no Good by the pious Books of this holy Man: For *Horatius* writ truly;—'Unless the Vessel be sweet, whatsoever you put therein will become sour.' In as much as he says, 'He could write a better Hierarchy, than that of St. *Dyonisius;*' pray let him brag of it when he has done it. In the mean while, he undertakes a Thing much more difficult, when he goes about to demolish that Hierarchy which is founded upon a solid Rock.

The Indignation we have conceived at that impious Fellow's casting such injurious Reproaches against the holy Man, has caused us somewhat to digress. But, as I begun to say, though St. *Dyonisius* had been the Man that had taught holy Orders to have been a Sacrament; yet that is, however, sufficient to convince *Luther,* when he asserts the Invention of the Sacraments to be but a new Thing; since he not only confesses *Dyonisius* to be antient, but also that all the Christian World honours him for a Saint. So that *Luther's* Anger against him, is caused merely through Malice, which suffers him to brook nothing contrary to his wicked Heresies.

But now, that his Vanity in every Place may the more plainly appear; I will shew, that not only St. *Dyonisius,* but also St. *Gregory,* and St. *Augustine,* (whom he falsely calls his Patron,) take Orders for a Sacrament. Moreover, this indefaceable Character (by him derided) though not called by that very Name; yet St. *Hierom,* in the Sacrament of Baptism, writes plainly enough of the Thing itself, to which also St. *Augustine* has had Regard, both in the Sacraments of Baptism and Orders.

cum Beliali? At quod e piis viri sancti libellis nihil pietatis hausit, impium ipsius caput erat in causa, quando quidem vere scribit Horatius:

"Sincerum est nisi vas, quodcumque infundis, acescit."

Nam quod ait sibi non operosum esse meliorem Hierarchiam scribere, quam fuerit illa Dionysii, postquam scripserit, tum istud jactitet. Interea vero rem aggreditur multo magis operosam, Hierarchiam alteram, quæ supra firmam fundata est petram, demoliri.

Longius aliquanto nos avexit indignatio, qua moleste ferimus in virum sanctum ab impio evomita tam contumeliosa convitia. Verum, ut cœpi dicere, etiamsi solus Dionysius docuisset Ordinem esse sacramentum, suffecisset illud ad revincendum Lutherum asserentem novam esse inventionem sacramentorum, quum Dionysium non solum Lutherus fateatur antiquum, sed et totus orbis Christianus veneretur ut sanctum. Cui quod Lutherus irascitur, non aliud facit, quam sola malitia, qua nihil ferre potest quod impiis ipsius hæresibus adversatur. At nunc, ut plane liqueat quam vanus undique sit Lutherus, ostendam non solum Dionysium, sed etiam Gregorium, et, quem sibi patronum Lutherus mentitur, Augustinum Ordinem habuisse pro sacramento; præterea characterem, quem Lutherus irridet, indelebilem, etiamsi non vocetur nomine, re tamen aperte describi et ab Hieronymo in sacramento Baptismatis, et rationem ejus haberi ab Augustino in utroque sacramento tam Baptismi, quam Ordinis.

I will therefore begin with St. *Hierom,* of the Character of Baptism, that the Character of Orders may more evidently appear; which for its Indebility, both St. *Augustine* and St. *Gregory* compare with the Sacrament of Orders. St. *Hierom,* therefore, on these Words of St. *Paul* to the *Ephesians, (Do not contristate the holy Spirit of God, in which you were signed in the Day of Redemption,)** writes thus, 'But we have been signed with the *Holy Ghost,* that our Spirit and Soul may be sealed with the Signet of God, and that we may receive that Image and Similitude, after which we were first created. This Seal of the *Holy Ghost,* according to the Words of our Saviour, is stamped by God himself: For, says he, This has God the Father signed:'† And a little after, 'He is therefore signed, that he may keep the Seal; and that he may, in the Day of Redemption, shew it pure, sincere, and unchanged; that therefore he may receive his Reward with those who are redeemed.' Amongst all those, who have ever writ of the Character of Sacraments, none could have more plainly expressed the Character, whereby God Almighty signs the Soul through the Sacraments, than St. *Hierom* has done in these Words; not by human Fiction (as *Luther,* that execrable Scoffer of Sacraments, feigns,) but by solid Testimonies of holy Scriptures.

For a Character is that Quality of the Soul, which God Almighty, (best known to himself, and to us inscrutable,) doth impress as a Seal, whereby to know his own Flock from Strangers: Which Character, though they stain it with Vices, and turn it from White to Black, from Perfect to Imperfect, from most Pure to Impure; yet can they never so raze it out, but that in the Day of Judgment, those therewith signed, will be known to all the World, to be of his Flock, who has marked

*Ephes. iv. 30.   †John vi. 27.

Incipiam igitur a Hieronymo de charactere Baptismatis, ut appareat manifestius character Ordinis, quem et Augustinus, et Gregorius ob indelebilem characterem cum Baptismo comparant. Igitur super illa Pauli verba ad Ephesios: *"Nolite contristari Spiritum sanctum Dei, in quo signati estis in diem redemptionis,"* Hieronymus in hunc scribit modum: "Signati autem sumus Spiritu Dei sancto, ut et spiritus noster, et anima imprimatur signaculo Dei, et illam recipiamus imaginem et similitudinem, ad quam in exordio conditi sumus. Hoc signaculum sancti Spiritus juxta eloquium Salvatoris Deo imprimente signatur: *Hunc enim,"* ait, *"signavit Pater Deus."* Et paulo post: "Idcirco signatur," inquit, "ut servet signaculum, et ostendat illud in die redemptionis purum, atque sincerum, et nulla ex parte mutilatum, et ob id remunerari valeat cum his qui redempti sunt." Quicumque scripsere de sacramentorum charactere nullis unquam verbis apertius expressere characterem, quem animæ per sacramenta imprimit Deus, quam verbis his beatus expressit Hieronymus, non humano figmento, ut Lutherus fingit sacramentorum exsecrandus irrisor, sed solidis Scripturæ sacræ testimoniis. Character enim est illa qualitas animæ, quam Deus sibi notam, nobis incogitabilem imprimit in signaculum, quo suum gregem discernit ab alienis, quod signaculum, etiamsi vitiis maculent, et e candido reddant atrum, ex integro mutilum, e purissimo reddant impurum, nunquam tamen ita poterunt eradere, quin illo characteris impressi signaculo, in cujus gregem signati sint, orbi toti maneant in judicii die cognoscibiles. Nec alia ratione tam constanter observat Ecclesia, ut quum alia sacramenta toties iteret (quod in Eucharistiæ sumptione facit ac Pœnitentia, Conjugio, et Unctione languentium), Baptisma, Confirmationem atque Ordinem nunquam iterari permittat. In iis enim sacra-

them with that Signet: Which is the only Reason, why
the Church so constantly observes; that, whereas she
renews so often other Sacraments, as the *Eucharist,
Penance, Marriage, Extreme Unction;* yet never suffers
Baptism, Confirmation, and *Holy Orders* to be renewed;
having learned from the Holy Ghost, that the Seal of the
Character is imprinted in these Sacraments, so that it
cannot be defaced, therefore ought not to be iterated.

But that it may more evidently appear, that Orders
are, in this Case, like to Baptism; let us hear St. *Gregory,* 'It is (says he) a ridiculous Thing to say, that he
who has received Holy Orders, ought to receive them
again; for, as he who has once been baptized, ought not
to be baptized again; so he, who has been once consecrated, ought not again to be consecrated in the same
Degree of Orders.' You see that the Church suffers not
the Sacrament of Orders to be iterated, any more than
that of Baptism, by Reason of its indelible Character.
But to shut *Luther's* Mouth, who calls that Character *a
feigned Thing, and that St.* Dyonisius *was the only
Man, of all the antient Fathers, that called Holy Orders
a Sacrament:* We will, as we have promised, give you St.
Augustine's Words; who, in treating of Baptism and
Holy Orders, speaks thus; 'They are both Sacraments,
and given to Man after certain Consecration; the one at
his Baptism, the other when he receives Holy Orders:
Therefore it is not lawful in the Holy Catholic Church
to iterate either of them. For when any heretical Minister is received into the Church, for the Good of Peace;
if, after the Error of Schism is corrected, it should
seem necessary, he should exercise the same Office, which
he had before: Yet is he not to be ordained again; for,
as Baptism remains intire in them, so Orders also; because the Vice consisted in the Separation, not in the
Sacraments, which are the same, where-ever they are:'

mentis, sancto docente Spiritu, didicit Ecclesia characteris conferri signaculum, quod quum deleri non possit, iterari non debeat.

Sed ut manifeste pateat Ordini hac in parte parem esse cum Baptismo conditionem, audiamus quid ait Gregorius: "Quod dicitis," inquit, "ut qui ordinatus est iterum ordinetur, valde ridiculum est." Ut enim baptizatus semel, iterum baptizari non debet, ita qui consecratus est semel, in eodem Ordine non valet iterum consecrari. Videtis ut Ordinis sacramentum non magis iterari patiatur Ecclesia quam sacramentum Baptismatis; quæ res, ut dixi, pendet ab indeleto charactere. Qua de re, ut os obstruamus Luthero, ne rursus obganniat figmentum esse characterem, et solum ex antiquis Dionysium Ordinem vocasse sacramentum, subjungemus, ut polliciti sumus hac de re, etiam divi Augustini sententiam. Is igitur, quum de Baptismo et Ordine disserit, in hunc modum scribit: "Utrumque enim sacramentum est, et quadam consecratione utrumque homini datur illud, quum baptizatur, et illud, quum ordinatur. Ideo non licet in Ecclesia catholica utrumque iterari. Nam si quando ex hæreticorum parte venientes etiam præpositi, pro bono pacis, correcto schismatis errore, suscepti sunt, et si visum est opus esse ut eadem officia gererent, quæ gerebant, non sunt rursus ordinandi, sed sicut Baptismus in eis, ita mansit ordinatio integra, quia in præcisione fuerat vitium, non in sacramentis, quæ ubicumque sunt, ipsa sunt." Et paulo post: "Neutri sacramento facienda est injuria." Et addit de sacramento Ordinis: "Sicut non recte habet qui ab unitate

And a little after, 'Injury must be done to neither of the two Sacraments.'

And of the Sacrament of Orders, he adds, 'That, as he that breaks off from Unity, has it not rightly, yet has it; so likewise he does not rightly give it, yet gives it:' And returning again to both, 'It hinders them not (says he) from being the Sacraments of Christ and his Church; because Hereticks and wicked Persons use them unlawfully; but these Men are to be corrected, and punished, and the Sacraments to be acknowledged and venerated.' You see how void of Truth it is, what *Luther* so boldly boasts, viz. *That the Sacrament of Holy Orders was unknown to the Church of Christ: That Character is an idle Fiction; That the Invention of Sacraments is a new Thing: That Holy Orders were no Sacrament among the Antients.* You see Nothing of what he has said, but has been rejected by the Testimony of such Persons, as he cannot separate from the Church of Christ; for they were illustrious therein by Doctrine of Faith and exemplary Lives; nor can he reckon them among the Moderns, if a thousand Years be not with him as one Day.* Notwithstanding this, he opposes himself against all the Reasons, Authority, and Faith of all, by this one Argument: We are all Priests (says he) according to that of St. *Peter. Ye are all a royal Priesthood, and priestly Kingdom;†* but as *one cannot be more a Man than another; so one can be no more a Priest than another: Those, therefore, who are called Priests, are no other but Lay-men, chosen by the only Consent of the People, or elected by the Bishop, not without the People: For to preach and ordain, are Nothing but mere Ministry, without any Thing of Sacrament.* We have not only faithfully repeated his Argument, but also freely set down whatever may support him: And yet who would not laugh at this doltish

*Ps. lxxxix. 4.			†I. Pet. ii. 9.

recedit, sed tamen habet, sic etiam non recte dat qui ab unitate recedit, et tamen dat." Et rursus ad utrumque reversus adjecit: "Non ergo ideo non sunt sacramenta Christi et Ecclesiæ, quia eis illicite utuntur non modo hæretici, sed etiam omnes impii; sed illi corrigendi sunt et puniendi, illa autem sunt agnoscenda et veneranda."

Videtis nunc quam verum sit illud, quod Lutherus tanta jactavit audacia, sacramentum Ordinis Ecclesiam Christi nescire, characterem inane figmentum esse, sacramentorum inventionem novam esse, Ordinem veteribus non habitum pro sacramento. Quorum omnium nihil dixit, quod non videtis eorum testimonio reprobatum, quos neque de Christi Ecclesia potest eximere (utpote quam illi et doctrina fidei, et exemplo virtutis illustrarunt), neque inter novos numerare, nisi talis sit, ut ei *mille sint anni, tanquam dies unus.*

Sed ille tamen adversus omnes omnium rationes, auctoritatem, fidem, uno se tuetur argumento. "Omnes," inquit, "sumus sacerdotes secundum illud Petri: *Vos estis regale sacerdotium et sacerdotale regnum.* Sed alius alio non potest magis esse sacerdos, quemadmodum alius alio non potest magis esse homo. Igitur sacerdotes qui vocantur, nihil sunt aliud, quam laici quidam, solo vel consensu populi, vel episcopi vocatione, non absque populo delecti ad concionandum, et Ordo nihil est aliud, quam merum sine sacramento ministerium." Recensuimus ejus argumentum non solum fideliter, sed etiam liberaliter adjicientes quod fulciat: et tamen cui non excutiat risum tam hebes theologantis argutia? Nam si

Divine? For, if the Order of Priesthood is therefore
Nothing, because every Christian is a Priest; by the
same Reason it will follow, that *Christ* had Nothing
above *Saul:* For *David* said of *Saul, Peccavi tangens
Christum Domini;* I have sinned in touching *(Christum)* the Anointed of our Lord: Or that Christ had
Nothing above them, of whom it is said, *Nolite tangere
Christos meos; Touch not mine anointed:* Finally,
that God had Nothing above all those of whom he said
by the Prophet, *I have said ye are Gods, and are all the
Sons of the most High.* In a Word, all Christians are
Kings in the same Manner that they are Priests: For it
is not only said, *Ye are a royal Priesthood;* but also, *a
priestly Kingdom.* Let us diligently observe what the
Serpent designs, who, I suppose, is more crafty than to
think this Argument of any Consequence, but only licks,
that he may afterwards bite: He extols the Laity to the
Priesthood, for this only Reason, that he may reduce
Priests to the Rank of the Laity; denying Priesthood to
be a Sacrament, but only a Custom of electing a
Preacher; and saying, 'That he who preaches, is no
more a Priest, than the other; nay, no more a Priest,
than a painted Man, is a Man:' Contrary to St. *Paul,*
who, writing to *Timothy,* says, *The Priests that rule
well, are worthy of double Honour, especially such as
labour in the Word and Doctrine.** The Apostle, by
this, evidently teaches, That though those are most
worthy of double Honour, who, being Priests, do labour
in the Word and Doctrine: Yet those who perform not
This, but can only govern well, are also Priests; and
merit double Honour. Otherwise, he would not have
said, *Especially those who labour in the Word and Doctrine;* but only such as labour therein.

Furthermore, that *Luther* may not be able to hold
what he says, viz. 'That the Priest's Office is nothing

*I. Tim. v. 17.

ideo nihil est Ordo sacerdotii, quia quilibet Christianus est sacerdos, eadem ratione sequetur ut nihil supra Saül habuerit Christus. Nam et de Saül dixit David: *"Peccavi tangens Christum Domini."* Nihil habuerit Christus supra quemquam eorum, de quibus dictum est: *"Nolite tangere Christos meos."* Nihil denique supra quemquam Deus eorum omnium, de quibus per prophetam dixit ipse: *"Ego dixi, Dii estis, et filii excelsi omnes."* Postremo, qua ratione Christiani omnes sacerdotes sunt, eadem etiam ratione reges sunt. Non enim solum dicitur: *"Vos estis regale sacerdotium,"* sed etiam *"sacerdotale regnum."*

Sedulo considerandum est serpens iste quid destinet, quem ego certe callidiorem puto, quam ut ullius esse momenti putet tam frivolum argumentum: sed qui tantum ideo lambit, ut mordeat, laicos ideo tollit in sacerdotium, ut sacerdotes redigat in classem laicorum. Nam sacramentum esse negat, et ritum tantum esse dicit eligendi concionatoris. Nam qui non concionantur, nihil minus ait esse quam sacerdotes, nec aliter sacerdotes esse, quam homo pictus est homo; contra Paulum apostolum, qui ad Timotheum scribens ait: *"Qui bene præsunt presbyteri, duplici honore digni sunt, maxime qui laborant in verbo et doctrina."* Apostolus hic manifeste docet, quanquam ii præcipue duplici honore digni sunt, qui quum presbyteri sint, laborant in verbo et doctrina, tamen et qui hoc non faciunt, non solum esse presbyteros, sed et bene præesse posse, et duplicem quoque honorem promereri. Alioqui non dixisset: *maxime qui laborant in verbo et doctrina,* sed solum *ii qui laborant in verbo et doctrina.*

Præterea ne possit dicere Lutherus id quod dicit, officium sacerdotis erga populum nihil esse, nisi prædi-

but to preach to the People: For to say Mass (says he) is nothing but to receive the Communion for himself:' I say, that it may appear how false this is; let us again hear the Apostle's Words, 'Every Priest (says he) that is taken out from amongst Men, is constituted for Men, in the Things which belong to God, that he may offer Gifts and Sacrifices for their Sins.'* Does not this plainly shew us that a Priest's Duty requires from him, to offer Sacrifices to God for Men? Though writing to the *Hebrews,* (yet not willing, that Christians should be any Thing Jewish,) it is evident that it is spoken of the Priesthood of both Laws; so that *Luther* is twice pressed by this Testimony: For he also teaches Mass to be a Sacrifice, and to be offered for the People: Seeing the Church offers no other; and he teacheth, that the Duty of offering it, is the chief Part of the Priest's Charge. And truly if *Luther's* Words were not false, how easily may you see it to follow; that since none but a Priest can consecrate our Lord's Body: of so many Thousand Priests, that have not the Gift of Preaching, if they were not truly Priests, but only equivocally so called, as a painted Man is called a Man; then would almost all the Christian World have no other God, or People but Idolators, adoring Bread for Christ, and bending their Knees to *Baal.*

In the Right of electing, as he calls it, he attributes the chief Power to the People; for though in one Place; he seems to give this Rite promiscuously to the Bishop and People, (when he says, 'That although it is certain all Christians are equally Priests, and that they have a like Power in all the Sacraments: Yet that none can lawfully exercise this Power, without the Consent of the Congregation, or the Vocation of a Superior.' Yet, in another Place, he gives the greatest Right to the People

*Heb. v. 1.

care: nam "Missas," inquit, "canere nihil est aliud,
quam communicare seipsum," hoc, inquam, ut appareat
quam falsum sit, rursus audiamus Apostolum: *"Omnis,"* inquit, *"pontifex ex hominibus assumptus pro
hominibus constituitur in his quæ sunt ad Deum, ut
offerat dona et sacrificia pro peccatis."* Annon Apostolus aperte declarat etiam pontificis officium istud pos-
cere, ut pro hominibus offerat sacrificium Deo? Quod
quum scribat, quanquam Hebræis, tamen Christianis,
quos nolit judaizare, clarum est loqui de pontifice legis
utriusque, atque ideo bis Lutherum suo premere testimonio. Nam et Missam docet esse sacrificium, et offerri
pro populo, quum Ecclesia nullum offerat aliud, et docet
offerendi officium præcipuam partem esse muneris pon-
tificii. Et certe, nisi falsum esset quod dicit Lutherus,
facile videtis consequi ut quum nemo nisi sacerdos possit
consecrare corpus Domini, si e tot sacerdotum millibus,
qui concionari nesciunt, nullus vere sacerdos est, sed
tantum vocatur æquivoce, quemadmodum homo pictus
vocatur homo, totus Christianus orbis clerum popu-
lumque ferme non habet alium quam idololatras, panem
pro Christo colentes, et genua sua curvantes ante
Baal.

In eligendi, ut vocat, ritu, præcipuum jus tribuit
populo. Nam licet uno loco tribuere videatur episcopo
aut populo jus promiscuum, quum dicit quod quanquam
certum sit omnes Christianos æqualiter esse sacerdotes,
et eamdem in verbo et sacramento quocumque habere
potestatem, non licere tamen quemquam hac ipsa uti,
nisi consensu communitatis aut vocatione majoris, alio
tamen loco, superiores partes tribuit populo, quum de
sacerdotibus dicit: "Qui si cogerentur admittere nos
omnes æqualiter esse sacerdotes, quotquot baptizati

when, speaking of Priests, he says, 'who, if they were
compelled to admit all of us, who have been baptized
equally to be Priests, as indeed we are; and that the
Ministry is only given to them by our Consent; they
should know also, that they have no Right of ruling over
us, but what we admit them of our own free Will.'
Which two Places being compared together, shews his
Opinion to be, 'That the People, without the Bishop,
but not the Bishop without the People, can ordain
Priests;' as appears by his saying, 'That the Ministry
only is permitted to the Priests, and that not without
the Consent of the People:' Which if true, a Priest
cannot be ordained, without the People's Consent; by
which alone, he says, 'That Bishops were formerly made
Rulers of the Church.'

'It cannot be denied, (says he) that the true Churches
were formerly governed by Elders, without the Ordi-
nations and Consecrations; being chosen to this, by
Reason of their Age and long Experience in Things of
that Kind.' Pray let him shew us where he finds these
Things? For my Part, I do not think them to be true.
For, if every Layman hath equal Power over any of the
Sacraments, with a Priest; and if the Order of Priest-
hood stands for Nothing, why writes the Apostle thus to
Timothy, 'Neglect not the Grace which is in thee, and
which has been given thee by Prophesy, by the Imposi-
tion of the Hands of the Presbytery?'* and in another
Place, to the same, 'I admonish thee, that thou stir up
the Grace of God that is in thee, by the Imposition of
my Hands:'† Again, 'Impose Hands suddenly on no
Man, neither be thou Partakers of other Men's Sins.'‡
Finally, these are the Words of the Apostle to *Titus;*
'For this Cause left I thee in *Crete,* that thou shouldest
correct the Things that are wanting; and constitute

*I. Tim. iv. 14.   †II. Tim. i. 6.   ‡I. Tim. v. 22.

sumus, sicut re vera sumus, illisque solum ministerium, nostro tamen consensu, permissum, scirent simul nullum eis esse super nos jus imperii, nisi quantum nos sponte nostra admitteremus."

Quæ duo loca si conferantur, ostendunt hoc sentire Lutherum, ut populus absque episcopo possit ordinare sacerdotem, episcopus sine populi consensu non possit, quum dicit sacerdotibus solum ministerium, nec id tamen, nisi populi consensu, permissum. Nam si hoc verum est, sacerdos fieri nisi populi consensu non potest, cujus consensu solo dicit olim præfectos Ecclesiis episcopos. "Negari non potest," inquit, "Ecclesias olim a senioribus fuisse rectas absque istis ordinationibus et consecrationibus, propter ætatem et longum rerum usum in hoc electis." Lutherus ubi ista reperit, ostendat ipse; mihi interim vera non videntur. Nam si laicus quisque æqualem habet potestatem cum sacerdote in quocumque sacramento, et Ordo sacerdotii nihil est, cur ita scribit Apostolus Timotheo: *"Noli negligere gratiam quæ est in te, quæ data est tibi per prophetiam, cum impositione manuum presbyterii?"* Et alibi ad eumdem: *"Admoneo te ut ressuscites gratiam Dei, quæ in te est per impositionem manuum mearum?"* Iterum: *"Nemini,"* inquit, *"cito manus imposueris, neque communices peccatis alienis?"* Denique hunc in modum Apostolus scribit ad Titum: *"Hujus rei gratia reliqui te Cretæ, ut ea quæ desunt corrigas, et constituas per civitates presbyteros, sicut et ego disposui tibi."*

Priests in the Cities, even as I have appointed thee.'*

Now Reader, you have, in a few Words, seen some Passages of the Apostle, by comparing of which, you may easily discover, that whatsoever *Luther* has thus disorderly vented against Order, are mere Fictions and Lyes: For what he says, 'is done by the People's Consent,' St. *Paul* shews to be done by the Bishop, while he says, 'He has left him *(Titus)* at *Crete,* to that End that he should ordain Priests in the Cities, and that not rashly, but as he himself, when present, had appointed.' You see, by this, that Priests are made by Imposition of Hands. And that it may not be doubted that Grace is also given at the same Time; you see, that it is conferred by Imposition of Hands: 'Stir up (says he,) the Grace of God; which has been given thee by the Imposition of my Hands:'† And this also, 'Neglect not the Grace which is in thee, and which has been given thee through Prophesy, by Imposition of the Hands of the *Presbytery'*‡——Take Notice of these Things——I admire that *Luther* is not ashamed to deny the Sacrament of Holy Orders, as he is not ignorant that the Words of St. *Paul* are in every Man's Hands; which teach, that a Priest cannot be ordained but by a Bishop, and not without Consecration: In which both the corporeal Sign is adhibited, and so much spiritual Grace infused, that he who is consecrated, not only receives the Holy Ghost for himself, but also the Power of imparting it to others. Can that which the Apostle has writ be new, though it is so affirmed by *Luther?* How can it be unknown to the Church, which is, and has at all Times been, read through the universal Church of Christ? By these Things, it is manifest, that of all that *Luther* has railed out so confidently against Holy Orders, not one Syllable is true, but all the mere lying Inventions of his Malice.

*Tit. i. 5.   †II. Tim. i. 6.   ‡I. Tim. iv. 14, 15.

Habes nunc, lector, semel sub oculis Apostoli pauca loca, et non multa verba, quibus inter se collatis facile potes deprehendere falsa fictaque esse omnia quibus tam inordinate Lutherus debacchatur in Ordinem. Nam quos dicit populi consensu fieri, Paulus ostendit fieri ab episcopo, quem in hoc ait se reliquisse Cretæ, ut oppidatim presbyteros constitueret, nec tamen temere, sed sicut ipse præsens disposuerat. Vides impositis manibus fieri sacerdotem. Et ne dubitari possit simul conferri gratiam, vides illam manuum impositione collatam. *"Ressuscita,"* inquit, *"gratiam quæ data est tibi per impositionem manuum mearum."* Et illud quoque: *"Noli negligere gratiam quæ in te est, quæ data est tibi per prophetiam, cum impositione manuum presbyterii; in iis te exerce."* Miror igitur non pudere Lutherum, quum negat sacramentum Ordinis: haud ignarus in manibus omnium versari verba Pauli, quæ doceant non nisi a sacerdote fieri sacerdotem, nec sine consecratione fieri, in qua et signum adhibeatur corporeum, et tantum spiritalis infundatur gratiæ, ut is, qui consecratur, non solum accipiat ipse Spiritum sanctum, sed etiam potestatem conferendi aliis. Novum vero qui potest esse, quanquam id Lutherus ait, de quo scribit Apostolus? Quomodo ignoratum Ecclesiæ, quod in omnibus Christi legitur, et nunquam non legebatur Ecclesiis? Quibus ex rebus manifestum est e tam multis quæ tanta cum confidentia pro compertissimis Lutherus deblateravit in Ordinem ne unam quidem syllabam fuisse veram, sed per malitiam ficta falsaque omnia.

CHAP. XIII

Of the Sacrament of Extreme Unction

In this Sacrament of Extreme Unction; that *Luther* might be twice derided himself, he twice scoffs the Church: First, because *Divines*, (says he) do call this Unction a Sacrament; (as if those he calls Divines, were the only Men who call it a Sacrament.) Again, because they call it Extreme; to which, as to the second, he himself objects, after a joking Manner, what he can never answer in earnest: For it may be rightly called Extreme, as being the last of four. Afterwards, to shew that it is no Sacrament, himself first objects, what he foresees every Body will object against him, viz. the Words of St. *James* the Apostle, 'If any be sick amongst you, let him send for the Priests of the Church, and let them pray over him, anointing him with Oil, in the Name of our Lord: And the Prayers of the Faithful will save the Sick, and our Lord will raise him up; and if he be in Sins, they shall be forgiven him.'* These Words, (which, according to his own Definition, most apparently testify Extreme Unction to be a Sacrament, as wanting neither a visible Sign, nor Promise of Grace) he immediately begins, with most impudent Confidence, to deride; as if they were of no Manner of Force. 'For my Part, (says he) I say, that if ever there was Folly acted, it is especially in this Place.' And I, again on the Contrary do affirm, that if ever *Luther* was mad at any Time, (as indeed his Madness appears almost in every Place,) he is certainly dis-

*Jas. v. 14, 15.

CAP. XIII

De Sacr. Extremæ=Unctionis

In sacramento Extremæ-Unctionis, Lutherus bis ipse
ridendus, bis irridet Ecclesiam. Primum, quod Theologi, ut ait, hanc unctionem appellent sacramentum
(quasi soli hoc dicant hi, quos ille vocat theologos),
deinde, quod appellent extremam. Et quod ad secundum pertinet, objicit sibi tanquam joco quod nunquam
solvet serio.

Nam et ideo quoque vere dici potest extrema, quod
extrema sit e quatuor. Postea, ut doceat non esse sacramentum, objicit sibi primum id quod neminem videt
non objecturum, apostoli Jacobi verba: *"Si infirmatur
quis in vobis, inducat presbyteros Ecclesiæ, et orent
super eum, ungentes oleo in nomine Domini: et oratio
fidei salvabit infirmum, et alleviabit eum Dominus, et
si in peccatis sit remittentur ei."* Hæc verba, quæ ex
ipsius etiam finitione apertissime declarant hanc unctionem sacramentum esse, quæ neque signo careat visibili, nec promissione gratiæ, protinus incipit Phormiana
confidentia, tanquam nihil haberent vigoris, eludere.
"Ego autem dico," inquit, "si uspiam deliratum est,
hoc loco præcipue deliratum est." At ego contra non
verebor dicere quod si uspiam delirat Lutherus (qui
fere delirat ubique) hic in sacramento Unctionis-
Extremæ ad extremam usque delirat amentiam.
"Omitto," inquit, "quod hanc epistolam non esse apostoli Jacobi, nec apostolico spiritu dignam, multi valde
probabiliter asserant, licet consuetudine auctoritatem,
cujuscumque sit, obtinuerit. Tamen," inquit, "si esset

tracted here, in the Sacrament of Extreme Unction, to
an extreme Height of Madness. 'I omit (says he) saying that many do probably assert this not to be the
Epistle of the Apostle St. *James,* nor worthy an apostolic Spirit, though by Custom, whosoever it be, it has
obtained Authority: Yet if it were certainly written
by the Apostle St. *James,* I should say that it is not
lawful for an Apostle to institute a Sacrament by his
own Authority; that is, to give a divine Promise, with
a Sign joined thereunto: This belongs to Christ alone.
So that St. *Paul* says that he received from our Lord the
Sacrament of the Eucharist; and that he was sent, not
to baptize, but to preach the Gospel: But of the Sacrament of Extreme Unction we read no where in the
Gospel.' You see how he endeavours here, two Ways,
to weaken the Words of the Apostle. First, he will not
have the Epistle to have been writ by the Apostle. Secondly, though it was by him written; yet will he not
have the Apostle to have Authority of instituting Sacraments. Although he has proposed these two Things in a
few Words, and passes hastily on to some other; yet are
they the chief Weapons, by which he intends to destroy
this Sacrament; for what else he says, are but Trifles,
whereby he takes Occasion to laugh, as if the Church
did not well in observing this Sacrament. But these
two do come both to the same Thing: For if the Epistle
had not been writ by the Apostle, or is not worthy an
apostolical Spirit; or if, for the Apostle's giving this
Unction for a Sacrament, it be not the more approved
to be one: Yet it should follow plainly, that nothing
could be effected by these Words. If he had said, that
it was formerly doubted whose Epistle this was, he had
said truly; for the Church admits Nothing rashly, it
discusses every Thing diligently: And this it doth, that
every Thing it receives, may be had for greater Cer-

apostoli Jacobi, dicerem non licere apostolum sua auctoritate sacramentum instituere, id est divinam promissionem cum adjuncto signo dare; hoc ad Christum
solum pertinebat. Sic Paulus sese accepisse a Domino
dicit sacramentum Eucharistiæ, et missum, non ut bap-
tizet, sed ut evangelizet. Nusquam autem legitur in
evangelio Unctionis istius extremæ sacramentum."

His verbis videtis ut apostoli verba duobus modis
enervare conatur, primum, quod epistola non sit apostoli, deinde quod, etiamsi sit apostoli, tamen apostolus
auctoritatem non habeat instituendi sacramenta. Hæc
duo quanquam proponat paucis, ac statim ad alia transi-
liat, tamen præcipua tela sunt, quibus instituit hoc
sacramentum perimere. Nam cætera quæ dicit omnia,
nugamenta sunt, ridendi occasionem captantia, tanquam
Ecclesia non recte sacramentum observet. Sed hæc duo
vivum tangunt. Nam si epistola non apostoli sit, nec
apostolico spiritu digna, aut si apostolo tradente Unctionem hanc pro sacramento, tamen nihilomagis probe-
tur sacramentum, consequeretur omnino ut hæc verba
nihil efficerent.

Si dixisset olim fuisse dubitatum cujus illa fuerit
epistola, dixisset vere: neque enim temere quicquam
recepit Ecclesia; omnia diligenter excussit, idque ipsum
facit, ut certiora deberent haberi omnia, quæ receperit,
etiamsi duntaxat humana prudentia regeretur Ecclesia.

tainty; though it were only directed by human Policy. But when he says, 'That many do assert this Epistle, not only, not to be of the Apostle's Writing; but also, unworthy of an apostolical Spirit; and that they not only assert, but probably assert this;' it is more than probable, he cannot prove what he says; otherwise let him name some of these many Persons; who if they be of the Church, I suppose they are not so many, nor of so great Authority, as to be able to stand out against the whole Church. But as yet he has produced none: I will therefore bring one who may suffice against his many, to wit, St. *Hierom;* who, in holy Scriptures, was the most learned of his Time, and has as exactly distinguished between dubious and real Things, as could be possible. This great Man, after he had for some Time remained doubtful, of the Epistle of St. *Paul,* (and that only at such Time as it was not confirmed by a full Consent of the whole Church.) Yet he pronounces the Epistle of St. *James* to be undoubtedly of his own Writing: His Words are these, 'St. *James,* St. *Peter,* St. *Jude,* and St. *John,* have published seven Epistles, as mystical, as they are succinct and short; yea, likewise long; short in Words, and long in Sentences, so that there are not many, who would not be blinded in the reading them.' The same St. *Hierom,* speaks thus of the seven canonical Epistles, 'The first of them is one of St. *James's,* the second, of St. *Peter's,* three of St. *John's,* one of St. *Jude's:'* You see how this Father has the same Opinion of St. *James's* Epistle that he has of St. *Peter's;* nor does he think it unworthy an apostolical Spirit: Truly if *Luther* had brought us any Reasons why this Epistle must not be accounted St. *James's,* (though of some other Person, who should speak in the same Spirit,) yet should he be in some Sort tolerable. But now he says, 'It is not probable it should

Verum quum dicat multos asserere hanc epistolam non solum non esse apostoli, sed esse præterea indignam apostolico spiritu, atque istud non asserere solum, sed asserere etiam probabiliter, probabile est illum istud probare non posse. Alioqui proferat e multis aliquos qui, si ex Ecclesia sunt, neque tam multi sunt, opinor, neque tam magni, ut pondus obtinere mereantur adversus reliquos omnes. Adhuc produxit nullum. Ego producam unum, qui sufficere debet adversus multos, beatum Hieronymum, quo neque doctior quisquam fuit in Scripturis sacris, neque qui veras ac germanas exactiore censura distinxit a dubiis.

Is igitur quum aliquandiu de epistola Pauli dubitasset, sed tunc dubitasset, quum res adhuc non esset tam pleno Ecclesiæ consensu firmata, Jacobi tamen, quæ vocatur epistola, ipsius esse sine ulla dubitatione pronuntiat. Nam hunc in modum scribit: "Jacobus, Petrus, Judas et Joannes, septem epistolas ediderunt, tam mysticas quam succinctas, et breves pariter et longas, breves in verbis, longas in sententiis, ut rarus sit qui non in earum cæcutiat lectione." Idem in prologo in septem epistolas canonicas sic ait: "Est enim prima earum una Jacobi, duæ Petri, tres Joannis, una Judæ."

Videtis ut beatus Hieronymus idem judicium de Jacobi profert epistola, quod de Petri, nec putat indignam apostolico spiritu. Certe si rationes attulisset Lutherus, quare epistola non esset Jacobi, sed tamen alterius cujuspiam, qui eodem loqueretur spiritu, potuisset utcumque ferri. Nunc vero dicit esse probabile ideo non esse, quod sit indigna spiritu apostolico. Qua in re non alium objiciam Luthero, quam Lutherum ipsum,

be St. *James*'s, because it is unworthy an apostolical
Spirit:' In which Thing, I will bring no Objections,
but *Luther*'s own against *Luther;* for none did ever
more frequently and strongly contradict himself, than
Luther. In the Sacrament of holy Order, he says, 'The
Church has Power given her to discern the Word of
God, from the Words of Men.'—How then does he say,
that this Epistle is unworthy an apostolical Spirit,
which the Church whose Judgment (as himself confesses) cannot err in this, has judged it to be full of
apostolical Spirit? Wherefore, he has now, by his own
Wisdom, so hemmed himself in on all Sides, that he
must necessarily consent that this Epistle belongs to the
Apostle, contrary to what he has affirmed to be probable;
or, that the Church can err in distinguishing Scripture,
which before he denyed. If he says that the Church has
approved, as worthy of an apostolical Spirit, what is
unworthy, then is he a Blasphemer against the Church:
If he hold that the Apostle has writ what is unworthy
an Apostle, then is he a Blasphemer against the Apostle.

We have therefore sufficiently confuted this: Indeed
he has sufficiently confuted himself, in denying the
Epistle to belong to the Apostle, or to be worthy an
apostolical Spirit. Now come we to that, in which, like
a valiant Man, he openly sets upon the Apostle himself,
saying, 'That though it was of the Apostle's Writing,
yet it is not lawful for an Apostle to institute a Sacrament by his own Authority; that is, To give a divine
Promise, with a Sign thereunto adjoined: For this (says
he) belongs to Christ alone.' O this happy Age! in
which *Luther,* this new Doctor of the Gentiles, is risen,
who will seem himself to follow the Example of St.
Paul, by resisting an Apostle to his Face,* as not going
the right Way to the Gospel of Christ, but (which is

*Gal. ii. 11–14.

neque enim Luthero quisquam aut sæpius ferme contradicit, aut validius, quam Lutherus. Is igitur in sacramento Ordinis ait Ecclesiam hoc habere datum, ut possit discernere verba Dei a verbis hominum. Quomodo ergo nunc dicit epistola apostolico spiritu indignam esse, quam Ecclesia, cujus judicium, ut ait, hac in re falli non potest, apostolico spiritu judicavit plenam? Quamobrem nunc ita se sua sapientia constrinxit undique, ut aut necessario comprobet epistolam esse apostoli (cujus contrarium dixit esse probabile) aut dicat Ecclesiam in Scriptura sacra posse dijudicanda falli, quod eam posse negaverat. Quod si dicat velut apostolico dignum spiritu comprobasse, quod apostolico spiritu sit indignum, blasphemus est in Ecclesiam. Si fatetur apostolum scripsisse quod apostolo sit indignum, blasphemus est in apostolum.

Satis igitur illud confutavimus, imo semet satis confutavit ipse, quod epistolam negavit aut esse apostoli, aut dignam apostolico spiritu. Veniamus nunc ad id in quo, ut fortem virum decet, aperte oppugnat apostolum, dicens, etiamsi sit apostoli Jacobi, tamen non licere apostolo sua auctoritate sacramentum instituere, id est, divinam promissionem cum adjuncto signo dare. "Hoc enim pertinet," inquit, "ad solum Christum." O nostri sæculi magnam felicitatem, quo novus iste Gentium doctor exortus est Lutherus, qui hoc sibi arrogans, tanquam Pauli sequeretur exemplum, in faciem resistat apostolo, quod non recta via ingrediatur ad evangelium Christi, sed, quod plus est, quam si gentes doceat judaizare, arroget sibi facultatem promittendi gratiam, et sacramenta condendi, hoc est, quod usurpet sibi potes-

more than if he should teach the Gentiles to Judaize)
arrogating to himself the Power of promising Grace,
and instituting Sacraments; usurping in that the Power
of Christ; like the proud and traitorous Angel, who said,
'I will establish my Throne in the North, and be like
to the most High.'* The Pope has no great Cause of
being vexed at his Reproaches, who charges such enor-
mous Crimes upon the Apostle himself: For, since it is
certain this Epistle belongs to the Apostle; what else
does he then, but manifestly accuse the Apostle of having (without Authority, and against all Right) instituted this Sacrament? Nay, when he denies the Epistle
to belong to the Apostle (lest he should leave off his
Calumny,) he professes, that he would say as much, if
it were of the Apostle's own Writing! Indeed, though
some think, that the Apostle received Power of instituting Sacraments, (not without the Power of the Holy
Ghost, which God sent them at Pentecost, and of which
Christ had foretold, 'The Holy Ghost which I will send
unto you, He shall teach you all Things.')† Yet shall
not I dispute it at this Time, whether an Apostle has
such Power or no, because it is now not necessary to
dispute it. But seeing it is evident, that the Apostle
gives us this Unction as a Sacrament, I do not doubt,
but it is really a Sacrament; and that the Apostle was
not so impiously arrogant, as to give the People, for a
Sacrament, what was in Reality no such Thing. But if
the Apostle had not the Power of instituting this Sacrament himself, then has he delivered it to the People in
these Words, as he received it from Christ, who, as he
would notify to the World some Things by St. *Matthew,*
some by St. *Luke,* some by St. *John,* and some by the
Apostle St. *Paul;* why is it not possible he should be

*Isai. xiv. 13, 14.   †John xiv. 26.

tatem Christi, ad modum superbientis et prævaricantis
angeli, qui dixit: *"Ponam solium meum ad aquilonem,
et ero similis Altissimo!"* Non est nunc quod ægre
ferat Pontifex ab illo reprehendi, qui de tam atroce
crimine reprehendit apostolum. Nam quum certum sit
epistolam esse apostoli, quid aliud quam manifeste dicit
apostolum sine auctoritate et contra fas instituere sacramentum? Imo quum neget epistolam illius esse, tamen
ne abstineret contumelia, dicit id se dicturum etiamsi
esset apostoli. Ego certe etsi nonnullis visum sit apostolis non sine Spiritu sancto, quem Deus in Pentecoste
misit, rationem traditam esse condendi sacramenti, de
quo spiritu Christus prædixerat: *"Spiritus sanctus
quem ego mittam, ille vos docebit omnia,"* tamen in præsente non disputabo, utrum apostolus auctoritatem
habeat instituendi sacramenti, quippe quod nunc disputari non opus est: sed quum plane constet apostolum
Unctionem istam pro sacramento tradere, non dubito
vere sacramentum esse, et apostolum non fuisse tam
impie arrogantem, ut pro sacramento traderet populo
quod sacramentum non esset; sed, si condendi sacramenti potestatem non habuit, verbis illis id tradidisset
populo, quod ipse acceperat a Christo, qui, ut alia
mundo volebat innotescere per Matthæum, alia per Lu-
cam, per Joannem alia, alia præterea per apostolum
Paulum, cur fieri non possit, ut quædam etiam doceri
voluerit per apostolum Jacobum?

pleased to make known some Things unto us, by the Apostle St. *James.*

Luther having thus strenuously behaved himself against the Apostle, begins now altogether to turn himself against the Church: 'Which (as he says) abuseth the Words of the Apostle, iu not administring this Unction to the Sick, but when at the Point of Death:' Whereas St. *James* says, 'If any be sick, not if any be dying.' As if the Church sinned in not exhibiting inconsiderately, in every light Fever, (contracted, perhaps, by too much Drinking) so great a Thing as a Sacrament; or, in not attributing to herself a Miracle in healing such Disease, as either Sleep, or Abstinence can cure; that it may not be doubted, though the Apostle writes sick, that yet he did not mean a Man in every light Sickness, but troubled with such Sickness, as, if cured, may shew to be taken away by Virtue of the Sacrament; and that this Sacrament is not to be adhibited, but in great Sickness; appears by all the Prayers which are said over the sick Person, which, no Doubt, are very antient, and not of the new Invention of those he calls Divines. And though they do not promise an assured Health of the Body, yet do they not despair of Health; nor do they (as *Luther* says,) come to such only, as are sure undoubtedly to die; for it should be in vain to pray for his Health, if they were sure of his Death.

Therefore the Church's Intention, is, not (as he impertinently cavils) that this should be the last Sacrament, although it is so called, but on the Contrary, and that the sick Person may recover his Health; which, if God is not pleased he should; yet that is no Prejudice to the Force and Virtue of the Sacrament, which tends more to the curing of the Soul, than to the Health of the Body.

Lutherus postquam se tam strenue quam videtis gessit adversus apostolum, jam totum se convertit ad ridendum Ecclesiam, quæ verbis apostoli, ut dicit Lutherus, abutitur, quod non ministret, nisi ad mortem usque ægrotanti, quum Jacobus dicat: *"Si quis infirmatur,"* non si quis moriatur: quasi ideo peccet Ecclesia, quod rem tantam, quanta est sacramentum, non adhibeat temere in qualibet levi febricula, quam aliquis nimium fortasse potando contraxerit, neque in eo morbo, qui vel dormiendo paululum, vel abstinendo curari possit, Ecclesia per sacramentum velit efflagitare miraculum! Ne dubitari possit, etiamsi duntaxat infirmum scripserit Jacobus, sensisse tamen haud ægrotantem leviter, sed eo morbo vexatum, cujus depulsio posset ostendere, si sanaretur, sanatum sacramento, orationes omnes quæ dicuntur super infirmum (quas nemo dubitat esse vetustissimas, non novum inventum eorum, quos iste vocat theologos), ostendunt non adhibendum hoc sacramentum, nisi in laborante graviter: et tamen ut non promittunt certam salutem corporis, ita non desperant salutem, nec veniunt, quod Lutherus ait, tanquam ad eos, qui jam tum sint omnino morituri. Frustra enim tot orationibus orarent salutem, si certo sibi sponderent mortem. Non igitur id agit Ecclesia, quod inepte cavillatur iste, ut sit Extrema-Unctio, licet vocetur extrema, sed agit ut non sit extrema, sed convalescat ægrotus. Quod si nolit eum Deus convalescere, id tamen non evacuat vim ac virtutem sacramenti, cujus præcipua cura non in corpus fertur, sed animam.

As for *Luther's* Reason, concerning the Efficacy of the Sign, it is altogether without Reason or Efficacy: 'If that Unction be (says he) a Sacrament, it ought, without Doubt, to be an effectual Sign of what it promises; but it promises the Health and Recovery of the Sick, as appears by the Words, The Prayers of the Faithful shall save the Sick, and our Lord will raise him up: Yet who sees not but this Promise is fulfilled in very few? What shall we say then? (says he), For either the Apostle speaks false in this Promise, or else this Unction is no Sacrament; for a sacramental Promise is certain, but this, for the most Part, fails.' It appears by this only Argument, that *Luther* cares not much how open his Calumnies are, so that he can but, under some Pretext of Truth, impose upon the Unwary: For he shames not to object against the Divines, (as said by them,) what they never spoke: A 'Sacrament (says he) is, according to their Sayings, an effectual Sign of what it promiseth; but this Sacrament gives not the Health of the Body, which it promiseth.' But Divines say no such Thing; they say it is an effectual Sign of Grace, defining it thus, 'A Sacrament is a visible Sign of invisible Grace:' They do not speak of the Health of the Body, which may be given without Grace. So that when he says, 'That if Unction be a Sacrament, the Apostle should lye;' it is *Luther* himself that lyeth: For the Sacrament, in as much as it is a Sacrament promiseth not the Health of the Body, but of the Soul, by a corporeal Sign. Nevertheless, *Luther* comprehends, under the same Lye, not only the Apostle, but Christ himself, though Unction were no Sacrament: For the Words and Promise ought to be true also, without the Sacrament. Therefore, when the Apostle says, 'The Sick shall be healed by Unction and Prayers;' And when Christ says, 'These Signs shall follow those that

Nam ratio illa Lutheri de efficacia signi nihil omnino rationis habet, aut efficaciæ. "Si unctio ista sacramentum est," inquit, "debet sine dubio esse, ut dicunt, efficax signum ejus quod signat et promittit. At sanitatem et restitutionem infirmi promittit, ut stant aperta verba: *Oratio fidei salvabit infirmum, et alleviabit eum Dominus.* Quis autem non videt hanc promissionem in paucis impleri? Quid ergo dicemus, inquit? Aut apostolus hac promissione mentitur, aut unctio ista sacramentum non erit; promissio enim sacramentalis certa est, at hæc majore parte fallit."

Vel ex hoc argumento patere potest nihil curare Lutherum quam apertas afferat calumnias, modo specie aliqua veritatis imponere possit incautis, quem non pudet ea contra theologos afferre, quasi ab ipsis dicta, quæ nusquam dicunt. "Sacramentum," inquit, "ut dicunt, est efficax signum ejus quod promittit: at hoc sacramentum sanitatem corporis non efficit, quam promittit." Theologi non istud dicunt, sed quod est efficax signum gratiæ. Sic enim definiunt: sacramentum est visibile signum invisibilis gratiæ; non dicunt salutis corporeæ, quæ dari possit et sine gratia. Quamobrem, quod ait consequi, ut, si hæc unctio sacramentum esset, apostolus mentiretur, Lutherus ipse mentitur. Nam sacramentum, quatenus sacramentum est, non salutem promittit corporis, sed animæ, per signa corporea. Alioqui Lutherus nihilominus eodem concludit mendacio, non apostolum solum, sed etiam Christum ipsum, quanquam unctio non esset sacramentum. Debent enim verba et promissiones etiam extra sacramenta veraces esse. Igitur quum apostolus dicat sanandum per unctionem et orationem, eum qui infirmus est, et Christus, signa illa secutura credentes, ut super ægros manus imponerent, et bene haberent, quis non videt hæc sic interdum fieri, ut tamen non fiant semper? Neque

believe in him, to wit, that they should lay Hands on
the Sick, and they should be healed;'* who sees not that
sometimes these Things are performed, but not always?
Neither yet are they false who promised them: For, in
whatsoever Words they promised corporeal Things; yet
every Body knows, they never promised them to be perpetual, when the Body, in which they are to be done,
cannot last always.   But spiritual Things are here to be
understood, because the Spirit is to live for ever.   For
Luther's Sentence (which exacts from the Divines, that,
if Unction is a Sacrament, it may always cure, that may
not be an ineffectual Sign) undertakes to prove that it
cannot be a Sacrament, if it renders not the Body immortal: Which, nevertheless, he himself promises to be
done by the Prayers of good Men, without the least staggering in Faith: For, (says he) 'There is no Doubt, but
at this Day, as many as we please may be cured:'
Which, if true, such a Faith as this may preserve Man
immortal: For, seeing this may be done by Faith, not
only Sometimes, but, as he affirms, always, if Faith be
stable and undoubtful; it is probable indeed, if any one
ever meet with such a Faith: And doubtless *Luther* was
a Man of such Faith, (having so much thereof, that in
Favour of it, in many Places, he almost bids Defiance to
good Works; being likewise one to whom God has revealed so many, and so great Mysteries, and who erects
a new Church, for which Miracles are absolutely necessary) it is therefore likely that *Luther* can perform
abundantly whatever can be done by Faith.   If this be
true, I wonder he cures not every dying Person!   We
look for News daily from *Germany* of his raising the
Dead: Yet, for all this, we hear that not only none are
cured by him, but that many good and innocent Priests
are killed, (by his Adherents) and cruelly murthered

*Mk. xvi. 17, 18.

tamen falsos esse qui promiserint, quum eos nemo dubitet corporalia, quibuscumque verbis promiserint, nunquam promisisse perpetua, quum corpus in quo fieri
deberent perpetuum esse non possit. Spiritalia vero,
quia sua natura spiritus æternum victurus est, perpetua
consecutura pollicentur.

Nam Lutheri sententia, quæ a theologis exigit ut, si
sacramentum sit Unctio, semper sanet, ne sit signum
inefficax, eo tendit ut sacramentum esse non possit, nisi
reddat corpus immortale, quod ipse tamen fieri posse
promittit per orationem factam a bonis viris nihil hæsi-
tante fide. Nam prorsus dubium non esse dicit, hodie
quoque, sic sanari posse quotquot vellemus. Hoc si
dicit verum, talis fides qualis est illius, hominem servare
potest immortalem. Nam quum ista fieri possint per
fidem, non solum interdum, sed, quod Lutherus ait,
perpetuo, modo sit fides indubia, quæ nihil hæsitet,
credibile est fidem istam, si cuiquam alteri, potissimum
contigisse Luthero, homini sic in fidem propenso, ut,
fidei favore, bonis operibus multis in locis propemodum
indicat bellum. Homini præterea, cui nunc tot et tanta
mysteria revelavit Deus, et qui novam condit Ecclesiam,
quam in rem opus est et miraculis. Igitur verisimile
est, quicquid fieri per fidem potest, abunde Lutherum
facere. Demiror igitur, si vera dicit, ipsum non curare
quoscumque morientes. Et quotidie auscultamus
rumores e Germania, qui referant ressuscitatos etiam
sepultos, quum interim semper audimus non modo sanatum nullum, sed etiam per illius quosdam satellites,
occisos et crudeliter trucidatos, ejus causa, bonos et
innocentes sacerdotes, ut exemplo doceret Ordinem
nihil esse, figmentum esse characterem, meticulosum

for his Sake; that, by his Example, he may teach, 'That
Holy Order is nothing: That Character is a Fiction:
That *David* was timorous for repenting himself to have
touched the Lord's Anointed.'*

These are *Luther's* Cures, wrought by his great Faith,
without good Works. For, seeing he kills, and cures
not; it appears plainly, (as he says, 'That Prayers are
to be made not only by Faith, but also by good Men,')
that *Luther,* not being a good Man, can therefore cure
no Body himself. 'This Unction, he says, is no Sacrament, because it does not always heal the Body:' But
himself is a holy Man, by whom, as it is reported, the
Body is killed, and certainly Souls are killed. St. *James*
writes nothing worthy an apostolick Spirit; but *Luther*
writes every Thing worthy such Spirit, and discerns
Things unworthy thereof, and that against the whole
Church: which, as he acknowledges, cannot be deceived
in discerning such Scripture. In which Thing, when I
had read St. *James*'s Epistle, and saw so many Things
worthy an apostolic *Spirit* therein, (as the Joy in over-
coming Temptations, Patience in Adversity, Wisdom to
be begged from God, Hopes to be placed in God without
staggering, with many such like; all which are read in
the Apostle) I much wonder what Reason *Luther* had
to think them unworthy to have been writ by an Apostle.
But perhaps *Luther* would that the Apostle had writ
such Things as these, to wit, 'That Mass is not profitable
to the People, that Order is a vain Fiction;' and such
like, as himself writes; which are all Things worthy an
apostolic Spirit.

But though, as I said, I admired why *Luther* should
be so much displeased at St. *James*'s Epistle; yet, hav-

*I. Ks. xxvi. 11, 23.

fuisse Davidem, quem pœnituerit tetigisse Christum
Domini.

Hæc sunt Lutheri sanationes, quas nihil vacillans
ejus fides operatur, absque bonis operibus. Nam quod
occidit, non sanat, inde plane accedit, quod, ut Lutherus
ait, oratio non tantum cum fide facienda est, sed etiam
a bono viro, quæ res Lutherum, qui vir bonus non est,
ne quemquam sanet, impedit. Unctio hæc sacramentum non est, quia non semper sanat corpus. Lutherus
vir sacer est, per quem et corpus, ut ferunt, occiditur,
et certe occiduntur animæ. Jacobus apostolus nihil
dignum scribit apostolico spiritu ; Lutherus apostolico
spiritu digna scribit omnia, et quæ sint indigna discernit, idque contra totam Ecclesiam, quam in talium
discretione Scripturarum falli, fassus est ipse non
posse.

Qua in re, quum epistolam Jacobi legerem, atque ibi
tam multa conspicerem apostolico digna spiritu, vehementer admiratus sum quid in mentem venerit Luthero,
ut gaudium in tentationibus, patientiam in adversis, a
Deo petendam sapientiam, in Deo fiducia nihil hæsi-
tante, sperandum, et hujusmodi multa (nam talia sunt,
quæ tota leguntur epistola) miratus, inquam, sum, cur
Lutherus putarit indigna quæ scriberentur ab apostolo :
an illa potius scribere debebat apostolus, populo nihil
esse fructus in Missa, et Ordinem inane figmentum
esse, et alia quæ Lutherus scribit hujusmodi ? quæ quanquam sint omnia dignissima spiritu apostatico, tamen
contemnere non debet, si minora scribant minores
apostoli.

Atqui licet aliquandiu, quod dixi, miratus sum cur
Luthero displiceat epistola Jacobi, tamen ubi legi
sæpius, et oculos intendi pressius, desii profecto mirari.

ing read it more attentively, I wonder not at all: For, by the Apostle's Writings, I find that he so narrowly touches *Luther* every-where, as if, by his prophetic Spirit, he had plainly foreseen him. For, when *Luther* under the Pretext of Faith, despises good Works; St. *James,* on the other Side, disputes, by Reason, Scripture, and Example, 'that Faith without Works, is dead:' Nor is it in one Place alone, that by bitter Words, he resists that prattling Petulancy of *Luther:* 'If any one (says he) esteem himself religious, not bridling his Tongue, but seducing his own Heart, his Religion is vain.'* Besides *Luther* frets at this, which 'he sees very fitly may be applied to his own Tongue.' The Tongue is a restless Evil, full of deadly Poison.† Finally, he perceives that what the Apostle has writ against contentious Persons, is truly spoken against his own Opinions: 'For (says the Apostle) who is wise and well-disciplined among you? Let him shew forth his Works by a good Conversation, in the Meekness of Wisdom; because, if you have the Zeal of Souls, and Contentions be in your Hearts, do not glory, being Lyars against the Truth. For this is not Wisdom descending from above, from the Father of Lights, but an earthly, beastly, and diabolical Wisdom: For where Zeal is joined with Contention, there also is Inconstancy, and every naughty Work. But the Wisdom which is from above, is first of all shamefaced, then peaceable, modest, complyable, agreeing with good Things, full of Mercy and good Works, judging with Dissimulation: And the Fruit of Justice is sown in Peace to the Workers of Peace.'‡

These, gentle Reader, are the Words which move *Luther* to Wrath against the Apostle: These, I say, are the Words whereby the Apostle as openly touches *Luther's* Petulancy, Railings, wicked and contentious

*Jas. i. 26.   †Jas. iii. 8.   ‡Jas. iii. 13 fol.

Nam ea scribit apostolus, ut plane videri possit prophetico spiritu prænovisse Lutherum: ita virum undique pungit ad vivum. Nam quum Lutherus fidei prætextu contemnat opera, Jacobus e diverso disputat, ratione, Scripturis, exemplis fidem sine operibus mortuam esse. Præterea garrulam istam Lutheri petulantiam non uno loco verbis invadit acerrimis. *"Si quis,"* inquit, *"putat se religiosum esse, non refrenans linguam suam, sed seducens cor suum, hujus vana est religio."* Accedit ad hæc quod in suam linguam Lutherus aptissime videt competere, quod illi frendit legens: *"Lingua inquietum malum, plena veneno mortifero."* Denique sentit in sua dogmata verissime dici quæ de contentiosis hunc in modum scribit pluribus ibi verbis apostolus: *"Quis sapiens et disciplinatus inter vos? Ostendat ex bona conversatione operationem suam in mansuetudine sapientiæ. Quod si zelum amarum habetis, et contentiones sint in cordibus vestris, nolite gloriari, et mendaces esse adversus veritatem. Non est enim ista sapientia desursum descendens a Patre luminum, sed terrena, animalis, diabolica. Ubi enim zelus et contentio, ibi inconstantia, et omne opus pravum. Quæ autem desursum est sapientia, primum quidem pudica est, deinde pacifica, modesta, suadibilis, bonis consentiens, plena misericordia, et fructibus bonis, non judicans, sine simulatione. Fructus autem justitiæ in pace seminatur facientibus pacem."*

Hæc sunt, lector, quæ Lutherum commovent ut ei non placeat apostolus. Hæc, inquam, sunt, quibus apostolus aperte Lutherum ac Lutheri petulantiam, maledicentiam, impia et contentiosa dogmata, non secus ac si vidisset virum, et verba legisset, attingit. Cujus epis-

Opinions; even as if he had seen him, and read his Words. I question not but his Epistle, though never so much despised by *Luther,* will sufficiently prove to all Christians the Sacrament of Extreme-Unction; nor shall *Luther* be ever so powerful, as to be able to abolish any Sacrament, which, for the Salvation of the Faithful, has been received by the Church, against which the Gates of Hell shall never prevail; much less this single Brother, who is but a sooty Wicket of Hell.

WE have in this little Book, courteous Reader, clearly demonstrated, I hope, how absurdly and impiously *Luther* has handled the Holy Sacraments: For, though we have not touched all Things contained in his Book; yet so far as was necessary to defend the Sacraments, (which only was our design) I suppose I have treated, though not so sufficiently as might have been done, yet more than is even necessary; insomuch that it behoves me not to insist any longer thereupon; else were it no hard Matter to enrich this Discourse with more plentiful Arguments, Laws, and Sentences of the Holy Fathers, and Scripture itself, if it were not in vain, upon *Luther's* Account, and for others more than necessary; for it is as easy for the *Æthiopian* to change his colour, or the Leopard his spots, as for *Luther* to be converted by teaching. But that others may understand how false and wicked his Doctrine is, lest they might be so far deceived as to have a good Opinion of him; I doubt not but in all Parts there are very learned Men, though I had said Nothing at all of this Matter, who have much more clearly discovered the same, than can be shewn by me. And if there be any who desire to know this strange Work of his, I think I have sufficiently made it apparent to them. For, seeing by what has been said, it is evident to all Men what sacrilegious Opinions he has of the Sacrament of our Lord's Body, (from which the Sanc-

tolam quantumvis eam contemnat Lutherus, non dubito
satis approbare Christianis omnibus Unctionis-Extremæ
sacramentum, nec tam potentem fore Lutherum, ut
ullum sacramentum possit evertere, quod in salutem
fidelium fides recepit Ecclesiæ, adversus quam nec portæ
prævalebunt inferorum, nedum fraterculus unus, in-
ferni fuliginosum posticum.

FECIMUS hoc libello tibi, lector, ut spero, perspicuum
quam absurde Lutherus et impie tractarit sacramenta.
Nam etsi non attigimus omnia, quæ liber ipsius conti-
net, tamen quod attinet ad tuenda sacramenta ipsa
(neque enim aliud erat institutum meum) tractasse rem
videor, si non quam multis fieri potuit, certe pluribus
ferme quam necesse fuit, tantum abest ut oporteat immorari diutius. Alioqui et rationibus, et legibus, et
Doctorum sententiis, et Scripturis ipsis non fuisset
difficile rem locupletare cumulatius, nisi erga et Lutherum frustra fecissemus, et erga cæteros supervacue.

Nam si Lutherum docendo conemur immutare, citius
et nigrorem Æthiops, et varietatem pardus immutabit.
Sin aliis ostendere quam falso et quam maligne sentiat,
ne quis ita fallatur, ut de illo sentiat bene, passim doctissimos viros esse non dubito, qui, vel tacentibus nobis,
id multo clarius perpendant, quam ipse queam ostendere, et si qui sint, qui alienam in id operam desiderant,
his abunde jam nunc opinor ostendisse me. Quum
enim ex his quæ disseruimus inclarescat omnibus, quam
sacrilega statuat dogmata de sacramento illo quod ipsius
Christi corpus est (e quo sacramenta reliqua quicquid
habent sacri promanat), quis dubitare potuisset, etiamsi
nihil adjecissem amplius, quam indignis ille modis

tity of all the other Sacraments flows) who would have
doubted, if I had said Nothing else, how unworthily,
without Scruple, he treats all the rest of the Sacraments? Which, as you have seen, he has handled in
such Sort, that he abolishes and destroys them all, except
Baptism alone; and that too, he has abused and deprived
of all Grace; leaving it for no other End, than in a
Contumely of Penance; in some, denying the Sign, in
others, the Matter itself: Neither proves he any Thing
in this so great a Matter; nor brings he any Thing in
Confirmation of his Doctrine; contenting himself in
only denying whatever the Church admits. What every
Body believes, he alone, by his vain Reason, laughs at;
denouncing himself to admit Nothing, but clear and
evident Scriptures: And these too, if alledged by any
against him, he either evades by some private Exposi-
tion of his own, or else denies them to belong to their
own Authors. None of the Doctors are so antient, none
so holy, none of so great Authority in treating of Holy
Writ: But this new Doctor, this little Saint, this Man
of Learning; rejects with great Authority. Seeing
therefore he despiseth all Men, and believes none, he
ought not to take it ill, if every Body discredit him
again. I am so far from intending to hold any further
Dispute with him, that I almost repent myself of what
I have already argued against him. For what avails it
to dispute against a Man, who disagrees with every one,
even with himself? who affirms in one Place, what he
denies in another; denying what he presently affirms;
who, if you object Faith, combats by Reason; if you
touch him with Reason, pretends Faith; if you alledge
Philosophers, he flies to Scripture; if you propound
Scripture, he trifles with Sophistry; who is ashamed of
Nothing, fears none, and thinks himself under no Law;
who contemns the antient Doctors of the Church, and

tractare cætera sacramenta non dubitet? Quæ sicut
videtis tractavit sic, ut præter Baptismum unum, et
illum quoque male vexatum, et omni privatum gratia,
nec in aliud relictum, quam in contumeliam Pœnitentiæ, tollat prorsus, atque evertat omnia, in aliis signum
negans, in aliis rem inficians, nec in tanta re probat
quicquam, nec affert aliquid, quo confirmet sua, sat
habens negare tantum quicquid recepit Ecclesia. Quicquid creditur ab omnibus, ratione futili solus eludit, ac
se denuntiat nihil admissurum præter claras et evidentes Scripturas. Quas ipsas tamen, si quis afferat,
vel aliquo repellit commento, vel auctoris esse, cujus
feruntur, negat. Doctorum vero nemo tam vetus est,
nemo tam sanctus, nemo tantæ auctoritatis in tractatu
sacrarum litterarum, quem non iste novus doctorculus,
sanctulus et eruditulus magna cum auctoritate rejiciat.

Quamobrem, quum Lutherus omnes contemnat, et
credat nemini, debet non indignari si nemo vicissim
credat illi. Cum quo tantum abest ut disputem pluribus, ut propemodum pigeat disputasse tam multis.
Quid enim prodest amplius cum illo disserere, qui
cæteris dissentit omnibus, et non consentit sibi? qui
quod alibi negat, alibi dicit; quod dicit, id rursum
negat? Qui si fidem objicias, ratione dimicat; si
ratione ferias, prætendit fidem. Si philosophos alleges,
appellat Scripturam; si Scripturam proponas, nugatur
sophismate. Quem neque pudet quicquam, neque timet
quemquam, neque legem putat tenere se ullam. Qui
veteres Ecclesiæ Doctores contemnit, novos e sublimi
deridet. Summum Ecclesiæ Pontificem insectatur convitiis. Ecclesiæ consuetudines, dogmata, mores, leges,

derides the new ones in the highest Degree; loads with Reproaches the chief Bishop of the Church: Finally, he so undervalues the Customs, Doctrine, Manners, Laws, Decrees, and Faith of the Church; yea, the whole Church itself; that he almost denies there is any such Thing as a Church; except perhaps such a one as himself makes up of two or three Heretics, of whom himself is Chief. Wherefore, since he is such a one, as will have no solid or certain Principle betwixt himself and his Adversary; but requires to be free in whatever pleases him, and as often as it pleases him lawfully to assert or deny; when, neither Reason, Scripture, Custom, Laws, human or divine Authority, binds him: I thought it not fit to dispute any longer with him, nor to contend, by painful Reason, against his Heresies, which he confirms by no Reason. But I rather advise all Christians, that, as the most exterminating of Plagues, they shun him, who endeavours to bring into the Church of Christ such foul Prodigies, being the very Doctrine of Antichrist. For, if he, who studies to move a Schism in any one Thing, is to be extirpated with all Care; with what great Endeavours is he to be rooted out, who, not only goes about to sew Dissention, to stir up the People against the chief Bishop, Children against their Parents, Christians against the Vicar of Christ; finally, who endeavours to dissolve by his Tumults, Brawls and Contentions, the whole Church of Christ, which he, in the Time of his precious Death, has bound together by the Bond of Charity and Love; and also to destroy, prophane and pollute, with a most execrable Mind, filthy Tongue, and detestable Touch, what is most sacred therein; who, if he did but give any Hopes of Cure in himself, or any Sign of Amendment, he would thereby move all People to regard Disposition, and to endeavour, by all good Means possible, to heal him, and

decreta, fidem, Ecclesiam denique ipsam adeo floccifacit universam, ut nec esse fere fateatur ullam, nisi fors Ecclesiam illam, quam facit ipse duorum vel trium hæreticorum, quorum sit ipse caput.

Quamobrem, quum sit ejusmodi, ut nihil statuat principii, quod certum sit ac solidum, quod ei cum disputante conveniat, sed sibi liberum relinqui postulet, ut quicquid libet, quando libet, quoties libet, id illi liceat et asserere vicissim, et negare : quum neque ratione sese, neque Scriptura, neque moribus, neque legibus, neque auctoritate demum vel humana, vel divina patiatur astringi, non constitui cum eo disserendum amplius, nec adversus eas hæreses, quæ nulla ratione firmantur, operosa ratione pugnandum, sed admonendos potius Christianos omnes, ut tanquam teterrimam pestem devitent illum, qui tam fœda portenta, ipsissima Antichristi dogmata, in Ecclesiam Christi conatur invehere. Nam si omnimodo curandum est ut extirpetur qui de quavis una re schisma suscitare studuerit, quanto studio conniti decet ut evellatur is qui non dissidium modo pergit serere, et populum in Pontificem, filios in parentem, Christianos in Christi vicarium provocare, totam denique Ecclesiam Christi, quam ille moriens amore et charitate colligavit, tumultu, rixis et contentione dissolvere, verum etiam quicquid est in ea sacrosanctum exsecrabili mente, spurcissima lingua, scelerato contactu rescindere, temerare, polluere ? Qui si quam tamen de se salutis spem, si quod emendandi sui signum daret, hortarer omnes ut hominis sic affecti curam susciperent, et in hoc incumberent, ut modis quam possent optimis, medicarentur, et sanitati mentis restitutum facerent ut hæreses a se propositas revocaret. Verum adhuc pro-

to restore him to Soundness of Mind, that he might
again revoke the Heresies he has broached. But indeed, as yet, I see in him all the Signs that precede
Death: I am not so much moved to think thus, by
Reason of his Disease, though never so mortal; as by
his admitting no Medicine, nor of any manual Opera-
tion of the Chyrurgion: For how can he be cured, who
will not suffer himself to be handled? Or in what Manner is he to be dealt withal; who, if you teach him,
trifles with you?——If you advise him, is angry?——If
you exhort him, resists?——If in any Thing you would
appease him, is incensed?—If you resist him, is mad?
Otherwise, if he could be cured, what has the pious
Vicar of Christ omitted, who, following the Example of
a good Shepherd, would seek, find, take on his Shoulders, and bring home to the Fold this lost Sheep? But,
alas! the most greedy Wolf of Hell has surprized him,
devoured and swallowed him down into the lowest Part
of his Belly, where he lies half alive, and half dead in
Death: And whilst the pious Pastor calls him, and
bewails his Loss, he belches out of the filthy Mouth of
the hellish Wolf these foul Inveighings, which the Ears
of the whole Flock do detest, disdain, and abhor.

For, first of all, being unprovoked in any Kind, he
proposed some Articles of Indulgences; in which, (under Pretence of Godliness,) he most impiously defamed
the Chief Bishop: Afterwards, that he might under
Pretence of Honour and Duty, cast on the Pope the
greater Aspersion, he transmitted them to *Rome,* as if
submitting himself to the Pope's Judgment; but he aug-
mented them with Declarations, much worse than they
were themselves; that it might appear to all Men, that
the Pope would not be counselled by a good and pious
Man, but derided by a knavish little Brother, as if so
stupid as to hold for an Honour such a Contumely, as

fecto, quæcumque solent ad mortem esse signa, omnia
huic esse video. Quod ut censeam non tam morbus ejus,
quantumvis lethalis, me movet, quam ipse : quippe qui
medicinam nullam, nullam prorsus manum medicantis
admittit. Quomodo enim curari potest qui se tractari
non patitur ? Aut quomodo tractari potest, quem si
quid doces, nugatur; si quid mones, irascitur; si quid
hortaris, obnititur; si quid placas, incenditur; si quid
adversaris, insanit ?

Alioquin si curari potuisset, quid omisit pientissimus
Christi vicarius, quo pastoris sui secutus exemplum,
ovem hanc errantem quæreret, inveniret, in humeros
tolleret, ac reportaret in stabulum ? Sed heu Lupus
averni pessimus, anteceperat, devoraverat, atque in
imum ventrem dimiserat, ubi semivivus adhuc in morte
jacens, adversus inclamantem se pastorem pium, et
perditionem ejus deplorantem, e spurco tartarei Lupi
rictu, fœdos illos latratus eructat, quos totius gregis
aures aversantur, abominantur, exhorrent.

Nam primum, nihil omnino lacessitus, articulos proposuit de Indulgentiis, quibus prætextu pietatis impie
traduceret summum Pontificem. Deinde, ut per honoris
eum et officii speciem majore contumelia perfunderet,
eos transmittit Romam, tanquam Pontificis judicio sub-
mittens, sed auctos ante declarationibus multo quam
essent ipsi deterioribus; ut plane liqueret omnibus,
Pontificem non a viro bono pioque consuli, sed a frater-
culo nebulone rideri, tanquam ita stupidum, ut pro
honore duceret insignem et nullius unquam exempli
contumeliam, barbamque, quod aiunt, vellendam præ-
beret irrisori. Si nihil mali commerebatur Pontifex,

the like thereof had never before been heard.   If the
Pope deserved no Ill, why has this degenerate Son, cast
a false and undeserving Scandal on his Father?   But if
any Thing had been done at *Rome,* which needed re-
forming; yet if *Luther* had been (as he would be accounted) an honest Man, and zealous Christian, he
should not have preferred his own private Glory before
the public Good of all others, nor have desired to have
had the Credit of a Scorner amongst the Wicked, laugh-
ing at the Nakedness of his sleeping Father,* uncover-
ing, and pointing thereto with his Finger; but, contrary-
wise, would have covered the same, and would have more
secretly advised him in his own Person by Letters, following the Example of the Apostle, who commands us
not to deride or reproach our Superiors, but to seek of
them:†   Which if *Luther* had done, I doubt not but the
more holy *Pope,* (so well is his great Benignity known
to all Men) being awakened, should have blessed his Son
Japhet; would have rendered him Thanks for his Piety;
and would not have cursed him in his Anger; who has
forborn to curse him when he was mocked by him; but,
pitying the miserable, and (more tender of a Son, than
mindful of a Scoffer) has dealt with him by most
honourable Men, in whose Presence he was not worthy
to appear, that he might desist from his Iniquity: To
which pious and wholesome Counsel, he was so far from
obeying, that he not only derided the Legate, careful for
his Salvation, but also immediately published another
Book, in which he endeavoured to overthrow the Pope's
Power: After which, he was summoned to *Rome,* that
he might either render Reasons of his Writings, or recant what he had inconsiderately written; having any
Security imaginable offered him, that he should not
undergo the Punishment which he deserved, with suffi-

*Gen. ix. 22 fol.   †I. Tim. v. 1.

cur filius degener immerentem patrem falsa conspersit
infamia ? At si quid Romæ fiebat, quod oporteret immutari, tamen si fuisset Lutherus, quod haberi volebat,
probus, et Christianæ rei studiosus, non præposuisset
privatam gloriam suam publico omnium commodo, nec
scurrandi famam sibi venatus esset apud improbos, dor-
mienti pudenda parentis irridens, et revelata common-
strans digito, sed adversus contexisset potius, et vel
coram, vel per epistolam secretius reverenter admonuis-
set, Apostoli præceptum secutus, qui jubet ut majores
non rideamus, non objurgemus, sed obsecremus. Quod
si fecisset Lutherus, haud dubito quin beatissimus Pontifex (tanta est ejus nulli non explorata benignitas) ex-
pergefactus benedixisset filio suo Japhet, et pietatis
retulisset gratiam, non maledixisset iratus, qui ne sic
quidem adhuc maledixit illudenti, sed misertus miseri,
magisque filii memor, quam irrisoris, egit cum eo per
viros honoratissimos, in quorum ille conspectum prodire
non erat dignus, ut ab iniquitate desisteret. Cui tam
pio ac salubri consilio tantum abfuit ut paruerit, ut non
solum deriserit legatum, de ipsius salute sollicitum, sed
etiam novum librum ederet e vestigio, in quo Pontificis
potestatem machinabatur evertere. Vocatus deinde
Romam, ut vel scriptorum causam redderet, vel temere
scripta recantaret, quavis oblata securitate non sube-
undi supplicii quod meruerat, oblato quod in rem satis
esset viatico, tamen, ut insignem declararet obedientis
viri modestiam, venire contempsit fraterculus ad Pontificem, nisi regio instructus apparatu, et bellico stipatus
exercitu. Sed homo cautus appellavit ad generale consilium, nec tamen quodlibet, sed quod proxime congre-
garetur in Spiritu sancto, ut in quocumque damnaretur,
ibi negaret esse Spiritum sanctum, quem homo sanctus
et spiritalis nusquam fatetur esse, nisi in sinu suo.

cient Expenses offered him for his Journey: Yet, for
all this, this silly Brother, to shew his great Modesty
and Obedience to the Pope, refused to go, unless in the
Equipage of a King, and guarded by a warlike Army:
But this wary Man made his Appeal to a general
Council; yet not to every Council, but to such as should
next meet in the Holy Ghost; that in whatsoever Council, he was condemned, he might deny the Holy Ghost
to be present therein; for this holy and spiritual Man
denies Him to be any where, but in his own Bosom:
Wherefore, being oftentimes advised to repent of his
Wickedness, the most conscientious Shepherd has at
length been forced to cast out from the Fold the Sheep
suffering with an incurable Disease, lest the sound Sheep
be corrupted by Contact, and to deplore the Death of his
son Absolom, whose Life he was unable to save, while
he sees him hanging from a Tree by his beautiful Hair,
of which he had stupidly grown proud.* So *Luther,*
realizing himself to be cast out from the Society of the
Faithful, began to do what the lamented Wicked Ones
do, who, when they have *fallen into Contempt,* contemn.† He has not uttered a Groan; he has not bewailed his Case, in which, exalted like Lucifer, like
Lightning he has fallen‡ and wrought Damage; but
having imitated the Despair of the Devil, himself a
Devil too, that is having become a Calumniator, he has
begun to rush into Blasphemies and Calumnies against
the Pope, and, jealous of others faithful, like the old
Serpent,§ to set up Nets of Infidelity, that he might get
them to taste of the forbidden Tree of harmful Knowledge and to be driven out of the Paradise of the Church
(whence he had fallen) onto an Earth bringing forth
Thorns and Briars. I indeed bear very ill this Man's

*II. Ks. xviii. 9.   ‡Lu. x. 18.
†Prov. xviii. 3.   §Gen. iii.

Quamobrem, iterum atque iterum admonitus ut ab impietate resipisceret, quum iterum atque iterum impietatem ad impietatem adjiceret, adactus est tandem pientissimus Pastor ovem immedicabili scabie laborantem, ne sanas attactu corrumperet, ex ovili procul ejicere, et filii sui Absolonis, cujus vitam servare non poterat, mortem deplorare, dum ab arbore pendentem conspicit decora cæsarie, qua stulte superbierat. Lutherus ergo sentiens ejectum se e societate fidelium, facere cœpit quod deplorati solent impii, qui *quum in profundum venerint, contemnunt.* Non ingemuit; non planxit casum suum, quo, sicut Lucifer exaltatus, sicut fulgur corruerat et allisus est, sed imitatus diaboli desperationem, diabolus etiam ipse, hoc est calumniator effectus, adversus Pontificem in blasphemias et calumnias cœpit erumpere, et reliquis invidens fidelibus, velut serpens antiquus infidelitatis laqueos tendere, ut eos e vetito scientiæ noxiæ ligno gustantes, ex Ecclesiæ paradiso, unde ipse deciderat, procuraret expelli in terram germinantem spinas et tribulos.

Ego profecto tantam hominis dementiam et miserrimum casum perquam moleste fero, cupioque ut vel adhuc, inspirante gratiam Deo, resipiscat tandem, *con-*

great Madness, and most lamentable State, and I wish that even now (God inspiring him by Grace) he may at length come to his Senses and be converted and live. And I do not wish this so much for his own Sake, (though for his too, as I wish all to be saved, if it be possible) as that at length being converted, and like the prodigal Son* returned to the Mercy of so benign a Father, and having confessed his Error, he may recall any whom he has made err.

But if he has sunken so deep in the Mire that now the Sink of Impiety and Despair shuts its Mouth upon him,† let him blate, blaspheme, calumniate, act as a Madman, so that "he that is filthy, let him be filthy still."‡

But I beseech and entreat all other Christians, and through the Bowels of Christ, (Whose Faith we profess,) to turn away their Ears from the impious Words and not to foster Schisms and Discords, especially at this Time when most particularly it behooves Christians to be concordant against the Enemies of Christ. Do not listen to the Insults and Detractions against the Vicar of Christ which the Fury of the little Monk spews up against the Pope; nor contaminate Breasts sacred to Christ with impious Heresies, for if one sews these he has no Charity, swells with vain Glory, loses his Reason, and burns with Envy. Finally with what Feelings they would stand together against the Turks, against the Saracens, against anything Infidel anywhere, with the same Feelings they should stand together against this one little Monk weak in Strength, but in Temper more harmful than all Turks, all Saracens, all Infidels anywhere.

*Lu. xv.   †Ps. lxviii.   ‡Apoc. xxii.

The End.

vertaturque, et vivat: nec id tam ipsius causa cupio (quanquam ipsius etiam, ut qui omnes cupiam salvos, si possit fieri) quam ut aliquando conversus, ac, velut filius prodigus, reversus ad misericordiam tam benigni Patris, et errorem suum confessus, in viam revocet, si quos effecit errare. Cæterum si is tam profunde se demersit, ut jam super eum puteus impietatis ac desperationis urgeat os suum, blateret, blasphemet, calumnietur, insaniat, ut qui sordet, sordescat adhuc!

Cæteros vero Christianos omnes obsecro, et per Christi viscera, cujus fidem profitemur, obtestor, ut ab impiis verbis avertant aures, neque schismata foveant et discordias, hoc præsertim tempore, in quo maxime oportebat adversus hostes Christi Christianos esse concordes. Neque adversus Christi vicarium probris et detractionibus auscultent, quas in Pontificem fraterculi furor eructat, neque sacrata Christo pectora hæresibus impiis contaminent: quas si seminat, charitate vacat, gloria turget, ratione friget, fervet invidia. Denique, quibus animis adversus Turcas, adversus Saracenos, adversus quicquid est uspiam infidelium consisterent, iisdem animis consistant adversus unum istum viribus imbecillum; sed animo Turcis omnibus, omnibus Saracenis, omnibus usquam infidelibus nocentiorem fraterculum.

Finis.

Translation of Index

NOTE. The references are to the pages of the Paris edition of 1562, by Desboys; every second or right-hand page is numbered, and that is "a"; the left-hand page is not numbered, but is "b"; the numbers only, not the letters, are printed in the body of the work.

Alphabetical Index to the "Defence of the Seven Sacraments"

A

Ambrose ordered married people to live continently during Lent, 48 b.

When the Apostles were ordained priests, 80 a.

Worthless Calling of Luther to the council, 100 a.

Occasion of mixing Water in the chalice, 32 a.

Shrewd interpretation of Luther, 18 b.

Arrogance of Luther, 51 b.

Argument from Christ's promise valid against Luther, 27 a.

Attrition greatly displeases Luther, 50 a.

Author's object, 96 b.

C

Open Calumny of Luther, 58 a.

Triple Captivity of Luther exploded, 26 b.

Reason of reserved Cases, 54 b.

In which sacraments a Character is imprinted, 68 b.

Circumstances of sins to be confessed, 56 b.

Luther condemns Celibacy of priests, 77 a.

Lord's Supper told of, 30 b.

Elegant and convincing Comparison of the sacrament, 19 a.

Beautiful Figure, 45 a.

Assertionis Septem Sacramentorum Index Alphabeticus

A

Ambrosius conjuges ab amplexibus in quadragesima jussit abstinere, 48 b.
Apostoli quando ordinati sint sacerdotes, 80 a.
Appellatio Lutheri ad concilium friuola, 100 a.
Aquæ miscendæ in calice, occasio, 32 a.
Argutula Lutheri interpretatio, 18 b.
Arrogantia Lutheri, 51 b.
Argumentum validum ex Christi promissione contra Lutherum, 27 a.
Attritio nimium displicet Luthero, 50 a.
Authoris institutum, 96 b.

C

Calumnia aperta Lutheri, 58 a.
Captivitas Lutheri trina excutitur, 26 b.
Casuum reservandorum ratio, 54 b.
Character in quibus sacramentis imprimatur, 68 b.
Circumstantiæ peccatorum confitendæ, 56 b.
Cœlibatum Sacerdotum damnat Lutherus, 77 a.
Cœna Dominica expensa, 30 b.
Comparatio elegans et efficax de Sacramento, 19 a.
Comparatio pulchra, 45 a.

G

Greece obeys the Roman Pontiff, 9 b.
That Grace is infused in the sacrament of Matrimony,
71 b; so too in the sacrament of Orders, 81 b, 88 b.

H

Most all Heretics rest on scripture, 79 b.
Helvidius, 62 a, 64 b.
Jerome for the character, 68 a.
How much Jerome defers to the Roman See, 9 b.
Hugh of St. Victor, 44 b, 62 b.

I

The Epistle of James is defended by the authority of
Jerome, 90 b.
The Epistle of James, how weighty and sacred, and
worthy of the apostolic spirit, 95 b.
The same can be taken and offered, 37 a.
Impudence is Luther's one reason for proving every-
thing, 106 a.
Little Children were formerly admitted to Communion,
14 b.

L

Laymen are the Lutheran priests, 86 a.
Leo the Tenth, 6 a.
The Liberty of Luther worse than the Egyptian bond-
age, 16 b.
The Liberty of those going over from the Church of
Christ to Luther, 42 a.
Luther fights against his mother, 3 b.
Luther is to be cautiously read, 4 b.
Luther contradicts himself, 6 a, 8 a, 13 a, b.

G

Græcia Romano paret pontifici, 9 b.
Gratiam in sacramento matrimonii infundi, 71 b; item in sacramento ordinis, 81 b, 88 b.

H

Hæreticos plerosque omnes scripturis niti, 79 b.
Helvidius, 62 a, 64 b.
Hieronymus pro charactere, 68 a.
Hieronymus quantum Romanæ sedi deferat, 9 b.
Hugo de Sancto Victore, 44 b, 62 b.

I

Jacobi epistola asseritur authore Hieronymo, 90 b.

Jacobi epistola quàm gravis ac sancta, apostolicoque spiritu digna, 95 b.
Idem potest sumi et offerri, 37 a.
Impudentia unica ratio est Luthero probandi omnia, 106 a.
Infantes olim ad communionem admittebantur, 14 b.

L

Laici sacerdotes Lutheriani, 86 a.
Leo decimus, 6 a.
Libertas Lutheri, Ægyptiaca servitute delerior, 16 b.

Libertas transfugientium ab ecclesia Christi ad Lutherum, 42 a.
Lutherus matrem oppugnat, 3 b.
Lutherus caute legendus, 4 b.
Lutherus sibi ipsi contrarius, 6 a, 8 a, 13 a, b.

Lutherus libros suos devovet igni, 8 a.
Lutherus nuper Bohemos detestabatur, 8 b.
Lutherus contrà facit ac docet, ibidem.
Lutherus unum tantum sacramentum admittit, 11 a.
Lutherus ut coluber vitandus, 11 b.
Lutherus quo tendat, 11 b, 12 b.
Lutherus fugam meditatur ad Bohemos, 16 a.
Lutherus adulterat Christi testamentum, 30 a.
Lutherus novus Esdras, 34 a.
Lutherus vel doctrina vel stultitia singularis, 39 a.
Lutherus Atlas, 40 a.
Lutherus populum a missa abigit, 40 b.
Lutherus Christianis summam decernit licentiam, 47 b.
Lutherus undequaque constrictus, 50 b.
Lutherus in labyrintho, 51 a.
Lutherus omnia confundit, 54 a.
Lutherus verborum prodigus, 57 b.
Lutherus ridicule ridet ecclesiam, 69 a.
Lutherus suis ipsius verbis victus, 79 a.
Lutherus cur irascatur Dionysio, 83 b.
Lutherus suo telo confossus de epistola Jacobi, 91 a.
Lutherus et corporum et animorum occisor, 95 a.
Lutherus apostatico spiritu digna scribit, 95 b.
Lutherus cur tam infensus epistolæ Jacobi, 95 b.
Lutherus reliquit baptismum in contumeliam pœnitentiæ, 97 a.
Lutherus qualis in disputando, 97 a.
Lutherus novus doctorculus, sanctulus et eruditulus, 97 b.
Lutherus ceu pestis vetandus, 98 b.
Lutherus Proteus, 97 b.
Lutherus immedicabilis, 98 b.
Lutherus qua via grassatur, 99 a.
Lutherus malitiosus, 111 a.

M

N

O

P

Penance a second plank, 43 b.

Lutheran Preparation for the Eucharist, 41 a.

The confidence of the Probity of Æmilius Scaurus, 55 b.

The Promises of the sacrifices of the Old Testament, 34 b.

Luther on Purgatory, 7 a.

R

Some things are to be Received which are not written, 61 b.

The right of Divorce denied married people by Christ Himself, 74 a.

A King is nobody to Luther, because all are kings with him, 86 b.

Authority of the See of Rome, 9 b.

S

Luther condemns the celibacy of priests, 77 a.

Priests are made only by bishops, 88 b.

The definition of a Sacrament according to Luther, 27 b.

The Sacrament of Marriage has existed among all races, 65 b.

Two opinions on the power of the Sacraments, 45 a.

How Luther treats the Sacraments, 44 b.

The Sacrifices of the Old Law were taken by the priests, 37 a.

Satisfaction is necessary to Penitents, 60 a.

Consideration of Satisfaction, 5 b.

The Holy Spirit withdraws from the deceitful, 5 b.

T

The Times prescribed by Luther for the people to communicate, 41 b.

Traditions also to be received, 61 b and fol.

How old the name of Transsubstantiation, 22 b.

V

Too great trust in the people of obtaining Pardon, 49 b.

Extreme Unction not to be given in every sickness, 93 a.

"You are a royal priesthood": how it should be understood, 86 a.

Votaries, 47 b.

The End.

Finis.

Printed by Benziger Brothers, New York.